STATE AND LOCAL
GOVERNMENT
Politics and Public Policies

STATE AND LOCAL GOVERNMENT
Politics and Public Policies

Fifth Edition

David C. Saffell
Ohio Northern University

McGraw-Hill, Inc.

New York   St. Louis   San Francisco   Auckland   Bogotá   Caracas
Lisbon   London   Madrid   Mexico   Milan   Montreal   New Delhi   Paris
San Juan   Singapore   Sydney   Tokyo   Toronto

STATE AND LOCAL GOVERNMENT: Politics and Public Policies

2 3 4 5 6 7 8 9 0 DOC/DOC 9 0 9 8 7 6 5 4 3

ISBN 0-07-054477-8

This book was set in Times Roman by the Clarinda Company.
The editors were Peter Labella and Fred H. Burns;
the production supervisor was Friederich W. Schulte.
The cover was designed by Rafael Hernandez.
The photo editor was Barbara Salz.
R. R. Donnelley & Sons Company was printer and binder.

Cover photo: © John Coletti, Stock, Boston
Town Hall Middleborough, MA

Library of Congress Cataloging-in-Publication Data

Saffell, David C., (date).
    State and local government: politics and public policies / David
C. Saffell.—5th ed.
        p.   cm.
    Includes bibliographical references and index.
    ISBN 0-07-054477-8
    1. State government—United States.   2. Local government—United
States.   I. Title.
JK2408.S17   1993
353.9—dc20   92-23653

CHAPTER-OPENER PHOTO CREDITS:

Chapter 1: Peter Menzel/Stock, Boston; *Chapter 2:* Tony Freedman/PhotoEdit; *Chapter 3:* John Jeregan/Impact Visuals; *Chapter 4:* Bob Daemmrich/Stock, Boston; *Chapter 5:* Robert Brenner/PhotoEdit; *Chapter 6:* Rick Reinhard/Impact Visuals; *Chapter 7:* Danny Lyon/Magnum Photos; *Chapter 8:* Mike Albans/AP Wide World Photos; *Chapter 9:* Michael Dwyer/Stock, Boston; *Chapter 10:* George Hall/Woodfin Camp & Associates.

ABOUT
THE AUTHOR

David C. Saffell is professor of political science at Ohio Northern University. He is the author of *Essentials of American Government: Change and Continuity* (1989), *The Politics of American Government,* fifth edition (1983), and *State Politics* (1984); editor of *Readings in American Government: The State of the Union* (1991), *Watergate: Its Effects on the American Political System* (1974), and *American Government: Reform in the Post-Watergate Era* (1976); and coeditor of *Readings in State and Local Government: Problems and Prospects* (1994) and *Subnational Politics: Readings in State and Local Government* (1982). Professor Saffell has been teaching state and local government to undergraduate students for the past twenty-seven years.

CONTENTS

PREFACE

As in previous editions, *State and Local Government,* fifth edition, examines the structure and operation of state and local government in a concise but thorough way. My hope is that by its reduced cost and size, this book will offer an alternative to the larger texts available, allowing instructors increased flexibility to assign other readings. While the main focus is on political parties, interest groups, legislatures, courts, and executive officials at the state level, their counterparts in cities also are discussed and evaluated. The book concludes with an examination of a variety of policy areas—education, welfare, housing, environmental protection. In each chapter the reader is reminded of the impact of political culture, tradition, levels of economic development, and the effects of political forces on government structure and policymaking.

The preface to the fourth edition of this book noted the resurgence of state government in the 1980s and the lead in political activism taken by states and cities in the face of cutbacks in federal domestic policy initiatives. States and localities have entered the 1990s in severe financial distress. The combination of reduced federal aid, an economic recession, and continued federal and state mandates has caused many states and cities to cut programs, lay off employees, and raise taxes. Unlike the U.S. government, all states (except Vermont) and all cities must balance their budgets each year. So long as the economy was going well, states were able to adjust to federal cuts in the 1980s, adding new programs and even cutting taxes. More recently, gloom and caution have overtaken most states and resurgence has turned to distress. Still, procedural and structural reforms of the 1970s and 1980s in state legislative, executive, and judicial branches remain in effect; and with cuts in federal aid and a very limited domestic agenda by the Bush administration, innovation in most domestic policy areas will continue to come from states and localities. Problems such as AIDS, homelessness, crime, and racial conflict must be faced daily by cities, and their governments are devising new approaches even as they face cuts in money and personnel.

Material has been added in this edition on the following subjects: the 1990 census, the financial crunch of the early 1990s, Bush's federalism proposals, city-state relations and mandates, politics in Chicago, the 1992 riots in Los Angeles, power of interest groups, voter registration, 1990 election campaigns, 1992 legislative redistricting, changing role of legislative leaders, women governors, veto power, role of city managers, privatization, Supreme Court decisions in civil rights and civil liberties cases, crime and prison statistics, criminal sentencing policy, state financial problems in the 1990s, Medicaid costs, Bush's education proposals, 1991 transportation legislation, annexation of land by cities in the 1980s, and the 1990 Clean Air Act.

A short reading is included in each chapter. These readings are current case studies in state and local government that seek to make the reader more aware of connections between academic interpretation and the "real world" of grassroots government. Each is new to this edition. Key words in the text appear in **boldface type** and are defined at the end of each chapter. Other important terms are given in *italic type* in the text.

The revision of this book was greatly helped by the insights of those who critiqued the fourth edition and those who reviewed this manuscript. In that regard I want to thank Bernard D. Kolasa, University of Nebraska; John McGlennon, College of William and Mary; Lou Morton, Mesa State College; Richard K. Scher, The University of Florida; and Randy Watkins, Lansing Community College. While their suggestions were incorporated throughout the book, I, of course, am responsible for any errors of fact or interpretation or omissions of material that should be included in an introductory textbook. Once again I want to thank Barbara Roberts for her help in preparing the manuscript.

David C. Saffell

STATE AND LOCAL GOVERNMENT
Politics and Public Policies

CHAPTER 1

THE SETTING OF STATE AND LOCAL GOVERNMENT

STATE VITALITY

During this century, the role of the federal government in public policymaking has expanded to a degree unimagined in earlier times. In fact, today the federal government can act on virtually any policy issue affecting our lives.[1] In those areas where Washington has refrained from action—for example, domestic relations, property, and contracts—the absence of legislation has been a matter of federal restraint rather than lack of constitutional authority.

The states dominated American government in the nineteenth century and the first decade of this century. However, several events in the first half of this century relegated the states to a position of secondary importance. Ratification of the Sixteenth Amendment (relating to income tax) in 1913 gave the federal government much greater ability to raise money and to centralize policymaking. The Depression showed the weaknesses of the states in responding to the nation's economic problems and led to greater focus on the president as the center of government. World War II further strengthened the authority of the president and the centralization of power in Washington.

State reform has been taking place since the early twentieth century, but the negative image of corrupt and incompetent state government persisted (and with good reason) into the early 1960s.[2] Since the mid-1960s, about forty states have ratified new constitutions or made significant changes in existing ones. Governors' terms have been lengthened and their powers increased. Legislatures have become more professional and more representative of urban interests, their rate of membership turnover has been lower, and nearly all meet in annual sessions. Court systems have been unified, and intermediate appellate courts have been added in many states. State bureaucrats are more professional, and the number of state employees under some form of merit system has increased from 50 percent in 1960 to nearly 80 percent. An increase in party competition in the states, coupled with legislative- and executive-branch changes, has led to more innovative policy. In addition, federal cuts in aid have caused local governments to look more to the states for financial help. Since 1980, states have shown a new creativity in several policy areas, including education, corrections, and hazardous waste disposal.

This resurgence of the states was well under way when Ronald Reagan was elected president in 1980. Reagan believed that the federal government had done too much and that more responsibility for policymaking should be turned over to the states. In addition, federal categorical grants-in-aid (see Chapter 2) were criticized by congressional conservatives and by state and local officials for their red tape and insensitivity to local problems. The timing of Reagan's changes in policy and philosophy thus caught the states at a point at which they were the most capable of assuming new policymaking responsibilities. Unfortunately, the states also found themselves without some of the financial assistance they had come to expect from the national government. As noted in the Preface, by 1990 states and localities faced severe financial pressures brought on by the recession and cuts in federal funds. A majority of states raised taxes in 1991, spending was cut, and employees were furloughed or fired. Thus, while states are doing more because of federal retrenchment policy, they are doing it with less money.

Only a few domestic functions—control of natural resources, management of the postal service, space research, and air and water transportation—are predominantly the responsibility of the federal government. In most of those policy areas where responsibility is shared among federal, state, and local governments, the federal financial share was reduced in the 1980s. The share of total state and local spending paid for by Washington declined from 25 percent in the late 1970s to 17 percent in the early 1990s. In comparison, the list of state responsibilities is long.

- *Education:* State and local governments administer public schools and colleges. The federal share of school expenditures rose from about 4.5 percent in 1960 to 9 percent in 1980. Under the Reagan and Bush administrations, it declined to about 6 percent by 1991.
- *Transportation:* Highway routes and construction are largely determined by state and local governments. Federal grants make up about 30 percent of all highway and mass transit expenditures. Federal aid to mass transit was cut form $4.6 billion in 1981 to $3.2 billion in 1991.
- *Welfare:* The states legislate welfare benefits paid to recipients and determine rules of eligibility. They also maintain homes for the aged, orphans, and the mentally ill. The federal government contributes about 55 percent of costs of Aid to Families with Dependent Children (AFDC), the major nonmedical welfare program. Eligibility standards for AFDC were tightened in the 1980s, reducing the number of recipients about 8 percent by the mid-1980s.
- *Criminal justice:* In an overwhelming number of cases, criminal defendants are tried in state rather than federal courts. Nearly 95 percent of all persons in the United States engaged in law enforcement are employed by state and local governments. New York city has nearly as many law enforcement agents as do all the federal agencies. More than 90 percent of all prisoners are held in state prisons and jails. Spending on corrections nearly doubled in the 1980s, with the federal share about 5 percent.
- *Commercial regulation:* Most regulation of industry, banking, and utilities is performed by the states.
- *Health:* States, cities, and counties run hospitals (New York City operates twenty-two hospitals) and they subsidize private hospitals. Their health departments inspect and license various types of businesses. Public health programs try to prevent disease and their nurses visit the elderly. The fastest-growing state expense is Medicaid (medical benefits to low-income persons); the federal share of costs is 56 percent.

State and local governments now provide many services that previously were provided by private agencies or were not provided at all. The growth of technology in communications and transportation has led to state regulation of such industries as electric power and trucking. Government services also have increased greatly as a higher percentage of our population has become urbanized. City residents require a host of services (health, police, sanitation) that were much less necessary when most of the population lived in rural areas. In addition, the concentration of large numbers of poor people in urban areas has contributed to the growth in public services. Since the Great Depression of the 1930s, public support of the poor (including racial and ethnic minorities) has expanded greatly.

In 1989, the states employed 4.2 million full-time workers, local governments employed 10.2 million, and the federal government employed 3.1 million (excluding military personnel). Thus over 80 percent of all public employees work for state

Why It Is Important to Teach State and Local Government

It is important to remember that during the Constitutional Convention there was never a question as to whether or not there would be states, but only if there was to be a national government. The balance of power between state and national governments may not be as much of a balance anymore, with the latter's power for all practical purposes unrestricted, but there remain important reasons for familiarizing our students with state and local governments.

It is at the subnational level that most people have contact with government. Most local services are people-related; the closeness of city hall and the ease of a local telephone call allow individuals the opportunity to observe government in action or to otherwise readily express their opinion on issues of direct interest to them. I often ask my students to imagine the three levels of government ceasing to exist as they arise one morning, and it is easy to see that the services first missed are local (water and sewage, traffic control, etc.). The most direct and intimate contact most people have with the national government is when they fill out their federal tax forms. Further, state and local governments offer even the introductory student the opportunity to conduct field work, to observe a city council or planning commission meeting, to interview a state or local director of finance. Such experiences can be extremely educational.

Both state and local governments have, on the whole, greatly modernized themselves over the past three decades. Many state legislatures are full time, governors' staffs have been expanded,

and civil service requirements have upgraded the educational background of executive agencies at all staff levels. Local governments have full-time chief executives with professional staffs. The once corruptible county assessor has been replaced in many localities by systems analysts who use computer programs to reassess properties. We should no longer fear that an understanding of, or contact with, these governments will in some way warp our students' perspectives about politics and government.

Furthermore, some of the most challenging policy problems and issues are being confronted at the state and local level. Efforts to improve our educational system, to deal with the problems of the homeless, to combat drug use, to determine and provide an adequate level of service while staying within a balanced budget—the front line is at the subnational level. One of the most controversial issues of all, whether or not to take someone's life for the commission of a crime, has been left to states to decide on an individual basis.

Finally, students who wish to get involved with government, whether in a campaign, internship or career, will have a much better chance of meaningful participation if they have been taught the particular workings of state and local governments. A meaningful inclusion of these topics in an introductory course thus provides not only additional insight into the general functioning of politics and government, it also better prepares the student to exercise his or her citizenship.

SOURCE: Bruce Wallin, "State and Local Governments Are American, Too," *Political Science Teacher*, Fall 1988, p. 3. Reprinted by permission.

and local governments. Total public sector employment increased slightly in the 1980s, with small gains at each level of government to reach all-time highs at each level by 1989. This stands in contrast to dramatic increases at the state and local levels in the 1970s. For example, state employment increased by about 33 percent in the 1970s but by only 6 percent in 1980–1988.

The states make significant monetary contributions to local governments—totaling $149 billion in 1988, up from $99 billion in 1983.[3] These payments represent about 35 percent of all state expenditures. There has been a virtually uninterrupted growth in state aid to localities in this century. This growth in state aid has been made possible by the changing nature of state tax systems, including the use of sales and income taxes. State aid also increased in the 1980s because the Reagan administration did away with a move that began in the 1960s to bypass the states and have federal grants go directly to the cities. By consolidating many categorical grants into block grants and giving the block grants to the states, the federal government has given the states new authority and control over federal funds. (These grants are explained in Chapter 2.)

The shift of responsibility to the states has increased concern about state **mandates** to local governments. Mandates arise from statutes, court decisions, and administrative orders that demand action from a "subordinate" government. The number and cost of state mandates have increased substantially, and local officials have become increasingly upset about underfunded mandates. A key issue involves guidelines from the states regarding such matters as how to deal with the environment and public employees. Just as federal mandates put pressure on states, state mandates put financial pressure on cities and counties and they call into question the matter of local self-government.

Current state vitality is part of a long history of innovative policymaking by state governments. Wisconsin serves as a classic example: In 1900–1914, that state initiated the direct primary, civil service regulations, a state income tax, conservation laws, and a variety of state regulatory commissions. More recently, New York has pioneered with water-pollution controls and antidiscrimination legislation far in advance of federal regulation. Minnesota state regulations continue to outdistance federal environmental protection laws, particularly in regard to waste material from nuclear power plants. California has been an innovator in community mental health treatment, air-pollution controls, and the development of community colleges.

Much more so than federal government policy, what states and localities do directly affects everyday life. Not only do they have the major responsibility for education, crime, AIDS and other health problems, and welfare administration, these governments also determine public university tuition charges, the price of subway fares, where and when we can purchase alcoholic beverages, whether soda bottles are returnable, and how much we pay for electricity. Most of these issues, even those that may appear trivial, generate strong political reactions from groups that have economic or ideological interests in public policy outcomes.

Political activity within the states is another indication of vitality. The activities of political parties and the management of campaigns and elections occur mainly in state and local settings. All elected public officials, except the president, are selected by voters within the states. Political parties have their organizational base in the states, with their power lodged most firmly in county committees and city organizations. Many members of the U.S. Congress initially held state or local office. Once elected, many senators and representatives devote much of their time (and the time of their staff members) to "casework"—that is, representing the interests of their local constituents in dealing with federal agencies. In election campaigns they often focus their attention on local issues. In electing a multitude of state and local officials (plus participating in federal elections) and in deciding special ballot issues, such as higher tax rates for schools, voters experience a nearly continuous process of campaigns and elections. By holding the first presidential primary, New Hampshire exerts a disproportionate influence on national politics.

STATE POLICYMAKING AND ECONOMIC DEVELOPMENT

Public policymaking is affected by a variety of factors operating outside the formal structure of state and local governments. A state's economic characteristics—including levels of urbanization, personal income, and education—influence political decision making as well as the nature of political participation and party competition.[4]

One example of the effects of economic factors on policymaking is in funding for education. Wealthy, urbanized states, such as Massachusetts, New Jersey, and New York, spend considerably more per capita on education than do less prosperous states. While wealthy states can obviously afford to spend more money per capita on social services than can poor states, their willingness to spend should be differentiated from their ability to spend. Thus in education, some relatively poor states, such as Maine and Vermont, make a stronger effort to assist their schools than do some rich states (i.e., their educational spending as a proportion of personal income is greater than that of wealthier states). Yet poor states, particularly in the South, are still unable to match the per pupil expenditure of wealthier states, such as Ohio and Connecticut, where the tax effort (or burden) is significantly less. The term *tax burden* refers to taxes as a percentage of personal income; it expresses a relation between total taxes and total income in a state. The tax burden is low in Connecticut because personal income is high while tax rates are relatively low.

The willingness to spend money is often tied to such political factors as the role of political parties, the influence of public opinion, and the leadership of the governor. These political factors operate at the margins of decision making and help to explain why differences in spending levels exist among rich states and why some poor states make substantially greater efforts than other poor states.[5] As we will see later in this chapter, willingness to spend money is also related to political culture and state tradition.

As far as political participation is concerned, party competition is usually stronger in the more wealthy, urbanized states, and voter turnout tends to be higher in those states as well. A few interest groups are more likely to dominate government in poor states, such as Maine, while in wealthier states a variety of interest groups tend to balance one another. The economically well-developed states have also been the most likely to adopt new policy ideas. Although there are many exceptions to economic explanations (see the two sections that follow), they do provide us with one of several useful approaches to understanding state politics.

STATE POLICYMAKING AND PHYSICAL SETTING

In a country as diverse as the United States, the physical environment affects the decisions of the state governments in many ways. Large states, such as Wyoming and Montana, often spend significantly more per capita to maintain their highways than do smaller states, such as Maryland and Massachusetts. In addition, the presence of natural resources may affect state policies significantly. Oil and natural gas interests have had a major impact on government in Oklahoma and Texas. For most of this century the Anaconda Company (copper) was the dominant political force in Montana. Unable to comply with new environmental standards in the 1970s, Anaconda ended all mining operations in Montana.[6] The distribution of water rights has had a tremendous influence on politics in such Western states as Arizona and California. Water shortage is a permanent circumstance in Los Angeles, where the annual rainfall is a scant 9 inches. Farms and cities from Salt Lake City to San Diego are literally drinking the Colorado River dry. Finally, the existence of such geographical features as mountains, deserts, and lakes within a state may cause special problems and influence the allocation of state resources.

Consider some of the physical features of California—features that subject its political decision makers to contrasting pressures from interest groups as well as force them to acquire knowledge about a wide array of technical matters. The state stretches for 650 miles, from the Mexican border to the Oregon state line. The Sierra Nevada Mountains extend for about 400 miles along the eastern border of the state. Temperatures range from harsh cold and deep snow in the High Sierras to unbearable heat in Death Valley. While northern California has ample water, southern California must import its water. The same state that has produced the Los Angeles freeway system also has the agriculturally rich Central Valley. The annual value of farm crops in California is $10.6 billion, nearly equal to the combined value of second-place Iowa (5.82) and third-place Illinois (5.8).

Population size and the presence of large metropolitan areas also have important effects on state politics. In the mid-1970s, the financial problems of New York City threatened the fiscal stability of New York State and involved the governor in extended negotiations with private bankers and the federal government to help "save" New York City. In the 1990s it is the state's budget deficit that will cut funding for projects in New York City. City dwellers demand more services— health care, welfare, sanitation, recreation, slum clearance, public housing—than do residents of small towns. These demands are transmitted to state legislative and gubernatorial candidates, who cannot ignore city voters as they campaign for office. In New York, Illinois, Pennsylvania, and Michigan, to name a few, serious conflicts between major cities and the rest of the state have long existed within state government.

STATE POLICYMAKING AND POLITICAL CULTURE

While explanations based on economics and physical characteristics are helpful in understanding state politics, there remain a significant number of exceptions to the rule. Economic conditions do not explain the high levels of voter turnout in Montana, Idaho, Wyoming, and Utah, where levels of income and urbanization are below the national average. Some states with low levels of personal income, such as Louisiana and Oklahoma, provide surprisingly high welfare benefits. In contrast, while Indiana ranked thirtieth in per capita personal income in 1988, it ranked thirty-sixth in per pupil expenditure for education. In the next section, we will note some of the vast differences that exist even among states within the same geographical area.

Sometimes states that have similar economic and demographic characteristics are very different politically. A case in point is the adjacent states of Michigan and Ohio. They are alike in terms of population, industrialization, and urbanization. Both have many small towns and rich farmland. In both states, there is a high level of party competition. In both, organized labor is a strong political force. Yet Michigan has been a much more progressive state than Ohio. It has allocated proportionately greater expenditures for social welfare services, and it has experienced significantly less corruption in government. In Ohio, on the other hand, the **spoils system** has persisted and the political parties have avoided dealing with the issue.

Another example is the neighboring states of Vermont and New Hampshire. Both are small and predominantly rural. Yet Vermont, the poorer of the two states, ranks among the highest in terms of tax burden, while New Hampshire ranks among the lowest. Vermont has been a center of public-spirited activism, while New Hampshire is characterized as a stronghold of stingy government.[7] Much of the reason for these differences appears to lie in the political cultures of the two states.

Political culture is defined by Daniel Elazar as "the particular pattern of orientation to political action in which each political system is embedded."[8] In the following analysis, political culture is understood to encompass political tradition and the rules governing political behavior. For students of state government, political culture helps explain differences in political attitudes and government concerns from state to state. In large part, political culture determines what policies can be expected from state government, the kinds of people who become active in political affairs, and the way in which the political game is played in particular states and their communities.

Each state has its own history and tradition, and this is reflected in differences in its population's concerns and attitudes toward political life. In many states, differences among nationalities are important to understanding politics. For example, Irish Catholics in Massachusetts and Jews in New York have played major roles in forming distinctive patterns of political participation in those states. The Civil War and Reconstruction left a lasting mark on the political systems of Southern and border states. The **Progressive movement** early in this century had a major impact on the political processes in Wisconsin, Minnesota, and the Dakotas. In particular, Progressivism created an intense distrust of party organizations and reliance on widespread citizen participation. Alaska and Hawaii have truly unique histories and cultures because of their geographical isolation and their mixtures of racial and ethnic groups. While residents of some states have a strong sense of identity with their state, it has been suggested that the dominant fact of political life in New Jersey is that residents do not and never did identify with their state.[9]

Elazar identifies three political cultures that can be found throughout the United States—**individualistic, traditional,** and **moralistic.**[10] These cultures have their roots in the three geographic regions of colonial America. The individualistic culture (I) developed in the business centers of New York, Philadelphia, and Baltimore; the traditional culture (T) developed in the plantation society of the Old South; and the moralistic culture (M) arose out of the tradition of Puritanism and town meetings in New England. As waves of settlers moved westward, these three cultures spread throughout the United States. In many instances, two or three cultures met, meshed together, and produced a variety of state and sectional cultural strains. In Illinois, Indiana, and Ohio, this mixing of political cultures produced complex politics and caused conflicts that have persisted over decades.

Politics in the three political cultures can be described with respect to (1) degree of political participation, (2) development of government bureaucracy, and (3) amount of government intervention in society. Of the three dimensions, degree of political participation (i.e., voter turnout and suffrage regulations) is the most consistent indicator of political culture. In individualistic political cultures, participation is limited because politics is viewed as just another means by which individuals may improve their economic and social position. Because corruption is accepted as a natural part of politics, its disclosure is unlikely to produce public protest. In moralistic cultures, political participation is regarded as the duty of each citizen in a political setting where government seeks to promote the public welfare of all persons. In traditional cultures, voter turnout is low and voting regulations are restrictive. Here government is controlled by an elite whose family and social position give it a "right" to govern. In many cases citizens are not even expected to vote. Corruption tends to be even more widespread in traditional than in individualistic states. This is so because politics is not oriented toward the **public interest,** and it is expected that payoffs will occur.

In traditional South Carolina a very strong legislature developed, controlled by a few political leaders working with the state's two dominant business interests. *The State,* Columbia's newspaper, noted in 1991 that "through most of South Carolina's history, the people who set up and ran state government have had two main priorities: Keeping power out of the hands of black people. Keeping power out of the hands of everybody else."[11] As late as the 1940s, less than 10 percent of the eligible voters voted in presidential elections. The political culture of South Carolina is blamed for a scandal in which fifteen state legislators were indicted in 1991 for taking bribes from undercover FBI agents.

In regard to the development of government bureaucracy, individualistic cultures limit government functions and provide only those few basic services demanded by the public. While bureaucracy is distrusted because of its potential to encroach on private matters, it is often used to advance the personal goals of public officials. In moralistic cultures, bureaucracy typically is permitted to expand to provide the public with the wide range of services it demands. Here government commitment to the public good, honesty, and selflessness leads to low levels of corruption. Traditional cultures tend to be antibureaucratic, because a professional bureaucracy would interfere with the established pattern of personal relations developed by politicians.

In regard to government intervention into community affairs, both individualistic and traditional political cultures strive to protect private activities by limiting government intrusions. The moralistic culture, in contrast, fosters a definite commitment to government intervention; government is viewed as a positive force. The moralistic political culture also differs from the other two cultures in that its political campaigns are marked by an emphasis on issues rather than personalities. Parties and interest groups are organized to direct policy in the public interest.

Each culture has made both positive and negative contributions. Elazar notes that the moralistic culture, although it has been a significant force in the American quest for the good society, tends toward fanaticism and narrow-mindedness—roughly parallel to groups that claim to have found the "true religion." In spite of widespread corruption, the individualistic culture of the Northeast and many large Midwestern cities did facilitate the assimilation of immigrant groups into American society. Moreover, some corruption occurs in all states and it does not necessarily affect the delivery of public services. Although the predominant traditional culture in the South has helped sustain racial discrimination and second-rate demagogues, it has also produced a significant number of first-rate national leaders and effective governors.

For the past twenty-five years Elazar's groundbreaking theory has helped explain variations in public policy and political behavior. As we would expect, his typology has been subjected to a wide variety of tests. Critics have noted that Elazar has never adjusted the mapping of his three subcultures, that what constitutes each subculture is a subjective judgment, and that his scheme relies on past behavior to predict current political behavior.[12]

Although culture has a strong effect on voter participation, its impact on government policymaking is less substantial. This is so because strong political leaders or dramatic events may divert the forms of public service from the pattern most consistent with the political culture. There is some evidence to suggest that distinctive state and local cultures are weakening because of population mobility, especially in the **Sunbelt** states—the fifteen states extending from southern California through Arizona, Texas, Florida and up the Atlantic coast to Virginia. The change has arisen because of the growing importance of the news media, especially television, nationwide and because federal grants have encouraged states to enact a variety of programs under which they can receive matching funds.

STATE POLICYMAKING AND SECTIONALISM

States that are located adjacent to each other tend to share some persistent political similarities. Elazar refers to this as the "geology" of political cultures.[13] States within particular areas, sharing a common cultural, economic, and historical background, exhibit clearly identifiable political tendencies. This is known as **sectionalism.** Major sections as defined by the U.S. Bureau of the Census are the Northeast, the North Central states, the South, and the West. Within each section we can identify several regions, such as the Southwest (West) and the Middle Atlantic (Northeast). The component states of the various sections and regions define problems and formulate public policy in a similar manner.[14]

The *South,* which includes the eleven former Confederate states plus the border states of West Virginia, Kentucky, Delaware, Oklahoma, and Maryland, has long been the most clearly identifiable section of America. Throughout most of the South, there is widespread poverty, levels of educational attainment are generally low, and government functions are centralized at the state level. In the South, state governments often perform many of the government functions typically carried out by cities and counties in other sections of the country. As in other sections, it often is difficult to tell whether policy is influenced more by geographic location or by economic factors. Moreover, as in other sections, major exceptions to the general rule can be identified. For example, West Virginia has had a high level of interparty competition; considerable wealth exists in parts of Texas, Virginia, and Florida; and politics in Atlanta is vastly different from politics in Yazoo County, Mississippi.

In the *Northeast* (the six New England states plus the Middle Atlantic states of New York, Pennsylvania, and New Jersey), most states share problems of congestion and industrialization. Levels of party competition and voter turnout are comparatively high. There is an emphasis on local government decision making stemming from the New England tradition of town meetings. As a result, government functions are much less centralized than in the South. On a regional basis, Boston continues to be the economic and educational hub of New England, while New York City dominates the Middle Atlantic states in terms of culture and business. In many Northeastern states a substantial number of children attend parochial schools. Yet major differences exist between the northern Northeastern states, which have been predominantly rural and Protestant (Maine, New Hampshire, and Vermont), and the southern Northeastern states, which have been predominantly urban and Catholic (Rhode Island, New York, Connecticut, Massachusetts, Pennsylvania, and New Jersey). There is a great contrast between the wealth of suburban Connecticut and the poverty of rural Maine and Vermont.

The eleven states of the *West* (including the Rocky Mountain, Desert, and Pacific Coast states), which comprise nearly 60 percent of the land mass of the continental United States, share problems of natural resource development, population diffusion, and water distribution. Most Western states have relied heavily on resource extraction with little economic diversity. This has produced a history of boom-or-bust economic cycles. Despite their political conservatism and dislike of the federal government, the Western states have depended heavily on federal aid, and government is the major employer in several of these states.[15] In each of the Western states, the federal government owns at least 30 percent of the land. The federal government owns 85 percent of the land in Nevada and 86 percent in Alaska. Still, as noted earlier, there is great geographical diversity in just one state, California, and there are vast cultural differences between residents of San

Francisco and Salt Lake City. Thus, as with other sections of the country, we need to be careful about stereotyping the West.

Typically, the Western states are marked by high levels of voter turnout and relatively weak party organizations. While Democratic–Republican competition is keen in state elections, these states have been strongly Republican in presidential elections. In the 1968 and 1972 presidential elections, Richard Nixon carried every Western state (except Washington in 1968). In 1976, Gerald Ford lost only Texas and Hawaii among all states west of Minnesota. In 1980 and 1984, Ronald Reagan carried all the Western states. And, in 1988, George Bush carried all the Western states except Washington and Oregon.

The *North Central* (Great Lakes and Great Plains) states each have a blend of agricultural, industrial, and urban areas. There is strong two-party competition and above-average wealth, particularly in the Great Lakes states. However, the twelve North Central states are the least homogeneous of the four sections. Because the North Central section borders on each of the other three sections, some of its regional areas share the characteristics found in other sections. As with the other sections, there are major internal contradictions. While politics in Indiana, Ohio, and Missouri often has centered on patronage, jobs, and personalities (a reflection of their Southern heritage), politics in Minnesota, Wisconsin, and Michigan has been issue-oriented and government has been essentially corruption-free.[16]

POPULATION SHIFTS AMONG SECTIONS

Americans are a highly mobile people, and movement from the cities to the suburbs and from one region to another has added a dynamic dimension to state politics. As of 1990, about 77 percent of Americans lived in metropolitan areas. There were a total of 284 **metropolitan statistical areas** (MSAs) in the United States in 1990. As defined by the Census Bureau since 1983, a county may qualify as an MSA if it contains a city of at least 50,000 population or if it contains an urbanized area of 50,000 or more population and a total metropolitan population of 100,000 or more. An MSA can be one county or group of counties. There is at least one MSA in every state. That the United States is becoming increasingly metropolitan can be seen in statistics showing that 56 percent of the population in 1950 lived in metropolitan areas and nearly 90 percent of the nation's population growth in the 1980s occurred in the thirty-nine largest metropolitan areas.

The density, heterogeneity, and interdependence of urban life have created obvious political problems in the areas of health, housing, and crime. The spread of the suburbs (in extreme cases creating vast, sprawling developments—as along the East Coast, southern California, and southern Lake Michigan) has fragmented government and made metropolitan planning and coordination extremely difficult. There are thirty-nine MSAs that have more than 1 million population and two with populations that exceed 10 million (see Table 1.1). Areas with more than 1 million residents are called consolidated metropolitan statistical areas. New Jersey is completely within MSAs and seven other states are over 90 percent metropolitan. The least metropolitan state is Idaho (about 20 percent), followed by Vermont and Montana.

Table 1.1   The Forty Largest Metropolitan Areas, 1990

METROPOLITAN AREA	Total Population (1,000)	PERCENT OF TOTAL METROPOLITAN POPULATION	
		Black	Hispanic Origin
New York-Northern New Jersey-Long Island, NY-NJ-CT CMSA	18,087	18.2	15.4
Los Angeles-Anaheim-Riverside, CA CMSA	14,532	8.5	32.9
Chicago-Gary-Lake County (IL), IL-IN-WI CMSA	8,066	19.2	11.1
San Francisco-Oakland-San Jose, CA CMSA	6,253	8.6	15.5
Philadelphia-Wilmington-Trenton, PA-NJ-DE-MD CMSA	5,899	18.7	3.8
Detroit-Ann Arbor, MI CMSA	4,665	20.9	1.9
Boston-Lawrence-Salem, MA-NH CMSA	4,172	5.7	4.6
Washington, DC-MD-VA MSA	3,924	26.6	5.7
Dallas-Fort Worth, TX CMSA	3,885	14.3	13.4
Houston-Galveston-Brazoria, TX CMSA	3,711	17.9	20.8
Miami-Fort Lauderdale, FL CMSA	3,193	18.5	33.3
Atlanta, GA MSA	2,834	26.0	2.0
Cleveland-Akron-Lorain, OH CMSA	2,760	16.0	1.9
Seattle-Tacoma, WA CMSA	2,559	4.8	3.0
San Diego, CA MSA	2,498	6.4	20.4
Minneapolis-St. Paul, MN-WI MSA	2,464	3.6	1.5
St. Louis, MO-IL MSA	2,444	17.3	1.1
Baltimore, MD MSA	2,382	25.9	1.3
Pittsburgh-Beaver Valley, PA CMSA	2,243	8.0	0.6
Phoenix, AZ MSA	2,122	3.5	16.3
Tampa-St. Petersburg-Clearwater, FL MSA	2,068	9.0	6.7
Denver-Boulder, CO CMSA	1,848	5.3	12.2
Cincinnati-Hamilton, OH-KY-IN CMSA	1,744	11.7	0.5
Milwaukee-Racine, WI CMSA	1,607	13.3	3.8
Kansas City, MO-KS MSA	1,566	12.8	2.9
Sacramento, CA MSA	1,481	6.9	11.6
Portland-Vancouver, OR-WA CMSA	1,478	2.8	3.4
Norfolk-Virginia Beach-Newport News, VA MSA	1,396	28.5	2.3
Columbus, OH MSA	1,377	12.0	0.8
San Antonio, TX MSA	1,302	6.8	47.6
Indianapolis, IN MSA	1,250	13.8	0.9
New Orleans, LA MSA	1,239	34.7	4.3
Buffalo-Niagara Falls, NY CMSA	1,189	10.3	2.0
Charlotte-Gastonia-Rock Hill, NC-SC MSA	1,162	19.9	0.9
Providence-Pawtucket-Fall River, RI-MA CMSA	1,142	3.3	4.2
Hartford-New Britain-Middletown, CT CMSA	1,086	8.7	7.0
Orlando, FL MSA	1,073	12.4	9.0
Salt Lake City-Ogden, UT MSA	1,072	1.0	5.8
Rochester, NY MSA	1,002	9.4	3.1
Nashville, TN MSA	985	15.5	0.8

SOURCE: U.S. Census Bureau.

Particularly during the 1950s and 1960s, great numbers of lower-income Southern blacks and Appalachian whites moved into Northern cities such as Chicago, Detroit, and New York, greatly compounding the financial problems of those city governments. In the 1980s there was a large increase in the number of Asians and Hispanics in many American cities. For example, New York City's Hispanic population increased by 29 percent in the 1980s, and nearly 1,400 immigrants arrive each month in New York's Chinatown, the largest Chinese community in the Western Hemisphere. At the same time, there has been an exodus of upper- and middle-class whites and of industries to the suburbs. Thus while the costs of public services multiplied, the tax base of many cities declined substantially. Currently, more than 80 percent of blacks and persons of Spanish origin live in MSAs.

In 1976, the Census Bureau reported for the first time that a majority of the United States population lived in the South and the West. The growth in these states has been accompanied by a variety of political and economic problems, which are discussed in Chapter 9. As in the 1970s, Nevada was the fastest-growing state in the 1980s (49 percent). It was followed in order by Arizona, Florida, California, Texas, and Utah, all up at least 18 percent. About 50 percent of the nation's population increase occurred in three states—California, Florida, and Texas. While only one state (Rhode Island) lost population in the 1970s, nine states, led by West Virginia (down 8.6 percent), lost population in the 1980s (see Table 1.2).

From 1940 through 1990, the population of Houston grew from 385,000 to 1,631,000; that of Phoenix from 65,000 to 968,400. San Diego gained 900,000 people, San Jose 714,000, and San Antonio 682,000. In that same period Chicago lost 714,000 people, Cleveland lost 373,000, and St. Louis lost over one-half its population (420,000). Virtually all the fastest-growing cities in the 1980s were mid-sized suburbs, close to interstate highways, and located in the Sunbelt. Of the twenty fastest-growing cities, eleven were in California (see Table 1.3). Curiously, several large Sunbelt cities, such as New Orleans, Louisville, Atlanta, and Memphis, lost population—because of either a downturn in the local economy (New Orleans) or a movement to the suburbs (Atlanta). Previously booming Denver lost 5 percent of its population in the 1980s (see Table 1.4). As noted in the reading for this chapter, population growth was especially strong in state capitals and in university towns. Several state capitals with large state universities, such as Columbus, Madison, and Tallahassee, had especially strong growth. In many cases, state government generates jobs and helps the economy of an entire metropolitan area. For example, in the 1980s Columbus grew by 12 percent, replacing Cleveland (down 12 percent) as Ohio's largest city. In several instances, urban public universities have spurred economic growth and have become community social leaders. For example, the University of Alabama at Birmingham is the largest employer in the state and has about a $1 billion annual impact on the region.

A controversial issue with the U.S. Census is the undercount and adjustment of population figures. Census takers missed about 5 million Americans in 1990, and they missed black and Hispanic men at more than twice the national rate. This has major significance for cities such as New York, Los Angeles, and Detroit, where minorities comprise a majority of the population and where the census count

Table 1.2   State Population Changes, 1990

Rank and State	1990	1980	Rank and State	1990	1980
1. California	29,839,250	23,667,902	28. Oklahoma	3,157,604	3,025,290
2. New York	18,044,505	17,558,072	29. Oregon	2,853,733	2,633,105
3. Texas	17,059,805	14,229,191	30. Iowa	2,787,424	2,913,808
4. Florida	13,003,362	9,746,324	31. Mississippi	2,586,443	2,520,638
5. Pennsylvania	11,924,710	11,863,895	32. Kansas	2,485,600	2,363,679
6. Illinois	11,466,682	11,426,518	33. Arkansas	2,362,239	2,286,435
7. Ohio	10,887,325	10,797,630	34. West Virginia	1,801,625	1,949,644
8. Michigan	9,328,784	9,262,078	35. Utah	1,727,784	1,461,037
9. New Jersey	7,748,634	7,364,823	36. Nebraska	1,584,617	1,569,825
10. North Carolina	6,657,630	5,881,766	37. New Mexico	1,521,779	1,302,894
11. Georgia	6,508,419	5,463,105	38. Maine	1,233,223	1,124,660
12. Virginia	6,216,568	5,346,818	39. Nevada	1,206,152	800,493
13. Massachusetts	6,029,051	5,737,037	40. Hawaii	1,115,274	964,691
14. Indiana	5,564,228	5,490,224	41. New Hampshire	1,113,915	920,610
15. Missouri	5,137,804	4,916,686	42. Idaho	1,011,986	943,935
16. Wisconsin	4,906,745	4,705,767	43. Rhode Island	1,005,984	947,154
17. Tennessee	4,896,641	4,591,120	44. Montana	803,655	786,690
18. Washington	4,887,941	4,132,156	45. South Dakota	699,999	690,768
19. Maryland	4,798,622	4,216,975	46. Delaware	668,696	594,338
20. Minnesota	4,387,029	4,075,970	47. North Dakota	641,364	652,717
21. Louisiana	4,238,216	4,205,900	48. Vermont	564,964	511,456
22. Alabama	4,062,608	3,893,888	49. Alaska	551,947	401,851
23. Kentucky	3,698,969	3,660,777	50. Wyoming	455,975	469,557
24. Arizona	3,677,985	2,718,215			
25. South Carolina	3,505,707	3,121,820	Total states	249,022,783	225,866,492
26. Colorado	3,307,912	2,889,964	D.C.	609,909	638,333
27. Connecticut	3,295,669	3,107,576	Total U.S.	249,632,692	226,504,825

SOURCE: U.S. Census Bureau.

missed 3 to 5 percent of the population. Population adjustment would help cities gain seats in state legislatures and give them more federal and state aid. However, Secretary of Commerce Robert A. Mosbacher decided *not* to adjust the 1990 census. He argued that adjusted figures would be increasingly unreliable for smaller communities and would increase cynicism about government by suggesting that the census process could be manipulated by statisticians in Washington.

In his provocative book *Power Shift,* Kirkpatrick Sale vividly describes the political implications of this population shift.[17] Sale argues that America's southern rim, or Sunbelt, has come to dominate American politics, as population, manufacturing, and capital have moved form the North to the South. From 1960 to 1992, New York lost ten seats in Congress and Florida gained eleven. In 1960, California had thirty-two electoral votes, the same number as Pennsylvania; in 1992, California had fifty-four electoral votes, Pennsylvania only twenty-three. Congressional redistricting for 1992 resulted in a switch of nineteen seats. All the gainers, except Washington (one seat), were in the Sunbelt and all the losers were

Table 1.3   The Twenty Fastest-Growing Cities and Largest Population Losers, 1980–1990

City	1980 Population	1990 Population	Percent Gain
Mesa, Ariz.	152,404	288,091	88.98%
Rancho Cucamonga, Calif.	55,250	101,409	83.54%
Plano, Texas	72,331	128,713	77.95%
Irvine, Calif.	62,134	110,330	77.57%
Escondido, Calif.	64,355	108,635	68.81%
Oceanside, Calif.	76,698	128,398	67.41%
Bakersfield, Calif.	105,611	174,820	65.53%
Arlington, Texas	160,113	261,721	63.46%
Fresno, Calif.	217,491	354,202	62.91%
Chula Vista, Calif.	83,927	135,163	61.05%
Las Vegas	164,674	258,295	56.85%
Modesto, Calif.	106,963	164,730	54.01%
Tallahassee, Fla.	81,548	124,773	53.01%
Glendale, Ariz.	97,172	148,134	52.45%
Mesquite, Texas	67,053	101,484	51.35%
Ontario, Calif.	88,820	133,179	49.94%
Virginia Beach, Va.	262,199	393,069	49.91%
Scottsdale, Ariz.	88,622	130,069	46.77%
Santa Ana, Calif.	203,713	293,742	44.19%
Stockton, Calif.	148,283	210,943	42.26%

City	1980 Population	1990 Population	Percent Loss
Gary, Ind.	151,968	116,646	−23.24%
Newark, N.J.	329,248	275,221	−16.41%
Detroit	1,203,368	1,027,974	−14.57%
Pittsburgh	423,959	369,879	−12.75%
St. Louis	452,801	396,685	−12.39%
Cleveland	573,822	505,616	−11.89%
Flint, Mich.	159,611	140,761	−11.81%
New Orleans	557,927	496,938	−10.87%
Warren, Mich.	161,134	144,864	−10.10%
Chattanooga, Tenn.	169,514	152,466	−10.08%
Louisville	298,694	269,063	−9.92%
Macon, Ga.	116,896	106,612	−8.80%
Erie, Pa.	119,123	108,718	−8.73%
Peoria, Ill.	124,160	113,504	−8.58%
Buffalo	357,870	328,123	−8.31%
Richmond, Va.	219,214	203,056	−7.37%
Chicago	3,005,072	2,783,726	−7.37%
Atlanta	425,022	394,017	−7.29%
Kansas City, Kan.	161,148	149,767	−7.06%
Birmingham, Ala.	284,413	265,968	−6.49%

SOURCE: U.S. Census Bureau.

Table 1.4   The Thirty Largest Cities, 1980–1990

1990 Rank	1980 Rank	City	1990 Population	1980 Population	Percent Change
1	1	New York	7,322,564	7,071,639	3.5%
2	3	Los Angeles	3,485,398	2,968,528	17.4%
3	2	Chicago	2,783,726	3,005,072	−7.4%
4	5	Houston	1,630,553	1,595,138	2.2%
5	4	Philadelphia	1,585,577	1,688,210	−6.1%
6	8	San Diego	1,110,549	875,538	26.8%
7	6	Detroit	1,027,974	1,203,368	−14.6%
8	7	Dallas	1,006,877	904,599	11.3%
9	9	Phoenix	983,403	789,704	24.5%
10	11	San Antonio	935,933	785,940	19.1%
11	17	San Jose, Calif.	782,284	629,400	24.3%
12	12	Indianapolis	741,952	711,539	4.3%
13	10	Baltimore	736,014	786,741	−6.4%
14	13	San Francisco	723,959	678,974	6.6%
15	19	Jacksonville, Fla.	672,971	571,003	17.9%
16	20	Columbus, Ohio	632,910	565,021	12.0%
17	16	Milwaukee	628,088	636,297	−1.3%
18	14	Memphis	610,337	646,174	−5.5%
19	15	Washington	606.900	638,432	−4.9%
20	21	Boston	574,283	562,994	2.0%
21	23	Seattle	516,259	493,846	4.5%
22	28	El Paso	515,342	425,259	21.2%
23	25	Nashville	510,784	477,811	6.9%
24	18	Cleveland	505,616	573,822	−11.9%
25	22	New Orleans	496,938	557,927	−10.9%
26	24	Denver	467,610	492,686	−5.1%
27	42	Austin, Texas	465,622	345,164	34.6%
28	33	Fort Worth	447,619	385,164	16.2%
29	31	Oklahoma City	444,719	404,014	10.1%
30	35	Portland, Ore.	437,319	368,148	18.8%

SOURCE: U.S. Census Bureau.

concentrated in a nearly unbroken line from Massachusetts west to Iowa. California, Texas, and Florida gained a total of fourteen seats.

Another issue of concern is the flow of federal dollars to the Sunbelt. As the amount of federal grants has increased, competition among the states for federal dollars has grown intense. In general, Western and New England states receive the highest levels of federal expenditures per capita (see Table 1.5). Southern states receive the lowest levels of federal expenditures.

Tensions among sections of the country have led to the formation of such organizations as the Western Governors' Policy Office and the Coalition of Northeastern Governors. In Congress, several informal groups—including the

Population Grows in State Capitals

WASHINGTON, Jan. 25—Expanding employment in state government and higher education in the 1980's fueled population gains in college towns and state capitals, according to 1990 census figures released today.

The population of cities like Lawrence, Kan., home of the University of Kansas, Columbus, Ohio, home of the state government and of Ohio State University, and West Lafayette, Ind., home of Purdue University, gained 20 percent or more even as the states around them stagnated. The new census figures show that North Dakota, for example, lost 1.7 percent of its population, but its capital, Bismarck, gained 10.7 percent.

This trend did not hold true in older cities in the East that are state capitals, like Boston or Atlanta. But generally, said John Connally, an assistant director of the Census Bureau, "You get one star if you have a state capital, two if you have a college or university, and three if there's a major medical center there."

DECLINE OF NORTHERN CITIES

In their overall depiction of the country, the new numbers reflected trends long tracked by demographers, most dramatically the 6-million gain in population registered by California, much of that on the immigrant- and industry-rich southern coast.

The new numbers also demonstrated anew the decline of many Northern urban centers, a decline now spreading to the inner suburbs of cities like New York, Washington and Detroit. And they reflected the continued decline of old industrial cities like Gary, Ind., which lost 26 percent of its population in the 1980's, and the quick expansion of suburban and satellite communities on the edges of metropolitan areas from Frederick County in Maryland to Orange County in California.

But, while the new figures provide a thorough confirmation of some of the population trends of the decade, particularly the impact that an influx of 7 to 9 million Latin American, Asian and European immigrants has had on the United States in the 1980's, demographers combing through the numbers today found other trends that have gone relatively unnoticed. Among them are these:

¶Older industrial cities in the South are joining their Northern counterparts in the cycle of decline. Atlanta, Birmingham, Ala., Macon, Ga., Chattanooga and Knoxville, Tenn., were among the Southern cities losing population. "About 25 percent of all the big cities lost, and half of those that lost were in the South," said William O'Hare, director of policy studies for the Population Reference Bureau, a Washington-based research organization.

¶Immigration has been a bulwark against decline in other major cities, he said, including Miami, New York and New Jersey communities like Elizabeth and Jersey City, both of which registered modest population gains of 2 to 4 percent. In the more suburban areas of Gloucester, Hunterdon and Middlesex counties, a combination of expanding suburbs and thousands of immigrants from India, China, the Philippines and the Dominican Republic pushed growth rates to near 15 percent, triple New Jersey's growth rate.

¶California's growth, while the best-told story of the 1990 census, continued to generate astonishing statistics: of the 29 cities that surpassed the population mark of 100,000, 18 were in California. Seven of the 10 fastest growing cities in the 100,000-plus group were in Southern California, including Chula Vista, Bakersfield, Irvine, Oceanside and Escondido. One American in eight now lives in California.

¶The stories in other big gainers, like Texas and Florida, were a mixture of growth and decline, although growth predominated. Texas, whose population swings tracked the roller-coaster fortunes of the oil industry, still had two cities among the 10 fastest population gainers—Plano and Arlington, both suburbs of Dallas. Austin, the state capital, gained 35 percent, a rate double that of the state as a whole.

¶The changes in rural America were more dramatic than earlier indications had shown. Half of all rural counties lost population in an exodus of more than two million people from dwindling mining communities in Wyoming and Kentucky, the cotton and catfish farms of the Mississippi Delta and the Great Plains, according to Calvin Beale, a demographer for the Department of Agriculture.

MOVE TO RURAL AREAS

But while these areas, which encompass more than a million square miles, emptied out, one-third of the nation's rural counties were growing quickly. Ocean-view communities, mountain resorts and farm land an hour's commute from urban areas were booming with long-distance commuters, vacationers and retired people.

In an article awaiting publication, Mr. Beale says the movement of retired people to rural areas is so pronounced that 20 percent of all rural counties may now be retirement areas. These counties grew by 15 percent in the 1980's,

compared with a national growth rate of 10.2 percent.

About two-thirds of all state capitals gained population. Those that lost were largely in the East: Albany, Harrisburg, Pa., Columbia, S.C., Augusta, Me., Trenton, Charleston, W.Va., and Richmond. Capitals that were both the seat of government and of a state university, like Madison, Wis., and Columbus, Ohio, which each grew 12 percent, far outstripped their states' growth.

State government experts and private statisticians say the population growth in state capitals parallels the 16.3 percent growth in state employment over the decade. And they say it may be a fragile trend, as many states like New York are wrestling with intractable budget deficits because of the current recession.

HEYDAY IN STATE CAPITALS

The 1990 census may be a picture of a heyday in state capitals that is now over, said Edward J. Spar, president of Market Statistics, a New York marketing and demographic analysis firm.

"The figures are a wonderful reflection of the Federal Government pushing more and more down to the states, which have to increase staff to handle the burden," said Mr. Spar. "But you can't project this data into the future with the current recession."

The similar, though less dramatic, boom in college communities may be tempered by declining numbers of college-age students as well as by shrinking budgets in the next few years. But in the 1980s, college towns in many states were population meccas. The population of Norman, Okla., seat of the University of Oklahoma, grew by nearly 18 percent, while the state as a whole grew by 4.2 percent.

Austin, Tex., benefited both by the presence of the state capital and the state university, but its 35 percent population growth rate was attributable in part to the annexation of new land. Immigration was apparently an important factor pushing up the population rate in southern Texas—four counties bordering the Rio Grande registered population increases from 34 percent to 48 percent.

Occasionally, a single company turned a city around. Although South Dakota suffered the same problems as its neighbors on the High Plains, Sioux Falls, now home to the billing operation of Citibank MasterCard, went from a population of 81,000 to 101,000, a 24 percent increase.

SOURCE: Felicity Barringer, *The New York Times,* January 26, 1991, pp. 1 and 10. Copyright © 1991 by The New York Times Company. Reprinted by permission.

Table 1.5   Federal Aid to State and Local Government, Per Capita, 1989

1.	District of Columbia	$2,521	28. Hawaii	475
2.	Alaska	1,258	29. Oklahoma	468
3.	Wyoming	1,018	30. Delaware	465
4.	New York	763	31. New Jersey	462
5.	Montana	693	32. Arkansas	460
6.	Rhode Island	686	33. Maryland	459
7.	North Dakota	654	34. Ohio	455
8.	South Dakota	649	35. Nebraska	440
9.	Vermont	629	36. Alabama	437
10.	Massachusetts	624	37. Illinois	428
11.	New Mexico	593	38. Iowa	416
12.	Maine	563	39. South Carolina	414
13.	Connecticut	574	40. California	411
14.	Pennsylvania	531	41. Colorado	410
15.	Louisiana	526	42. Missouri	394
16.	Mississippi	521	43. North Carolina	380
17.	Minnesota	521	44. Indiana	378
18.	West Virginia	513	45. New Hampshire	371
19.	Oregon	506	46. Arizona	367
20.	Kentucky	497	47. Kansas	363
21.	Idaho	494	48. Texas	352
22.	Michigan	491	49. Nevada	351
23.	Washington	482	50. Virginia	347
24.	Utah	482	51. Florida	323
	UNITED STATES	481		
25.	Georgia	480		
26.	Tennessee	476		
27.	Wisconsin	475		

SOURCE: Edith Horner, ed., *Almanac of the Fifty States* (Palo Alto, Calif.: Information Publications, 1991).

Northeast–Midwest Economic Advancement Coalition, the Sunbelt Caucus, and the Great Lakes Conference—have been established since the early 1970s.

CONSTITUTIONAL AND LEGAL LIMITS ON STATE ACTION

The U.S. Constitution on the one hand provides certain guarantees to the states and on the other hand imposes certain restrictions on state actions.[18] For example, political integrity is protected by federal constitutional provisions that states cannot be divided or consolidated without state legislative consent. In addition, amendments to the Constitution must be ratified by three-fourths of the states. The Constitution limits state action by denying to the states the power to coin money or pass **ex post facto laws.** Treaties with foreign nations are binding on the states as the law of the land; and the Constitution and all laws made under it are the supreme law of the land.

The American system of federalism (discussed in detail in Chapter 2) distributes power in such a way as to deny the central government authority in only a few areas. However, the central government must rely on the cooperation of state and local governments to achieve most of its objectives. As a result, there is a great deal of sharing in policymaking between the states and the federal government. Because the constitutional division of power between the states and the federal government is not precise, a dynamic relationship exists that has allowed the federal government in recent years to move into many areas traditionally reserved to the states. Federal administrative actions, congressional statutes, and court decisions have imposed national standards that in some instances replace previously controlling local standards. Specifically, federal grants-in-aid (see Chapter 2) have given the national government the means to exercise powers concurrent with the states in many areas of policymaking.

Federal court decisions have limited state action from the earliest days of the republic. In *McCulloch* **v.** *Maryland* **(1819)** and *Gibbons* **v.** *Ogden* **(1824),** the Supreme Court supported the supremacy of national law and broadly interpreted congressional power in interstate commerce (these decisions are discussed in Chapter 2). More recently, decisions in the areas of civil rights, school integration, rights of criminal defendants, and voting qualifications have expanded federal authority while limiting that of the states. As an instrument of the national government, the Supreme Court under Chief Justice John Marshall and in most instances since the late 1930s has broadly construed the implied powers of Congress vis-à-vis the states and ignored the so-called reserved powers of the states (see the **Tenth Amendment**). Under court order, federal registrars have replaced local voting officials in Southern states and state legislatures have been ordered to reapportion themselves on the basis of "one man, one vote."

THE STATE CONSTITUTIONS

State constitutions prescribe the structure of government, the powers granted various public officials, terms of office and means of election, and the way in which constitutional amendments shall be enacted. Like the U.S. Constitution, state constitutions take precedence over any state laws that are in conflict with them.

It is difficult to generalize among the fifty state constitutions (see Table 1.6). The oldest is that of Massachusetts, adopted in 1780; Georgia, Illinois, Louisiana, Montana, and Virginia have adopted new constitutions since 1970. The 1982 constitution in Georgia replaced a document well known for its excessive length (48,000 words) and excessive amendments. The new Georgia constitution eliminated approximately 1,200 local amendments added by voters over the years.

Probably the most unusual of all state constitutions is a proposal for the new state of New Columbia, which was approved by voters of the District of Columbia in 1982; a revised document was submitted to Congress in 1987. The proposed government structure calls for a unicameral legislature and a limitation on principal executive departments to twenty. In addition, the document permits public employees to strike, guarantees a right to employment, and would give state benefits to persons unable to work because of pregnancy. The chances of congressional approval are slim at best.

While twenty states have had only one constitution, Louisiana has had eleven. The constitution of Alabama contains approximately 174,000 words, while the constitutions of five states have less than 10,000. Vermont has added about 50 amendments to its 1793 constitution, while California has added more than 470 amendments. Most state constitutions were written in the nineteenth century, when government power was distrusted. Only eighteen are twentieth-century documents. The reform movement of the early twentieth century was reflected in modern constitutions that sought to limit partisan influences in government. More recent constitutions have strengthened the governors and unified state judicial systems.

In spite of their differences, a general framework of state constitutions can be presented. Most constitutions have a separate section to give effect to the doctrine of separation of powers. All state constitutions have a preamble and a bill of rights. Often these sections contain obsolete provisions. For example, according to the Pennsylvania and Tennessee preambles, a state officeholder must not only believe in God but also in a future state of rewards and punishments. And in seven of the bills of rights, the honorable art of dueling is at issue. A record-high number of changes were made in state bills of rights in the 1980s.[19] A majority of the changes concerned rights of criminal defendants, although four states added rights for victims of crime.

The newer constitutions, such as Alaska's and Hawaii's, omit any specific reference to the mutual exclusiveness of legislative and executive functions. Legislative articles have been strengthened in recent years so that most legislatures are considered to be in continuous session and empowered to meet annually. Executive articles limited the power of governors by creating large numbers of boards and commissions whose members often were independent of the governor. For example, before Michigan wrote a new constitution in 1963, the executive branch consisted of the governor, six major elected officials, twenty-three executive departments, four elected boards, sixty-four appointed boards and commissions, six ex-officio boards, and five retirement boards. Judicial articles typically have been marked by detail, multiplicity of courts, overlapping jurisdictions, and low salaries. Here, too, many amendments have been added to establish new courts, alter the way in which judges are selected, and create a unified state judicial system.

Other constitutional articles deal with suffrage and elections, local government, particular economic interests (such as farming), and amendments. Although most rules and regulations regarding voting have been established by the states, a series of amendments to the U.S. Constitution (Fifteenth, Seventeenth, Nineteenth, Twenty-third, Twenty-fourth, and Twenty-sixth) have provided a degree of uniformity throughout the nation. Nevertheless, a few interesting examples may be cited. In Vermont, for example, the constitution requires "quiet and peaceable behavior" as a voting qualification. In some Southern states before 1965, a person of "good character" might have been excused by the local voting registrar from taking a literacy test or complying with other regulations specifically established to disenfranchise blacks.

Most newer state constitutions have separate articles on policy areas, such as education and welfare. Recently, several states have made changes to eliminate gender-bias language in their constitutions. Most constitutions have a Miscellaneous or General Provisions article to lay out provisions that do not fit elsewhere or that apply to more than one section of the constitution.

In contrast to the U.S. Constitution, most state constitutions are long, detailed, and heavily amended. There is a strong feeling that much of their detail should have been left to legislatures to determine by passing bills. While length and detail are not necessarily bad, these characteristics have had great political significance in the operation of state government. Excessive detail is due in part to the successful efforts of interest groups to have constitutions specifically recognize and protect their economic concerns. Indeed, constitutions are longest in those states with the strongest interest groups. Unless amended, these provisions may hinder government regulation as changes in society occur. Duane Lockard notes that the complexity of state constitutions invites litigation and thus plays into the hands of those resisting change.[20] Opponents can often challenge new laws on the grounds that some detail of constitutional procedure was not properly followed. State courts have often tended toward a narrow interpretation of state constitutions, particularly limiting legislative and executive authority. Indeed, Lockard suggests that courts have often been so opposed to change that they reach beyond specific to general provisions in order to invalidate laws.

Recently, state supreme courts have been forces for change, not obstruction. Several state courts have interpreted their own constitutions independently of the U.S. Constitution, especially in civil rights cases, to support reformist goals. We need to remember that state constitutions are changed by judicial interpretation as well as by amendments. Very detailed constitutions make it more likely that amendments will be added as circumstances change and explicit provisions leave less leeway for change through interpretation. As a result, length and detail beget greater length through amendments.

Many state constitutions reveal a strong suspicion of government power, and they act as roadblocks to change. In particular, constitutional restrictions on gubernatorial power have made activist government in the twentieth century difficult. In

Table 1.6 General Information on State Constitutions
(As of January 1, 1990)

State or Other Jurisdiction	Number of Constitutions*	Dates of Adoption	Effective Date of Present Constitution	Estimated Length (number of words)	NUMBER OF AMENDMENTS Submitted to Voters	Adopted
Alabama	6	1819, 1861, 1865, 1868, 1875, 1901	Nov. 28, 1901	174,000	726	513
Alaska	1	1956	Jan. 3, 1959	13,000	31	22
Arizona	1	1911	Feb. 14, 1912	28,876 (a)	198	109
Arkansas	5	1836, 1861, 1864, 1868, 1874	Oct. 30, 1874	40,720 (a)	164	76 (b)
California	2	1849, 1879	July 4, 1879	33,350	781	471
Colorado	1	1876	Aug. 1, 1876	45,679	239	115
Connecticut	4	1818 (c), 1965	Dec. 30, 1965	9,564	26	25
Delaware	4	1776, 1792, 1831, 1897	June 10, 1897	19,000	(d)	119
Florida	6	1839, 1861, 1865, 1868, 1886, 1968	Jan. 7, 1969	25,100	79	53
Georgia	10	1777, 1789, 1798, 1861, 1865, 1868, 1877, 1945, 1976, 1982	July 1, 1983	25,000	35 (e)	24
Hawaii	1 (f)	1950	Aug. 21, 1959	17,453 (a)	93	82
Idaho	1	1889	July 3, 1890	21,500	187	107
Illinois	4	1818, 1848, 1870, 1970	July 1, 1971	13,200	11	6
Indiana	2	1816, 1851	Nov. 1, 1851	9,377 (a)	70	38
Iowa	2	1846, 1857	Sept. 3, 1857	12,500	51	48 (g)
Kansas	1	1859	Jan. 29, 1861	11,865	115	87
Kentucky	4	1792, 1799, 1850, 1891	Sept. 28, 1891	23,500	58	29
Louisiana	11	1812, 1845, 1852, 1861, 1864, 1868, 1879, 1898, 1913, 1921, 1974	Jan. 1, 1975	51,448 (a)	51	27

Table 1.6 General Information on State Constitutions (As of January 1, 1990) *Continued*

State or Other Jurisdiction	Number of Constitutions*	Dates of Adoption	Effective Date of Present Constitution	Estimated Length (number of words)	NUMBER OF AMENDMENTS Submitted to Voters	Adopted
Maine	1	1819	March 15, 1820	13,500	186	157 (h)
Maryland	4	1776, 1851, 1864, 1867	Oct. 5, 1867	41,349 (a)	233	200
Massachusetts	1	1780	Oct. 25, 1780	36,690 (a,i)	143	116
Michigan	4	1835, 1850, 1908, 1963	Jan. 1, 1964	20,000	47	16
Minnesota	1	1857	May 11, 1858	9,500	206	112
Mississippi	4	1817, 1832, 1869, 1890	Nov. 1, 1890	24,000	133	102
Missouri	4	1820, 1865, 1875, 1945	March 30, 1945	42,000	115	74
Montana	2	1889, 1972	July 1, 1973	11,866 (a)	25	15
Nebraska	2	1866, 1875	Oct. 12, 1875	20,048 (a)	283	189
Nevada	1	1864	Oct. 31, 1864	20,770	175	108 (g)
New Hampshire	2	1776, 1784	June 2, 1784	9,200	274 (j)	142 (j)
New Jersey	3	1776, 1844, 1947	Jan. 1, 1948	17,086	52	39
New Mexico	1	1911	Jan. 6, 1912	27,200	231	120
New York	4	1777, 1822, 1846, 1894	Jan. 1, 1895	80,000	274	207
North Carolina	3	1776, 1868, 1970	July 1, 1971	11,000	34	27
North Dakota	1	1889	Nov. 2, 1889	20,564	222 (k)	125 (k)
Ohio	2	1802, 1851	Sept. 1, 1851	36,900	245	145
Oklahoma	1	1907	Nov. 16, 1907	68,800	274 (l)	133 (l)
Oregon	1	1857	Feb. 14, 1859	26,090	367	188
Pennsylvania	5	1776, 1790, 1838, 1873, 1968 (m)	1968 (m)	21,675	25 (m)	19 (m)
Rhode Island	2	1842 (c)	May 2, 1843	19,026 (a,i)	99	53
South Carolina	7	1776, 1778, 1790, 1861, 1865, 1868, 1895	Jan. 1, 1896	22,500 (n)	647 (o)	463

Table 1.6 General Information on State Constitutions
(As of January 1, 1990) *Continued*

State or Other Jurisdiction	Number of Constitutions*	Dates of Adoption	Effective Date of Present Constitution	Estimated Length (number of words)	NUMBER OF AMENDMENTS Submitted to Voters	Adopted
South Dakota	1	1889	Nov. 2, 1889	23,300	185	97
Tennessee	3	1796, 1835, 1870	Feb. 23, 1870	15,300	55	32
Texas	5	1845, 1861, 1866, 1869, 1876	Feb. 15, 1876	62,000	483	326
Utah	1	1895	Jan. 4, 1896	11,000	126	77
Vermont	3	1777, 1786, 1793	July 9, 1793	6,600	208	50
Virginia	6	1776, 1830, 1851, 1869, 1902, 1970	July 1, 1971	18,500		20
Washington	1	1889	Nov. 11, 1889	29,400	23	86
West Virginia	2	1863, 1872	April 9, 1872	25,600	153	62
Wisconsin	1	1848	May 29, 1848	13,500	107	124 (g)
Wyoming	1	1889	July 10, 1890	31,800	168	57
					97	
American Samoa	2	1960, 1967	July 1, 1967	6,000		7
No. Mariana Islands	1	1977	Jan. 9, 1978	11,000	13	45 (p,q)
Puerto Rico	1	1952	July 25, 1952	9,281 (a)	47 (p)	6

*The constitutions referred to in this table include those Civil War documents customarily listed by the individual states.

(a) Actual word count.

(b) Eight of the approved amendments have been superseded and are not printed in the current edition of the constitution. The total adopted does not include five amendments that were invalidated.

(c) Colonial charters with some alterations served as the first constitutions in Connecticut (1638, 1662) and in Rhode Island (1663).

(d) Proposed amendments are not submitted to the voters in Delaware.

(e) The new Georgia constitution eliminates the need for local amendments, which have been a long-term problem for state constitution makers.

(f) As a kingdom and a republic, Hawaii had five constitutions.

(g) The figure given includes amendments approved by the voters and later nullified by the state supreme court in Iowa (three), Kansas (one), Nevada (six) and Wisconsin (two).

(h) The figure does not include one amendment approved by the voters in 1967 that is inoperative until implemented by legislation.

(i) The printed constitution includes many provisions that have been annulled. The length of effective provisions is an estimated 24,122 words (12,400 annulled) in Massachusetts and, in Rhode Island before the "rewrite" of the constitution in 1986, it was 11,399 words (7,627 annulled).

(j) The constitution of 1784 was extensively revised in 1792. Figures show proposals and adoptions since the constitution was adopted in 1784.

(k) The figures do not include submission and approval of the constitution of 1889 itself and of Article XX; these are constitutional questions included in some counts of constitutional amendments and would add two to the figure in each column.

(l) The figures include five amendments submitted to, and approved by the voters which were, by decisions of the Oklahoma or U.S. Supreme Courts, rendered inoperative or ruled invalid, unconstitutional, or illegally submitted.

(m) Certain sections of the constitution were revised by the limited constitutional convention of 1967-68. Amendments proposed and adopted are since 1968.

(n) Of the estimated length, approximately two-thirds is of general statewide effect; the remainder is local amendments.

(o) As of 1981, of the 626 proposed amendments submitted to the voters, 130 were of general statewide effect and 496 were local; the voters rejected 83 (12 statewide, 71 local). Of the remaining 543, the General Assembly refused to approve 100 (22 statewide, 78 local), and 443 (96 statewide, 347 local) were finally added to the constitution.

(p) The number of amendments is from 1984-1989.

(q) The total excludes one amendment ruled void by a federal district court.

SOURCE: *The Book of the States 1990–91* (Lexington, Ky.: Council of State Governments, 1990), pp. 40–41. © 1990/91 The Council of State Governments reprinted with permission from *The Book of States*.

many of the constitutions written in the last century, governors were limited to two-year terms; legislatures met as infrequently as every other year and only for a limited period (sixty to ninety days); legislative salaries were specified; most state officials, such as the attorney general and auditor, were elected rather than appointed by the governor; significant restraints were placed on borrowing; many special interests were exempt from taxation; and reapportionment in some cases required constitutional amendment. As noted in Chapter 6, much of the history of state governors can be written in terms of constitutional amendments to give them powers comparable to those of the president of the United States.

State constitutions also impose major limitations on the powers of local governments, which legally are only subdivisions of the state. The government structure of cities, counties, and townships generally is prescribed by the states. State constitutions often delegate responsibility for certain services, such as police, fire, and health, to particular units of local government; but local taxes are prescribed and debt limits are established. All this, of course, adds to the detail of state constitutions. While there has been a concerted drive toward granting **home rule** to cities (in the form of charters that allow cities to adopt the kind of government structure they prefer and perform services as they see fit), in many cases local officials still must turn to state legislatures for approval of government programs.

Local governments are clearly subordinate to the state. In a classic statement, Judge John F. Dillon formulated **Dillon's Rule** (1868), which says that municipal corporations can exercise only those powers expressly granted by state constitutions and laws and those necessarily implied from granted powers. If there is any question about the exercise of power, it should be resolved in favor of the state. Although this rule has been accepted by the U.S. Supreme Court, Daniel Elazar notes that more than 80 percent of the states have rejected Dillon's Rule or have changed it to recognize the residual powers of local government.[21]

An effective state constitution—that is, one allowing government to take an active role in the initiation and implementation of policy—should include the following three fundamental characteristics.

1. It should be brief and to the point. Constitutions are not legislative codes; all they should do is establish the basic framework within which state officials can act.
2. It should make direct grants of authority so that the governor and legislators can be held accountable by the voters for their actions.
3. It should be receptive to orderly change. The amendment process should not be too cumbersome, and the constitution should include enforceable provisions on reapportionment. Unfortunately, legislators often have a built-in resistance to change, and voters often defeat new constitutions at the polls when they are asked to accept or reject in total a new constitution.

To most people, state constitutions are painfully boring documents. They are not read by those seeking examples of stirring phrases or eloquent prose style. However, as we shall see throughout this book, there are few if any problems of state government for which the suggested solution will not sooner or later run head-long into constitutional prohibitions, restrictions, or obstructions. Constitutions are necessarily conservative documents that limit the exercise of political power. Because of the nature of state constitutions, there has been a strong reform movement in this century to pass constitutional amendments aimed at increasing the power of legislators, governors, and judges and at providing an independent basis of power for local governments.

There are four methods of changing state constitutions: legislative proposal, constitutional initiative, constitutional convention, and constitutional commission. **Legislative proposal** is available in all states, and it is by far the most commonly used means of change. In most states, a two-thirds or three-fifths vote of the legislature is required as the first step in approving an amendment. In seventeen states, only a majority vote is necessary. While most states require approval in only one legislative session, twelve require approval in two consecutive sessions. Following legislative approval, the amendment is typically placed on the ballot, where a majority vote is needed for ratification. Only Delaware does not require voter approval of amendments. State legislators initiate about 90 percent of all proposed amendments. The number of legislative proposals in the 1980s was down substantially from the 1970s. About 75 percent of those proposed by state legislatures were approved by the voters.

The **constitutional initiative** may be used in seventeen states. It allows proponents of reform to have suggestions for limited change placed on the ballot. The process is time-consuming and often expensive for reform groups, especially in large states. Still, the number of constitutional initiatives rose to all-time highs during the 1980s (initiatives will be discussed in Chapter 5). Proponents must first get signatures on an initiative proposal. In California, for example, the number required is 8 percent of the total number of voters for governor in the last election. In a few states, the signatures must come from people distributed across the state. Thus in Massachusetts no more than one-fourth can come from any one county. As a final step, there is a referendum vote, in which most states require a majority vote on the amendment for it to be approved. The most famous action of this type in recent years was the 1978 approval of Proposition 13 in California, which limited state taxing ability.

Constitutional commissions may be formed to study the state constitution and make recommendations for change, or their purpose may be to make arrangements for a constitutional convention. Most have acted as study commissions. Commission size varies from as few as five members to as many as fifty. Members are usually appointed by the governor, legislative leaders, and chief justice of the highest court in the state. A few states mandate a convention every eight or nine years. No new constitution was proposed to the voters in the 1980s, although the Georgia constitution was adopted in 1982.

Constitutional conventions were convened in five states in the 1980s and nine states had constitutional commissions that operated in the 1980s. Delegates to most conventions are elected on a nonpartisan basis. In Texas the legislature constituted a constitutional convention in 1974. After action by the convention delegates, voters are asked to approve their proposals in a referendum.

THE STATES CONTRASTED AND COMPARED

This chapter has pointed out the great diversity among the states in terms of culture, socioeconomic characteristics, population, and geography. In the chapters that follow, the reader should develop a clearer picture of *similarities* among the states. Most states have virtually the same patterns of government structure—they have bicameral legislatures, organized by parties and by committees; their governors exercise similar constitutional powers in such areas as the budget and veto; and their judicial systems are organized in a common three- or two-tier arrangement of trial and appellate courts.

Although personalities differ and unique styles can be identified, political campaigns and elections proceed in the same general pattern in all the states. Particular circumstances dictate how each state and community will respond to demands for public policy. Yet every state must confront common problems in education, housing, transportation, welfare, health, and safety. Differences in political culture are becoming less distinct as people grow more mobile, as means of communication improve, and as a more national economy develops.

Comparative analysis of politics in the fifty states reveals both similarities and differences. Because the states are alike in many ways, they offer social scientists the opportunity to make a wide range of comparisons. Because there also is great variety among the states and the thousands of local governments, it gives us the opportunity to study why structural and behavioral differences occur at particular times and under particular conditions. In the chapters that follow, the reader should be careful to note both similarities and differences among the states and relate this to particular patterns of policymaking.

KEY TERMS

Constitutional commission A group selected to study state constitutions, propose changes, and prepare for a constitutional convention.

Constitutional convention A group of people selected to rewrite a state constitution.

Constitutional initiative Means by which citizens can petition to have a proposed amendment put on the ballot for voter approval.

Dillon's Rule A general guideline formulated for courts in 1868 stating that municipal corporations can exercise only those powers specifically granted them by state constitutions and laws.

Ex post facto law A law that makes an act a crime although it was not a crime when committed, or increases the penalty for a crime after it was committed. The U.S. Constitution prohibits the federal government and the states from enacting such laws.

***Gibbons* v. *Ogden* (1824)** A Supreme Court decision that broadly interpreted the power of the national government to regulate commerce and thus limited state authority.

Home rule Power given local governments to draft charters and manage their own affairs; limits the ability of state legislatures to interfere in local affairs.

Individualistic culture A pattern of political orientation characterized by distrust of government bureaucracy, low levels of political participation, and above-average corruption in government. Often found in large cities.

Legislative proposal Means by which state legislators propose constitutional amendments, which then must be approved by the voters.

Mandates State statutes, court decisions, and administrative orders that demand action (and often expenditures) from cities and counties.

***McCulloch* v. *Maryland* (1819)** A Supreme Court decision that extended federal authority by supporting the creation of a national bank and ruling against state taxation of a federally established instrument.

Metropolitan statistical area A population center of at least 50,000, generally consisting of a city and its immediate suburbs, together with adjacent communities that have close economic and social ties to the central city. First developed for the 1950 census.

Moralistic culture A pattern of political orientation characterized by high levels of political participation, support of government intervention in social and economic affairs, and little public corruption. Found in the upper Midwest.

Political culture The predominant way of thinking, feeling, and believing about the political system.

Progressive movement Reform in the early twentieth century that advocated government ownership of railroads, the right of labor to bargain collectively, and the use of direct-democracy techniques such as the initiative and recall.

Public interest Actions taken in the public interest to support measures that benefit the whole community rather than narrow economic interests.

Sectionalism The division of the nation into geographical areas, such as the South, in which the people share common cultural, economic, and historical backgrounds.

Spoils system Awarding government jobs to political supporters and friends. Now replaced in most cases by merit systems of government employment.

Sunbelt The area stretching east from southern California through the Southwest and South to Florida and north along the Atlantic coast to Virginia. It has been marked by exceptional population growth and economic development during the past thirty years.

Tenth Amendment "The powers not delegated to the United States by the Constitution, nor prohibited by it to the States, are reserved to the States respectively, or to the people." This amendment was added to the Constitution to define the principle of federalism.

Traditional culture A pattern of political orientation characterized by low levels of political participation, little government interference in social and economic affairs, and a dislike of formal bureaucracy. Typically found in the South.

REFERENCES

1. See Michael Reagan and John G. Sanzone, *The New Federalism,* 2d ed. (New York: Oxford University Press, 1981), pp. 11–15. They note that "no sphere of life is beyond the reach of the national government" with the exception of the continuance of the state's present boundaries. Here the Constitution (Article IV, Section 3) provides that a state's boundaries cannot be changed without its consent. In *Garcia* v. *San Antonio Metropolitan Transit Authority* (1985), Justice Brennan's majority opinion stated that "with rare exceptions" the Constitution does not impose affirmative limits on federal power to intrude in the affairs of state and local governments.
2. Larry Sabato, *Goodbye to Goodtime Charlie,* 2d ed. (Washington, D.C.: Congressional Quarterly Press, 1983), p. 8.
3. David Kellerman and Henry Wulf, "State Aid to Local Governments," *The Book of the States 1990–91* (Lexington, Ky.: Council of State Governments, 1990), p. 549.
4. See Thomas R. Dye, *Politics, Economics, and Public Policy: Policy Outcomes in the American States* (Chicago: Rand McNally, 1966). Dye regards urbanism, industrialism, and education, in addition to income, as economic measures. See also Dye, *Understanding Public Policy,* 6th ed. (Englewood Cliffs, N.J.: Prentice-Hall, 1987).
5. Virginia Gray, "Politics and Policy in the American States," in Virginia Gray, Herbert

Jacob, and Kenneth N. Vines, eds., *Politics in the American States,* 4th ed. (Boston: Little, Brown, 1983), p. 20.

6. Thomas Payne, "Montana: From Copper Fiefdom to Pluralist Polity," in Ronald J. Hrebenar and Clive S. Thomas, eds., *Interest Group Politics in the American West* (Salt Lake City: University of Utah Press, 1987), p. 77.

7. See Neal Peirce and Jerry Hagstrom, *The Book of America: Inside 50 States Today* (New York: Norton, 1983).

8. Daniel J. Elazar, *American Federalism: A View from the States,* 3d ed. (New York: Harper & Row, 1984), p. 109.

9. Maureen Moakley, "New Jersey," in Alan Rosenthal and Maureen Moakley, eds., *The Political Life of the American States* (New York: Praeger, 1984), pp. 219–220.

10. Elazar, *American Federalism,* pp. 114–122. As a handbook for further reading into the elements and patterns of political cultures and subcultures of the United States, see Daniel Elazar and Joseph Zikmund II, eds., *The Ecology of American Political Culture: Readings* (New York: Crowell, 1975). See also John Kincaid, ed., *Political Culture, Public Policy, and the American States* (Philadelphia: Institute for the Study of Human Issues, 1982).

11. Quoted in Peter Applebome, "Scandals Cloud Life in South Carolina," *The New York Times,* May 12, 1991, Sec. 1, p. 16.

12. See Joel Lieske, "Political Subcultures of the United States: A New Measure for Understanding Political Behavior." Paper delivered at the 1991 meeting of the Midwest Political Science Association.

13. See Elazar, *American Federalism,* pp. 122–123.

14. Among the many excellent regional studies, see John H. Fenton, *Midwest Politics* (New York: Holt, Rinehart and Winston, 1966), and a series of books by Neal Peirce.

15. See Hrebenar and Thomas, eds., *Interest Group Politics in the American West,* p. 144.

16. See Fenton, *Midwest Politics.*

17. Kirkpatrick Sale, *Power Shift: The Rise of the Southern Rim* (New York: Random House, 1975).

18. See Elazar, *American Federalism,* Chapter 2.

19. Janice C. Mays, "State Constitutions and Constitutional Revision: 1988–89 and the 1980s," in *The Book of the States 1990–91* (Lexington, Ky.: Council of State Governments, 1990), p. 25–26.

20. Duane Lockard, *The Politics of State and Local Government,* 3d ed. (New York: Macmillan, 1983), Chapter 4.

21. Elazar, *American Federalism,* p. 203.

CHAPTER 2

STATES AND CITIES IN THE FEDERAL SYSTEM

FEDERALISM AS A POLITICAL CONCEPT

Most textbooks in the past discussed federalism in terms of structure and legal principles. This approach stressed the constitutional division of authority and functions between the national government and the states. As such, it was a static view of power being assigned to units of government and remaining fixed over long periods of time. The current approach suggests a much more dynamic notion of intergovernmental relations.[1] Thus interpretation focuses not on *structure* but on *politics*. According to this view, levels of government share authority and power in an interdependent and constantly changing relationship of joint action. Federalism is regarded, in part, as a state of mind. For example, although the national government has the *legal* authority to take a wide range of actions, it is constrained by political and social forces that support state autonomy and resist centralization.

We need to be reminded that there never was a time when federal, state, and local government affairs were completely separate. Thus, the traditional analogy of the American federal system as a "layer cake," with clear divisions between layers of government, was never true. Instead, it is more accurate to speak of the federal system as a "marble cake," in which government functions are shared by all levels.[2] Cooperative efforts by federal, state, and local governments have become increasingly common in the last twenty years.

This sharing of functions is most clearly seen in federal grants-in-aid (which are discussed in detail later in this chapter). Most Americans favor the decentralization of power. At the same time, they want to solve problems. Grants-in-aid are a practical solution: The programs are funded by the national government but administered by state and local governments and even by nonprofit business firms. Virtually every function of local government has a counterpart federal program.[3] As we shall see in this chapter, fiscal federalism provides the means by which the congressional majority's sense of basic policy needs directs and shapes public policymaking in states and cities.

The Reagan administration believed that the expansion of grants-in-aid in the 1960s and 1970s represented a serious overreaching of federal authority. It was concerned that state and local governments had become too dependent on federal funds and that federal regulations had become too intrusive. Also, the Reagan administration was convinced that state and local aid was taking too high a percentage of the federal budget (it reached an all-time high of 17 percent of all federal spending in 1978). As we shall see later in this chapter, Reagan's proposals to change the nature of intergovernmental relations fostered the impression that "federalism" was simply a code word for making budget cuts.[4] President Bush shared Reagan's concern about federal authority. In 1991 he proposed to "move power and decision making closer to the people" by giving states control of $15 billion worth of federal programs.

CREATION OF THE AMERICAN FEDERAL SYSTEM

The decision by the framers of the Constitution in 1787 to create a federal system of government may be viewed as a compromise between those who wanted to continue with a confederate form of government and those who wanted to change to a centralized system as existed in England. Under the Articles of Confederation, the national government lacked the authority to manage effectively the economic and international affairs of the nation. The population had strong loyalties to the states, and there was a general fear of centralized authority as it had been manifested in colonial America. A federal system offered unity without uniformity. By reserving to the states considerable power, it lessened the likelihood of centralized tyranny. A federal system is appropriate for any developing country because it is flexible and permits changes in the distribution of power among government units and in the balance of power without changing the fundamental charter of government.

A **federal system** may be distinguished from a **confederacy** in the following ways: (1) in a federal system, the central government is stronger than its member states in regard to the size of its budget and the scope of its jurisdiction; (2) in a federal system, national law is supreme; (3) in a federal system, the central government acts directly upon individuals in such matters as taxation and raising an army, whereas in a confederacy, the central government must act indirectly through the states when dealing with individual citizens; and (4) in a federal system, states may not withdraw from the union, but in a confederacy, they may secede.

A less flexible sort of system is the **unitary nation-state,** in which local governments can exercise only those powers given them by the central government. Unitary government exists in such nations as Great Britain, France, and Israel. In physically small countries, a unitary structure provides efficiency in dealing with national problems and ensures that national values will prevail. In the United States, cities and counties exist as extensions of state governments except when allowed home rule by state constitutional provisions.

As discussed in Chapter 1, the U.S. Constitution provides guarantees to the states and imposes limits on their actions. The powers of the states are limited because substantial powers are delegated to Congress, and the supremacy clause makes very clear the subordinate relationship of the states to the national government:

> This constitution, and the laws of the United States which shall be made in pursuance thereof; and all treaties made or which shall be made under the authority of the United States shall be the supreme law of the land; and the judges in every state shall be bound thereby, anything in the constitution or laws of any state to the contrary notwithstanding.

At the same time, certain constitutional powers are reserved to the states (e.g., ownership of property, regulations of domestic relations, control over local government) and some powers (such as passing ex post facto laws or **bills of attainder**) are denied to both the national and the state governments. To underline the limits of federal authority, the Tenth Amendment states:

> The powers not delegated to the United States by the Constitution, nor prohibited by it to the States, are reserved to the States respectively, or to the people.*

---

*One view of the Tenth Amendment suggests that it reserves to the states all powers not specifically granted to the national government in the Constitution. However, such an interpretation ignores the elastic clause which follows the enumerated powers of Congress and states that Congress may "make all laws which shall be necessary and proper for carrying out the foregoing powers." The more widely accepted view of the Tenth Amendment, as expounded by the Supreme Court, is that it is simply a truism—"that all is retained which has not yet been surrendered." From this second perspective it follows that there is not a constitutionally binding permanent division of power between the national government and the states. In *United States* v. *Darby* (1941) the Supreme Court specifically repudiated the doctrine of dual federalism in favor of national supremacy.

In the American federal system, the distribution of power between national and state governments has never been fixed. There has been a continual reshuffling of power, followed by considerable resistance when one level is forced by legislative or judicial action to give up power. In recent years, for example, some states have been reluctant to relinquish the authority to apportion their legislatures and integrate their schools. In 1985, the Supreme Court held in *Garcia* v. *San Antonio* that federal wage and hour standards apply to municipal and state workers and that the Tenth Amendment does not shield states from this federal regulation of "traditional government functions." The decision was reinforced in *South Carolina* v. *Baker* (1988), in which the Court ruled that Congress could tax interest on bonds sold by state and local governments.

THE EVOLUTION OF AMERICAN FEDERALISM

We have noted that relationships among governments in the United States have been dynamic, rather than stable. Figure 2.1 illustrates the changes in the distribution of power between the states and the federal government, and the general expansion of government powers in the United States during the past 200 years. As conceived by the framers (Figure 2.1a), federal authority was limited largely to foreign affairs while state authority was relatively broad, and there was little overlap or cooperation between the two levels of government. Over time (Figure 2.1b), both federal and state authority have expanded, and federal activities are now greater than those of the states. The overlap in power between the states and the federal government has also expanded greatly. The loss of power has been in those

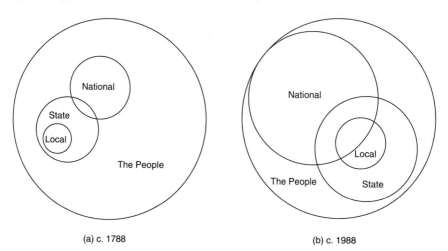

(a) c. 1788   (b) c. 1988

Figure 2.1   The Distribution of Constitutional Authority in the United States

SOURCE: Russell L. Hanson, "Intergovernmental Relations," in Virginia Gray, Herbert Jacob, and Robert B. Albritton, eds., *Politics in the American States,* 5th ed. (Glenview, Ill.: Scott, Foresman/Little, Brown, 1990), p. 46. Copyright © 1990 by Virginia Gray, Herbert Jacob, and Robert B. Albritton. Reprinted by permission of HarperCollins Publishers.

areas originally reserved to the people. Expanded government activity and regulation in such areas as environmental control and occupational safety inevitably limit the authority of private persons and businesses.

The increase in federal authority has been the result of various factors. Congress has enacted legislation, and presidents have supported broad federal enforcement of laws and constitutional provisions. This, in turn, has led to a series of challenges in federal courts. As a result, federal courts (especially the Supreme Court) have acted as umpires in the federal system to decide where power should reside.

McCulloch v. *Maryland* (1819) was the first judicial review of state-federal relations. The background of the case is as follows: Maryland had levied a tax on notes issued by all banks not chartered by the state of Maryland. McCulloch, the cashier in the Baltimore branch of the United States Bank, refused to pay the tax, and Maryland brought suit against him. After losing in Maryland state courts, McCulloch (as directed by the secretary of the treasury) appealed and the case was reviewed by the Supreme Court, headed by Chief Justice John Marshall.

Regarding the first issue—"Does Congress have the authority to charter a bank?"—the Court ruled that while this was not among the enumerated powers of Congress, it could be *implied* from the **"necessary and proper" clause** of the Constitution. Marshall reasoned that while the chartering of a bank was not absolutely indispensable in the performance of delegated Congressional responsibilities, it was, nevertheless, "convenient or useful to another objective." On the second issue—"Can the states tax an instrument of the national government?"—the Court ruled no. The power to tax, said the chief justice, is the power to destroy, and states cannot interfere with operations of the national government.

Shortly after *McCulloch,* the Marshall Court had another opportunity to rule in favor of a broad interpretation of national authority. *Gibbons* v. *Ogden* (1824) concerned the desire of New York and New Jersey to control shipping on the lower Hudson River. The states argued that the definition of **commerce** should be narrowly construed so as to include only direct dealings in commodities. Thus the regulation of shipping on inland waterways would be beyond the constitutional power of Congress. Marshall, however, ruled that the power of the national government to regulate commerce included all commercial activity. The Court stated: "This power, like all others vested in Congress, is complete in itself, may be exercised to its utmost extent, and acknowledges no limitations other than are prescribed in the Constitution."

Of course, the most serious threat to national authority came with the Civil War. Prior to 1860, John C. Calhoun proposed the concept of **concurrent majority.** In Calhoun's model each interest group (or state) had the right to decide independently whether to accept or reject national policy affecting it. Calhoun's idea was similar to the doctrine of **nullification,** under which each state could veto national legislation with which it disagreed.* Ultimately, the Southern states seceded from the

---

*Following the passage of the Alien and Sedition Acts of 1798,the Jeffersonians developed the idea of "interposition." Under this doctrine, states were given the power to "interpose" themselves between their citizens and the national government if they believed that a national law affecting their citizens was unconstitutional. The Alien and Sedition Acts were repealed in 1801, and interposition was never reviewed by the courts.

Union. After the issue had been decided on the battlefield, the Supreme Court ruled in 1869: "Ours is an indestructible union, composed of indestructible states."

The first federal money grants to states were made in 1837, whens surplus funds were sent to the states with no restrictions regarding their use. Before that, federal land grants had been made to assist in the construction of schools, canals, roads, and railroads. The first Morrill Act, passed in 1862, provided land to states to establish agricultural colleges; these institutions became land-grant universities. Terms of the legislation foreshadowed more modern grants-in-aid because they required colleges to make annual reports and required governors to account for the use of federal funds.

During the years between the Civil War and 1937, the Court followed the doctrine of **dual federalism,** in which the distribution of powers between the federal government and the states was seen as fixed. This meant that the states were allowed to operate within their own exclusive jurisdiction, and the national government could not intervene. In particular, the Court narrowly defined commerce so as to exclude manufacturing. The effect was to prevent the state and national governments from regulating such matters as wages, hours, and child labor.

Since 1937, the Court has reverted to the views of the Marshall era that the national government has broad authority under its implied powers and that the reserved powers under the Tenth Amendment do not limit national action. As a result, the modern Supreme Court has upheld provisions of the 1965 Voting Rights Act calling for federal registrars to replace state officials in several Southern states; it has ordered apportionment of both houses of state legislatures on the basis of population; and it has ordered busing to achieve racial integration in school districts where previously segregation was imposed by law.

During the 1920s, the federal government turned away from social concerns and the states were left to take action regarding such problems as care of dependent children. Federal domestic programs in the late 1920s were so limited that state spending was double federal spending and local government expenditures were five times greater.[5] Innovative state programs were used as models for new federal programs enacted under President Franklin D. Roosevelt's New Deal of the 1930s. The modern-day structure of categorical grants-in-aid came into being in the 1930s.[6] Federal aid was provided almost exclusively to states. It required them to submit plans for the use of the funds, to provide matching funds, and to allow federal audit and review of the programs. Under President Harry Truman, more federal aid went directly to local governments. Federal grants continued to expand under President Dwight Eisenhower, although there was some concern about the proper division of responsibility between Washington and the states. Although federal aid tripled from 1952 to 1961 (reaching $7.3 billion), dramatic change in the federal system did not occur until the mid-1960s.

FEDERALISM SINCE 1965

From 1965 to 1969 federal aid to state and local governments nearly doubled, to $20.2 billion. Under President Lyndon Johnson's "creative federalism," over 200 new grant programs were created. In many cases, states were bypassed and aid went directly to cities, counties, school districts, and nonprofit organizations. Although the first two block grants (fairly general grants) were created in 1966 (Partnership in Health Act) and 1968 (Safe Streets Act), the Johnson administration relied heavily on categorical grants (grants made for a specific purpose) to further national objectives.

In the 1968 campaign, Richard Nixon stressed his commitment to return power to the states and to cut administrative red tape. In fact, however, federal grants grew from $24 billion in 1970 to nearly $50 billion in 1975. Nearly 100 new categorical grants were created under the Nixon and Ford administrations. Nixon's **"new federalism"** did, however, establish general revenue sharing, which gave state and local governments greater discretion and flexibility in spending federal funds. Three new block grants, giving recipients more freedom, were also established.

The 1970s were marked by several significant changes in intergovernmental relations. We have noted the continued growth of federal grants. Grant eligibility was extended to virtually all local governments and many nonprofit organizations. As a result, by 1980 about 30 percent of all federal aid bypassed state governments, compared with 8 percent in 1960. Federal aid became available for a host of projects (e.g., libraries, historic preservation, snow removal, and development of bikeways) that previously had been totally state-local responsibilities. Thus state-local reliance on the federal government grew significantly. More procedural strings were attached to grants-in-aid, and more substantive strings were added to block grants.

According to David B. Walker, cooperative federalism was replaced by "dysfunctional federalism," or congressional federalism, in the 1970s.[7] New federal regulations became more intricate and more pervasive than the conditions attached to grants in the 1950s and 1960s. Responding to pressure from government lobbyists, more money went directly to substate governments. These changes placed Congress at the center of intergovernmental relations. This, says Walker, is why Nixon's "new federalism" failed to change the relative power positions of the states and the federal government. The result was more managerial confusion and overloading of the intergovernmental network.

As president, Jimmy Carter spoke of a "new partnership" in referring to federal-state-local relations. Essentially, this was a return to Johnson's policies. Carter called for a greater urban focus, expanded intergovernmental programs, and a leadership role for the federal government. Categorical grants remained dominant, and the federal government maintained direct access to local governments. It is significant that there was a clear shift in federal aid policy in the second half of Carter's term. Carter pulled back from his urban aid proposals, and the national political mood (as evidenced in "tax revolts" across the country) began to call for cuts in government programs. This shift became a focal point of the Reagan administration.

Under Ronald Reagan's "new federalism" plan the first substantial effort was made to reduce the tide of centralization that had been growing since the 1930s. After his first year in office, Reagan cut federal aid to state and local governments by about $6.5 billion. About sixty categorical aid programs were dropped and more than seventy-seven others were consolidated into block grants. Essentially, the administration sought to retrench by cutting the federal budget and to "devolve" domestic programs back to state and local governments.

At the beginning of his second year in office, President Reagan announced plans to shift most domestic programs to state and local governments by 1990. Reagan's new "new federalism" program, if enacted, would have given the federal system its most dramatic change since the New Deal brought big government to Washington in the 1930s. In his 1982 State of the Union message, the president declared, "In a single stroke we will be accomplishing a realignment that will end cumbersome administration and spiraling costs at the federal level while we insure these programs will be more responsive to both the people they are meant to help and the people who pay for them." President Reagan called for the federal government to take full financial responsibility for Medicaid, while the states would take full responsibility for food stamps. In addition, forty other federally assisted programs were to be phased out over a period of several years and federal excise taxes would have been eliminated to encourage states to increase their taxes and fund the former federal aid programs.

These proposals were not even given serious considerations by Congress, and they were strongly attacked by Democrats and minority groups. In his 1983 State of the Union message, the president dropped the idea of transferring major federal programs to the states. By its second term the Reagan administration had lost much of its enthusiasm for radical reform of intergovernmental relations.[8] Emphasis shifted to more conventional reform, such as reducing federal regulations regarding grant applications and evaluation.

The relative lack of success of Reagan's proposals (there is a more detailed evaluation at the end of this chapter) can be attributed to several factors. One was bad timing. The national recession in 1982 diverted attention away from debate about the nature of American federalism, and it also put additional financial pressure on the states. Politically, many liberals in Congress wanted to maintain control over federal programs, and they resisted cuts in social services when the president was asking for money for military spending. At the state and local levels, governors called for a federal takeover of the Aid to Families of Dependent Children (AFDC) program, rather than devoting it to the states. Mayors feared that states would not deliver federal funds that were designed to be used to finance the turnback programs. Politically, the administration was not able to build a coalition broad enough to support a revolutionary restructuring of our federal system, and it had less control over Congress after 1982.

President Bush's federalism proposal in 1991 was similar to Reagan's "new federalism," but less ambitious. Rather than impose new responsibilities on states with less money, Bush would guarantee the continuation of $15 billion in a "single consolidated grant" to be used for specific programs in health, education, housing, transportation, and environmental protection. Many mayors feared that city funds might be reduced as they filtered through state capitals. Bush believed the program would permit "states to manage more flexibly and more efficiently." Bush has conferred with state and local governments to a greater extent than Reagan in trying to develop domestic programs. On the negative side for states and cities, the decline in federal dollars in the early 1990s has been accompanied by an increase in nonfiscal federal mandates and regulations. As a result, states and localities are being forced to spend more money in areas such as environmental control and health care. The biggest federal cuts have come in programs for mass transit, economic development, and waste treatment.

INTERGOVERNMENTAL RELATIONS

The evolution of American federalism shows that the nation has moved from separate levels of government, acting almost as sovereign entities, to levels of government that interact and cooperate in an increasingly interdependent system. Intergovernmental relations involve interactions between the federal government and the states, between states, and between states and their localities.

Grants-in-Aid

We have briefly examined the changing relationships between the national government and the states. In large part, **grants-in-aid** have been the vehicle by which federal authority has greatly expanded since the early 1950s. **Fiscal federalism**—grants of money from the national government to the states and from the states to local governments—is at the center of intergovernmental relations and enables Congress to exert considerable influence over the states. For example, the threat of withholding funds from the states allowed Congress to set such national standards as the 55 m.p.h. speed limit and has led to increasing the legal age for drinking alcoholic beverages. Federal grants create **vertical coalitions** of administrators at several levels of government who are much more effective in creating policy changes than local groups acting alone.[9]

One argument for increased federal involvement in traditional state and local activities has been that it provides a degree of national uniformity (in the form of minimal standards) in a system divided by interstate competition. Also, because of great differences in state wealth, spending for such programs as education and public assistance varies greatly from one part of the country to another. Federal aid can make things more equal and provide more nearly uniform benefits by transferring money from rich states to poor states (the "Robin Hood effect"). As a result, the federal grants-in-aid program has provided a politically acceptable way of providing needed money to state and local governments while keeping the formal structure of federalism.

Increasingly in the 1950s and 1960s, both state and local governments were faced with pressing demands to solve social problems at a time when their financial base was either dwindling or expanding only a little. Cities often found state legislatures unwilling or unable to come to their aid. As a result, they turned directly to Congress for help. Congress responded to cities and states by greatly expanding the grants-in-aid programs already existing while keeping state and local administration of government programs. Grants provide the means by which the federal government exerts some effect on state programs without taking over the entire function and removing it from state or local control.

Grants-in-aid are by no means new. They began with the Land Ordinance Act of 1785, which provided land grants for public schools in the developing Western

Table 2.1   Federal Grants-in-Aid in Relation to State and Local Outlays, Total Federal Outlays, and Gross National Product, 1955–1993 (billions of current dollars)

			GRANT AS A PERCENTAGE OF		
Fiscal Year	Amount	Percent Increase or Decrease (−)	Total State-Local Outlays	Total Federal Outlays	Gross National Product
1955	$3.2	4.9%	10.2%	4.7%	0.8%
1956	3.6	15.6	10.4	5.0	0.9
1957	4.0	8.1	10.5	5.2	0.9
1958	4.9	22.5	11.7	6.0	1.1
1959	6.5	32.7	14.1	7.0	1.3
1960	7.0	7.7	14.5	7.6	1.4
1961	7.1	1.4	13.7	7.3	1.4
1962	7.9	11.3	14.1	7.4	1.4
1963	8.6	8.9	14.2	7.7	1.5
1964	10.2	17.4	15.4	8.6	1.6
1965	10.9	7.9	15.1	9.2	1.6
1966	12.9	19.3	16.1	9.6	1.7
1967	15.2	16.9	16.9	9.7	1.9
1968	18.6	22.4	18.3	10.4	2.2
1969	20.2	9.1	17.8	11.0	2.2
1970	24.1	18.2	19.0	12.3	2.4
1971	28.1	17.1	19.7	13.4	2.7
1972	34.4	22.4	21.7	14.9	3.0
1973	41.8	21.5	24.0	17.0	3.3
1974	43.4	3.8	22.3	16.1	3.1

territory. Throughout the nineteenth century, grants were made available for railroads and canals. However, they did not become politically significant until after World War II. In 1950, federal grants to state and local governments amounted to only $2 billion annually. By 1970, there were 530 grants-in-aid programs paying out about $24 billion every year. In spite of President Nixon's campaign oratory about decentralizing government, about 100 grant programs were created by the Nixon and Ford administrations. The federal grant program continued to increase sharply under the Carter administration.

In fiscal 1982, federal grants had their first absolute decline in more than twenty-five years (see Table 2.1). As noted earlier, this was consistent with President Reagan's desire to cut federal spending and reduce government regulation. Grants increased after 1982, but they dropped in 1987. There was a substantial increase in 1990 and an even larger increase projected for 1991.

There are two types of federal grants. **Categorical grants** are made for specific purposes, such as job training, highway safety, prevention of juvenile delinquency,

Table 2.1 Federal Grants-in-Aid in Relation to State and Local Outlays, Total Federal Outlays, and Gross National Product, 1955–1993 (billions of current dollars) *Continued*

Fiscal Year	Amount	Percent Increase or Decrease (−)	GRANT AS A PERCENTAGE OF		
			Total State-Local Outlays	Total Federal Outlays	Gross National Product
1975	49.8	14.7	22.6	15.0	3.3
1976	59.1	18.7	24.1	15.9	3.5
1977	68.4	15.7	25.5	16.7	3.5
1978	77.9	13.9	26.5	17.0	3.6
1979	82.9	6.4	25.8	16.5	3.4
1980	91.5	10.4	25.8	15.5	3.4
1981	94.8	3.6	24.7	14.0	3.2
1982	88.2	−7.0	21.6	11.8	2.8
1983	92.5	4.9	21.3	11.4	2.8
1984	97.6	5.5	20.9	11.5	2.6
1985	105.9	8.5	20.9	11.2	2.7
1986	112.4	6.1	19.9	11.3	2.7
1987	108.4	−3.6	18.0	10.8	2.5
1988	115.3	6.4	17.7	10.8	2.4
1989	122.0	5.7	17.3	10.7	2.4
1990	136.9	12.2	17.9	10.9	2.5
1991*	158.6	15.8	n.a.	11.2	2.8
1992*	171.0	7.8	n.a.	11.8	2.9
1993*	184.1	7.7	n.a.	12.7	2.9

*Office of Management and Budget estimate.

SOURCE: *Significant Features of Fiscal Federalism 1991,* vol. 2 (Washington, D.C.: Advisory Commission on Intergovernmental Relations, 1991), p. 50.

and agricultural extension. The recipient of such a grant has little choice about how the money is to be spent, so the federal government retains more control. Categorical grants made up about 80 percent of all federal grants in 1980. **Block grants** are much broader in their scope. They allow greater choice by the recipient, and they reduce or end matching requirements. For example, Community Development Small Cities Block Grants create a "package" of grants to deal with a series of problems previously covered by separate, categorical grants. As discussed in the next section, President Reagan's "new federalism" program stressed the development of block grants. Because of the large number of categorical grants now available to state and local governments, it is possible for public officials to build their own packages of specific grants to fight problems within a general area of concern. In this way officials can virtually create their own block grants.

Another way of categorizing grants is according to their terms for distribution. **Formula grants** are distributed to all eligible recipients on the basis of established guidelines. For example, in aid to the blind, all needy blind persons in every state can receive federal aid as a matter of "right." **Project grants,** however, require specific congressional approval;they are not distributed equally among all potential recipients. Instead, under grants such as urban renewal, specific programs are funded in only some of the areas in which problems exist. Nearly 80 percent of all grants are project grants. In contrast to states, local governments receive most of their federal aid in project grants. This means they must rely heavily on "grantsmanship" in obtaining categorical grants. A balance sheet evaluating the grants-in-aid system would contain the debits and credits shown below.

Grants-in-Aid

Advantages	Disadvantages
1. Provide funds needed by state and local governments.	1. Large number and complexity of grants imposes administrative burdens on recipients.
2. Help to equalize resources in rich and poor states.	2. Uncoordinated grants often overlap or are at odds with one another.
3. Encourage local initiative and experimentation.	3. They dull local initiative and distort planning by directing attention to
4. Are based on the progressive tax structure of the federal government.	available grants rather than proposing solutions for problems in fields not
5. Can concentrate attention in a problem area and provide valuable technical assistance.	covered by grants.
	4. Duration of grants is often too long or too short.
6. Allow introduction into the federal system of national values and standards.	5. They encourage "grantsmanship"—the ability to fill out the forms in a way that pleases federal officials.
	6. Categorical grants leave little room for state and local discretion regarding expenditures and require increased federal supervision.

Although states have the option of *not* participating in the grants-in-aid programs, there is strong pressure to take advantage of the opportunity to get programs for half cost or less. This, in turn, places a great financial burden on states (particularly poor ones) to earmark much of their discretionary money as matching funds for grants-in-aid. This fiscal federalism also puts strong pressure (some would say coercion) on the states to comply with federal regulations. For example, in the 1970s, states had the option of complying with a 55 m.p.h. speed limit for their highways or losing federal highway funds. They all complied, just as all states raised the legal drinking age to 21 in the 1980s when faced with the loss of federal aid.

Let us look at the *economic rationales* that support the entire grants-in-aid system. As noted earlier, it is easier to raise revenue at the national level than at the state and local levels. This is so because the federal tax structure is more elastic than that of the state and local governments. Federal revenues rise in direct proportion to overall economic growth in the United States. As a result, federal revenue expands greatly without any increase in tax rates. In contrast, state and local taxes are less elastic; they do not respond well to economic growth. Thus city councils and state legislatures must create new taxes or raise existing tax rates to get added funds necessary to respond to their constituents' demands for more services. In addition, federal taxes are more *progressive* than state and local taxes. (Chapter 8 deals more specifically with state and local financing.)

The economic fact of **elasticity** has strong political implications. All public officials are very aware that voters resist higher taxes. While many state and local governments have increased taxes in recent years, the easiest course is to pass on their financial problems to Congress. An interesting change in the federal tax structure since 1964 has been the *reduction* of taxes while total expenditures were increasing.

A second economic rationale for grants-in-aid is what one observer refers to as **spillover benefits.** This means that the benefits obtained from a program administered in one government area may extend into other government areas. Thus it seems fair that all who benefit should share in the cost. Education is an example of how spillover benefits work. If a person educated in New York, where per pupil spending is far greater than the national average, moves to a state such as New Jersey, where per capita spending for education is lower, the second state benefits from educational programs for which it has not paid. Federal grants that support education make certain that all states share in the cost of any single program by the national government.

An additional benefit of federal grants is that they have helped reduce corruption by requiring review of state and local financial records by federal auditors. A final economic rationale is that grants reduce unnecessary administrative expense by requiring recipients to improve their administrative structures.

Regarding *political* expediency, it may be easier to mount a national campaign for a mixed federal-state program than to manage campaigns throughout the fifty states. Labor, for example, has its membership centered in about one-third of the states. It therefore has little effect in many of the other state capitals. Yet labor's strong influence in urban, industrial states gives it a great deal of bargaining power with Congress and the president. It also exerts pressure on the national government to respond to such problems as poverty, community mental health, and environmental protection—problems that otherwise would not receive political support because of the unresponsiveness of local political elites. From another perspective, political scientist David Mayhew argues that categorical grants provide "particularized benefits" to congressional constituencies and thus allow members of Congress to claim credit for benefits in their districts.[10] Since this helps their chances for reelection, it is not surprising that members of Congress are reluctant to cut categoricals.

More and more, traditional state and local political problems can be viewed as having national implications. With an interdependent economy, including transportation and communications systems, most problems do not have a purely local impact. As a result, the federal system involves plans in which federal and state officials join in fighting such problems as air pollution and urban decay. Federal grants allow Congress to form national objectives, which are put into effect through cooperation between federal officials and state and local governments. Such grants have also been an effective way for strong presidents, such as Franklin D. Roosevelt and Lyndon Johnson, to centralize their political aims.

Block Grants

Earlier we considered block grants in contrast to categorical grants. More accurately, block grants may be thought of as a middle ground between categorical grants, which provide for strong congressional control, and general revenue sharing, which gives states greater independence. As such, block grants represent a balance between national goals and greater recipient flexibility.[11] Block grants are programs in which federal funds are provided to "general purpose governments" for use in a broad functional area, largely at the recipient's discretion.

Prior to 1981, only five block grants had been created. No new block grants were enacted during the Ford and Carter administrations. In each case, the block grant consolidated existing categorical grants, the aim being increased efficiency. Local officials were given greater control over selecting activities to be funded, and there were fewer federal regulations.

The Reagan administration abruptly reversed past practice in 1981 by converting seventy-seven categorical programs designed to achieve specific goals in health, education, transportation, and urban aid into nine block grants. These changes began with the 1982 fiscal year. President Reagan originally proposed consolidating eighty-six categorical grants into seven major block grants, but Congress retained many of the categoricals. However, the Omnibus Reconciliation Act, which created the block grants, also terminated sixty-two other categorical grants. As a result, the total number of federal programs was reduced by nearly 25 percent in one year.[12] Most of the new block grants gave almost unlimited discretion to state recipients, and no funds were sent directly to local governments. Timothy J. Conlan suggests that there has been a change in the rationale supporting block grants and that this change helped get support from conservatives in Congress to support 1981 reform. Conlan notes that "block grants have been politically transformed from a predominantly management-oriented device for simplifying program administration and enhancing adaptation to varying local conditions . . . to a concept more closely identified with conservative ideology and sometimes strident opposition to federal involvement in a range of domestic activities."[13]

Revenue Sharing

Dissatisfaction with the restrictiveness of grants-in-aid and a desire to return power to the states prompted the creation of revenue sharing. Essentially, **revenue sharing** is the return of federal tax money to states and localities, with minimum restrictions on its use, permitting the local decision-making process to determine which programs will be funded. Passage of a revenue-sharing bill was delayed for several reasons. First, the Vietnam War removed an expected federal revenue surplus. Second, liberals, including organized labor, feared that states would not "pass through" enough funds to cities. Third, Representative Wilbur Mills (then chairman of the House Committee on Ways and Means) delayed the bill. He argued that when one level of government spends money raised at another level, it encourages irresponsible behavior free from voter scrutiny. Once Mills's opposition was removed, the Nixon revenue-sharing plan—the State and Local Fiscal Assistance Act of 1972—was quickly approved.

The 1972 revenue-sharing act provided about $30 billion to be given to states and localities over a five-year period. Roughly one-third of the funds were allocated to the states, two-fifths to cities, and one-fourth to counties. (Special-purpose districts, such as school districts, were not eligible to receive these funds.) Some 39,000 government units received revenue-sharing money. The funds were given out under a very complex formula that looked at such factors as total population, state and local tax revenue, state income tax, personal per capita income, federal tax liabilities, and degree of urbanization. As a result, there was not a direct population equation.

In 1976, Congress overwhelmingly voted to extend the revenue-sharing program through September 30, 1980. In an election year, few members of Congress wishes to make changes in a program that had gained strong support throughout the country. The original act's formulas for allocating funds to recipient governments were continued as well as the provision that one-third of the funds go to state governments and two-thirds to local governments. The 1976 act repealed parts of the original act that did not permit using revenue-sharing funds to match federal grants under other programs. Provisions under the 1976 act called for greater citizen participation in deciding how revenue-sharing funds would be spent.

In 1980, another election year, mayors and governors strongly supported keeping the program at full funding. Early in the year, the Carter administration called for the termination of revenue sharing as part of a move to balance the federal budget. However, this position was later changed when it became clear that the budget would remain unbalanced. In one of its last actions, the Ninety-sixth Congress extended revenue sharing for local governments. State governments were not eligible for funding in fiscal 1981 but were authorized for 1982 and 1983. However, the funds were never appropriated. In 1983, general revenue sharing was extended through 1986 and the states continued to be excluded. Because of the expanding federal deficit, revenue sharing was completely eliminated in 1986.

Because cities have been eliminated from revenue sharing more recently than states and revenue-sharing funds comprised a much higher percentage of city budgets (about 5 percent of cities' general fund revenues), the impact has been felt more at the local level than in the states. Although the impact has been less than some feared, many cities have raised property taxes and increased user fees in order to cope with the loss of revenue-sharing funds. Unfortunately for cities, concurrently with this cut came reductions in federal grants-in-aid and then a national recession in the early 1990s.

Horizontal Federalism: Interstate Cooperation

The U.S. Constitution attempts to encourage cooperation among the states in the following ways:

1. States are to give *"full faith and credit . . .* to the public acts, records, and judicial proceedings of every other state." This clause requires a state to recognize the validity of civil actions, such as a contract for sale of property, which originate in another state. In the area of domestic relations—divorce, child custody, alimony—the situation is complicated by state refusal on occasion to accept as binding civil judgments of other states.
2. States are to extend to residents of other states all **"privileges and immunities"** granted their own residents. This includes allowing residents of one state to acquire property, enter into contracts, and have access to the courts in a second state. It does not include the extension of political rights such as voting and jury service. In 1984 the Supreme Court held that New Hampshire could not exclude nonresidents from admission to the bar and the practice of law.
3. States are to return to another state fugitives who have fled from justice. It is the governor who signs **extradition** papers to deliver a fugitive to the state having jurisdiction over the criminal act. Although governors usually comply with requests for extradition, the Supreme Court during the Civil War ruled that this was a matter of executive discretion and a governor may refuse to deliver a fugitive upon request from another state. More recently the Court held that states must return fugitives. In 1934, Congress made it a federal crime to cross state lines to avoid prosecution or imprisonment.
4. States may enter into **compacts** with one another provided that Congress approves. There has been only one case in which congressional approval of a proposed interstate compact was denied. A state cannot withdraw from a compact unless the other-party states agree. The provisions of compacts take precedence over any state laws that conflict with their provisions.

The most significant use of interstate compacts has developed since World War II. Only 35 compacts were created between 1783 and 1920. There were 58 by 1940. Between 1941 and 1975, however, more than 100 compacts were enacted and the coverage was broadened. There are now over 170 compacts dealing with the management of problems that cross state lines, such as transportation, environmental protection, taxes, and health care. The best-known interstate compact is the Port Authority of New York and New Jersey, established in 1921, which controls much of the transportation in greater New York City. Beginning with the Delaware Basin Commission in 1961, the federal government has joined with states—here Delaware, New York, New Jersey, and Pennsylvania—in "federal-interstates." More than thirty compacts are open to participation nationwide. Although the growth of interstate compacts has slowed, new compacts have been formed in recent years dealing with such areas as hazardous waste and natural resources management. The proposed Environmental Compact of the States would be a national clearinghouse for environmental and natural resource information. In most instances compacts are viewed as a way to improve problem solving without involving the federal government.

States also cooperate through the exchange of information. An ever-growing number of associations—governors, attorneys general, welfare officials, lieutenant governors—hold regular conferences. Many of these organizations are associated with the Council of State Governments, which provides a framework of organization and also publishes materials (including *The Book of the States*) on a wide range of state government issues. State and local police cooperate with each other and with the FIB in the exchange of information regarding criminals. Some states have developed reciprocal programs in higher education. For example, residents of northwestern Ohio can attend Eastern Michigan University and pay Michigan in-state tuition. In turn, residents of southeastern Michigan can attend the University of Toledo and pay Ohio in-state tuition.

In spite of the availability of formal means of cooperation, interstate relations often are marked by *competition* and *conflict,* rather than by accommodation. In the field of taxation, states sometimes cite their low tax rates as a means of luring businesses from other states. Increasingly, environmental issues are causing interstate conflict. These include disposal of hazardous waste, dumping of pollutants in waterways, and acid rain in New England that is caused by air pollution in the Midwest.

In spite of federal encouragement of cooperation, the states differ considerably. For example, even though legislators and attorneys general attend regular conferences, and even though the National Conference of the Commissioners on Uniform Law has existed since 1892, there remains a significant lack of uniformity in commercial law. Differences also exist in divorce laws, legal marriage age, and voting residency requirements. At one time, California legislators attempted (unsuccessfully) to bar paupers from moving into their state. Truckers are confronted with a variety of state rules regulating lights, load limits, and licensing as they travel cross-country. One might expect that in a "reasonable" system such confusion would have been eliminated by now. However, in the name of federalism Americans continue to support state and local autonomy and are therefore willing to live with the inconveniences that inevitably result.

State-Local Relations

As we have seen, states and cities in the United States exist in a unitary relationship. Thus, unlike the federal government's relations with the states, each state can coerce its cities to comply with policy objectives. For example, in the Aid to Families with Dependent Children (AFDC) program, federal matching funds are made available to states and their participation is voluntary.[14] Because of fiscal incentives, all states participate in the program. However, states have considerable control because they are free to establish eligibility requirements and benefits beyond federal minimum standards. On the other hand, states may require localities to administer the AFDC program and contribute to its costs. State mandates have become an increasingly irritating factor in state-local relations.[15] By 1989 thirteen states had exacted constitutional provisions to restrict the power of legislatures to mandate local expenditures. In some states, cities must submit their entire budgets to a state agency for approval.

State financial contributions to local governments have been increasing throughout this century. As noted in Chapter 1, state aid to localities increased from $99 billion in 1983 to $149 billion in 1988 and it constitutes over one-third of local expenditures. In 1930 state aid was 10 percent of local expenditures. The states' role has become more significant since the early 1980s because of the withdrawal of the federal government from many domestic programs. As a result, states have become the dominant factors in many policy areas by providing services directly.

At the same time, the federal aid being sent to state governments gives states the responsibility to allocate funds to and mandate actions from localities. Either way, state centralization of policy occurs.

FEDERALISM IN THE 1980s AND 1990s

Earlier in this chapter, we examined President Reagan's "new federalism" proposals. Although his "big swap" of federal-state programs did not occur, fundamental change did take place. States were given more control over the grant-in-aid program, and the federal government sent a clear signal to the states that they could not expect future federal initiatives in domestic policy.[16] As we have seen, the shift to retrenchment in domestic spending began in the 1970s under the Carter administra-

The Reagan Revolution: Effects on Federalism

Part of the first-year legislative success of the Reagan presidency involved a dramatic reconstruction of recent intergovernmental patterns of relationships in the American federal system. A number of categorical grant programs, especially in health, were folded into less munificently funded block programs that granted greater discretion to the states. In addition, because of the revenue shortfalls and pressure on the federal budget, numerous federal subsidy programs to states (revenue sharing, for example), local communities, or authorities (mass transit subsidies, for instance) were either ended or sharply curtailed. Between fiscal 1980 and 1985, for example, federal grants in aid to states and localities decreased in absolute terms by $10 billion, and as a percentage of state and local expenditures, they decreased from 26.3 to 21.0 percent.

It was anticipated at the time that once responsibility for expenditures was placed on the states, they would be less likely to be sustained. As one might expect from a federal system,

though, there was a good deal of variation among the states in the extent to which they were willing to finance new or heavier burdens. In fact, the extent to which a good many states increased taxes to pay for additional obligations created an ironic set of circumstances for the Reagan administration.

As with most Republican administrations, the Reagan presidency was in favor, at least theoretically, of more devolution of discretion at the state level. In the American federal system that typically means variety—an outcome displeasing to national Democrats who favor programs with standards manufactured in Washington. This particular Republican administration, however, has been imbued with a strong flavor about what types of policies are good for the country overall. Some of these policy objectives conflict with the idea of greater discretion at other levels of government.

Thus, while the Reagan administration promoted the supply-side economics of lowering tax rates at the federal level and lopping off expenditures—at tion. When Reagan took office in 1981, cuts were made in entitlement programs to the poor (Medicaid, food stamps, and Aid to Families with Dependent Children) and in operating grants to the states. In addition, the creation of new block grants gave the states greater flexibility in administrating federal funds. After 1982, federal aid funding in constant dollars remained stable under the Reagan administration.

Nathan and Doolittle state that Reagan's cuts in federal aid fell disproportionately on the poor.[17] Cuts were made in entitlement programs and public service, jobs for the poor were eliminated, child nutrition programs were reduced, funding for community development in large cities was diminished, aid to schools in low-income urban areas was reduced because of changes in block grants, and public housing rents increased. Thus most of the Reagan cuts came in federally controlled grant-in-aid programs. Where state governments play a stronger role, as in Medicaid policy, cuts were less substantial (see Chapter 9).

---

which it only modestly succeeded—many states increased taxes and took on additional responsibilities. While the federal deficit climbed at a dizzying pace through the first term of Reagan's presidency, the states, overall, ran a fiscal surplus—although much of this was apparently the result of pension fund investments. Since a national economy does not obey political jurisdictions, the fiscal and tax policies of the federal government possibly were countered at other levels of government.

The commitment of the Reagan administration to a diminished public sphere and a lower taxing federal government undoubtedly was reflected in its initial 1985 proposals to eliminate state and local tax deductions from the federal income tax. In his early reactions to criticism of this aspect of the tax reform proposal, President Reagan indicated that individuals facing this penalty either would be better off moving to lower tax states or pressuring their state governments to reduce taxes. One could infer that the objective behind this sort of proposal was to create a national policy rather than enhance

state and local discretion. That also seems to be the reason why the administration went to court seeking to overturn some local affirmative action agreements that failed to reflect the Reagan administration's strongly expressed opposition to quotas based on race or gender.

Federal relations will continue to undergo transformation, but at least for the immediate future, any considerable increase of either federal government grant-in-aid burdens to other levels of government or revival of categorical programs from eliminated programs appears unlikely. The federal government owes too much money to consider giving more money back to states, counties, and cities. This legacy will outlive the Reagan presidency for some time. To that extent, the Reagan administration has achieved its goals. Local units of government no longer beat a path to Washington as frequently. Diversity among states and localities appears to reign—in some respects, to a greater degree than some of the policy missionaries in the Reagan administration might prefer.

SOURCE: B. B. Kymlicka and Jean V. Matthews, *The Reagan Revolution?* (Chicago: Dorsey Press, 1988), pp. 197–198. Reprinted by permission of Brooks/Cole Publishing Company.

The accompanying reading evaluates the impact of the Reagan presidency on relations between the federal government and states and localities. It notes the "ironic set of circumstances" in which states responded to federal cuts by increasing taxes and by continuing programs that Reagan preferred to be eliminated. We have examined the financial distress faced by states and localities in the early 1990s because of federal cuts and an economic recession. Given the large federal deficit and the philosophical position of the Bush administration, states and cities cannot expect more aid from Washington. Bush's proposal to give more flexibility to state governments may not adequately compensate for the cuts in federal aid. Cities fear that as more aid is funneled through the states, they will have less money to deal with the pressing problems of inner-city neighborhoods. Cities also are concerned that the federal government will shift responsibility to them, as in the war on drugs, without transferring additional funds. The frustration of the states was expressed by former Vermont governor Madeleine Kunin when she said, "The federal government really has created a myth that you can have it all, that you don't have to raise taxes and life can go on as usual and give people what they want without any pain or sacrifice. It is a very powerful message because it is so simple and desirable. But it's creating expectations that are impossible to meet."[18]

FEDERALISM EVALUATED

Critics of federalism offer a number of serious changes. Some suggest that because it gave Southern states independent power federalism helped foster racism in America;[19] that the states cannot deal effectively with social problems that cross state boundaries; that relations between states are marked more by conflict than by cooperation; that the unequal distribution of wealth among the states creates a system in which social benefits vary greatly from state to state; and that with more than 80,000 units of government, duplication of effort is unavoidable and makes it difficult for citizens to hold officials accountable for their actions.

In this chapter we have examined the lack of cooperation and the unequal distribution of social services among the states. While businesspeople and lawyers often get financial rewards from "the system," it is the poor—both black and white—who are its victims.

Considering the defects of the American federal system, the reader might well ask, "Why not scrap it and create a unitary system?" Centralization of authority under a unitary form of government might produce more efficiency in operating social programs and in overcoming racial discrimination.[20] The problem is that a unitary system might actually create more problems than it would solve.

Lockard argues that a unitary government might not be able to cope with controversial problems now left largely to the states. Of course, a unitary government could impose racist policies on a national basis. The misuse of the FBI and CIA by the Nixon administration shows how close the nation came to the establishment of a police state even under federalism. In a unitary system, a president seeking power might more easily have succeeded when directing a national police force. A unitary system possibly would create an even more dehumanized and routinized bureaucracy than already exists in city halls and county courthouses.

As we shall see in Chapter 9, Americans are questioning more and more the growth and centralization of government authority. Smaller units of government permit more citizens to participate and make possible greater economic control for residents of urban areas. Thus the costs of giving up federalism appear to be greater than any possible advantages to be gained by a unitary system.

Federal systems offer a number of benefits.[21] These include the flexibility to respond to regional differences; the prevention of abuse of power because no single group is likely to gain control of government at the state and local levels; the encouragement of innovation by testing new ideas at the local level; and the creation of many centers of power to resolve conflict and to handle administrative burdens. Of course, most of these benefits will occur only if state and local governments are energetic and respond to public demands. As we shall see throughout this book, there is strong evidence that the states have made the necessary structural changes and that elected officials have sufficient personal commitment to enable them to respond effectively to their policy needs.

KEY TERMS

Bill of attainder A legislative act that determines the guilt of an individual and hands down punishment without a trial. The United States Constitution prohibits the national government and the states from taking such action.

Block grants Grants made to cover broad, general areas of policy, such as health care, which allow the recipient freedom in the allocation of funds.

Categorical grants Grants made for a specific purpose; the recipient has little choice in deciding how to spend the money.

Commerce The buying and selling of commodities, transportation, and commercial exchange.

Compacts Arrangements made by two or more states to cooperate in the management of a common problem, such as flood control.

Concurrent majority A proposal made by John C. Calhoun prior to the Civil War that all segments of the country must concur in decisions of the national government. If concurrence is lacking, individual states may accept or reject national decisions. This concept has been accepted only by extreme supporters of states' rights.

Confederacy A loose organization of independent states in which the central unit of government (unlike in a federation) cannot act directly upon individuals.

Dual federalism The belief that the powers of the states and the national government are fixed and that grants of power to the national government do not destroy power reserved to the states. This doctrine has been rejected by the Supreme Court.

Elasticity In tax matters, this refers to the ability of a tax to raise revenue in direct proportion to increases in personal income; for example, if income increases 2 percent, tax revenues will increase at least 2 percent.

Extradition The return of a fugitive to the state in which it is alleged that he or she committed a crime. This is done at the discretion of the governor.

Federal system A system in which a national government shares power with state and regional governments; supremacy rests with the national government.

Fiscal federalism The use of federal funds (often the threat to cut them off) to force states to take actions favored by Congress.

Formula grants Grants made available to everyone who qualifies under the guidelines established for eligibility, such as blind persons.

Grants-in-aid Federal programs in which funds are made available by Congress to state and local governments. The recipient must accept prescribed standards and usually must make a contribution from its own funds. States provide grants to local governments.

"Necessary and proper" clause The so-called elastic clause of the U.S. Constitution, which allows Congress broad authority to carry out its enumerated powers.

"New federalism" A way of viewing federalism that focuses on political interrelationships rather than on government structure. Stresses cooperation among government units.

Nullification As supported by Southern states prior to the Civil War, the doctrine that individual states might declare a national law null and void and secede from the Union. This was based on the belief that the states are the final judges of their authority.

"Privileges and immunities" The provision of the U.S. Constitution that compels states to extend to residents of other states the same legal rights, such as the right to enter into contracts, as they extend to their own residents. Some *political* rights may be denied to out-of-state residents.

Project grants Grants that require specific congressional approval; not every unit of government that is generally qualified will receive funds.

Revenue sharing A federal program of returning tax dollars to state and local governments to be spent largely as they desire; this contrasts with grants-in-aid, under which money must be spent for specific programs as approved by the federal government. Revenue sharing ended in 1986.

Spillover benefits The benefits of a federal program in one state that "spill over" and benefit a second state.

Unitary nation-state A system in which states or regional governments can exercise only those powers given them by the central unit of government—as in Great Britain.

Vertical coalitions Individuals working at federal, state, and local levels who form alliances to accomplish policy objectives.

REFERENCES

1. See Michael D. Reagan and John G. Sanzone, *The New Federalism,* 2d ed. (New York: Oxford University Press, 1981), Chapter 1, "Is Federalism Dead?"
2. See Morton Grodzins, "Centralization and Decentralization in the American Federal System," in Robert A. Goldwin, ed., *A Nation of States* (Chicago: Rand McNally, 1963).
3. Neal R. Peirce, "The State of American Federalism," *Civic Review,* January 1980, p. 32.
4. David R. Beam, "New Federalism, Old Realities: The Reagan Administration and Intergovernmental Reform," in Lester M. Salamon and Michael S. Lund, eds., *The Reagan Presidency and the Governing of America* (Washington, D.C.: The Urban Institute, 1984), p. 423.
5. Russell L. Hanson, "Intergovernmental Relations," in Virginia Gray, Herbert Jacob, and Robert Albritton, eds., *Politics in the American States,* 5th ed. (Glenview, Ill.: Scott, Foresman/Little, Brown, 1990), p. 48.
6. Richard P. Nathan, Fred C. Doolittle, et al., *Reagan and the States* (Princeton, N.J.: Princeton University Press, 1987), p. 31.
7. David B. Walker, "Dysfunctional Federalism—The Congress and Intergovernmental Relations," *State Government,* vol. 54, no. 2 (1981).
8. Peter M. Benda and Charles H. Levine, "Reagan and the Bureaucracy: The Bequest, the

Promise, and the Legacy," in Charles O. Jones, ed., *The Reagan Legacy: Promise and Performance* (Chatham, N.J.: Chatham House, 1988), p. 123.

9. See Thomas J. Anton, *American Federalism and Public Policy: How the System Works* (New York: Random House, 1989), pp. 83–85.
10. David Mayhew, *Congress: The Electoral Connection* (New Haven, Conn.: Yale University Press, 1974), p. 129.
11. Reagan and Sanzone, *New Federalism,* pp. 124–125.
12. Timothy J. Conlan, "The Politics of Federal Block Grants: From Nixon to Reagan," *Political Science Quarterly,* Summer 1984, p. 260.
13. *Ibid.,* p. 269.
14. Hanson, "Intergovernmental Relations," pp. 62–63.
15. See Joseph F. Zimmerman, "Developing State-Local Relations: 1987–1989," in *The Book of the States 1990–91* (Lexington, Ky.: Council of State Governments, 1990), pp. 533–548.
16. Nathan, Doolittle, et al., *Reagan and the States,* p. 45.
17. *Ibid.,* p. 65.
18. Quoted in Jeffrey L. Katz, "State Tax Politics, 1990: No Place to Hide," *Governing,* June 1990, p. 29.
19. William H. Riker, *Federalism: Origin, Operation, Significance* (Boston: Little, Brown, 1964), p. 155.
20. Duane Lockard, *The Perverted Priorities of American Politics,* 2d ed. (New York: Macmillan, 1976), pp. 125–128.
21. See David C. Nice, *Federalism: The Politics of Intergovernmental Relations* (New York: St. Martin's Press, 1987), pp. 13–16.

CHAPTER 3

POLITICAL
PARTIES AND
INTEREST GROUPS

POLITICAL PARTIES AND FEDERALISM

The same adjectives—loose, fragmented, and decentralized—may be applied to both the federal system and political parties in the United States. Indeed, political scientists have long debated the causes and effects of this situation. Some argue that because the United States has a federal system, it follows that political parties will be fragmented and decentralized. Others, however, contend that it was loose, unstructured, locally oriented political parties that caused the American federal system to develop as it has. Regardless of how this chicken-or-egg question is answered, a significant effect of both federalism and the nature of political parties in America has been to strengthen the role of states and localities to the detriment of the nationalization of policymaking.

Political parties have their bases in the states, where more than 500,000 public officials are elected to serve the nearly 100,000 different state and local governments. Political parties have built their organizations to match voting districts within states, and their power tends to be strongest at the local level of ward and county committees. In most cases, individuals run for office with only minimal ties to national (or state) party organizations. As a result, elected officials are often independent of control from above and their primary concern is to formulate policies that will appeal to local constituents and local party leaders.

Even members of the U.S. Congress consider issues largely in terms of state and local interests. Most of them owe their election to the efforts of state and local political organizations, not the national party, and they are well aware that continued electoral success is closely tied to serving local interests. Frequently, campaign organizations are put together by the individual candidates and not even local party organizations are involved.

Political parties and federalism are interrelated systems that support and sustain each other. Because of federalism, Americans place strong emphasis on decentralized political decision making. Constitutional federalism has led to the creation of a multitude of state and local government units. In a similar manner, political parties have fostered a tendency toward localism, and they have helped create an electoral system in which thousands of public officials are dependent on state and local support if they are to remain in office—even national office. The decentralizing effects of federalism also influence the nature of the electorate. States have the authority to set a minimum voting age, determine residence requirements, and restrict the right to vote for reasons of criminal or mental incompetence.

PARTIES AND POLITICAL CULTURE

In Chapter 1 the impact of political culture on state politics was discussed in general. More specifically, it was pointed out that distinct patterns of attitudes toward political parties prevail in different states. Party loyalties appear to be much stronger in the East than in the West. Voters in some states appear more willing to follow the party over a long period of time and to allow the party organization to control the nomination process. In other states, such as California, party organizations are weak, voting patterns are less stable, and nominations are more likely to be determined by primary elections. Indeed, California deliberately tried to weaken parties by establishing cross-filing and open primaries.

Styles of politics also are affected by state history and tradition. For example, ethnic differences may influence the way in which party factions develop, the balancing of party slates, and the degree of allegiance to parties. The style of political leaders, such as the Longs in Louisiana, can leave a strong imprint on state political parties. In other states, political movements can have lasting effects. For example, politics in Minnesota and Wisconsin continue to be influenced by the **Progressive movement** of the early twentieth century and its distrust of political parties. The Progressive movement sought to replace boss-dominated city government with a structure that would be less partisan and less corrupt. It favored nonpartisan elections, city managers, and primary elections. The movement was especially strong in the Upper Midwest and in California. Nationally, its high point came in 1924 when Senator Robert M. La Follette of Wisconsin ran as a third-party candidate for president.

Political conflict has a much stronger **ideological** base in some states than in others. That is, there is a reasonably clear division between liberals and conservatives. In general, **liberals** support government regulation, increased government spending, and civil rights legislation. **Conservatives** tend to oppose those positions, and they favor more effective crime control and lower taxes. In some states, political corruption seems to be tolerated as a way of life. Higher turnover in office and the degree to which patronage is used also are affected by the political culture. In some cases, these patterns of behavior are extremely difficult to explain other than by accepting the statement, "That's just the way we do it here."[1]

PARTY ORGANIZATION AND STRUCTURE

Political party structures may be viewed as having three components. One component is the **party in the organization**—the formally chosen leaders in ward clubs, county committees, and state central committees plus the activists who donate time and energy to the support of party causes. (The party in the organization is examined in the paragraphs that follow.) A second component is the **party in the electorate**—the great mass of people who identify casually with a party and usually vote for its candidates. (This component is discussed in Chapter 4.) The third component is the **party in government**—those individuals who serve in the legislative and executive branches of government and organize themselves along party lines. (Party organization in the legislature is discussed in Chapter 5 and the roles of governors and mayors as party leaders are examined in Chapter 6.)

We have noted that political parties are built on the smallest voting districts within the states. As a consequence, formal state party organization can be described as in Figure 3.1, with rank-and-file party supporters at the bottom and the state party chairman at the top. This is not a hierarchical structure, in which power flows from top to bottom. Instead, each unit operates independently of those units

Figure 3.1   Diagram of the Typical Formal State Party Organization

SOURCE: Adapted from Paul Allen Beck and Frank J. Sorauf, *Party Politics in America,* 7th ed. (New York: HarperCollins, 1992), p. 74. Reprinted by permission of HarperCollins Publishers.

above and below it. State politics has been dominated in most parts of the country by county committees. In some cases city organizations may be the center of power. Paul Allen Beck and Frank J. Sorauf suggest that this is so because the county as a political unit elects a large number of public officials; its officials continue to control substantial political patronage; the boundaries of many larger electoral units, such as congressional districts and state legislative districts, follow county lines; county chairpersons usually serve as members of the state central committee; and state constitutions often recognize county committees as the key political units.[2]

While counties remain the basic organizational unit of state political parties, local party activity appears to be declining. William Crotty notes, "Few local parties are active and even fewer exercise any influence."[3] As we will see later in this chapter, declining local party influence is especially evident in the weakening of urban political machines. County parties are much more poorly organized than is commonly believed. Most are part-time, voluntary operations without paid staff, a permanent headquarters, an annual budget, or even a telephone listing.[4] Just filling the posts of 6,000 Republican and Democratic county chairpersons with intelligent, energetic people is a difficult task. Still, there are some very effective county organizations, such as Cook County (Chicago), Illinois, that are more active than their state-level parties. Where they function at all, congressional district committees often exist only for the purpose of selecting nominees for Congress. They exercise little power and at best operate for only a few months every two years.

There are two basic patterns of party organization. In the more common, the **precinct** chairperson is elected either by a precinct caucus or by voters in the party primary. The precinct chairperson becomes a member of the county committee, which elects the county chairperson (see Figure 3.1). In the other pattern, the city or ward is the lowest level of organization. In this case, if precincts are organized (as in Chicago), it is done by appointment from the ward level. Although attendance at precinct caucuses has been very low (perhaps less than 1 percent of those eligible), participation has increased greatly in states such as Iowa, where substantial media attention has been directed to party caucuses in presidential election years.

In contrast to local party organizations, state parties were strengthened in the 1980s.[5] Most have become substantially more active in the past twenty years, conducting public opinion polls, publishing newsletters, and providing services to candidates. Virtually all have a permanent headquarters and a paid, permanent staff.

Of course, there are differences in state party organizations across the country and between the two parties. For example, Republicans in California, Florida, Indiana, Minnesota, New Jersey, and New York have annual budgets over $1 million. State party organizations have been weak in most Southern states because the Democrats are factionalized and the Republicans are unable to win statewide elections. In general, state Republican parties are much better financed than their Democratic counterparts. Republicans have received more help from their national party, and they have used more sophisticated means of fund-raising.

The state party chairperson performs a variety of tasks, including building the party organization, raising money, recruiting candidates, and planning campaign strategy. The relationship between the holder of this position and the governor is perhaps the most critical element in defining the nature of the job. In some cases, the chairperson has been selected by the governor and serves as the governor's agent. In such cases, he or she exercises little independent judgment. In other cases, the chairperson has a base of political power that is independent of the governor. While this sort of chairperson may cooperate with the governor, he or she can devote proportionately more time to broad-based party activities. Of course, half of the chairpersons are members of the out-party and would tend to work more closely with the state central committee. A substantial number of chairpersons have gone on to hold elective office.

Often *informal* organizations composed of elected officials and influential business leaders compete with formal party leaders for power and influence in directing the party's policies and controlling nominations. In addition, the party itself must compete with a variety of auxiliary groups such as the Young Republicans, ward or district clubs, or, in California, the California Democratic Council, for members and for policymaking leadership. The party organization is also weakened by the short tenure of chairpersons, which averages about two and one-half years. The tenure of national party chairpersons also averages about that length.

Often there is conflict between the **"professionals"** in the party organization and the **"amateurs"** who are active in party clubs. Amateurs are usually more reform-minded than are professionals. They tend to live in suburbs, have higher incomes, and have more years of education than party professionals. Amateurs, more often than professionals, are motivated to enter politics because of their desire to further particular political causes. Professionals are more interested in winning elections and are therefore more willing to compromise and use political patronage than are amateurs.

STATE REGULATION OF POLITICAL PARTIES

The U.S. Constitution does not mention political parties, and Congress has made little effort to regulate them. As a result, states are relatively free (the U.S. Supreme Court has occasionally overruled state practices such as the whites-only primary in Texas) to regulate party activity by provisions in their constitutions and by state law.

Some states have extensively regulated the structure and activities of political parties. In others, particularly in the South, there is a minimum of regulation. Regulation began in the 1880s, when states required a secret ballot. Prior to that time, voters orally indicated the candidates they supported, a practice that led to voter intimidation and bribery. Later reforms in the Progressive period (1900–1920) were directed to parties' internal structure and procedures. This was also when the direct primary began to be used. As discussed in Chapter 4, the direct primary undercut the parties' ability to control nominations through party conventions.

Currently most states regulate party membership organization, the selection method of state central committee members, access to the ballot, methods of nomination, and campaign finance.[6] Of course, party leaders would prefer a minimum of regulation. Not surprisingly, the greatest dissatisfaction with state laws is by minority parties, such as the Republicans in the South and Democrats in the Rocky Mountain states, where one party is clearly dominant in the state legislature.

RECRUITMENT OF CANDIDATES

A major role for parties is to seek candidates to run for office. This may be an especially difficult task for the minority party in strong one-party areas. For example, without strong persuasion from the party organization, the Republican party in many parts of the South might not be able to field any candidates against the Democrats. It requires a very effective statewide organization for a party to recruit and support legislative candidates in areas where the party's candidates receive little support.

In several states, the parties make informal endorsements of primary candidates. Even with the advent of primaries, state conventions continue to be held and endorsements made. In Connecticut, a candidate must receive at least 20 percent of the vote on a state party convention ballot in order to be placed on the primary ballot. In other states, such as New York and Colorado, candidates who win a certain percentage of the convention's support are automatically placed on the primary ballot while others must have petitions signed in order to be on the ballot. From the perspective of political parties, states that either require or permit preprimary endorsements do the most to build strong party organizations. Only California and Florida prohibit preprimary endorsements by political parties. The convention system gives parties greater control of the nominating process by making it difficult for outsiders to be nominated. However, as will be seen in Chapter 4, the use of primary elections has not weakened parties as much as was originally anticipated.

URBAN POLITICAL MACHINES

"I seen my opportunities and I took 'em."

—George Washington Plunkett,
TAMMANY HALL POLITICIAN IN NEW YORK

"Two things you can't let an opponent get away with—telling lies about
you or telling the truth about you."

—Anonymous Chicago politician

Although political parties are generally weak and undisciplined, tightly disciplined
party organizations have existed in the form of the **urban political machine.** Most
of the strong urban machines—Tammany Hall in New York, the Pendergast machine in Kansas City, and the organizations of Frank Hague in Jersey City, James
Michael Curley in Boston, and Ben West in Nashville—have fallen at the hands of
reformers. The organization of the late Richard J. Daley in Chicago has become
weaker since he died in 1976. Some machines have survived or reemerged in smaller Eastern cities such as Albany, New York, and Atlantic City, New Jersey. In addition, a new kind of mayor-centered machine has come into existence in several
cities. As with Mayor Coleman Young in Detroit, mayor-centered machines get
much of their power from federally funded programs that provide the mayor with
political workers and with resources to build support from neighborhood groups
and downtown development interests.[7]

Urban political machines have a historical importance. They performed a wide
variety of urgently needed social services in virtually every large American city between 1860 and 1930, and their method of operation has had a continuing effect on
the behavior of contemporary party leaders.

Fred I. Greenstein notes that nineteenth-century political machines developed
because of five major factors:

1. In the second half of the nineteenth century, the American urban population increased
   sixfold. This increase in population created a need for improvement in such public
   services as transportation, public health, firefighting, and police.
2. The structure of city government, marked by weak mayors and the presence of many
   elected officials, made it virtually impossible for the city to respond to the challenges
   of growth by upgrading public services and assuming the management of urban life.
3. From 1860 until World War I, more than 25 million immigrants came to the United
   States and most of them settled in cities. There was an almost complete absence of
   social planning to meet the needs of these dependent people.
4. Businesses increasingly needed public services, such as street repair, and they also
   needed freedom from strict enforcement of ordinances controlling such matters as job
   safety and waste disposal.
5. Oftentimes, immigrants were naturalized and registered to vote soon after arriving in
   this country. Their votes were easily purchased by the machines.[8]

The party machine operated by providing employment (patronage jobs), financial assistance, and recognition to the urban poor. The machine was organized with
the boss, assisted by ward leaders and precinct leaders, presiding over a well-disci-

plined party. Precinct leaders were responsible for an area of several city blocks, containing about 600 voters. Ward leaders were often city councilors and were responsible for the several precincts that made up their ward. Although the machine bosses were often the mayors, sometimes they were nonelected people who operated behind the scenes to control local government.

While the classic power of the machine derived from its control of patronage jobs, it could also help the poor by securing jobs in private business or by acting as a friend in court. The party secured votes (often simply because of friendship established between the precinct captains and their neighbors) and limited nominations to its own politicians. The machine assured itself continuance in office, it centralized public decision making, and it provided much-needed social services (e.g., shelter for residents of an apartment gutted by fire) at a time when government assumed little responsibility for social welfare.

The Democratic party organization in Chicago has been the most celebrated example of a contemporary political machine. Richard J. Daley was first elected mayor in 1955 as a reform candidate. As mayor of Chicago and chairman of the Cook County Democratic party, Daley is estimated to have controlled as many as 30,000 public jobs and perhaps 10,000 private jobs.[9] Most of the key projects supported by Daley—road building, a new airport, a convention hall—were noncontroversial and benefited the county as well as the city. Unlike many other bosses, Daley did not fall victim to personal greed. He died in office in 1976 and was replaced as mayor by a hand-picked member of the city council.

The machine had been losing power since the late 1960s. It began with violence at the 1968 Democratic party convention and was followed in the mid-1970s by the defection of members of the growing black community. Daley's successor was defeated in a 1979 primary election when Democratic leadership splintered. In 1983 black U.S. Congressman Harold Washington defeated the incumbent mayor, Jane Byrne, in a primary election. Washington faced strong opposition from white ethnic members of council (aldermen), many of whom had been part of the Daley organization. After being largely ignored by Daley in the 1960s and 1970s, black and Hispanic community groups gained new access to government in the 1980s. Washington died in office in 1988 and a black alderman, Eugene Sawyer, was named to replace him. However, he was defeated in a 1989 special election by Richard M. Daley, son of Richard J. Daley. Richard M. Daley revived the machine, projected himself as a "good government" reformer, and was easily reelected in 1991. In 1989 and 1991 Daley defeated four top black candidates who each claimed to be the successor to Harold Washington. While Daley campaigned hard in black neighborhoods, blacks were divided and no strong leader emerged. As a result, in 1991 for the first time in twenty years blacks did not hold any of the three citywide elective offices in Chicago.

In many ways, political machines were victims of their own success. As urban residents became better educated and better off financially, **patronage** jobs ceased to be attractive and they moved to better-paying jobs in private business. Individuals began to place a greater value on their vote and were less willing to tolerate corruption in government. Even for those who remained poor, federal welfare programs ended the machine control of social services.

Machine politics in Chicago and across the county has been dealt a setback by two Supreme Court decisions limiting the use of patronage. In *Elrod* v. *Burns* (1976) the Court held that two non-civil-service employees of the newly elected Cook County (Illinois) sheriff had been improperly fired simply because they did not support the party in power. In *Rutan* v. *Illinois Republican Party* (1990), the Court decided that party affiliation could not be a factor in hiring, promoting, or transferring state employees. This decision affected the treatment of 60,000 employees in Illinois and has led to changes in personnel practices in several states and cities. The accompanying reading looks at *Rutan* as a threat to political parties. In his dissent, Justice Antonin Scalia lamented the weakening of political parties and suggested that we continue to use patronage as a means of supporting the two-party system. *Rutan* was a 5–4 decision with the majority opinion written by former Justice William Brennan. With its strong conservative majority, the Court might overturn *Rutan* in the near future.

Patronage Ruling: Threat to Political Parties, Promise to Individual Rights

Illinois is frequently called "the most political state in the union." It is little wonder, then, that its patronage practices should eventually need scrutiny by the U.S. Supreme Court, and that the decision should send shock waves across the nation. Civil libertarians hailed the decision as strengthening the constitutional guarantee of freedom of association. The severest critics saw it as ending the two-party system and thus strengthening the influence of special interest groups.

The facts are simple. In November 1980 Gov. James R. Thompson proclaimed a hiring freeze on all employment under his control. Affected were approximately 60,000 positions, more than 5,000 of which become available each year because of resignation, retirement, reorganization, expansion, etc. His "express permission," granted through the Governor's Office of Personnel, was needed for new hires, promotions, transfers and recalls after layoffs.

Four state employees brought suit, claiming that their failure to support the Republican party caused denial of promotion, transfer or recall after layoff. They held jobs as rehabilitation counselor, equipment operator, garage worker and dietary manager. In addition, one applicant for a job as prison guard claimed that he was denied employment because of his lack of Republican party affiliation.

In the version that reached the U.S. Supreme Court, *Rutan et al v Republican Party of Illinois et al* (Docket No. 88-172, issued June 21) the court held, 5–4, that Illinois' patronage system abridged First Amendment rights of free speech and association. Two earlier decisions had forbidden firing of government employees because of party affiliation (see *Elrod v Burns*, 427 U.S. 347 (1976)—also an Illinois case—and *Branti v Finkel*, 445 U.S. 507 (1981), and the court here extended the prohibition to other employment decisions.

In *Elrod* and *Branti* the court held that making party allegiance, including work for candidates and money contributions, a condition of employment was impermissible because it could cause unwanted association or inhibit desired association. Certainly the government must require efficient work, but the court saw no connection between party membership and poor performance on the job, and it observed that there are less drastic measures than dismissal to correct inadequate performance. Although government jobs are not a matter of right or entitlement, the government may not deny them for reasons that infringe basic constitutional rights. Party affiliation may be required as a condition of government employment only at policymaking levels.

In *Rutan* the court called denial of promotion or transfer, failure to recall after layoff and rejection of initial hire "deprivations less harsh than dismissal that nevertheless press state employees and applicants to conform their beliefs and associations to some state-selected orthodoxy." It said, "These are significant penalties and are imposed for the exercise of right guarantees by the First Amendment."

Critics of the decision see it as threatening the democratic process. Indeed, said the court, "Respondents, who include the Governor of Illinois . . . do not suggest any other overriding government interest in favoring Republican Party supporters for promotion, transfer, and rehire." The court observed that political parties are managing to survive and noted "the declining influence of election workers when compared to money-intensive campaigning, such as the distribution of form letters and advertising."

Justice Brennan wrote for the majority, which included Justices White, Marshall, Blackmun and Stevens. Justice Scalia, joined by Chief Justice Rehnquist and Justices Kennedy and, in part, by Justice O'Connor, filed a dissenting opinion. Justice Stevens filed a special concurrence that was, in large part, a rebuttal of Scalia who, in turn, responded in frequent, often voluminous footnotes. Scalia attacked at many points, but two issues were central: the degree to which patronage has been historically accepted and the damage that weakening it will do to our democratic process.

On the history of patronage Scalia said, "[W]hen a practice not expressly prohibited by the text of the Bill of Rights bears the endorsement of a long tradition of open, widespread and unchallenged use that dates back to the beginning of the Republic, we have no basis for striking it down." Stevens responded by pointing out that most of the founding fathers hardly accepted patronage since they vigorously opposed political parties. Quoting President John Kennedy's famous "Ask not . . ." statement, he added, "This case involves a contrary command: 'Ask not what a job applicant can do for the State—ask what they can do for our party.' Whatever traditional support may remain for a command of that ilk, it is plainly an illegitimate excuse for the practices rejected by the Court today."

On the democratic process Scalia made the rather astounding statement, "As . . . the Boss Tweeds, the Tammany Halls, the Pendergast Machines, the Byrd Machines and the Daley Machines have faded into history . . . political leaders at all levels increasingly complain of the helplessness of elected government, unprotected by 'party discipline,' before the demands of small and cohesive interest groups." According to his reading of recent history, the legislative process has been open to undue influence of interest groups precisely because the absence of patronage has destroyed the symbiotic interdependence of officeholder and party faithful beholden to him for their jobs. The party cannot deliver the vote, so the candidate needs the big bucks of the PACs (political action committees) to get the vote through expensive media campaigns.

Scalia says that patronage specifically fosters a two-party system, which makes for efficient expression of the will of the people. He also argues that it is via patronage that minority groups enter the political system and eventually achieve power. He is quite aware of the well-known evils of patronage, but he is apparently willing to make a trade-off for "the systemic effects of patronage in promoting political stability and facilitating the social and political integration of previously powerless groups."

Branti established the principle that high level appointments to policymaking jobs could be conditioned upon party affiliation, and *Rutan* affirmed this. An initial reaction of some government officials was puzzlement as to where the line occurs, and Scalia underlines this by including a laundry list of seemingly conflicting decisions on areas in which government has a legitimate interest in interfering with basic rights of its employees. While lawyers would probably observe that each case cited "turns on the facts," *Rutan* may open the door to a series of court actions.

The implications for Illinois are complicated by the certainty that there will be a new governor next year. There is no question that existing decisions permit him to name his own top officers, but the aftermath of *Branti* seems not to have clarified how far down the bureaucratic job chain the definition extends. Like *Branti, Rutan* is criticized for failing to provide guidelines, and Scalia's dissent underlines the wide divergence in precedent decisions in the various states. In other words, employees previously secure in their jobs still are, but at some undefined levels there may still be the historic election year uneasiness.

An immediate effect was the issuance by Gov. Thompson on July 17 of Executive Order No. 1 (1990), strictly implementing the principles embodied in *Rutan*. About the past it says, "It has been the policy and practice of this administration to fill positions in the state only with individuals who are qualified for their positions." Indeed, recommendations to the governor's office have been made from lists of those qualified under civil service regulations, but apparently the attitude has been, "All other things being equal, hire the Republican." Now the record of past party affiliation, activity and voting is not to be considered. The order does not prohibit recommendations for those seeking employment by party officials, but these must deal strictly with the candidate's qualifications for the job and not with party loyalty.

Anyone who lives in Springfield will have to wonder whether job dispensers will be able to ignore the known party affiliation of the recommenders—but at least the Republicans have stopped attaching application forms for party membership to job application forms.

SOURCE: F. Mark Siebert, *Illinois Issues,* August–September 1990, pp. 14–15. Copyright *Illinois Issues,* published by Sangamon State University, Springfield, Ill. 62794-9243. Reprinted by permission.

THE REFORM MOVEMENT

In a more direct way, machines declined because they were attacked by reformers or so-called **good-government organizations.** In many cities reformers succeeded by the early twentieth century in establishing civil service commissions, instituting the direct primary and nonpartisan elections, and creating procedures for auditing government funds and monitoring the letting of government contracts. Good-government groups drew their support from upper- and middle-class Anglo-Saxon Protestants who believed they had the "right" answers to political problems. Today, reform administrations have replaced machines in most cities. Yet, as we have seen, some political machines have survived. By appealing to business leaders, working with blacks, and controlling patronage jobs, organizations such as the Daley machine in Chicago adapted to change and have continued to maintain power.

One of the municipal reforms at the turn of the century was to switch from ward elections of council members to **at-large elections.** It was hoped that this would elevate the tone of elections, produce better candidates, and break the local bias of ward elections. Today, about 60 percent of all cities have at-large elections. No change ever receives universal acclaim: Current reformers argue that at-large elections hurt minorities by diluting their vote in citywide elections. They also contend that at-large elections produce long ballots that make intelligent voting difficult and that these elections weaken legislator-constituency links. This is also a major issue in reapportionment, which is discussed in Chapter 5.

When reformed and machine-run cities are compared, some clear differences in policymaking can be identified. Reformed cities, with New York City as a glaring exception, generally have lower taxes and spend less money for public purposes than do nonreformed or machine cities. Reformed cities are less responsive to the needs of ethnic minorities, as is reflected in their taxing and spending policies. Social divisions of race, religion, and ethnicity are more clearly visible in nonreformed cities.

Reformers assumed that there was an interest ("the public interest") that should control the way in which citywide decisions were made. They argued that this interest should prevail over the **"private-regarding" interests** pursued by racial, religious, and ethnic groups. Government decision making was to be isolated from the impact of socioeconomic cleavages.

STATE PARTY SYSTEMS: LEVELS OF COMPETITION

Political scientists have devoted considerable attention to measuring the *intensity* of interparty competition and to speculating on the effects of competition on policymaking. Regardless of the measurement techniques employed to determine the degree of competitiveness between Democrats and Republicans (usually the popular votes for governor and for the two houses of the state legislature are averaged together and a percentage of Democratic and Republican success is calculated), the results show a pattern in which the states can be grouped into four categories:

Democratic majority, Republican majority, Democratic dominant, and competitive two-party (see Figure 3.2). Malcolm Jewell and David Olson state that the only **one-party dominant states** are some Southern Democratic states where the Republican party has been able to win only a few legislative seats and occasionally elect a governor.[10] **Majority party states** are those in which the minority party usually gets at least 40 percent of the vote and about one-fourth of the legislative seats. In these states the majority party typically controls both the governorship and the legislature. Only two states, South Dakota and New Hampshire, were classified as Republican majority, and none was Republican dominant in 1988. In **competitive states,** on the other hand, the legislature may be controlled by one party, while the governor's mansion is occupied by a member of the opposing party. In the North, substantial changes have recently occurred in Kansas, North Dakota, and Vermont, where Democratic strength has grown.

It is easy to dismiss third parties as though Democrats and Republicans had a complete monopoly on state politics. From 1950 to 1988, only one state (Maine) elected an independent governor and there has been only a handful of independent state legislators. Still, in recent years minor party support in state legislative races has been as high as 9 percent in New York, where the Liberal and Conservative

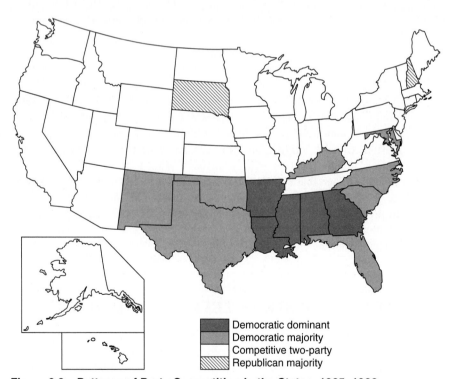

Figure 3.2   Patterns of Party Competition in the States, 1965–1988

SOURCE: Malcolm E. Jewell and David M. Olson, *Political Parties and Elections in the American States,* 3d ed. (Chicago: Dorsey Press), p. 29. Copyright 1988 The Dorsey Press. Reprinted by permission of Brooks/Cole Publishing Company, Pacific Grove, California 93950.

parties are a constant pressure, and 7 percent in Alaska, where support has been strong for the Libertarian party. In 1990 independent governors were elected in Connecticut and Alaska. In general, support for minor parties has been strongest in Western states and weakest in the South.[11]

In spite of changes in the voting pattern in recent presidential elections (George Bush carried all the Democratic dominant and Democratic majority states in 1988), five Southern states remain Democratic dominant when only state offices are considered. Since 1960, however, Tennessee, North Carolina, Texas, Alabama, Louisiana, South Carolina, Virginia, Arkansas, and Florida each elected at least one Republican governor, and Republicans made significant gains in their state legislatures. Change has been greatest in Tennessee and Virginia, whose classifications have changed from Democratic dominant to competitive two-party. Voters in West Virginia, Alabama, Mississippi, Georgia, Arkansas, and Louisiana continue to vote overwhelmingly for Democratic candidates in state and local elections. For example, in 1990, 19 of the 100 members of the Arkansas house were Republicans, and there were only 24 Republicans among 154 legislators in West Virginia. Mississippi and Georgia have yet to elect a Republican governor. From 1900 to 1960, the Republicans in Georgia did not even run a candidate for governor, and Republicans have never controlled a single Southern state legislature since Reconstruction. Democrats gained governors in Florida and Texas in 1990 to control all Southern states except Alabama, North Carolina, and South Carolina.

The prevalence of one-party control is greater at the county and city levels. While the Republican party has controlled many rural Midwestern counties throughout this century, the Democratic party has dominated most large cities nationwide. This imbalance in party competition has led many cities to establish nonpartisan elections (discussed later in this chapter) as a way of providing more equitable access to political office.

The increase in party competition throughout the nation is due to several factors. The population shift from rural to urban areas has reduced the strength of rural counties, where one party has traditionally been dominant. Also, movement across state lines has weakened party loyalties. At the national level, the **New Deal** had a powerful effect in increasing the strength of the Democratic party in the North. Since 1952, presidential candidates Eisenhower, Goldwater, Nixon, Reagan, and Bush have helped increase Republican support in the South. However, outside of Arkansas in the 1960s and Virginia in the 1970s, the Republican party has not been able to win any consecutive gubernatorial elections there. In only four Southern states has the Republican party been able to win as many as one-fourth of the seats in one legislative house. As recently as 1978, all 144 members of the Alabama legislature were Democrats.

The process by which party competition increases in a state may be described as follows: (1) voters who consistently supported the dominant party begin to split their tickets and vote for some minority party candidates in state and national elections; (2) voters (especially younger persons) begin to shift their party identification, perhaps first to independent and then to the minority party; and (3) voters shift their party registration. A variety of factors may work to retard change. In states with closed, competitive primaries, voters will be more hesitant to change registration because of the importance of primary elections and the fact they are committed to vote in their party's primary. In other states, the leaders of the minority party have become content with the status quo and their role as a dispenser of federal patronage when their party's presidential candidate is successful. In many cases, Republicans are frustrated in the South because Democratic incumbents compile very conservative voting records, giving the people little incentive to switch parties. An excellent example of this strategy was Charles Robb's successful 1981 gubernatorial campaign in Virginia, in which he stressed his broad agreement with President Reagan before conservatives, but showed selective disagreement when appearing before liberal audiences. Party competition has, of course, increased because of the movement of Northern Republicans into Southern states.

Even with President Reagan's strong popularity, Republican gains at the state level were modest in the 1980s. Although Republicans made an impressive gain of 8 governorships in 1986, they lost 179 legislative seats and controlled both houses

Table 3.1   Mean Percentage of Voting-Age Population Voting for Presidential, Gubernatorial, and Congressional Candidates, 1981–1988

Rank	State[*]	Overall	President	Governor	U.S. Senator	U.S. Representative
1	Montana	61.7	63.7	64.1	60.6	58.5
2	North Dakota	60.6	62.1	63.7	57.3	59.3
3	South Dakota	59.5	62.0	56.8	60.1	58.9
4	Minnesota	59.5	67.2	52.6	64.4	53.7
5	Maine	58.3	63.5	52.2	60.6	57.1
6	Utah	56.0	60.8	60.6	51.3	51.4
7	Idaho	55.9	59.1	52.4	57.2	54.9
8	Oregon	55.7	60.2	52.9	56.5	53.4
9	Alaska	54.7	55.6	55.3	54.1	53.8
10	Vermont	53.5	59.4	52.9	49.9	51.6
11	Iowa	52.6	60.8	46.3	51.8	51.8
12	Nebraska	52.0	56.2	47.8	52.6	51.5
13	Wisconsin	51.6	62.7	44.7	49.3	49.7
14	Missouri	51.4	56.0	56.9	45.3	47.3
15	Washington	51.0	56.3	58.5	42.4	46.8
16	Indiana	50.7	54.6	55.0	45.2	47.7
17	Connecticut	49.9	59.5	43.4	46.9	49.8
18	Massachusetts	49.8	57.8	42.3	53.5	45.5
19	Kansas	49.7	55.6	44.7	50.4	48.3
20	Rhode Island	49.7	54.4	48.5	50.5	45.3
21	Delaware	49.6	53.2	53.2	47.6	44.3
22	Wyoming	49.5	51.8	47.2	50.5	48.5
23	Colorado	48.8	55.1	43.0	49.6	47.4
24	Michigan	48.4	56.0	41.3	51.1	45.4
25	Ohio	47.8	56.7	40.9	45.8	47.7
26	Illinois	47.1	55.2	40.5	46.7	46.0
27	West Virginia	46.5	49.2	52.2	45.2	39.2
28	New Jersey	45.2	54.3	38.2	47.3	41.2

of the legislature in only ten states. In the 1988 elections Democrats gained one state governorship to hold a 28 to 22 advantage over Republicans. Democrats also made modest legislative gains in 1988. In 1990 Democrats gained control of six new legislative chambers, while suffering a decline of one governorship. However, Republicans also lost one governorship because two independents were elected. While the overall party balance remained largely changed, there was a swing in party control of 14 governorships in 1990. Legislative elections were particularly disappointing to the Republican party because it had made state races a top priority in a bid to gain control of the congressional redistricting process for 1992 elections.

There is a strong correlation between higher levels of party competition and voter turnout (see Table 3.1). Voter turnout is markedly lower in the eight Southern states that have the strongest dominance by the Democratic party. Those eight states also have low levels of education and income, which depress voter turnout. It is interesting to note, however, that the states with the highest turnout are *not* the wealthiest.

Table 3.1   Mean Percentage of Voting-Age Population Voting for Presidential, Gubernatorial, and Congressional Candidates, 1981–1988 *Continued*

Rank	State*	Overall	President	Governor	U.S. Senator	U.S. Representative
29	New Hampshire	45.2	53.9	41.7	42.0	43.1
30	Mississippi	44.6	51.6	39.9	46.1	40.5
31	Arkansas	44.5	49.4	46.4	45.7	36.4
32	New Mexico	44.3	49.3	40.2	45.7	42.2
33	Pennsylvania	44.3	52.0	39.4	41.8	43.9
34	North Carolina	43.2	45.4	48.5	41.2	37.6
35	California	42.8	48.5	40.0	40.7	42.2
36	Alabama	42.7	47.8	40.9	44.3	37.7
37	Oklahoma	41.9	50.4	37.5	43.5	36.1
38	Hawaii	41.8	43.7	42.7	40.7	40.2
39	Maryland	40.3	50.3	34.3	37.5	39.1
40	New York	40.3	49.6	36.1	37.3	38.1
41	Tennessee	39.9	46.9	35.1	42.2	35.2
42	Virginia	39.8	49.5	31.7	42.5	35.4
43	Louisiana	39.6	52.9	51.0	37.3	17.3
44	Nevada	39.1	43.2	36.2	38.6	38.6
45	Arizona	38.9	45.1	34.9	37.6	37.8
46	Kentucky	38.1	49.5	33.3	36.4	33.4
47	Texas	36.7	45.7	29.1	39.2	32.6
48	Florida	36.4	46.5	35.0	37.4	26.5
49	South Carolina	34.7	39.8	30.0	35.3	33.9
50	Georgia	32.8	40.4	27.7	33.7	29.5

*In some states the vote may be understated because election returns are not reported in uncontested races.

SOURCE: Virginia Gray, Herbert Jacob, and Robert Albritton, eds., *Politics in the American States,* 5th ed. (Glenview, Ill.: Scott, Foresman/Little, Brown, 1990), p. 89. Copyright © 1990 by Virginia Gray, Herbert Jacob, and Robert B. Albritton. Reprinted by permission of HarperCollins Publishers.

While it is generally taken for granted that two-party politics is preferable to one-party politics, political scientists disagree regarding the *effects of competition* on government performance. Thomas R. Dye, for example, indicates that education, welfare, taxation, and highway programs appear to be more closely related to the socioeconomic factors in a state than to the degree of party competition itself. Dye notes that "party competition itself does not necessarily cause more liberal welfare policies."[12]

In contrast, other political scientists, among them John H. Fenton, have identified "a significant statistical relation between two-party competition and expenditures for education and welfare [they are greater]."[13] In his study of state politics in New England, Duane Lockard found that the more competitive states in southern New England had programs that were more liberal toward the poor than did the less competitive states of northern New England did. Others have found that competitive states provide higher welfare and education benefits. V. O. Key believes that competition forces parties to become more responsible and that it facilitates the expression of lower-class viewpoints in the political system.[14] Because the more competitive states are often more wealthy and thus can more easily afford to spend more money than the less wealthy one-party states, it is difficult in many cases to distinguish economic capacity from levels of competition. Nevertheless, some relatively poor competitive two-party states, such as Montana and Utah, make a strong effort to support social welfare and educational services. If party competition does not always affect *total* state expenditures, it does seem to affect the *direction* of expenditures toward education and welfare rather than toward capital projects such as highways. Lockard evaluates the influence of competition as follows:

> I am led personally to believe that the competition factor has some significance here because of the evidence we have of party leaders actually behaving as if they were afraid of the next election and pressing their followers to take specific actions because of that fear. I have myself witnessed party leaders often angering their own followers when they insist on certain policies as necessary for winning the next election. Indeed, I have seen leaders do this even when the policy in question was very distasteful to them. Because they were in the spotlight of publicity they acted, as they believed, to save the greater cause: winning the next election. How often this happens and how much it may contribute to policies responsive to the have-nots there is no way of demonstrating by any statistical means, but it can hardly be irrelevant.[15]

Sara McCally Morehouse concludes that it is not so much the degree of party competition, but the *cohesiveness* of political parties that influences policy outcomes in the states.[16] Morehouse has found that in states with **cohesive parties**— where the governor heads the state ticket and other candidates run on an established platform—the quality and distribution of public services are improved.

As a final note on state party systems, it should be pointed out that **nonpartisan elections** are dominant in small cities across the country and that Nebraska elects state legislators in elections where party labels are removed. Nonpartisanship is often found in cities with a council-manager form of government, and it is especially prevalent in the West (see Chapter 6).

Nonpartisanship was part of the general reform movement of the early twentieth century that led to the decline of political machines. It sought to eliminate the evils of "politics" by attacking the parties in the most direct way possible. In spite of the goals of reformers to recruit "better" candidates and to "democratize" politics, there are some surprising parallels between nonpartisan politics and politics in multifactional one-party states. First, many studies indicate that without party labels to guide voters, the personal qualities of candidates—celebrity status, ethnicity, familiar-sounding names—become very important influences on voter decisions. Second, in both systems, interest groups gain in power. For example, without party financial resources candidates must turn to other sources for help. As a result, instead of becoming more independent they become even more indebted to other groups besides parties than are candidates in two-party states. Finally, voter turnout decreases in nonpartisan situations. In part, this is because protest voting is made difficult by the absence of party labels, and incumbents, who are better known to the public than their opponents, are frequently returned to office.

INTEREST GROUPS

Earlier, it was noted that relatively few persons are active participants in party organizations. Only about 25 percent of American adults have ever worked for a political party or for a candidate in an election, and fewer than 10 percent have been members of a political club or organization. In contrast, about 60 percent of the American people are members of organized interest groups (for example, local parent-teacher organizations), which take stands on various public issues and try to affect government decision making. Lobbyists representing interest groups communicate the goals of their organizations to policymakers in the hope of influencing the establishment of public policy. Organized interests working in state capitols run the gamut from well-financed national groups, such as local affiliations of the American Medical Association (AMA) and the AFL-CIO, to local groups represented by a single part-time lobbyist. Interest groups perform a major political function of channeling demands into policy by serving as brokers between the people and the government. As suggested earlier in this chapter, there is evidence that interest groups exist in larger numbers and have more influence in those states where party organization is the weakest.

Interest groups differ from parties in the following ways. Most significantly, they—in the United States, at least—do not contest elections by running candidates for office. Although they may work closely within parties in an attempt to control nominations and elect officials who will support their goals, they do not run their own candidates for office nor do they serve as symbols of voter loyalty.

Second, although political parties are committed exclusively to political action, interest groups engage in both political and nonpolitical activity. For example, while the AMA makes major financial contributions to political campaigns, it also maintains a wide variety of professional services for physicians. In regard to political activities, the two major parties take positions on a vast array of social and economic issues confronting the nation or the state. Interest groups, in contrast, are often concerned about only a single issue or a limited number of policy matters. Because of their broad commitment to public policies and their concern for winning elections, parties must appeal to the broadest possible spectrum of the electorate. The political positions taken by interest groups are much less inclusive, and their appeal is often limited to a small percentage of the American people.

Third, the history of the major political parties reflects a remarkable degree of stability and consistency over the past century. Interest groups, on the other hand, are usually short-lived, forming around a single issue and quickly disappearing when the issue either is resolved or simply fades away.

In spite of their differences, parties and interest groups both serve as basic representational mechanisms. While parties provide virtually unlimited representation, interest groups accommodate specific points of view. Because of their more narrowly defined goals and the greater unity among members, interest groups generally have been more effective representatives for particular points of view than political parties.[17]

Since the 1960s, there has been significant expansion in the number of groups that are politically active in virtually all states. While business, labor, agriculture, education, and government continue to be the major interests, new groups representing women, specific issues such as abortion, minorities, religion, tourism, environmental protection, and the elderly have become increasingly influential. Within the traditional categories of interest groups there have been major changes to reflect greater economic diversity in most states (the rise of new technologies, for example) and a relative decline in the strength of labor and agricultural interests. Education and public employee unions have become much more politically active and powerful in the states. For example, government is the major employer in several Western states, and some legislators believe that the most effective lobbyists represent their state university system.

Interest-Group Tactics and Effectiveness

Interest groups are involved in all stages of political activity. In many states, registered lobbyists outnumber elected representatives by two to one. For convenience, their tactics may be divided into three categories: public relations, electioneering, and lobbying.

Interest groups may initiate a proposal by carrying out a *public relations* campaign in which they attempt to publicize an issue and then seek support for their position. Often an interest group will attempt to mobilize public opinion in opposition to a proposal initiated by another group or political party. In many instances, the most successful interest groups are those whose basic strategy is defensive—they wish to preserve the status quo rather than initiate change. In this regard, the more conservative business and manufacturing groups typically have an advantage over labor unions, which seek to alter the distribution of resources in their favor. Moreover, because there is a close connection between interest-group public relations and commercial advertising, groups representing the business community have an advantage in expertise and available personnel, not to mention money.

As noted previously, interest groups may participate in political campaigns by providing assistance to political parties or individual candidates—that is, by **electioneering.** Some groups may assume a position of neutrality and give money to candidates from both parties. Others may be closely tied to partisan politics. Labor unions, for example, are intimately connected to the Democratic party in most of the large, industrial states, such as New York, California, Illinois, Pennsylvania, Ohio, Michigan, and New Jersey. In these states, however, interest groups occasionally endorse Republican candidates, especially incumbents whose voting records they like.

The most basic election function of interest groups is to provide an opportunity for candidates to acquire friendships and build reputations. Most candidates are members of several groups, and they believe they can translate friendship into votes. This may be especially important in nonpartisan contests, where the "politics of acquaintance" can help win elections. Interest groups may assist candidates by publicizing elections. Candidates may be invited to appear before the group or they may respond to questionnaires. Most directly, interest groups may provide staff assistance in running a campaign. Mailing lists of members can be provided to candidates and office material and equipment made available for their use.

At a third stage in the political process interest groups employ **lobbyists** to communicate specific policy goals more directly to legislators. Communication may be in the form of testimony before legislative committees or, more indirectly, through entertainment, where social contacts are established. Very often state interest groups are affiliated with national groups (such as the National Education Association) that lobby in Washington.

In many states there is a growing influence of *contract lobbyists,* who may represent ten or more clients. This is part of a growing professionalization of state lobbyists who are better educated, better informed, and less likely to use pressure tactics than their predecessors. This growing professionalization of lobbying parallels a similar legislative trend and has helped keep interest groups strong in the face of political change in the legislative and executive branches. As political issues become more complex, legislators need more technical information, and they are less likely to be influenced by social lobbying.

In addition to contract professionals, Thomas and Hrebenar identify four other categories of lobbyists.[18] The largest group of state lobbyists (nearly 50 percent) is comprised of employees of organizations who devote full time or part of their job to lobbying. Another large category (25 to 40 percent) is comprised of employees of state, local, and federal agencies who represent their agencies to the legislature. These are sometimes referred to as "hidden lobbies" because most states do not require government employees to register as lobbyists. Perhaps 10 to 20 percent of lobbyists are volunteers who represent citizen and community organizations on a part-time basis. The final 3 to 5 percent consist of self-styled lobbyists, or "hobbyists," who act on their own behalf to support pet projects. The number of hobbyists is hard to estimate because few are required by law to register.

Because state legislators are often inexperienced and short legislative sessions require them to act quickly on many bills with which they are unfamiliar, they may rely heavily on technical information presented by lobbyists. Information ranges from a political analysis of voting blocs forming on bills to a projection of the economic impact of a state income tax. In addition to testimony at committee hearings (the primary channel of information for most legislators), lobbyists communicate by working through sympathetic legislators, who they hope will influence other lawmakers. Because most bills are controlled by a few committees or by party caucuses (meetings of party members in the House and Senate to discuss legislative business), lobbyists make a strong effort to establish contacts with the select number of legislators who dominate those committees.

In many instances, lobbyists find they have built-in representation in legislative bodies. Because most legislators continue to pursue their private interests as, for example, farmers, bankers, business executives, or teachers, they need not be pressured to vote as an interest group wishes. In fact, the legislators themselves act as lobbyists to persuade their colleagues.

As at the national level, there has been a great increase in the number of single-interest groups operating at the state and local levels. Groups such as Right to Life are able to raise substantial amounts of money and focus their attention on a single social issue. Such groups cut across party lines, making uncompromising, all-or-nothing demands on legislators. The threat to legislators is that if they do not vote 100 percent for the positions favored by the single-issue group, the group will cut off all support. Other interest groups, in contrast, give money to legislators of both parties in hopes of developing a cordial relationship and easy access. Single-issue groups may find access more limited because legislators hesitate to promise an explicit vote that could hurt them politically.[19] Single-issue groups are also weakened by the fact that they often deal with highly emotional issues that are difficult to resolve.

Another significant state-level change that parallels a national trend has been the recent expansion of political action committees (PACs). Many interest groups have formed PACs as a means of contributing money to political campaigns. Because many states prohibit unions or business corporations from making direct contributions to political campaigns, labor and business PACs have been formed in order to collect and distribute funds legally. In most cases their contributions go to incumbents and legislative leaders. Political scientist Frank J. Sorauf found that in the mid-1980s in California nearly two-thirds of the campaign receipts of incumbent state legislators came from PACs and business. On the other hand, challengers who had much smaller receipts received only about one-third of their money from such sources.[20]

PACs have become the dominant source of campaign funds in virtually all states as the pressure to spend more money has intensified. In general, groups that spend the most money have the greatest political influence. While some ideological PACs give money only to Democratic or Republican candidates, others tend to ignore party labels and "go with the power." Nearly half the states attempt to regulate PACs, but these regulations have not had much impact on PAC operations or effectiveness. Most states require all interest groups to register and to report specific expenditures. However, there seldom are limits on the total amount of money they can spend. In some states, regulation of PACs is so limited that their contributions are not compiled individually or in the aggregate.

After laws are passed, interest-group activity continues as lobbyists contact administrators, who are usually given considerable discretion in executing the law. Administrators interact very little with the general public, and they have a tendency to identify very closely with the goals of the groups they are supposed to oversee. As noted in Chapter 1, detailed state constitutions invite litigation by opponents charging that a new law violates part of the constitution. This provides yet another tactic for interest groups that hope to negate laws or render their provisions meaningless through narrow judicial interpretation.

Cities and states and organizations such as the National League of Cities, the National Association of Counties, and the National Governors Association have maintained a substantial lobbying presence in Washington since the 1960s. When federal aid to states and cities increased in the 1960s and 1970s, states and localities reaped the benefits of expanded federal programs. As noted in Chapter 2, federal aid has declined in recent years and the focus of government activity has shifted to the states. Yet lobbying efforts have not been redirected.[21] Cities and counties need to maintain a strong lobbying presence in Washington in order to get their fair share of grants and ease the burden of federal mandates, but they would be well advised to devote more resources and personnel to statehouses.

Interest-Group Power

Conventional wisdom among political scientists has suggested a relationship in which interest-group power is greatest in states that have weak political parties, less professionalized legislatures and bureaucracies, and less well-developed socioeconomic conditions. Morehouse argued that states with strong political parties have less access open to lobbyists, and thus interest groups have less influence on public policy.[22] When legislatures are more professional—that is, when they have more staff and work full time (see Chapter 5)—legislators tend to be less reliant on lobbyists for information and group power is limited. In states with well-developed economic systems, this would lead to a proliferation of groups, and no single group or small number of groups could dominate state government. Of the twenty-two states that Morehouse listed with "strong" interest groups, eleven were in the South. On the other hand, the ten states with "weak" interest groups were all Northern and included such urbanized states as Connecticut, Massachusetts, Michigan, New Jersey, New York, and Rhode Island.

A recent, comprehensive study of interest groups by Thomas and Hrebenar found that interest groups were much stronger in Northern states than was previously believed.[23] They defined the power of an interest group as the "ability to achieve its goals as it defines them." While no state today is run by one or two interests, as once was the case in Montana with the Anaconda Company, Thomas and Hrebenar believe that the increase in interest groups (political pluralism) and the fragmentation of the business community have not lessened the overall power of interest groups. The need for more campaign money and the rise of PACs have increased the power of interest groups in virtually all states.

If legislatures have become more professionalized, so too have interest groups become more sophisticated in the use of computers, mass mailings, and other public relations techniques. Even as government has become more professionalized, its expansion, Thomas and Hrebenar believe, has produced new information gaps that are filled by lobbyists.

Rather than classify interest-group systems as "weak" or "strong," Thomas and Hrebenar suggest referring to interest groups within a state as dominant, complementary, or subordinate. Table 3.2 classifies the states according to the impact on policymaking made by interest groups. Interest groups are more powerful than political parties in a majority of states, and it is likely that their power will continue to increase so long as the demand for campaign funds and information continues. As we will see in the concluding section of this chapter, interest-group strength is checked, in large part, by competition among an increasing number of groups.

Regulation of Interest Groups

All states have some regulation of interest groups. In most cases, states have slowly increased the degree of regulation since the mid-1970s, when the Watergate scandal brought a wave of reform in campaign finance laws passed by Congress and state legislatures. Laws generally take the form of (1) registration by lobbyists and disclosure of expenses, (2) campaign finance disclosure, (3) PAC regulations, and (4) conflict-of-interest provisions limiting the activities of state legislators and executive officials.

**Table 3.2   Classification of the Fifty States According
to the Overall Impact of Interest Groups**

| | STATES WHERE THE OVERALL IMPACT OF INTEREST GROUPS IS | | | |
Dominant (9)	Dominant/ Complementary (18)	Complementary (18)	Complementary/ Subordinate (5)	Subordinate (0)
Alabama	Arizona	Colorado	Connecticut	
Alaska	Arkansas	Illinois	Delaware	
Florida	California	Indiana	Minnesota	
Louisiana	Hawaii	Iowa	Rhode Island	
Mississippi	Georgia	Kansas	Vermont	
New Mexico	Idaho	Maine		
South Carolina	Kentucky	Maryland		
Tennessee	Montana	Massachusetts		
West Virginia	Nebraska	Michigan		
	Nevada	Missouri		
	Ohio	New Jersey		
	Oklahoma	New Hampshire		
	Oregon	New York		
	Texas	North Carolina		
	Utah	North Dakota		
	Virginia	Pennsylvania		
	Washington	South Dakota		
	Wyoming	Wisconsin		

SOURCE: Clive S. Thomas and Ronald J. Hrebenar, "Interest Groups in the States," in Virginia Gray, Herbert Jacob, and Robert B. Albritton, eds., *Politics in the American States,* 5th ed. (Glenview, Ill.: Scott, Foresman/Little, Brown, 1990), p. 147. Copyright © 1990 by Virginia Gray, Herbert Jacob, and Robert B. Albritton. Reprinted by permission of HarperCollins Publisher.

How much disclosure is required and how well laws are enforced are the main differences among the states. For example, about 1,000 lobbyists are registered in both California and Montana. Not surprisingly, where interest-group power is greater, there usually is less regulation. Political culture affects regulation in that moralistic states such as Minnesota and Oregon place more restraints on what is acceptable political behavior and regulate lobbying more than do individualistic and traditional states, which have less active government and more tolerance of corrupt behavior. In some moralistic states, such as North Dakota, standards of behavior are so high that they do not need strong laws to control political behavior. As with federal law, the main goal of state lobbying regulations is simply to require disclosure of information so that interest-group activities are open to public view.

Urban Interest Groups

Although the discussion so far has focused on state legislatures, it should be noted that interest groups operate in essentially the same way at the local level. The difference is that the same groups are not equally active in state capitols and city halls. Lobbyists representing real estate groups, downtown merchants, and liquor dealers have been more influential at the city level than at the state level. Farmers, of course, direct their communication to state legislators and governors.

Urban interest groups may be classified as follows:

1. *Occupational interests:* Groups are organized on the basis of common work, trade, or business interests. Often individual occupations are organized in trade associations or professional societies. In most cities there are "peak associations" such as chambers of commerce and central labor councils.
2. *Problem-oriented interests:* Some groups come together to solve a particular social problem. This category includes groups dealing with housing, parks, schools, or welfare problems.
3. *Neighborhood interests:* These groups are most often concerned with local, territorial issues. In the past, they were usually found in upper-class areas where residents wanted to preserve the character of their neighborhood. Since the mid-1960s, community-action groups have been formed in many inner-city neighborhoods to support such causes as day-care and health-care centers.
4. *Good-government interests:* These are reform or improvement groups such as city clubs and the League of Women Voters.

The strength of urban interest groups comes from their willingness to take action, their pooled resources, and their numbers. Business groups often form nonpartisan research organizations to study a local problem. Their emphasis on expertise and their nonpartisan stance give them a high level of respectability. Although the poor find it much more difficult to organize than the affluent, they have been effective in many cities. Their tactics include legal action (instigating class-action suits), constant pressure on city officials to follow their own rules, and the threat of violence. Political organizer Saul Alinsky speaks of making the "enemy" live up to its own set of rules.[24] For example, by mastering the rules for welfare eligibility, neighborhood organizers can influence city officials to alter the way in which they administer the welfare program. Chapter 4 discusses some "extraordinary" forms of political participation, including demonstrations and violence.

The reform movement in American cities has been aided by a variety of so-called good-government groups. These citizens' groups have lobbied for lower taxes and lower city expenditures, and they have supported reform goals such as a council-manager plan, professional civil service, and nonpartisan elections. The League of Women Voters has also worked for these objectives.

Where strong party organizations do not exist, downtown merchants are often the dominant force in city politics. They are concerned about such matters as lower taxes, increased downtown parking, and zoning restrictions. The local chamber of commerce frequently speaks for all business interests. Banks and public utilities also exert pressure on local government. Matters related to business regulation, taxation, zoning, and housing are of utmost importance to each of these business groups. Contractors, who may do business with the city and who are affected by the city's inspection policies, engage in substantial lobbying.

Organized labor often lobbies for public policies that are opposed by the business community. These include subsidized public transportation, public housing, rent control, and higher wages for city employees. On some occasions, however, labor and business present a common front. For example, both support large construction projects that provide jobs and stimulate the local economy and highway construction. In recent years, unions representing city workers have had a major influence on city budgets, and they have utilized strikes to push for their demands. Because of the financial difficulties faced by many large cities, the bargaining position of public employee unions has been weakened. Indeed, the unions have been blamed for creating financial crises as wages grow and pension funds expand.

WHO GOVERNS? ELITISM VERSUS PLURALISM

The above discussion of political parties and interest groups leaves unanswered the crucial question of which groups control the making of public policy. Political scientists and sociologists have studied community power structures in great detail, and their conclusions are nearly as numerous as the individual cities and towns studied. Generally speaking, the researchers fall into one of two categories: the **elitists** (who find that a few top leaders form a power structure that dominates decision making) and the **pluralists** (who object to the idea of a **power structure** and instead view power as a process that is shared by a variety of competing groups).

In the classic elitist studies,[25] community power is believed to be concentrated in the hands of a few old families and business leaders. Community leadership is viewed as a rigid system in which those at the top are a relatively permanent group. There is a one-way flow of power, with the elite dictating policy to subordinates. In many cases, the "power elite" does not exercise control openly but operates by manipulating more visible public officials. Although there are occasional disagreements among the elite membership, their common economic interests unite them on most basic issues. In such a system, public opinion and elections have little effect on policymaking. Elitist studies are usually the work of sociologists.

Pluralist studies,[26] on the other hand, are usually the work of political scientists. Pluralists conclude that power is shared by a variety of groups that are in conflict with one another. The groups are often short-lived—they form around an issue and then disappear. Thus pluralists do not see a power structure existing; rather, they perceive a fluid system of leadership. Persons or groups who dominate decision making in one area are seldom equally effective in other areas. In the pluralist model, public decisions are influenced by public opinion, and elections are an important means of transferring power from one group to another.

As one might expect, elitists and pluralists are critical of each other's methodology. Pluralists charge that elitists begin by assuming the existence of power relations. Elitists often rely on an interview method in which the respondents are asked, "Who has power in Gotham City?" Such a *reputational* approach, suggest the pluralists, often results in confusing groups with high potential for power (i.e., groups that have high status) with groups that actually exercise power. If obvious leaders do not emerge in their studies, elitists can resort to the argument that there are top leaders simply operating behind the scenes. A great many people believe that "they"—bankers, merchants, old families—run cities, so the elitist argument has strong appeal: It is simple, dramatic, and "realistic."

Elitists argue that the pluralist method of focusing on decision making has some major drawbacks. They contend that "key decisions" are not easily selected for analysis, and they suggest that an observer cannot always be sure whose interests have prevailed in those situations selected. Furthermore, elitists note that political influence is not always seen in the public decision-making process. Those with power may be able to exclude an issue from public discussion altogether and thus exercise control through prevention of decision making.[27] The ability to keep issues off local political agendas is, of course, the ultimate power that individuals or groups can exercise. However, it is very difficult to study nonevents. Finally, even pluralists agree that it is difficult to *compare* power in different situations. Thus the exercise of power on a zoning decision may differ greatly from the exercise of power on a decision regarding water fluoridation.

It is crucial to the pluralist model that many people in many small groups participate in public decision making. Yet even the leading pluralist, Robert A. Dahl, concedes that in many cases only a handful of leaders participate in decision making in such areas as urban renewal, party nominations, and public school matters. Although 60 percent of the American people belong to interest groups, it is significant that those most likely to be participants are white, better educated, and middle class. And two of every five Americans are not represented directly by any group. Regarding this last point, public interest groups such as Common Cause are serving the purpose of representing many consumer groups that previously did not have a voice in government decision making.

No definitive answer can be given to the question "Who governs?" Particular mixtures of social, economic, and cultural patterns clearly influence the distribution of power within different cities. In many old towns and cities, elites clearly have dominated public policymaking. There is, however, some evidence to suggest that pluralism is becoming more widespread and probably is the dominant pattern in American cities.

In traditional political cultures, government has functioned to limit power to a small, self-perpetuating elite, which gains the power to govern through family or social ties. As noted in Chapter 1, this culture has been particularly strong in the South, where it was supported by racial segregation and a predominantly nonindustrial economy. While socioeconomic changes have weakened elite structures throughout the nation, this trend has been particularly evident in the Sunbelt states. Increased industrialization results in economic diversity, which typically weakens elites. As social cleavages become deeper—for example, when black Americans push for equal representation in government—elites lose power. In larger cities and rapidly growing cities, the influx of new people creates greater competition for leadership. Finally, higher levels of education and the spread of middle-class values regarding participation in government have the effect of pushing traditional cultures in the direction of moralistic cultures. Perhaps the most likely places for elite structures to continue to exist inside and outside the South will be in white, upper-class suburbs, where political party organizations are ordinarily weak.

The next chapter continues the discussion of political participation in terms of the development of partisan ties by citizens and citizen involvement in campaigns and elections. Participation in citizen-action groups is also examined.

KEY TERMS

"Amateurs" Party members who are issue-oriented and often unwilling to compromise on basic goals.

At-large election Election in which the members of a legislative body are elected by all the members of a community, rather than by subdivisions such as wards.

Cohesive parties Unified political parties whose members agree on basic issues.

Competitive state A state in which the major parties compete on an equal footing.

Conservatives Individuals who generally oppose government regulation, increased government spending, and civil rights legislation. They tend to favor strong crime control policies and lower taxes.

Electioneering Activities of an interest group aimed at securing the election of candidates who are sympathetic to the group.

Elitists Those who believe that a few top leaders form a power structure that dominates government decision making.

Good-government organizations Reform groups, active at the turn of the century, that sought to overthrow political machines, institute efficient government, and eliminate partisan politics.

Ideological Pertaining to attitudes and actions on social, political, and economic issues.

Liberals Individuals who support government regulation, increased government spending, and civil rights legislation.

Lobbyists Individuals employed by organized *interest groups* who seek to bring about the passage or defeat of legislative bills or to influence their content.

Majority party state A state in which the majority party usually wins about three-fourths of the legislative seats.

New Deal The liberal economics program advanced by Franklin D. Roosevelt in the 1930s.

Nonpartisan elections Campaigns in which the candidates do not use party labels. Typically found in small-town elections and the election of judges and school board members. This was one of the goals of good-government groups.

One-party dominant state A state in which the majority party consistently wins nearly all the legislative seats and nearly always elects the governor.

Party in government Those persons holding office in the legislative and executive branches who are organized along party lines and often announce policies in the name of the party.

Party in the electorate Those members of the general population who identify themselves as members of political parties.

Party in the organization That part of political parties which includes state and local party committees and their leaders.

Patronage The ability to make political appointments or grant special favors on the basis of party loyalty.

Pluralists Those who believe that political power is shared by a large number of competing groups, rather than concentrated in an elite.

Power structure An "establishment" composed of the elite members (those with wealth, family status, or political power) who dominate a community.

Precincts Polling districts, containing 200 to 1,000 persons, into which cities and counties are divided. Political parties organize within these precincts and select leaders to register voters, manage party business, and get out the vote on election days. Several precincts constitute a *ward,* which is another unit for elections and party activity.

"Private-regarding" interests The narrow economic interests of groups and individuals; contrasted with the *public interest.*

"Professionals" Traditional party members, who use patronage and compromise to accomplish their main political goal—winning elections.

Progressive movement An early twentieth-century reform movement whose program called for government ownership of railroads, farm-relief measures, the right to collective bargaining, and various devices for direct democracy.

Urban political machine A party organization that has remained in power over a long period of time in a large city. It is headed by a boss or small group of leaders. Often synonymous with corruption.

REFERENCES

1. Malcolm E. Jewell and David M. Olson, *American State Political Parties and Elections,* 3d ed. (Chicago: Dorsey Press, 1988), p. 11.
2. Paul Allen Beck and Frank Sorauf, *Party Politics in America,* 6th ed. (Glenview, Ill.: Scott, Foresman, 1988), p. 79.
3. William Crotty, *Party Reform* (New York: Longman, 1983), p. 45.
4. *The Transformation in American Politics: Implications for Federalism* (Washington: Advisory Commission on Intergovernmental Relations, 1986), p. 110.
5. See James Gibson, Cornelius Cotter, John Bibby, and Robert Huckshorn, "Assessing Party Organizational Strength," *American Journal of Political Science,* May 1983, pp. 194–205.
6. *The Transformation in American Politics,* p. 127.
7. Bernard H. Ross, Myron A. Levine, and Murray S. Stedman, *Urban Politics: Power in Metropolitan America,* 4th ed. (Itasca, Ill.: F. E. Peacock, 1991), pp. 128–130.
8. Fred I. Greenstein, *The American Party System and the American People,* 2d ed. (Englewood Cliffs, N.J.: Prenctice-Hall, 1970).
9. Milton Rakove, *Don't Make No Waves . . . Don't Back No Losers: An Insider's Analysis of the Daley Machine* (Bloomington, Ind.: Indiana University Press, 1975),

p. 112. Other colorful studies of Mayor Daley include Mike Royko, *Boss: Richard J. Daley of Chicago* (New York: Signet, 1971); Milton Rakove, *We Don't Want Nobody Sent: An Oral History of the Daley Years* (Bloomington: Indiana University Press, 1979); and Eugene Kennedy, *Himself: The Life and Times of Richard J. Daley* (New York: Viking, 1978).

10. Jewell and Olson, *American State Political Parties,* p. 29.
11. Euel Elliott, Gerald S. Gryski, and Bruce Reed, "Minor Party Support in State Legislative Elections," *State and Local Government Review,* Fall 1990, pp. 123–125.
12. Thomas R. Dye, *Politics in States and Communities,* 7th ed. (Englewood Cliffs, N.J.: Prentice-Hall, 1991), p. 135.
13. John H. Fenton, *People and Parties in Politics* (Glenview, Ill.: Scott, Foresman, 1966), p. 49.
14. V. O. Key, Jr., *Southern Politics* (New York: Knopf, 1949), p. 308.
15. Duane Lockard, *The Politics of State and Local Government,* 2d ed. (New York: Macmillan, 1969), p. 179.
16. Sara McCally Morehouse, *State Politics, Parties and Policy* (New York: Holt, Rinehart and Winston, 1981), p. 88.
17. Clive S. Thomas and Ronald J. Hrebenar, "Interest Groups in the States," in Virginia Gray, Herbert Jacob, and Robert B. Albritton, eds., *Politics in the American States,* 5th ed. (Glenview, Ill.: Scott, Foresman/Little, Brown, 1990), p. 127.
18. *Ibid.,* pp. 149–151.
19. L. Harmon Zeigler, "Interest Groups in the States," in Virginia Gray, Herbert Jacob, and Kenneth N. Vines, eds., *Politics in the American States,* 4th ed. (Boston: Little, Brown, 1983), pp. 118–119.
20. Frank J. Sorauf, *Money in American Politics* (Glenview, Ill.: Scott, Foresman/Little, Brown, 1988), p. 267.
21. Jonathan Walters, "Lobbying for the Good Old Days," *Governing the States and Localities,* June 1991, pp. 33–37.
22. See Morehouse, *State Politics,* and Zeigler, "Interest Groups in the States," pp. 97–131.
23. Thomas and Hrebenar, "Interest Groups in the States," pp. 123–158.
24. Saul Alinsky, *Rules for Radicals* (New York: Random House, 1972), pp. 128, 138.
25. Robert Lynd and Helen Lynd, *Middletown* (New York: Harcourt, Brace, and World, 1929); Robert Lynd and Helen Lynd, *Middletown in Transition* (New York: Harcourt, Brace, and World, 1937); Floyd Hunter, *Community Power Structure* (Chapel Hill: University of North Carolina Press, 1953); and W. Lloyd Warner et al., *Democracy in Jonesville* (New York: Harper & Row, 1949).
26. Robert A. Dahl, *Who Governs?* (New Haven: Yale University Press, 1964); Aaron Wildavsky, *Leadership in a Small Town* (Totowa, N.J.: Bedminister Press, 1964); Frank J. Munger, *Decisions in Syracuse* (Bloomington: Indiana University Press, 1961); Robert Agger, Daniel Goldrich, and Bert Swanson, *The Rulers and the Ruled* (New York: Wiley, 1964); and Robert Presthus, *Men at the Top* (New York: Oxford University Press, 1964).
27. Peter Bachrach and Morton S. Baratz, *Power and Poverty: Theory and Practice* (New York: Oxford University Press, 1970).

CHAPTER 4

POLITICAL
PARTICIPATION
AND ELECTIONS

KINDS OF POLITICAL PARTICIPATION

In discussing political parties and interest groups, the generally low level of involvement of the American people in political activities has been noted. When participation is defined as "those activities aimed at influencing government in some way," only a small minority of Americans (less than one-third) undertake any endeavor other than voting (see Table 4.1). For most people, *voting* is their only form of participation. Yet voter turnout in state and local elections is often less than 40 percent, and turnouts for primary elections are frequently less than 30 percent. As a general rule, turnout for state elections and for off-year (nonpresidential) congressional elections is about 15 to 20 percent below turnout rates in presidential elections.

In their classic study of American political behavior, Verba and Nie found that 22 percent of Americans were **inactives,** who took "almost no part in political life."[1] Members of this group voted occasionally or not at all and seldom engaged in any other kind of political activity. Persons of lower socioeconomic status were predominant in this group. Another 21 percent were **voting specialists,** people who voted regularly but engaged in little other political activity. About 20 percent were identified as **communalists.** These people were active in neighborhood projects, but seldom were involved in political campaign work. **Campaigners** made up 15 percent of the total. In contrast to communalists, these people were active in campaigns but were not involved in neighborhood issues. A small group (4 percent) was comprised of **parochial participants,** average voters who made contact with government officials, but only about issues that directly affected their lives. Finally, 11 percent were identified as **complete activists,** who frequently engaged in a variety of political activities.

Levels of voting turnout, interest-group participation, and political party activity are all closely related to socioeconomic status. Clearly there is an upper-class bias, with those people who are better educated and hold higher-status jobs more likely to be politically active. Because they feel closed out of mainline political parties and interest groups, lower-status people may be involved in extralegal protest demonstrations and riots. This has been true for minority groups in several cities

Table 4.1   Political Participation in the United States

Type of Participation	Percentage of American Adults
Have interest in political campaigns*	73
Vote for president (1988)	50
Vote for Congress (1990)	33
Attempt to persuade others how to vote*	28
Have ever contacted a local government official about an issue or problem*	20
Have ever given money to a party or candidate*	13
Presently a member of a political club or organization*	8

* Self-reported percentages. These generally overstate the degree of participation.

and for some Native Americans on reservations. However, higher-status people are just as likely to get involved in demonstrations. In most cases antiwar, proenvironment, and abortion (both pro-and antichoice) demonstrators have been predominantly white, middle-and upper-class people.

Clearly, there is a concentration of political participation in the hands of a few people. An examination of Table 4.1 shows an interrelated cumulative structure of participation: People who are members of a political club have almost certainly given money to a candidate in an election; in turn, financial contributors have often attended political meetings, and virtually all of those people will vote in primary and general elections.

Voter Turnout

The most prevalent form of political participation is voting. Yet, as has been noted, less than half the American people vote in state and local elections. Even in federal elections turnout is low—only about 50 percent of those eligible voted in the 1988 presidential election, and in 1990 the turnout for congressional elections (33 percent) was the lowest since 1942. Voter turnout in nonpresidential elections in the 1980s ranged from under 40 percent in ten Southern states to about 60 percent in Montana, North Dakota, South Dakota, and Minnesota (see Table 3.1, p. 70). In general, turnout is highest in the West and lowest in the South, with Midwestern and Northeastern states in the middle. In states that elect governors in presidential and nonpresidential years, the turnout is about 15 percent higher in presidential years. Voter turnout in contested gubernatorial primaries is about 30 percent. Primary turnout is highest in the West and the South. Because of the dominance of the Democratic party in the South, primary turnout has averaged about 130 percent of the party turnout for the general election.[2]

Voter turnout is lowest in local (city and county) elections—often under 30 percent. A variety of factors are responsible, including the lack of media attention paid to these elections, the absence of opponents to challenge incumbents in many races, and the overwhelming number of positions to be filled by election. In most cases there is little excitement, because local officials deal largely with such noncontroversial issues as road repair and other basic services. In most small towns, officials avoid controversy and support the status quo. Campaigns are low-key events and center on name identification. Rates of participation are down even in fabled New England town meetings.

There are a variety of reasons for the different rates of voter turnout. People higher on the socioeconomic ladder are more likely to vote because they are more familiar with political issues and realize that election results will make a difference in their lives. Moreover, they tend to have an ingrained sense of their obligation to vote. Among people at lower socioeconomic levels, however, voting may be threatening to their self-esteem because they frequently know little about politics. They differ from the middle class in that they usually do not possess a sense of **political efficacy**—that is, they do not believe that their vote will make any difference or that they can affect public policymaking.

There has been a steady decline in voter turnout since the early 1960s, when

62.8 percent voted in the 1960 presidential election and 46.3 percent voted in the 1962 gubernatorial elections. One reason has been the addition of eighteen- to twenty-one-year-olds to the electorate. Only about 40 percent of those in the eighteen- to twenty-four-year-old age bracket have voted in the last three presidential elections. But many political scientists believe that the major reasons for the recent decline in voter turnout are (1) the increased belief that government is not responsive to people and their needs and (2) a decline in the percentage of people who identify with one of the two major parties.[3] When people do not see much difference between the Democratic and Republican parties, nonparticipation results. Thus the decline in allegiance to political parties has helped lower turnout.

In the past, those least likely to vote have been Southern, black, and female. For example, in 1952 more than 80 percent of Southern black women and nearly 70 percent of Southern black men had never voted.[4] By 1980 these percentages had dropped to less than 25. Obviously, legal restrictions held down the black vote in the South, and the traditional culture of the South discouraged political participation by women. Southern voter turnout continues to be lower than turnout in the rest of the country because of lower educational levels in the South, and the continued dominance of the Democratic party in Southern state and local elections means that candidates in general elections there often run unopposed. In the North, blacks and women now have turnout records equal to that of white men.

Registration procedures in many states have been the single greatest impediment to higher voter participation. Most states require registration from ten to thirty days before elections. Only Maine, Minnesota, and Wisconsin permit registration on an election day. Half the states allow mail registration, and some states offer "motor-voter registration," in which people applying for a driver's license (or license renewal) can register to vote as well. Most states automatically cancel registration for failure to vote in a four-year period, although a few cancel registration for those who do not vote in one general election. Highly mobile people are affected by registration cutoff dates and the hassle of reregistration. Others find it inconvenient to go to registration centers, or they are dropped from the rolls for not voting.

There is no question that registration requirements reduce voter turnout. Still, it is curious to note that even in North Dakota, which has no personal registration, voter turnout declined by about 20 percent from 1960 to 1988. Thus the problem of turnout is more complex than just changing the electoral machinery. In a study published in 1990, the Library of Congress could not come to any conclusion about the impact of motor-voter and mail registration on voter turnout.[5] Congress is considering a bill that would require all states to register voters by mail, offer motor-voter registration, and report registration practices and results to Congress.

Curiously, as campaign spending has increased in recent years, voter turnout has declined. One explanation is that candidates increasingly are spending money to hire private political consultants to manage their campaigns. In turn, many consultants have developed campaigns that focus on personality, not issues, and that include negative attacks on opponents. When campaigns are nasty and relevant issues are not discussed, it is not surprising that turnout is low.

During the past thirty years, voter turnout in the South has been dramatically influenced by actions of Congress and the federal courts. Most significantly, the

Voting Rights Act of 1965 has added nearly 1 million blacks to the voter lists of the six Deep South states. In the period from 1964 to 1968, the percentage of voting-age blacks registered to vote increased from 6.7 to 59.4 in Mississippi; from 19.2 to 57.6 in Alabama; and from 57.7 to 83.1 in Texas.

The Voting Rights Act of 1965 applied to counties or states where a literacy test was used as of November 1, 1964, and where fewer than 50 percent of the eligible voters either were registered or cast ballots in the 1964 presidential election. In those areas (Alabama, Alaska, Georgia, Louisiana, Mississippi, South Carolina, and Virginia, plus thirty-four counties in North Carolina), the U.S. attorney general was empowered to abolish literacy tests and replace local registrars with federal agents who would register voters under federal procedures. The act also bars states from changing their election systems unless they have received approval from the U.S. attorney general or the U.S. District Court for the District of Columbia. This means that reapportionment of legislative bodies or a change from single-member districts to at-large elections must be cleared with the U.S. attorney general or the U.S. District Court for the District of Columbia. The Voting Rights Act effectively ended literacy tests. (Before 1965, twenty states, mostly in the South, had such tests.) Because of voluntary compliance in registering voters, federal registrars were sent to only a few counties. In 1966 the Supreme Court upheld the constitutionality of the Voting Rights Act.

When the Voting Rights Act came up for renewal in 1982, President Reagan proposed to change it so that those suing under it would have to prove that the defendant had *intended* to discriminate. Civil rights groups protested that intent would be difficult to prove and that, in any case, discrimination that is not deliberate still adversely affects blacks. The president did not press the issue, and the act was extended for a further twenty years. As amended in 1982 the Voting Rights Act "forbids *any* government to use any procedures related to voting, regardless of intent, that result in the denial of the vote to any person because of race or color or the *dilution* of the voting power of members of a protected class."

The Twenty-fourth Amendment, approved in 1964, ended **poll taxes** in federal elections. Until that time Alabama, Mississippi, Texas, Vermont, and Virginia still required payment of a poll tax in order to vote. The 1965 Voting Rights Act invalidated poll taxes in all elections. In 1966, the Supreme Court ruled that the Virginia poll tax denied individuals equal protection of the law as guaranteed in the Fourteenth Amendment. This decision (*Harper* v. *Virginia State Board of Elections*) upheld the 1965 act and also made the Twenty-fourth Amendment superfluous.

As noted in Chapter 1, *political culture* affects voter turnout. States with a moralistic culture consistently lead the nation in rates of turnout. In these states individuals have the strongest belief that they can accomplish something positive through the political process. Traditional states have the lowest turnout, and individualistic states fall in the middle.[6] In traditional states, the political culture holds that political participation should remain in the hands of a social elite. These states have made voter registration difficult, and turnout is low even among whites. It is interesting to note that while turnout is high in moralistic states, individuals in those states are no more likely to take an active role in political organizations or campaigning than are people in other states.

Party Activists[7]

Although the percentage of people who are members of political organizations is very low (less than 10 percent), hundreds of thousands of people around the country work actively for political parties. Since parties only rarely pay a salary even to county officials, the incentive to devote time and energy to political organizations must come in other forms of rewards.

As discussed in Chapter 3, the classic form of reward for the urban political machine was *patronage*. The Daley machine in Chicago, for example, controlled over 30,000 patronage jobs as rewards to the party faithful. Most patronage jobs are unappealing to the well educated, however, and parties must look to other inducements to attract substantial numbers of middle-class people. For some, an elective office may be the reward for party service. In many cases, the organization controls nominations and primaries and thus can "give" public office to the candidate willing to accept control by the party once he or she is elected. For business, the party may be able to provide rewards in the form of public contracts or freedom from the close application of regulatory or inspection policies. Parties that are issue-oriented may attract workers simply because those people agree with certain ideological positions taken by the party. Frequently this kind of support is more strongly directed to a candidate (e.g., Eugene McCarthy, George McGovern, Ronald Reagan, or George Wallace) than to the party as an organization.

Other Forms of Political Participation

In many instances, groups find the established means of participation—political parties or interest groups—closed to them. At the local level, citizen-advocacy groups are often formed to combat a specific problem to which public officials have been unresponsive. Individuals concerned with problems such as air pollution, lack of adequate police protection, or safety crossings for school children have formed ad hoc groups that attempt to gain publicity and force public officials to respond to their demands. Their tactics have also included demonstrations, rent strikes, and sit-ins.

In recent years, a variety of groups that have been frustrated by "the system" have attempted to alter the status quo. The pattern followed by black Americans is typical of methods historically used by politically disadvantaged groups in America. Finding state and local authorities unresponsive, blacks turned to the federal government for redress of grievances. Because of the control exercised by Southern whites in both the House and the Senate, they initiated action in federal courts rather than in Congress. Eventually, blacks became involved in more direct forms of political protest, including sit-ins, marches, boycotts, and riots. College students also have turned to extraordinary political action when faced with a lack of responsiveness from both government and school officials. In recent years the most emotional political confrontations have been between antiabortion and free-choice activists. Antiabortion forces have tried to block entrances to abortion clinics and, in a few instances, they have bombed clinics.

Beginning in New York in 1964, riots spread to many American cities by the late 1960s. The worst violence occurred in Detroit in 1967, when forty-three people were killed during seven days of rioting. In every city in which riots occurred, the needs of low-income, poorly educated groups were not being met. Protesters typically demanded better housing, greater police protection, jobs, and better municipal services, such as sanitation and street lighting. Curiously, in most riot cities, formal means existed for citizens to present their grievances to public officials. These formal organizations were not used because officials were distrusted and there was a feeling of frustration based on a history of unresponsiveness by public agencies.

Following a period of relative calm in the 1970s, violence broke out in Miami in 1980. Fourteen people were beaten or shot to death and 3,800 National Guardsmen patrolled a forty-by-sixty-block area of the city. In New York (1964), Los Angeles (1965), Cleveland (1966), Newark (1967), and Detroit (1967), relatively minor, isolated instances of police action against blacks ignited rioting. Rioting in Miami broke out in 1989 for the fourth time in the decade when a police officer shot a black motorcyclist. Also in 1989 a 16-year-old black youth was killed in the Bensonhurst area of Brooklyn. In 1991 black activist Al Sharpton was attacked in Bensonhurst, and violent confrontations broke out between blacks and Jews in the Crown Heights section of Brooklyn. Rioting in Los Angeles in 1992 after a jury found four police officers not quilty of beating Rodney King resulted in the deaths of forty-one people and $550 million in property damage. Over 4,500 fires were set in Los Angeles County. The Los Angeles police department was strongly criticized for its slow response to the racial explosion. Other major rioting followed in San Francisco, Atlanta, and Seattle.

In response to the actions of protesters, many cities have established a variety of new means for residents to express their political feelings and have revitalized older channels of communication. Information and complaint centers have been set up in city halls, and officials have been instructed to follow up on all complaints. Several cities have initiated public information programs to make residents aware of the existence of such centers and how they can be used.

Other cities have created neighborhood service centers where inner-city residents can walk in for advice on immediate problems and referrals to appropriate agencies. Some of these centers have been funded by federal grants; others receive aid from private foundations. **Community-action programs,** funded by the federal government, have encouraged maximum participation by local residents in the planning and implementation of urban-development programs in such areas as housing, education, and employment. These programs are directed by boards with some members elected by local residents. Board members are to communicate with public officials and to reflect the views of their local constituents.

THE NOMINATION PROCESS

The nomination process is crucial to political parties because candidates' images and stands on policy issues will be identified as those of their party. During the nomination process, factions within the party vie for the power to control the party organization and to manage future nominations. If the party fails to nominate candidates who will be successful in the general election, it will be unable to organize and control the legislative and executive branches of government. This, in turn, will greatly affect the party's ability to shape public policy.

Until the beginning of the twentieth century, parties as organizations managed the nomination of candidates free from outside control. In the early days of the American republic, this was accomplished by party caucuses in legislative bodies. By the mid-nineteenth century, nominations were made by party conventions. Since 1902, state governments have increasingly regulated and administered elections, and citizen participation in the nomination process has been expanded significantly by the use of the direct primary. As a result, political parties have much less control of nominations than they once had. Until the 1970s, conventions were the only method for nominating governors in New York, Indiana, and Delaware. Now, only in those few states where parties are very strong are nominees even slated by local leaders and committees.

Although laws vary among the fifty states and no two systems are exactly alike, some basic pattern of laws regarding nominations and elections can be identified. As discussed in Chapter 3, the states control voting choices by establishing regulations concerning the conditions under which a political organization is entitled to have its candidates' names appear on election ballots. All states have established some form of primary elections as a means for nominating candidates, and state law defines the basis for voter eligibility in those elections. In primary elections, state regulations provide access to the ballot for those who obtain a certain number of signatures on a petition or pay a modest fee. All states regulate party finance by such means as establishing procedures for reporting publicly on income and expenses and by setting regulations on who may contribute to party funds as well as how much money may be spent in particular campaigns.

Although party conventions continue to be used in some states to nominate candidates for public office, since 1903 all states have followed the lead of Wisconsin and instituted some form of **direct primary.** By 1917 most states had adopted the primary. In primaries, nominations are made directly by the voters, rather than indirectly by those selected to attend party conventions. They are administered by state officials, rather than by party leaders.

There are four basic types of primaries:

1. **Closed primaries** are used in twenty-seven states. Voters declare their party preferences when they first vote in a primary, and they are then bound to vote only in that party's primary unless they publicly change their affiliation within a given period prior to an election. Ten states that have closed primaries allow considerable flexibility in changing parties. For example, in Iowa a record is kept of voter registration but voters can switch registration on the day of the election.
2. **Open primaries** are used in twenty states. Voters do not declare a party affiliation and in each primary may choose either a Republican or Democratic ballot. This, of course, allows "crossover" voting in which members of one party vote in the other party's primary. While some states require the voter to express a preference for the ballot of one party at the polls, in others the mechanics of the voting process keep party preference completely secret.
3. **Blanket primaries** are used in Alaska and Washington. These differ from open primaries in that the voter may vote for candidates from both parties, crossing back

and forth as he or she wishes while moving through the lists of candidates for various offices. The only restriction is that the voter can indicate only one preference for each office.

4. The **nonpartisan primary** has been used in Louisiana since 1975. All candidates, regardless of party affiliation, are required to appear on the same ballot. Candidates may, and usually do, list their party affiliation. If needed, there is a runoff between the top two candidates, and this serves as a general election. Louisiana's nonpartisan primary seems to have helped the Republican party more than Democrats, since the first Republican governor was elected under the system.

Most of the states that have open primaries are in the Midwest and West, the regions where the Progressive movement was strongest. There appears to be a trend toward adopting open primaries or at least changing closed primaries to permit voters to shift registration more easily. As a result, the distinction between the two systems is becoming less clear. A few states allow independents to vote in either party primary. In 1986 the U.S. Supreme Court upheld the proposal of the Connecticut Republican party to permit independents to vote in the Republican closed primary. Although this decision seems to raise questions about the ability of states to mandate closed primaries, the impact is likely to be minimal because the decision applies only to situations in which a political party chooses to permit independents to vote in its primary.

In New York, Delaware, and Connecticut, a **challenge primary** is used, which combines the party convention with the primary. Each party holds a convention and nominates candidates for office. If no one challenges the party nominees, their names go directly on the ballot and a primary is not held. If anyone does challenge the party nominee, that person must have sought the nomination in the party convention and received at least 20 percent of the convention votes in Connecticut, 25 percent in New York, and 35 percent in Delaware. It is obvious that such a system is intended to protect the ability of the party to nominate candidates. Colorado and Utah use a preprimary convention system in which the party convention endorses candidates. In Colorado the winner is listed first on the ballot and others receiving at least 20 percent of the convention vote are also on the primary ballot. Utah designates two candidates for each office. If candidates receive 70 percent or more of the convention vote, they are automatically declared the primary winner.

The spread of the direct primary has weakened party organizations. This, of course, is just what its founders, the Progressives, had intended. Primaries open the political process by removing the monopoly of power once held by party leaders to hand-pick candidates and to direct their behavior once they are elected to office. Primaries open the way for the nomination of well-financed candidates who are opposed by the party leadership. This lessens the ability of the party to reward its faithful members with nominations. It may lead to the election of an individual who is opposed to some or virtually all of the party's major programs. Having run against the party in the primary, the successful outsider may not feel any obligation to support the party once in office. It is also possible that a handful of primary voters will nominate a candidate who has little chance of gaining the broad support needed to win the general election. In any event, there is concern among those who value the contributions of parties to American political history that primaries will divide the party, add to the overall cost of campaigns, and lessen the party's chances of presenting a strong, united front in the general election.

Despite the widespread use of primaries, political parties in most states have managed to retain a considerable degree of control over the nominating process. Very often state parties continue to endorse candidates at a series of local conventions. In many cases, particularly when an incumbent is running, there is a complete lack of competition in primaries. Competition is greatest in Southern one-party states where the Democratic party's chances of winning the general election are virtually 100 percent. Because so many of the elections are uncontested, parties are often assured that the candidates they have recruited will win. The parties themselves may contribute to the lack of competition by arbitrating among prospective candidates and promising patronage jobs or future endorsements to those who choose not to enter the primary. If there is a primary contest, the party will support its endorsed candidates with money, workers, and campaign strategy, making it very difficult for outsiders to win.

Because of the importance of primary elections in Southern states and the factionalization of the Democratic party, there often are several Democratic candidates, and it is likely that the winner will receive less than a majority of the total votes. To cope with this problem, nine Southern and border states plus Arizona have **runoff primaries** if the winner in the regular primary gets less than 50 percent of the vote. In Iowa and South Dakota, if no candidate gets a majority of the primary vote, a party convention meets and picks the party's candidate. Some civil rights organizations claim that runoff primaries help white candidates, because white voters will vote for a white candidate in cases where a black has won the regular primary. Although runoff primaries are constitutional, the U.S. Supreme Court has ruled in some instances that they violate the Constitution and the Voting Rights Act.

Parties are also helped by the low level of voter turnout in primary elections. Outside the South, turnouts have averaged less than 30 percent in primary elections. Particularly in urban areas, well-organized parties can mobilize voters and manage the outcome of primary elections by controlling as little as 15 percent of the total eligible electorate. In part, turnout is low in primaries because media coverage of state and local races is often minimal or nonexistent and voters are not motivated by party loyalty to go to the polls.

Turnout has been somewhat higher in open primary states than in closed primary states. Turnout is particularly high in those states that have a blanket primary. Primary voting is higher among college graduates, professional persons, and those over age thirty. A low and unrepresentative turnout of primary voters may lead to the selection of candidates who stand little chance of winning the general election.

Political reformers' hopes of democratizing the nominating process by the use of the direct primary have suffered because of the lack of competition and low voter turnout. Outside the South, primaries have had only a minimal effect on increasing participation in the selection of political candidates. Nevertheless, primaries have had the effects of weakening party organization and further decentralizing political power. When candidates appeal to local primary voters, this situation lessens the ability of state or national party organizations to control or discipline their representatives in government.[8]

RUNNING FOR THE LEGISLATURE

Every two years, about 14,000 people run for state legislative seats. Most have had a long-term interest in politics, and many come from politically active families. (More will be said in Chapter 5 about the kinds of people elected.)

The conditions of individual campaigns differ greatly depending on the nature of the district. District size varies from about 750,000 people in California senate districts and 375,000 in California house districts to 15,000 in Wyoming senate districts and 2,800 in New Hampshire house districts. Urban house districts may be very small geographically, while many rural senate districts are very large. Strategy will also vary depending on the relative strength of political parties and the presence of an incumbent. As in congressional races, most legislative races are not very competitive. That is, the majority party can count on winning by a margin of over 55 percent. Campaigning in single-member districts differs from that in **multimember districts** (those in which more than one person is elected). In twenty states some or all house members are elected in multimember districts, and multimember districts are used for senate elections in twelve states. Although the number of multimember districts has declined since 1970, about 25 percent of all house members are elected in multimember districts.[9] The U.S. Supreme Court has held in several states that multimember districts discriminate against black or Hispanic voters. Elections in multimember districts take two forms: In some, voters cast separate votes for each seat to be filled in a geographical area; in others, voters may cast as many votes as there are seats to be filled and the top two or three vote-getters win seats.

Candidates may consciously weigh their "opportunity costs."[10] The risks, including some sacrifice of their private careers and of time spent with their families, are balanced against increases in social esteem and political influence. Of course, the opportunity costs include the chances of winning, the presence of an incumbent, and the financial cost of running a campaign.

Because political parties are usually weak, most legislative candidates are on their own to develop a personal following that will volunteer for campaign work. In most cases, interest-group endorsements are of little significance.

In states where political parties are strong, party leaders often play a major role in recruiting candidates to run for the legislature. In several states legislative leaders, often the House Speaker, may control as much as $2 or 3 million that they can allot to their party's candidates.

The level of professionalism (and, in turn, the amount of money spent) varies greatly in legislative campaigns across the country. In California, races are often professionally managed, with widespread use of television and mass mailings. In other states, races are very informal, with the focus on face-to-face contact. In the early 1980s, average campaign spending per seat ranged from over $380,000 in California to about $10,000 per seat in Missouri.[11] Challengers need to spend more money than incumbents to activate voters and gain political visibility, but they find it more difficult to raise funds than do incumbents. For example, in 1986 state senate incumbents in California outspent challengers by a ratio of 58 to 1. California voters responded in 1988 by approving Proposition 73, which established limits on campaign contributions but rejected public financing.

Samuel C. Patterson notes that there is a significant difference in the skills needed to *run for* the legislature and those needed to *govern* once elected.[12] Campaigning emphasizes personal characteristics such as ambition, drive, and attention to local needs. Governing, in contrast, puts a premium on skills in collective action, including bargaining, negotiation, and compromise. Because of these differences, some legislators may find they are not well equipped to govern the states. As a result, Patterson suggests that they may withdraw from legislative work and concentrate on the needs of their districts, or they may be reluctant to do either district or lawmaking work. A few members, of course, do not find any incompatibility in their roles as campaigners and lawmakers, and can function actively on both fronts.

RUNNING FOR GOVERNOR

Gubernatorial campaigns have increasingly come to resemble presidential and U.S. Senate campaigns, with their use of more sophisticated technology and escalating costs. Candidates can no longer sit back and let party organizations deliver the votes. Larry Sabato discusses the new technology as including the following elements.[13] Computerized lists permit candidates to pinpoint mass mailings to particular groups across the state. Banks of several hundred telephones permit direct contact with thousands of potential voters. Media advertising ("image making") has become the largest subindustry in campaigns. In second place is polling, in which several dozen national firms vie to represent candidates. Sabato speaks of technology being used to create an instant political organization, which serves as a party substitute: "Targeted blocks of households are randomly called until a willing 'block captain' volunteer is identified who will organize the neighborhood. Various motivational devices, including repeated mailings and candidate communications, are used to keep the block captains committed for the duration of the campaign."

In addition to raising ethical questions about image making, the new technology has weakened political parties. Paid consultants have replaced party leaders, and polls may reflect voter sentiment better than precinct captains are able to do. In some states, parties are fighting back by developing their own technology and using it to assist candidates.

As one would expect, gubernatorial campaign spending has skyrocketed in recent years. New technology campaigns require big outlays for consultants, opinion polls, direct-mail operations, and rapid travel across the state. The largest reported expenditures in gubernatorial elections were about $50 million in Texas and $53 million in California in 1990, where there were open-seat elections.[14] We would expect large expenditures in New York, Texas, and California, but there were also expenditures of significant size (over $10 million) during the 1980s in gubernatorial elections in West Virginia, Kentucky, and Louisiana. In 1990 races in which incumbents were reelected in New York and Pennsylvania, total expenses in both states were under $9 million. Malcolm Jewell notes, "In races among well-known, strong candidates, money is seldom decisive."[15] Yet many races do not match equally strong candidates, and those with the most money (often incumbents) usually win. In 1990, however, successful women candidates were outspent by male opponents in Texas, Kansas, and Oregon. Joan Finney, the Kansas winner, spent only $300,000 compared with the $2 million spent by her opponent. In a 1990 race between two men in Florida, the winning Democrat was outspent 2 to 1.

RUNNING FOR MAYOR

Because of the great diversity of cities, it is impossible to generalize about mayoral campaigns. For example, running for mayor of Chicago differs greatly from running for mayor of San Francisco. Small-town campaigns in one-party areas or with nonpartisan elections obviously are very different from highly partisan elections in large or medium-size cities. This section will focus on new techniques used by mayoral candidates in cities of more than 100,000 population.

Mayoral candidates in large cities are using many of the same techniques— polling, television advertisements, direct mail—as gubernatorial candidates to build their images. As a result, campaign costs have skyrocketed. The use of new techniques and the employment of political consultants to manage campaigns are especially prevalent in the South and West, where local party organizations are weak.[16] Even in large Northern cities, old-time bosses have lost power because candidates can use television effectively to go directly to the voters. For example, Republican George Voinovich spent nearly $1 million in his first successful campaign in 1979 to win election in Cleveland, where most voters are Democrats.

As in statewide campaigns, political action committees have begun to contribute to mayoral campaigns. Typically mayoral candidates have received the bulk of their funds from businesses, real estate developers, and labor unions. Real estate investors and developers continue to be a major source of funding in fast-growing Sunbelt cities. Labor unions typically support Democratic candidates. Increasingly the American Federation of State, County, and Municipal Employees of the AFL-CIO has been a major force in city elections through endorsements and financial contributions.

Because nearly 70 percent of cities have nonpartisan elections, the personality of the candidates will be even more important than in gubernatorial elections. In addition, many cities with nonpartisan elections also have city managers and few, if any, patronage jobs. This means that mayoral candidates must rely on volunteer workers who cannot be promised jobs or other special favors if their candidate is elected.

RUNNING FOR JUDGE

As we will see in Chapter 7, judges in many states are selected by merit appointment systems or they are appointed directly by the governor or legislature. Where there are elections, they are often nonpartisan or incumbents resign before their terms expire to allow an appointment to be made by the governor. Even in partisan elections there is seldom strong competition. In some states, as many as nine of ten judges who seek reelection run unopposed. Local bar associations discourage challenging incumbent judges for purely partisan or personal reasons. When there is opposition, few sitting judges are defeated. Henry R. Glick paints this picture of judicial elections.[17]

> About the most that judicial candidates promise is to improve the efficiency of the courts, to be fair and just, to avoid personal conflicts of interest, etc. Moreover, the candidates usually look alike: typically white, middle-aged men who dress in conservative business suits with respectable and publicized careers in law, business, or government. To most voters, they are not exciting and are hard to distinguish. Only 10 or 15 percent of the electorate bother to vote. Given the general lack of information and interest in the election, incumbent judges have an enormous advantage. They are the candidates with the prestigious title in front of their names, and the voters are more likely to remember or recognize them. Since the voters have heard so little about the judges before the campaign started, they are likely to assume that they must be doing a good job on the bench.

Of course, there are occasions when incumbents are opposed and defeated in elections. Alleged incompetence or immoral behavior that generates some negative publicity in the local press may lead to defeat. In some states, such as Michigan, there is a tradition of hard-fought partisan battles. Increasingly, it seems that judicial elections are marked by mud slinging, gimmicks, and outright scandal.[18] As a result, there are renewed calls for merit selection of judges. (The Missouri Plan is discussed in Chapter 7.) However, even in merit selection systems the voters have an opportunity to turn sitting judges out of office and campaigns can be expensive and hard-hitting. For example, in 1986 voters defeated California Supreme Court Chief Justice Rose Bird and two associate justices in an election marked by high spending, personal attacks, and a new hairstyle for the chief justice. What may be needed are better education of the electorate and revised codes of conduct for all judicial elections.

WOMEN CANDIDATES FOR POLITICAL OFFICE

Although there has been a substantial increase in the number of women elected as state legislators and mayors (see Chapters 5 and 6), women still hold only a small minority of those positions. Only three state governors, all elected in 1990, are women and, though the number of women judges nearly doubled in the 1970s, their numbers remain small and a majority are on trial courts of limited jurisdiction. Opportunities for women candidates increased in 1992 as men and women voters reacted to the perception of legislative bodies as "old boy" networks. In particular, the U. S. Senate hearings on Clarence Thomas were seen by many as evidence that legislators are insensitive to women's issues. Women candidates are hampered by the basic fact that most incumbents are men and the power of incumbency in elections is very strong. Women have been helped in running for state houses of representatives by the relatively high levels of turnover and the availability of open seats. As more women become lawyers and have positions in business—the traditional steppingstones to public office—we can expect that more of them will enter

For Women Candidates, an Upbeat Election Day

On the morning after the night before, an assortment of political analysts came out, red-eyed and bleary to check the condition of the portrait they had drawn. This was the season they had entitled "The Year of the Woman."

In 1990, they said, more women were running for office then ever before. In 1990, "their issues" would be hot. In 1990, "their votes" would count.

In the early light, the big picture was still littered with undigested data, with gender issues and gaps, with women candidates and voters. The post-election image was a bit more complicated than the simple strokes that had been made earlier. But a pretty interesting portrait was emerging.

How did women do as candidates? Looking at the top of the ticket, Wendy Sherman, the executive director of Emily's List, a women's fund-raising outfit, said: "We haven't exactly shattered the glass ceiling. But we've thrown a few sizable boulders through it."

The most sizable boulders were the three women who made it into the governor's mansions: Ann Richards of Texas, Barbara Roberts of Oregon, and Joan Finney of Kansas.

The Richards victory was especially sweet. After a brutal and battering Texas-style campaign, she beat the Bubba and his bank account and did it with the votes of women. The women's vote went for her 61 per cent to 39 per cent, with a gender gap as big as the state.

On the other hand, Dianne Feinstein, even in defeat, came within a whisker—100,000 votes out of 7 million—of being governor of California. And most of the women who ran and lost for the Senate against incumbents proved they were serious contenders instead of sacrificial lambs.

But the news is in what sports-casters like to call "the field." As Sherman says, "We're beyond the tokens and beyond 'The Remarkable Woman' who breaks through the pack. It's not like there are five women out there and that's all we've got. The field is very deep."

This year there were 85 women running for statewide offices. Of these, 51 women won. There were so many women running for lieutenant governor—19 in all—that the races sometimes looked like the evening news-anchor team. In five states, coed teams ran against each other. There are now six women lieutenant governors, 10 secretaries of state, three attorneys general, and 12 women in charge of the coffers as state treasurers.

The long, slow process of waiting and running, the stop and start of politics has begun to work in women's favor. When the openings come, women are in the pipeline.

At the same time, the old arguments used against women seem to have lost some of their clout. Ten years ago the very word "competence" was a synonym for male. "The concern about whether women could do the job," says political analyst Ethel Kelin, "seems pretty much eliminated."

In fact, says Ms. Kelin optimistically, "the voters are more than happy to have women run. Corruption and honesty are much more salient issues. And there is an added edge that women have about honesty and hard work."

"Leadership" is still sometimes used as a code word to help male candidates, especially in races that hinge on the so-called "macho issues" of war and foreign policy. But that, too, seems to be losing its certainty.

Even "money" is gradually changing hands. Few women candidates raised as much as their male opponents, but they are finally getting serious money. The most visible, like Ms. Richards and Ms. Feinstein, broke the gender record for donor dollars.

As for the year of the woman as voter? Women's votes made the difference not only for Ann Richards, but for Barbara Roberts, and a number of men, including the new progressive senator, Paul Wellstone of Minnesota. In Massachusetts, in the last week of the governor's race, women seemed to lead the undecided away from John Silber to help Bill Weld squeak to victory.

The picture for 1990, then, was not exactly a revolutionary poster. The Year of the Woman collided with another Year of the Incumbent. When the sentiment is toss-'em-all-out-but-mine, seatholders have a powerful edge and most of them are male. So the Senate next year will have only two women out of 100. The House will have only 29 women out of 435, and there will still be only three women in the governor's job.

But if you're looking for the boulders, keep your eyes on the ranks. There are a lot of women aiming for the glass ceiling.

public life. In the accompanying reading, newspaper columnist Ellen Goodman discusses how women candidates did in 1990 and their prospects for the future.

CAMPAIGN FINANCE AND REGULATION

Earlier we examined the high cost of legislative and gubernatorial campaigns. Because such large sums of money are difficult to raise if they come in amounts of $10 and $20, candidates typically turn to the business community (if they are Republicans) or to labor unions, teachers' associations, or public employee unions (if they are Democrats) to secure substantial contributions. State employees, family members, and banks are other major sources of funds. Unlike the federal government, about half the states permit corporations to make campaign contributions. Candidates for statewide office use many of the same fund-raising techniques—dinners, personal visits, mail solicitation, cocktail parties, "voluntary" contributions from state employees—that those running for federal office use.

Almost all the states made major changes in their election laws in the 1970s. All states have disclosure requirements, which usually include identification of contributors and the amount and date of the contribution. About half the states place limits on the amount of individual contributions. Twenty-five states place some restrictions on contributions by labor unions, and thirty-three states restrict corporate contributions. About two-thirds of the states either regulate or prohibit political contributions from state-regulated industries.[19]

We have noted that PACs have raised and distributed increasingly greater amounts of money to campaigns in the past ten years. In 1978, the Supreme Court ruled unconstitutional a Massachusetts law that prohibited corporations from spending money to influence tax referenda. Since then there has been greater business involvement on referenda and initiative issues. Most states have established bipartisan, independent commissions to oversee election regulations. In some states there are nearly ten times as many PACs as there were fifteen years ago. As the number of PACs has increased, so too has their percentage of overall contributions to political campaigns. For example, in the 1980s PACs accounted for about 60 percent of all contributions given to Democrats and Republicans running for the New York legislature. As noted earlier, PACs tend to give most of their contributions to incumbents. A Common Cause study in 1984 found that the top ten PACs in California gave 96 percent of their campaign contributions to incumbent state legislators.[20]

These developments in campaign financing tend to fragment state legislative leadership because they permit independent funding of legislative campaigns. On the other hand, in some states legislative leaders have gained control of PAC funding and they have used this power to strengthen their leadership of the party.

In 1988, twenty-one states provided some distribution of public funds either to candidates or to political parties (see Table 4.2). Funding is provided in exchange for limits on campaign spending. It is made available through general appropriations in a few states. Typically there is a checkoff system ($1 or $2) as part of the state income tax form at no cost to the taxpayer or there is a surcharge that adds to the taxpayer's liability. Participation in states where residents agree to add to their tax burden is less than 5 percent. Where checkoff plans are used, participation averages more than 20 percent. Distribution ranges from gubernatorial candidates only in New Jersey to all statewide offices and the legislature in Minnesota. Seattle, Tucson, and New York City have local publicly financed campaign systems. For example, New York City paid about $1 million to the two 1989 candidates for mayor during the general election. Running contrary to the move to expand public financing, California has prohibited such action at all levels within the state.

State laws have been affected by a 1976 decision of the Supreme Court *(Buckley* v. *Valeo)* that voided some sections of the federal campaign law. The Court struck down federal limits on total spending in campaigns and also voided provisions limiting the amount of money a candidate or his or her family could contribute to a campaign. Furthermore, the Federal Election Commission, as originally established, was held to be appointed unconstitutionally. The Court did, however, uphold federal limits on individual contributions by nonfamily members. As a result, state laws setting spending limitations have been discarded. Also, some state election commissions whose members were selected by the legislature have been reorganized. As state politicians find the new laws difficult to live with and as the memory of Watergate fades away, there is concern that lawmakers will use the Supreme Court decision as a pretext for weakening state financial regulations.

Daniel Elazar notes that campaign costs are affected by variations in political culture.[21] His evidence indicates that on a per capita basis, costs are highest in

Table 4.2   **Public Financing of State Elections (as of January 1988)**

State	Source of Funds	Distribution of Funds
Alabama	Surcharge	Party designated by taxpayer
California	Surcharge matched by state	Parties and candidates for statewide elections
Hawaii	Checkoff	Candidates in all nonfederal elections
Idaho	Checkoff	Party designated by taxpayer
Indiana	Motor vehicle license plates	Divided equally between qualified candidates
Iowa	Checkoff	Party designated by taxpayer
Kentucky	Checkoff	Party designated by taxpayer
Maine	Surcharge	Party designated by taxpayer
Maryland	Direct appropriations	Governor and lieutenant governor only in 1990
Massachusetts	Surcharge	Candidates in statewide elections
Michigan	Checkoff	Gubernatorial candidates in primary; governor and lieutenant governor in general election
Minnesota	Checkoff	All statewide candidates and legislature
Montana	Surcharge	Candidates for governor, lieutenant governor, Supreme Court
New Jersey	Direct appropriations and checkoff	Gubernatorial candidates
North Carolina	Checkoff	Divided among political parties by registration
Ohio	Checkoff	Equally to parties
Oregon	Surcharge	Party designated by taxpayer
Rhode Island	Credit/checkoff	Party designated by taxpayer
Utah	Checkoff	Party designated by taxpayer
Virginia	Surcharge	Party designated by taxpayer
Wisconsin	Checkoff	Candidates for state executive office, supreme court, legislature

SOURCE: *The Book of the States 1990–91* (Lexington, Ky.: Council of State Governments. 1990), pp. 259–260.

states that have an eroding traditional political culture. In such states (e.g., Kentucky, Tennessee, and West Virginia) "vote buying" is common because political issues do not serve as a strong incentive to bring voters to the polls and because the electorate does not exhibit the sense of civic duty to vote that is seen in moralistic cultures.

KEY TERMS

Blanket primary A primary in which voters may vote for candidates from both parties in the same primary election. Used in Alaska and Washington.

Campaigners People who are active in political campaigns, but have little interest in neighborhood issues.

Challenge primary Parties hold conventions and nominate candidates. If no one challenges for the nomination at the convention, the party nominees' names go directly on the general election ballot and a primary is not held.

Closed primary A primary in which voting is restricted to those registered as members of a particular political party.

Communalists People who are active in neighborhood projects, but have little interest in political campaigns.

Community-action programs Federally funded urban-development programs that involve local residents in the planning and administration.

Complete activists About 11 percent of the population who are involved in a wide variety of political activities.

Direct primary An election in which voters determine who the candidates will be in the general election.

Inactives About 22 percent of the population who take almost no part in political life.

Multimember districts Legislative districts from which two or more legislators are elected. Most districts are single-member.

Nonpartisan primary A primary in which all candidates, regardless of party affiliation, are required to appear on the same ballot.

Open primary A primary in which voters participate regardless of their party affiliation.

Parochial participants A small number of people who contact public officials about matters that affect them personally.

Political efficacy The belief of individuals that they can influence the nature of public policy.

Poll tax A special tax to be paid as a qualification for voting. It was used in some Southern states until 1966. The Twenty-fourth Amendment outlawed poll taxes in federal elections, and the Supreme Court has ruled against the use of a poll tax in any election.

Runoff primary A second primary that is held if no candidate wins a majority of the total vote in the first primary election. Used only in Southern states.

Voting Rights Act of 1965 A federal law that helped significantly increase black voter turnout in the South by suspending literacy tests and authorizing registration of voters by federal officials.

Voting specialists People who vote regularly but seldom engage in other forms of political activity.

REFERENCES

1. Sidney Verba and Norman H. Nie, *Participation in America* (New York: Harper & Row, 1972), pp. 77–81. For those of you adding the percentages, 7 percent were unclassifiable.
2. Malcolm E. Jewell and David M. Olson, *Political Parties and Elections in American States*, 3d ed. (Chicago: Dorsey Press, 1988), p. 110.
3. Paul R. Abramson and John H. Aldrich, "The Decline of Electoral Participation in America," *American Political Science Review*, September 1982, pp. 502–521.
4. William H. Flanigan and Nancy H. Zingale, *Political Behavior of the American Electorate*, 6th ed. (Boston: Allyn and Bacon, 1987), pp. 20–22.
5. Richard G. Smolka, "Election Legislation," in *The Book of the States 1990–91* (Lexington, Ky.: Council of State Governments, 1990), p. 230.

6. Daniel J. Elazar, *American Federalism: A View from the States*, 3d ed. (New York: Harper & Row, 1984), pp. 152–153.
7. This section is based on material from Frank J. Sorauf and Paul Allen Beck, *Party Politics in America*, 6th ed. (Glenview, Ill.: Scott, Foresman, 1988), pp. 101–112.
8. *Ibid.*, p. 268.
9. Malcolm E. Jewell and Samuel C. Patterson, *The Legislative Process in the United States*, 4th ed. (New York: Random House, 1985), pp. 21–22.
10. Alan Rosenthal, *Legislative Life* (New York: Harper & Row, 1981), p. 27.
11. Frank J. Sorauf, *Money in American Elections* (Glenview, Ill.: Scott, Foresman/Little, Brown, 1988), p. 264.
12. Samuel C. Patterson, "State Legislators and the Legislatures," in Virginia Gray, Herbert Jacob, and Robert B. Albritton, eds., *Politics in the American States*. 5th ed. (Glenview, Ill.: Scott, Foresman/Little, Brown, 1990), p. 163.
13. Larry Sabato, "Gubernatorial Politics and the New Campaign Technology," *State Government*, Summer 1980, pp. 148–152. See also Coleman B. Ransone, Jr., *The American Governorship* (Westport, Conn.: Greenwood Press, 1982).
14. Thad Beyle, "Costs of the 1990 Gubernatorial Campaigns," *Comparative State Politics*, October 1991, p. 3.
15. Malcolm E. Jewell, "Political Money and Gubernatorial Primaries," *State Government*, vol. 56, no. 2, p. 72.
16. Jerry Hagstrom and Robert Guskind, "Mayoral Candidates Enter the Big Time Using Costly TV Ads and Consultants," *National Journal*, April 6, 1985, pp. 737–742.
17. Henry R. Glick, *Courts, Politics, and Justice*, 2d ed. (New York: McGraw-Hill, 1988), p. 87.
18. See Tom Watson, "The Run for the Robes," *Governing*, July 1991, pp. 49–52.
19. *The Book of the States 1990–91* (Lexington, Ky.: Council of State Governments, 1990), pp. 242–245.
20. Herbert E. Alexander, "The Resurgence of Election Reform in States and Cities," *Comparative State Politics Newsletter,* December 1988, p. 31.
21. Elazar, *American Federalism*, p. 153

CHAPTER 5

LEGISLATURES
IN THE
STATES

Once again we are faced with the problem of making comparisons among fifty very different states. At first glance, most state legislatures appear similar—they pass laws; all but one have two houses; they are organized by parties and committees; they respond to pressure from interest groups and constituents; they oversee administrative agencies; and they compete for power with the state governor. Nevertheless, legislatures are significantly different in regard to how actively they are involved in policymaking, their degree of professionalization, the extent of one-party control, the amount of dominance by the governor, and the existence of regional conflicts.

Although it is reasonably safe to make generalizations about legislative structure, the *political process* within these fifty groups defies simplification. As a result, the challenge is not only to *describe* the legislative process, but to *explain* the wide variation among the states.

It should be remembered that socioeconomic factors and political culture strongly influence legislative activity. The extent of urbanization, levels of income and education, the general pattern of the state's economy, and the dominant political culture affect the selection of legislators, the nature of government policymaking, attitudes toward legislative professionalism, and willingness to institute reform measures.

Prior to the mid-1960s, state legislatures were accurately described as holdovers from the nineteenth century, when their state constitutions were written and attitudes about the role of state government were formed. Most were malapportioned and dominated by rural political interests. Only twenty met in annual sessions. Legislators had few, if any, staff and seldom were they provided offices. Legislative procedures and committees were based on a time when activist state government was seen as undesirable. Sessions were short and there was heavy turnover of members. In short, state legislatures were characterized as a "series of sometime governments: their presence is rarely felt or rarely missed."[1]

Change began about 1965, following the Supreme Court's early rulings on legislative apportionment. At that time districts in both houses of state legislatures were redrawn based on equal population. Rural power was diminished and more urban and suburban legislators were elected. A series of studies conducted by national organizations and state legislatures recommended changes in lawmaking procedures, more staff, and higher pay. As governors gained more power (see Chapter 6), legislators felt a need to improve their budget and oversight powers in order to maintain a check on executive authority. In the 1980s Reagan's "New Federalism" energized legislatures by turning over the administration of many programs to the states. At the same time, federal funds were cut, forcing legislators to do more with less. As we move into the 1990s, states are the focal point for initiatives in most policy areas, including education, the environment, and welfare. State legislators must deal with increased interest group pressure because they are "where it's happening."

A PROFILE OF LEGISLATORS

Americans are, at best, only vaguely aware of what their state legislatures are doing. Newspapers and television pay less attention to state government than to national and local (city) news. Moreover, when the press does report state politics, it tends to focus on the governor. When legislatures are featured by the media, it is often to point out their faults rather than to note their accomplishments. If members of the public have a view of the legislature that is faint and often distorted, they are even less familiar with the actions of individual legislators.

Such unfamiliarity has several unfortunate consequences. Operating without close public or media scrutiny, legislators may shape their decisions to benefit particular interest groups or to further their personal economic well-being. As noted in Chapter 4, legislative elections are marked by low voter turnout and reasonably strong party identification by the electorate. Due to overwhelming local control by one political party, as many as 20 percent of the seats in some legislatures are uncontested in the general election. Because of such factors as low prestige and inadequate salaries, there has been a high turnover in state legislatures (about one-fourth of the members are new in each session of the average state legislature), and it has been difficult to attract the most capable people to legislative service.

In competitive, two-party states, it is the political party that serves as the major agent to recruit legislative candidates. Where party organizations are weak, legislators are recruited by friends, financial backers, or constituents. Although they are reluctant to admit it, some legislators are **self-starters**—people who seek the job by approaching party leaders or by running in primaries. Among individual legislators, motivation for running may range from a desire for free advertising to a strong sense of community service.

State legislators have similar social characteristics. Most are college-educated, middle-aged, white, and male, and have lived in the district all their lives. Although lawyers constitute the largest single occupational group, there are fewer lawyers now than at any recent time. The percentage of lawyers dropped from 22 to 16 in the period 1976 to 1986. As legislative work becomes more full-time and as states tighten financial disclosure laws, the number of lawyers has decreased. In addition, some former lawyers now list themselves as full-time legislators.[2] The largest percentage of lawyers is in the Southern states (45 percent of the Virginia legislators in 1988 were lawyers); the smallest percentage is in New England. Business and professional people dominate most legislatures, with only a few members coming from labor or agriculture. But increasingly members are listing their occupation as "government professional"—indicating a full-time commitment to the legislature.

As many legislatures have become full-time bodies, many lawyers and merchants are unwilling to pay the price of extended absences to serve in them. About 17 percent of legislators are women. Their number increased from 301 in 1969 to 1,261 in 1989. Women have been more likely to serve in New England and in the Western states, where legislative service tends to be part-time and salaries are low. Blacks constitute about 6 percent of all state legislators, and 2 percent are Hispanic. Not surprisingly, blacks are most likely to get elected in urban districts and in predominantly black districts in the South.

State legislatures have been noted for their high rates of turnover. But membership turnover has decreased steadily in the past twenty years as conditions for legislators have improved (see the section on "Legislative Procedures, Rules, and Organization" later in this chapter). Jumps in turnover occurred at the start of the

1970s and 1980s following reapportionment. Turnover jumped to over 40 percent in the mid-1960s when the first wave of reapportionment hit the states.[3] Legislators voluntarily leave office for a variety of reasons. Most often cited are weariness from criticism, family pressures, the feeling they have served long enough, and the desire to run for other office. Almost 60 percent of governors and 33 percent of members of Congress have served in state legislatures.

James David Barber classifies state legislators as spectators, advertisers, reluctants, and lawmakers.[4] **Spectator legislators** seem to find legislative life "interesting," but they are hesitant to become active participants. **Advertiser legislators** tend to be ambitious young lawyers who run to advance their private careers. **Reluctant legislators** are often those who were pressured into running. Seeking to avoid "politics," they may become masters of procedural rules. **Lawmaker legisla-**

State Capitals

Just as the geographical environment of a state may influence the nature of its political process (see Chapter 1), so too the nature of the state capital may have an effect on the social-psychological environment in which legislators work.

In about one-third of the states (fifteen), the capital is the largest city. Major cities that serve as state capitals include Atlanta, Boston, Denver, Indianapolis, and Phoenix. At the other extreme are capitals that had a population of less than 35,000 in 1990. These include Augusta, Maine; Dover, Delaware; Olympia, Washington; Frankfort, Kentucky; Helena, Montana; Juneau, Alaska; Montpelier, Vermont (8,247); and Pierre, South Dakota (12,906). Olympia is the sixteenth largest city in Washington and Frankfort is the tenth largest city in Kentucky. The knowledge that Trenton is the capital of New Jersey may make you a winner in "Trivial Pursuit." In some instances, states seem to have gone out of their way to locate the capital away from the diversions of big-city life. Here, places such as Springfield, Illinois, Harrisburg, Pennsylvania, and Sacramento, California, come to mind.

While many states have tried to locate their capitals near the geographical center of the state (e.g., Columbus, Ohio, and Indianapolis), others, such as Alaska, Massachusetts, and Minnesota, have their capitals far from the state's center.

In many states fierce political battles were fought to decide where to locate the capital. For example, Michigan legislators knew they did not want to keep the capital in Detroit, and several towns competed for the honor. When they picked Lansing, it barely existed as a community. Detroit, with a population of 10,000, was the capital in the late 1830s.

Expanded government activities and employment in the 1980s helped several state capitals grow in population. For example, while the state of North Dakota lost 1.7 percent of its population, Bismarck gained 10.7 percent in the 1980s. In a state capital that also claims the main state university population (such as Columbus, Ohio, or Madison, Wisconsin), increases were especially high, whereas the rest of the state experienced little gain.

tors are those few who do the full work of the legislature. They are the most likely to seek reelection and to have had active membership in organizations before running for the legislature.

The electoral process, particularly the drawing of legislative boundaries, may go far to determine the kinds of persons elected to the legislature. In turn, this may have a significant effect on the influence in the legislature of various pressure groups (e.g., labor versus business and manufacturing) and ultimately on the nature of public policy in the state.

LEGISLATIVE APPORTIONMENT

Electoral rules concerning the waging of political campaigns were discussed in Chapter 4. We turn now to the electoral rules governing the way in which legislative district boundaries are drawn. **Legislative apportionment** has been a major issue in state government since 1962, when the Supreme Court handed down the first of a series of decisions setting forth guidelines for legislative districts. It is still uncertain what the effects of reapportionment have been on the kinds of persons recruited for legislative service and the nature of the changes, if any, in state policymaking.

Before 1962, many state legislatures were grossly malapportioned—that is, districts were drawn in such a way that some legislators represented many more people than did other legislators. In part, this problem was caused by the legislatures' failure to change boundaries as population growth and shifts occurred. As a result, cities (and minority groups living in them) were underrepresented in legislatures dominated by rural and small-town interests. State senates were particularly malapportioned because of a tendency to give equal representation to geographical areas, often each county, rather than to base representation on population.

Illustrations of malapportionment could easily fill an entire book of this size. In California, 10.7 percent of the state's population could have elected a majority of the members of the state senate in the mid-1960s—one senator represented 6 million people and another represented only 14,294 people. In Vermont, 11.9 percent of the state's population could have elected a majority of the members of the state's house of representatives—one representative served a district with 24 people while another served a district with 35,531 people. In Nevada, 8 percent of the state's population could have elected a majority of the members of the state senate. Equal apportionment to each county was guaranteed in the senates of eight states and to each town in the lower house of Vermont. After 1901, Illinois did not reapportion its state legislature until 1955. Before 1962, Alabama and Tennessee had not reapportioned since 1901, and Vermont's house and senate apportionment had not been changed since the adoption of the state constitution in 1793.

Prior to 1962, the Supreme Court held that the issue of malapportionment of state legislatures was a political question, meaning that change would have to come through the action of legislators themselves rather than by directives from state or federal courts. This, of course, produced the practical effect of essentially no change, since the legislators were unlikely to vote themselves out of a job. In many states, legislatures were not constitutionally required to reapportion on a regular basis. Moreover, even when reapportionment was required, legislative boundaries were often subject to **gerrymandering** to give unfair advantage to the dominant political party. (Figure 5.1 shows an example of "creative cartography," drawn up by the California legislature to create a Democratic district in Orange and Los Angeles counties.)

In *Baker* v. *Carr* (**1962**) the Supreme Court for the first time ruled that federal courts have jurisdiction in cases challenging legislative apportionment. The Court declared that malapportioned state legislatures may violate the equal protection clause of the Fourteenth Amendment, and remanded the case to a federal district court in Tennessee (where the suit had originated) to take jurisdiction and enforce the provisions of the Tennessee constitution. The Supreme Court soon became more directly involved in setting down specific guidelines in a series of reapportionment decisions.

In 1963, the Court struck down Georgia's rule that in primary elections for governor and for Congress the person who carried a majority of counties would be the winner (*Gray* v. *Sanders*). In 1964, the Supreme Court made a clear statement that when drawing up congressional districts, state legislatures should make certain "as nearly as practical, one man's vote in the congressional election must be worth as much as another's" (*Wesberry* v. *Sanders*). In *Reynolds* v. *Sims* (1964), the Court

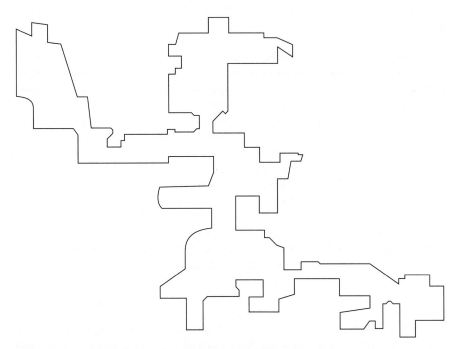

Figure 5.1   California: Proposed 69th Assembly District

SOURCE: Gordon E. Baker, "Redistricting in the Seventies: The Political Thicket Deepens," *National Civic Review,* June 1972, p. 281. Reprinted with permission.

ruled that *both* houses of state legislatures must be apportioned on the basis of population—that is, "one man, one vote."* Also in 1964, the Court in *Lucas* v. *Colorado* overturned a referendum overwhelmingly approved by the voters of Colorado that would have allowed legislators to consider factors other than population in preparing an apportionment plan. The Court stated that "An individual's constitutionally protected right to an equally weighted vote cannot be denied by a majority of the state's electorate, if the apportionment adopted by the voters fails to measure up to the requirements of the equal protection clause."

The Supreme Court has elaborated on the population standard of *Reynolds* v. *Sims* by permitting greater flexibility in state legislative redistricting. In *Mahan* v. *Howell* (1973), the Court approved a Virginia plan in which one district was overrepresented by 6.8 percent and another underrepresented by 9.6 percent over an ideal plan in which each house district would contain the same number of people. The Court suggested that applying the "absolute equality" test to state legislative redistricting might impair the normal functioning of state and local governments. In their dissent, the Court's liberal justices (Brennan, Douglas, and Marshall) questioned the need to preserve the integrity of county boundaries, doubting seriously whether local legislation amounted to a significant proportion of the Virginia legislature's business.

In general, the courts have stated that legislative districts should be nearly equal in population, compact in size, and contiguous. Yet even when these standards are met (e.g., a computer can turn out hundreds of equal-districting plans for a state), other, more complex political problems remain. These concern the impact of partisan groups and interests, as well as the impact of racial and ethnic groups. For example, should district lines be drawn to create an equitable balance between Democrats and Republicans in state legislatures? Should they be drawn to ensure the election of black or Hispanic legislators? Such procedures have been referred to as "affirmative gerrymandering."[5]

The Supreme Court has upheld some plans deliberately intended to predetermine the composition of state legislatures. In a 1973 case involving Connecticut, the Court upheld a plan devised to create a certain number of Democratic and Republican districts roughly in proportion to the overall political division in the state. The Court noted that "benevolent, bipartisan gerrymandering" was not only permissible but commendable. In 1977 (*United Jewish Organizations of Williamsburg* v. *Carey*), the Court upheld a districting plan in New York City that purposely concentrated blacks and Hispanics in several Manhattan and Brooklyn districts to help ensure the election of minority legislators. The Court held by a vote of 7 to 1 that the state had a legal right (here an obligation imposed by the 1965 Voting Rights Act) to draw district lines with the specific purpose of maximizing minority legislative representation.

Until 1986, the Supreme Court used population equality almost exclusively as the grounds for evaluating the constitutionality of state legislative and congression-

---

*In *Reynolds* v. *Sims* the Court rejected the "federal analogy"—that is, like the United States Senate, one house of a state legislature could be apportioned on the basis of geography rather than population. The Court held that political divisions of states are not "sovereign entities" as are the states themselves. The Court's majority classically stated that "legislators represent people, not trees or acres."

al districting plans. In *Davis* v. *Bandemer* (1986), the Court for the first time held that partisan gerrymandering (that is, drawing legislative district lines to benefit a political party) may violate the Constitution. However, in this instance (the case involved a districting plan for the Indiana legislature) the majority held that relying on a single election was too soon to make a judgment that unconstitutional partisan gerrymandering had occurred. Because the decision did not set clear guidelines for defining a partisan gerrymander, it left the matter very unclear. *Davis* v. *Bandemer* placed a heavy burden of proof on those seeking to show that a violation has occurred. It remains to be seen how the ruling will be interpreted by courts when cases are filed challenging reapportionment on the basis of the 1990 census.

Besides malapportionment, there is another major issue in redistricting—the continued use of multimember districts. Liberals contend that multimember districts disadvantage minorities by diluting their political strength. They also claim that multimember districts weaken the tie between legislators and their constituents, and that the long ballots used for elections serve to confuse voters. In 1980, the Supreme Court, however, upheld the use of multimember districting in Mobile, Alabama. In a plurality opinion, the Court noted that such plans could be overturned only if their *intent* was to dilute minority voting strength. Although blacks comprised 40 percent of Mobile's population, they had never elected a black representative to its three-member city commission. The standard of proof (intent and not impact) in the Mobile case was changed by Congress in 1982 amendments to the Voting Rights Act. Section 2 now allows courts to review the "totality of circumstances" in applying the "results" test.

By 1968, every state had reapportioned at least one house of its legislature since the *Baker* v. *Carr* decision, and redistricting was implemented in every state following the 1970 census. Several consequences of reapportionment can be noted, but the verdict still is not in regarding its effects on the nature of public policy. The following consequences were generally identified throughout the country:

1. Younger, better-educated people, often with little political experience, have been elected to state legislatures.
2. The number of urban and especially suburban representatives is markedly increased. In some Southern states where cities had been grossly underrepresented, urban representation has increased by a factor of ten. There also has been an increase in the number of black legislators in both the North and the South.
3. Democrats have gained some seats, but the impact on party strength has been less than Republicans feared.

The redistricting process for the 1992 elections faced many of the same racial and political issues that were litigated in the 1980s. The availability of computers meant that virtually all interested parties submitted redistricting plans, and this slowed the process even more than usual. In most states legislatures draw congressional as well as legislative boundaries. Although it is always difficult to reduce seats (Illinois, Michigan, New York, Ohio, and Pennsylvania all stood to lose two or more seats), there can be problems adding seats. For example, California gained seven seats for 1992 and in 1990 there was approval of a voter initiative limiting the terms of state legislators. As a result, running for Congress was on the minds of many of California's 120 legislators as they drew new districts for 1992.

As we have seen, Congress has made it easier for racial groups to prove violations of the Voting Rights Act—a move that is expected to increase litigation in the 1990s. Because of their history of discrimination, nine Southern states and portions of seven others are required to obtain approval from the U.S. Justice Department or a federal court before they make any change in voting laws or election procedures. The Justice Department reviewed over 1,000 redistricting plans in 1991. In several Northern states a tactic of Republicans has been to increase the number of blacks and Hispanics in urban districts and hope to win suburban districts that are predominantly white and supposedly more Republican.

V. O. Key noted that one consequence of malapportionment was to divide party control between governors and legislators.[6] This was particularly true in the North, where small-town, rural Republicans were overrepresented in the legislature and Democratic governors were elected because of their party's strength in big cities. Although Democratic strength in state legislatures increased in the 1970s (e.g., Minnesotans elected a majority of Democrats to both houses of their legislature for the first time ever in 1972), ticket splitting has become more prevalent, there are more candidate-centered campaigns, the Republican party has become stronger in Southern states, and even after reapportionment there are more cases of divided legislative-executive control.

Morris Fiorina notes that the increase in divided state government is due largely to the fall in unified Republican government over the past forty-five years.[7] As in presidential elections, minority party governors have been successful in elections across the country. Thus Democratic governors have been elected in strongly Republican Rocky Mountain states and Republican governors have been elected in predominantly Democratic states such as Oregon and Washington and even West Virginia.

Following the 1990 elections, divided control existed in twenty-seven states. The two houses of state legislatures had split party control in twelve states, and in fifteen other states the governor was of the opposite party from the majority controlling both legislative houses. In part, this results from the election of several Republican governors in the South (Louisiana, Alabama, North Carolina, and South Carolina), but it is difficult to discern a national pattern. Party unity in 1991 was also affected by the presence of independent governors in Alaska and Connecticut and by evenly divided senates in Alaska and Idaho. Whereas many Southern state legislatures are overwhelmingly Democratic, other states also are strongly one-party. In Hawaii, 67 of 76 legislators are Democratic, as are 134 of 150 legislators in Rhode Island. Utah is perhaps the most Republican state. In 1991 it had a Republican governor and 63 Republicans out of 104 state legislators; George Bush won 67 percent of the state's presidential vote in 1988. In 1991 only Utah, South Dakota, and New Hampshire had both houses of their legislature and the governor under Republican control.

Most political scientists are cautious in regard to the policy implications of reapportionment. However, the more urban and suburban representatives there are in a state legislature, the more likely it will be as a body to take liberal positions on such matters as housing, welfare, education, and mass transit. In a few states, however, new suburban legislators have joined with rural legislators in opposing liberal social policies.

Some statistical studies indicate that reapportionment is associated with higher spending for education, public health, hospitals, and highways. Reapportioned legislatures were found to be more responsive to majority views on civil rights, gun control, and public employee labor rights. State legislators believe that policy has become more liberal and more urban-oriented.[8]

A major factor limiting the impact of reapportionment on policymaking is that within metropolitan areas, legislators are often strongly divided between city and suburbs, blacks and whites, Republicans and Democrats. In contrast, rural legislators are more homogeneous (white, Protestant, and Republican) and thus comprise a much more effective voting bloc than do metropolitan legislators.

INITIATIVE, REFERENDUM, AND RECALL

As noted, the 1970s were marked by the most extensive restructuring of state legislatures in American history. In theory, reapportioned legislatures would enact legislation desired by a majority of the people and, in turn, restore public faith in representative bodies. Yet the 1970s saw a renewal of interest in the techniques of direct democracy—initiative, referendum, and recall—by which citizens are able to bypass legislatures and act directly on policy matters. Although tax limitations, such as Proposition 13 in California, were the most publicized uses of initiative and referendum, citizens in many states were actively involved with such issues as nuclear power regulation, the death penalty, and gay rights.

State and local election laws differ from federal laws in that they often permit the use of the techniques of initiative, referendum, and recall. These procedures allow voters to exert direct control over government without waiting for public officials, such as legislators, to assume leadership in public policy. Although the techniques of direct democracy were available in colonial America and their use can be traced back to ancient Greece, they are largely a product of the Progressive movement in the early twentieth century. Reformers distrusted partisan politicians and wished to introduce the means by which citizens could check government excess and incompetence. Because of widespread corruption and incompetence, turn-of-the-century reformers had good reason to want to bypass legislatures.

The **initiative** is a technique whereby citizens can bypass legislatures and propose new statutes or changes in government charters. The proposals for change are then placed on the ballot for voter approval. In most states, petitions to place an issue on the ballot are circulated (often an interest group and its attorneys organize the initiative) and if a certain percentage of registered voters (usually about 10 percent) sign the petition, the issue will appear on the ballot in the next election. In some states an *indirect initiative* is used, by which the issue is submitted to the legislature once the required number of signatures is obtained. If the legislature fails to act on the matter within a specified period of time, the proposal is then placed on the ballot for direct voter approval or disapproval. Twenty-three states permit use of the initiative. Seventeen of those states are located west of the Mississippi River, where political parties typically are weaker and nonpartisan good-government groups have been stronger than in the East.[9]

Proponents of the initiative contend that it (and the referendum) increases voter interest and turnout. They believe that the initiative improves government responsiveness and that it opens up debate on issues that otherwise would not be publicly discussed. In short, they place great confidence in the ability of the average citizen to understand politics and to participate in elections. Opponents respond that citizens are not well enough informed about complex matters to make intelligent decisions. They are critical of the yes-no format of initiatives, which precludes the kind of compromise that often occurs in legislatures. Experience has shown that voters are reluctant to approve initiatives. Less than 30 percent of initiatives have received a majority vote. Moreover, voter turnout in Northern states without initiatives has been higher than in Northern states with initiatives.

Curiously, although the initiative was established to counter the influence that special interests have on legislatures, in some states interest groups have become the dominant force in the initiative and referendum. Organizing and financing a petition drive are very difficult, and these are skills for which interest groups are very well equipped. In initiative elections interest groups help mobilize opinion and turn out voters.

In 1990 Oklahoma, Colorado, and California voters approved initiatives to limit service in state legislatures. The proposal in California, which was upheld by the California supreme court in 1991, limited members of the state assembly to six years and senators, the governor, and other elected state officials to eight years. It also required deep cuts in the legislature's operating budget. Elsewhere, voters in Oregon defeated two measures to restrict abortion, Alaskans reestablished criminal penalties for possession of marijuana, Arizonans rejected a state holiday for the birthday of Martin Luther King (thus making it unlikely that the Super Bowl will be held in Phoenix in the near future), voters in Massachusetts rejected a major tax-cutting proposal, and voters in California, Oregon, Washington, and Missouri defeated environmental protection measures. In 1991 voters in Washington state defeated a measure designed to limit the terms of state legislators and members of Congress.

A **referendum** gives voters the opportunity to approve or reject statutes or constitutional changes that have been proposed by the legislature. In a few states citizens may petition the legislature to force a referendum on a legislative proposal before it becomes law. The more common referendum procedure is for the legislature to direct a proposal to the voters for their approval. Such a method often is used for approval of local school bond issues and amendments to state constitutions. In California voters may be confronted with fifteen to twenty referenda issues in a single statewide election. The process of forcing responsiveness and using the petition process is similar to the initiative.

Voter response varies greatly on referenda issues. Support for referenda involving innovation and increased taxes is greater in high-income districts than in working-class areas. Technical propositions and matters dealing with government organization typically draw few voters. However, moral issues concerning such matters as liquor, gambling, and Sunday closing draw large turnouts. Health matters, such as fluoridation of water, also draw heavy voter turnout as rival groups compete against each other. Occasionally groups will try to avoid publicity, in hopes that their issue will be adopted as a "sleeper." If there is little awareness of the issue, opposition may not be prodded into an organized attack.

The **recall** is the least used and least available of the three techniques of direct democracy. Although twenty-five states allow for a referendum and twenty-three provide for a statewide initiative, only fifteen state constitutions include a provision for a statewide recall. In addition, fifteen other states allow local recall. Of the fifteen states providing for statewide recall, only three do not have a statewide initiative or referendum. Six states that provide for recall exclude judges from removal.

While recall is usually discussed with initiative and referendum and is historically a product of the same Progressive reform movement, it is distinctive in that it is directed against public officials. Under the recall procedure, voters circulate petitions calling for the removal of a public official. If a sufficient number of signatures is obtained (the percentage usually is high—about 25 percent of the vote cast for the office in the last election), an election is held in which the voters choose either to keep the official or remove him or her from office. Recall is authorized primarily in Western states. Only one governor, Lynn Frazier of North Dakota in 1922, has been recalled from office. He was subsequently elected to the U.S. Senate from North Dakota. In 1988, a scheduled recall election in Arizona was canceled when the state legislature impeached Governor Evan Mecham and removed him from office.

THE FUNCTIONS OF STATE LEGISLATURES

The performance of state legislatures can be measured by the way in which they perform three basic functions.

1. Individual legislators must represent the interests of their constituents. They provide service functions by helping people in their dealings with state administrative agencies and answering other personal requests. Legislators also respond to demands for policymaking and explain voting decisions to their constituents.
2. Legislatures review and evaluate actions of the governor and they oversee the administration of state programs. This oversight function is performed through the legislature's approval of a state budget, the holding of committee hearings, and the approval of executive personnel appointments. Since the legislature controls appropriations, it has the potential to review all agency programs before approving budget items. In particular, new program proposals are closely scrutinized by legislative committees before approval is given.
3. The most important function of the state legislature is to participate in making policy. Here a self-respecting legislature should not be content merely to deal with the governor's program or routinely approve members' bills. It has a responsibility to initiate action and to consider seriously a wide variety of proposals dealing with the most important and controversial problems of the day—abortion, drug law reform, and capital punishment. (Specific areas of policymaking are discussed in Chapters 8, 9, and 10.)

In making public policy, each legislator is confronted with a wide range of issues, ranging from the trivial (whether the ladybug should be designated the "state insect" in Ohio) to the enormously complex (the annual general expenditures for California, which are over $70 billion). In committees, in caucuses, and on the floor, the legislator faces a continuous array of decision-making situations. Moreover, legislators clearly realize their political vulnerability and the need to please their party, the governor (if he or she is of the same party), their constituents, and various interest groups. Since many legislators wish to advance their political careers beyond the statehouse, the need to compromise and accommodate the desires of many groups is a political necessity.

To help understand legislative decision making, political scientists have suggested that legislators look for cues to simplify certain decision-making situations. Legislators are most likely to consult friends in the legislature and those described as "legislative specialists" when making decisions. Although they frequently contact committee leaders, members of their own party who represent similar districts, and party leaders, legislators are more likely to consult lobbyists than these people.[10]

Policy initiation remains largely the function of state governors. As we shall see in the next section, the structure of legislatures and their rules and procedures equip them best for deliberation, discussion, and delay rather than initiation of policy. In addition, legislators must reflect local interests if they wish to be reelected. In contrast, the governor reflects the interests of a statewide constituency and is therefore able to focus on broad issues and to balance off the interests of many localized economic and social groups. Under the best of circumstances, legislators share their lawmaking power with several groups. Governors issue executive orders and, with administrators, interpret vague statutory laws. Courts "make law" by their interpretation of state constitutions and statutes. The public is directly involved in lawmaking by the use of the initiative and referendum.

THE CONSTITUTIONAL STRUCTURE OF LEGISLATURES

The *size* of state legislatures varies from 20 members in the upper house of Alaska to 67 in the upper house of Minnesota. New Hampshire has 400 members in its lower house to represent about 1.1 million people (in the New England states, assemblies use the town as a representative unit), while California has 80 members to represent over 30 million people. In a majority of states (thirty-one), the lower house has more than 100 members, and in several others the lower house has 98 or 99 members. In forty-four states, the upper house has at least 30 members. Although most students of state government conclude that legislatures are too large, it is impossible to say what the "ideal" size should be. Large bodies often become impersonal and more dedicated to staging debates than to taking action. On the other hand, in larger bodies the representational function is generally improved as legislators represent smaller numbers of people. There is also evidence that larger legislatures are more efficient because of their more hierarchical organization and greater specialization in committees. A disadvantage of small legislatures is that members have a tendency to become too cozy in a kind of social club atmosphere. Moreover, racial and ethnic minorities are less likely to be represented among the members of small legislatures. In terms of practical politics, it is unrealistic to expect legislators to vote themselves out of their jobs by decreasing the number of seats. Nevertheless, since 1979, Massachusetts, Illinois, and New Hampshire have reduced the size of their lower houses. In contrast, the legislatures of several states have been enlarged to facilitate reapportionment.

Terms of office also vary among the states. The most common pattern is for representatives to serve two-year terms and senators to serve four-year terms. In most states, members of each house receive equal pay. Legislative salaries range from $100 per year in New Hampshire to $57,500 per year in New York. In nine states (all low-pay), salaries are still set by state constitutions. Although ten states pay legislators over $30,000 a year, several states, including Texas, still pay legislators less than $10,000. In all but five states legislators receive a per diem allowance when the legislature is in session, and forty-two states provide extra compensation for legislative leaders.

Part-time service has also been encouraged by the length of legislative *sessions.* As recently as the beginning of World War II, only four states held annual sessions. Today, most state legislatures hold an annual session, and only seven states have biennial sessions. At one extreme, the New Mexico legislature meets for sixty calendar days one year and thirty calendar days the next, so that at most the legislature is in session from mid-January to mid-March. Session restrictions were originally established to guard against legislatures irresponsibly enacting too much legislation or to prevent interference with planting time and harvest. They were also a response to widespread concern about "riotous" living at public expense. Because of the demands of contemporary state government, most legislatures find ways to circumvent constitutional limits and thus remain in session during most of each calendar year. Twenty-nine legislatures can call themselves into special session without action by the governor. As part of the same kind of antilegislature sentiment in which three states have limited the tenure of legislators, voters in Colorado and Oklahoma have approved constitutional amendments limiting the length of legislative sessions. Other states, including Michigan and New Hampshire, have considered returning to biennial sessions.

With the exception of Nebraska, every state has a **bicameral** (two-house) **legislature.** The strong bicameral tradition originated when most legislatures in colonial America adopted the upper and lower house model of the British Parliament. (But Georgia, Pennsylvania, and Vermont had unicameral legislatures in the eighteenth century.) The U.S. Constitution, of course, provides for two chambers, a House and Senate, and this influenced the states. In the early years, many of the state legislatures included an economic class aspect, in which extra property requirements were imposed for service in the state upper chamber. Concern for irresponsible legislative behavior is reflected in John Adams's warning that "A single assembly is liable to all the vices, follies, and frailties of an individual; subject to fits of humor, starts of passion, flights of enthusiasms, partialities or prejudices, consequently productive of hasty results and absurd judgments."

It is significant that separation of powers did not exist in the early state governments. Governors had little power and were often appointed by the legislature. Legislatures exercised broad powers of economic management and occasionally even overrode the courts in some property-dispute cases. In such circumstances, a bicameral legislature offered greater protection against the abuse of power and undue influence by strong interest groups. As noted in the discussion of reapportionment, having two legislative chambers made it possible for the state to apportion one on the basis of geography, rather than population, and thus protect rural, conservative interests.

Due largely to the well-organized campaign of Senator George Norris, Nebraska adopted a **unicameral** (one-house) **legislature** in 1934. Although no state has followed Nebraska's lead, it is not outlandish to suggest that unicameral plans could be adopted in other states. Jess Unruh, former Speaker of the California Assembly, believes that the most effective way to improve state government is to consolidate state legislatures into one house each.[11] Unruh asks, "Does any corporation have *two* boards of directors? Would there be any point to it?" Unruh suggests that three major benefits would result from the adoption of unicameralism. First, the delay and buck passing found in bicameral legislatures would be lessened, making it easier to enact "progressive" legislation. Second, there would be an economic saving once duplication of costs in terms of staff time was eliminated and the total number of legislators was reduced. (The costs for lobbyists would also be reduced.) Third, a unicameral legislature would be more visible to the public and would help restore public confidence in state legislatures.

The case for unicameralism has been made at several recent state constitutional conventions. Although the idea appears logical to many academics, arguments for unicameralism have failed to move politicians who fear radical change and the loss of legislative seats. The longstanding tradition of bicameralism will undoubtedly continue, with the Nebraska experiment serving only to illustrate the exception to the rule.

LEGISLATIVE PROCEDURES, RULES, AND ORGANIZATION

In general, all state legislatures follow a similar procedure for passing bills into laws. In addition, the ways their committees are structured and the roles the political parties play in organizing the legislatures closely resemble the pattern found in Congress. Because most readers are familiar with how a bill becomes a law, only a brief outline is provided here to summarize the chain of events in a typical legislature.

Once a bill has been introduced in the upper or lower house, it is assigned to a committee. The committee holds public hearings on important bills and then meets in executive session to discuss and amend the bill. If the committee action is favorable, the bill is reported out and placed on the chamber's calendar. If party organization is strong, the bill is discussed at a regular caucus and a position is agreed upon. The bill is then given a second reading on the floor (its introduction constitutes a first reading), following which there is debate, amendment, and vote. After a usual delay of one calendar day, a third reading occurs and a final vote is taken. If the vote is affirmative, the bill then moves to the other legislative chamber, where the process of committee and floor action is repeated. If the second chamber approves the bill without amendment, it goes to the governor for his or her signature or veto. If the bill is approved in a different form by each house, a conference committee is selected to work out an agreement and both houses must approve the conference report before the bill is sent to the governor.

Most state legislatures have between twenty and thirty standing committees, established on a subject basis, to consider bills introduced by legislators and to monitor the activities of particular administrative agencies. The trend in recent years has been to reduce the number of committees, which range from six in Massachusetts and Rhode Island to fifty-eight in the North Carolina house. In Connecticut and Maine, all committees are joint house-senate bodies. As in Congress, it is in committees that the real work of the legislature is accomplished and here that many bills die for lack of action. The number of bills introduced in each two-year session ranges from about 30,000 in New York to 1,000 in Vermont and Colorado. Overall, legislatures pass about one-fifth of the bills that are introduced.[12] New York typically passes fewer than 1,000 bills (3 percent), whereas California has passed over 3,000 bills in a session. A few states have limited the number of bills that members can introduce. For example, individual Colorado legislators are limited to introducing six bills the first year and four bills in the second year of each session. The role of committees in reducing the legislative workload by providing a division of labor varies among the states. In Illinois, a significant number of bills are not reported to a committee at all, and most bills sent to committee are subsequently reported to the floor. In thirteen states, committees are required to report out all bills referred to them, but this rule gets only technical compliance.[13] Some states guarantee a floor vote for the governor's proposals.

Although it is convenient to compare the operation of committees in state legislatures with that of congressional committees, several factors help make state committees less influential than their federal counterparts. State legislative committees are weaker because the legislative sessions often are too short to permit deliberation and careful review of bills; members have little staff assistance; legislators often transfer from one committee to another or have short tenure in the legislature and thus do not develop expertise in a given subject area; and seniority usually does not play as strong a role in determining committee assignments and chairmanships as it does in Congress. In addition, because state legislative committees are so numerous and individual assignments so heavy, it is often difficult to get a quorum or even to find a room in which the committee can meet. The workloads of state committees vary greatly. In some states, two to three committees may deal with 25 percent of all legislation.[14] Because member participation is very limited, the chairperson often *is* the committee.

As state legislatures have become more professional (discussed below), their committees have become stronger. Many states have reduced the number of committees and organized them more effectively along functional lines. This, along with lower turnover, has permitted legislators to acquire greater expertise and influence in policy areas. Committees have added professional staff and they have become much more active in interim periods when the legislature is not in session.

If state legislative committees and their heads have been relatively weak, the presiding officers in the states frequently exercise more power than their counterparts in Congress. However, as committees are gaining power, legislative leadership has declined in several states. One reason for the decline is that individual legislators now have greater access to information through lobbyists and their personal staff and to campaign finances than they did in the past, and this has reduced the ability of legislative leaders to control information, favors, and money. Turnover among leaders is increasing, while turnover among all legislators is decreasing.

In the lower house, a speaker is elected by the entire membership. In twenty-eight states the lieutenant governor is the president of the senate, and in the remaining states the president is elected or confirmed by the members. Voting for these officials is nearly always along strict party lines, with the heads of the majority party being elected to the leadership posts. In New York, for example, the assembly speaker and the senate majority leader have near-dictatorial power, allowing them to appoint all committee heads, set the agenda for floor debate, and recognize speakers on the floor. They also control the awarding of part-time staff positions, which are used as party patronage. In most states, the speaker names members to committees, is a member of the rules committee, and is the major strategist for the majority party. If they are of the same party, the governor and speaker often work closely to secure passage of the governor's program.

With a few notable exceptions, such as New York, Ohio, and Illinois, domineering leaders are becoming a thing of the past.[15] As old leaders leave office, their successors face a new breed of legislators who ran election campaigns independently of the party and whose staffs provide a strong base of support. Legislators have acted to modernize legislative procedures and to reduce the formal powers of floor leaders. As a result, Rosenthal believes the next generation of leaders will manage more by consensus and will need superior interpersonal skills to be effective.

In addition to formal procedures and organization, *informal* or unwritten rules may be equally important to understanding how a legislature operates. Committees may not receive the bills their titles imply; speakers may merely do the bidding of other strong party leaders; even the length of the session may be extended by "covering the clock" (pretending that the time limit has not expired). Whether the rules are formally or informally established, they are adhered to not because of threats to discipline uncooperative members but because the members believe that the rules further the best interests of making the legislature work.

There has been a major drive in recent years toward **"professionalized" state legislatures.** By increasing salaries, expanding and improving legislative facilities (this includes new office buildings and more sophisticated information system technology), providing more staff assistance, reducing the number of committees, lengthening sessions, making rules and procedures more flexible, and improving oversight of the executive, legislatures are trying to become more professional. As more demands are placed on state government, legislatures cannot longer afford the luxury of part-time operation. Even in states where salaries, staff, and sessions have remained about the same (often the case in the South), legislators are working harder and developing more policy expertise. Thus they see themselves as more "professional."

With increased staff, a legislature is better able to initiate its own programs and to work with the governor in confronting the state's financial problems. All ob-

Lawyers, Building Contractors, and Legislators

One of the saddest days in David Diamont's life came in 1990 when he had to quit his job as a high school football coach. His father had been a coach for 36 years, and Diamont had been planning plays and teaching for over two decades in Pilot Mountain, N.C., a tiny textile-producing town. But, the 45-year-old Diamont had to give up the gridiron because it conflicted with his other, part-time job. Diamont is also cochair of the powerful appropriations committee of the North Carolina House of Representatives, which runs the state's $12 billion budget process. Diamont is one of a breed that may steadily disappear over the next couple of decades in all but a handful of states: the citizen legislator. Straight out of *Mr. Smith Goes to Washington,* these are the doctors, teachers, pharmacists and farmers who trundle off to their state capitals for a few months a year to pass laws. They're paid little—often under $12,000 a year. Folks like Diamont are still common fixtures in most of the 50 state legislatures, but they're caught in a squeeze. They are paid too little to devote themselves year-round to the work of government, but the growing complexities of running a state are forcing them in that direction. With the federal government regularly dumping more and more responsibility on the states, legislatures now allocate around a third of a trillion dollars annually to schools, highways, prisons, public welfare, health care, local government and a host of other needs and causes. "The inevitable trend is to a full-time legislative body," says Alan Rosenthal, director of the New Jersey-based Eagleton Institute of Politics at Rutgers University.

The first step for many states has been to add staff at a rapid clip to help their legislatures handle the burden. Legislatures now employ over 33,000 staff members, up over 25% from 10 years ago. In a number of states, these employees work year-round, even when the legislatures are out of session.

Since many states operate under constitutional constraints that limit the number of days they are allowed to serve, they have also added a variety of special sessions. Without them, it can be very difficult to get the work done.

"We have some 650 bills a year that need to be voted on," says Ted Strickland, president of the Colorado Senate. "And we have a 120-day limitation. That takes its toll. Yesterday afternoon, there were three bills dealing with the right-to-die issue and there were 24 witnesses who wished to testify. The committee chairman had to tell each of those individuals that his time was limited to a three-minute testimony. People don't get beyond the shouting in three minutes."

As the work load gets heavier, legislatures are increasingly populated by recent college graduates who are happy to take relatively low pay to plant their feet firmly on the first step toward a political future. Many are tantalized by the fact that about half of all U.S. Congressmen were once state legislators. Unfortunately, states lose something in the process. "They sacrifice the experience of people in nonpolitical life. People who have met a payroll, cooked a meal in a restaurant, done something real," says Rosenthal.

Consider Wisconsin. A couple of decades ago, its legislature was dominated by dairy farmers and other laymen. Now, its made up of career politicians who have helped keep the legislature's role in government intact. "As the size of government grew, it became imperative to have a full-time legislature if we were going to continue to hold the reins of government," says David Helbach, Wisconsin's senate majority leader. "Otherwise, you would have a much stronger executive branch, in relation to the legislature."

Often dominated by the executive branch, legislatures are increasingly determined to stand head-to-head with the governor. "Legislatures have made a conscious effort over the last quarter of a century to establish themselves as co-equal with the executive branch," says Karl Kurtz, director of state services at the National Conference of State Legislatures. "That is as it's described in most state constitutions. And they've made deliberate efforts to build up their staff capacity, spend more time in session, and they have more sophisticated committee systems."

In fact, in such states as Texas, Colorado and South Carolina, the legislature has more institutional power than the governor does—especially in budgetary matters. "We basically ignore the governor's budget," says one Texas legislator. "Well, some of us don't ignore it. Some of us file it."

The rancor between the executive and legislative branches has grown, as well. In most of the large states, at least one of the houses is of a different party than the governor, thus making disagreements between the branches of government all but inevitable. Just ask New York Governor Mario Cuomo, who has been unable to get a budget out on time for seven years.

What's more, this year, congressional redistricting has given legislators sufficient temporary power over Congress to inspire political columnist David Broder to observe, "They can make the life of any member of Congress miserable—or end his or her career—by the way they draw district lines."

But just when legislatures appear to be ready to consolidate their gains, they are coming under fire on a number of fronts.

In California, the state with the most professional legislature in the country, general voter dissatisfaction has led to an unrivaled assault on legislative power.

Proposition 140, passed in November, limited the members of the assembly to three two-year terms and the senators to two four-year terms. The proposition also put through budget cuts that will require a reduction of about 40% of the legislature's $190 million budget. Even Willie L. Brown Jr., California's assembly speaker and for many years one of the most powerful men in the state is personally losing about 30 staff members.

In a handful of states, including South Carolina, Tennessee and Arizona, claims of illegal activities have soiled the legislature's reputation. Although there's no evidence that legislatures are more corrupt than they used to be, heightened scrutiny has certainly given the public the impression that many legislators are on the take. In fact, Justice Department figures show that the number of state officials indicted in federal investigations grew from 10 in 1970 to 71 in 1989.

"It amazes me that legislators are so stupid," says the Eagleton Institute's Rosenthal, "because the risk of taking bribes today is so great."

The situation in Arizona was particularly messy. A handful of senators and representatives were videotaped taking money—sometimes stuffing it into gym bags—in exchange for their votes. "I like the good life and I'm trying to position myself so that I can live the good life," said one state representative on camera. "I sold way too cheap," complained another when told that his bribe of $12,105 was less than that paid to another legislator.

"We have been painted with a broad ugly brush, and there is a tremendous lack of confidence in elected officials in this state," says Senator Jamie Gutierez of Arizona, head of the senate ethics committee. "We have a great deal of damage control to do at home."

As a result of such unpleasant disclosures, many states have passed or considered ethics laws in the past few years. Texas, for example, is currently debating new rules that would prohibit the standard practice of legislators accepting prepaid vacations from lobbyists.

Partially as a result of such public improprieties, legislatures are repeatedly given negative ratings in public polls; often with under a third of the populace saying they are satisfied with their performance. According to one recent Gallup poll, the public ranked the ethical standards of state officeholders below those of lawyers and building contractors, and only marginally ahead of labor leaders and stockbrokers. One dubious honor: The legislators scored considerably higher than car dealers.

"There was a period in the middle of the 1970s when legislatures were developing as modern political institutions," says Rosenthal. "Now, things are more complex. And the problems for these institutions are not going away soon."

SOURCE: *Financial World,* May 28, 1991, pp. 56–57. Reprinted with permission.

servers believe that increased staffing for individual members and committees has been one of the most significant changes in state legislatures since the 1960s. Staff grew by about 25 percent in the 1980s. There is some fear that expanding legislative staff will add to the power of incumbency because the staff will be used more to assist in campaigns than to engage in legislative research. Should this be the case, policy alternatives might be limited instead of expanded.

Annual sessions and additional working days do not necessarily mean that legislatures will increase their output. There is a strong tendency to rush legislation through in the last few days of a session rather than to even out the workload over several months. Thus structural reforms may not change traditional approaches to legislation.

Political scientist Alan Rosenthal speaks of the "congressionalization of the legislature" as committee systems are strengthened, staff is increased, the number and variety of interest groups grow, tenure is longer, salaries increase, and the number of full-time professional politicians in statehouses expands.[16] As in Congress, power tends to be more fragmented as party and committee leaders find it more difficult to control members. Campaigns are more candidate-centered and party designation becomes less important. As costs increase, legislators spend more time raising money and less time on legislative matters. The accompanying reading discusses the changing nature of state legislatures from part-time to full-time employment and their growth in power relative to the governor. It then points out that as legislatures have gained power they also increasingly have come under attack, and their standing with the public has deteriorated.

POLITICAL PARTIES IN THE LEGISLATURE

As noted in the previous section, legislatures organize by party to elect floor leaders (speaker and majority leader); all committee heads are selected from among the majority party in the legislature; and in some states, members of each party caucus on a regular basis to determine a party position on various pieces of legislation.

A basic goal of the party organization is to produce the votes necessary to pass specific bills. However, the degree to which parties are successful in controlling their members' votes varies greatly among the states. In urban, industrial states with strong two-party systems, party control of voting behavior is clearly evident. As state politics becomes dominated by one party, factions develop and party discipline weakens. Often it is difficult to measure party unity in voting because many roll call votes are unanimous and there are few instances in which one party is pitted against the other in voting. In spite of these problems, party membership remains the single most important influence on legislative voting.

Party control has been weakening as legislators become more independent from state and local party organizations and as voters become more independent and less likely to vote a straight party ticket. In the past it was assumed that legislators elected from safe districts would be most likely to follow the party line in voting and those in the most competitive districts would be the most deviant. Various studies indicate, however, that the degree of interparty competition has relatively little effect on legislators' voting behavior. There does seem to be a positive correlation between the results of the gubernatorial race in a legislative district and party loyalty. In Pennsylvania, Ohio, and Michigan, where parties follow a clear urban-rural alignment, party cohesion is strong. In states such as California and Missouri, where Democrats and Republicans are not divided sharply along urban-rural lines, party cohesion is weak. Also, in California there is a strong tradition of nonpartisanship in which legislators do not wish to be perceived as captives of their party. Daily caucuses occur in about 15 percent of state legislatures while about half the states have weekly caucuses. There seems to be less direct influence by interest groups on legislators in states that have strong party cohesion.

In many two-party, competitive states, party discipline far exceeds that found in Congress. Several factors at the state level help explain this.[17] Because state committee heads have relatively less power than those in Congress and because there is less deference to seniority in state legislatures, there are fewer competing sources of power with which the party must contend. Patronage continues to be an effective way for state party leaders to reward loyalists. In Congress little patronage remains. State party organizations are able to control legislators more effectively than national parties because of the legislators' electoral dependence on the state party. Occasionally, state party leaders such as Jess Unruh may also occupy legislative leadership posts. State legislators are less able than members of Congress to build their own campaign organizations and therefore must rely more heavily on the party for electoral support. Finally, when state parties are divided along urban-rural and socioeconomic lines, legislators of each party are likely to share common backgrounds and are likely to have a common view of policy priorities. Because of their close personal relations, they are tolerant of party discipline. By contrast, in Congress, the Democratic party, for example, must attempt to accommodate the ideas of representatives from rural Southern districts as well as those from urban Northern districts.

Although party discipline often is stronger in states than in Congress, there also are cases where state legislatures are organized and controlled by **cross-party coalitions.** For example, in 1989 the Florida senate was run by a coalition of conservative Democrats and Republicans. In North Carolina and Connecticut, Democrats and Republicans joined forces to replace longtime House speakers. Coalitions are more likely to exist in Southern states because of the organizational weakness of the Democratic party and the fact that liberal-conservative differences are more important than party designations.[18]

Although there is a built-in antagonism between political parties, former Iowa governor Harold E. Hughes believes there is a deeper split between the legislature and the governor than between the parties.[19] Hughes feels that neither the governor nor the legislature understands the problems of the other. He argues that legislative reforms such as annual sessions, additional staff, and research assistance will help bridge the gap between the two branches of government, because the public will demand more constructive action from the legislature and legislators will be forced to work more closely with the governor.

THE LEGISLATURE AND THE GOVERNOR

Much of the history of state government can be written in terms of reforms that have changed weak governorships into strong executive offices modeled on the presidency. Governors, like presidents, act as "chief legislators" who develop legislative programs and set the agenda for legislative action. Assisted by ever-expanding numbers of staff, governors are constitutionally empowered to prepare state budgets, present messages to the legislature, call special legislative sessions, and veto bills.

Another similarity between governors and presidents is that governors often exercise their most effective legislative leadership by informal means. As the head of his or her state's party, the governor can bring pressure on legislators to support a program or face a loss of electoral support. With party leaders, governors also control sizable numbers of patronage jobs. Sorauf and Beck estimate that Pennsylvania had 50,000 patronage positions in 1970.[20] Although patronage jobs are declining in number, they still give governors, particularly in low-income states, considerable leverage in creating feelings of obligation among legislators whose constituents benefit directly from the awarding of patronage positions. Seeking similar results, governors may influence the awarding of contracts and the location of public works projects that will benefit local economic interests and indirectly give political support to legislators who can claim credit for helping their constituents. As the most visible and newsworthy political figure in the state, the governor can gain valuable media attention and take his or her programs directly to the people if legislators appear reluctant to respond to gubernatorial initiatives.

Just as in Washington, there are basic clashes in perspective between legislators and the chief executive. As Rosenthal points out, these include:

1. *District/state difference,* in which, of course, the governor's concern must be much broader than that of a legislator who represents a relatively small district.
2. *Special-interest/general-interest difference,* in which legislators may feel they must represent some narrow interests if they want to get reelected.
3. *Piecemeal/comprehensive difference,* in which legislators are less likely than governors to look at the "big picture" and instead focus more on the operational level of policymaking.
4. *Compromise/coherence difference,* in which legislators put more emphasis on backroom compromise, following the path of least resistance.
5. *Short-range/long-range difference,* in which legislators focus more on immediate concerns—getting their own bills passed in a session—than does the governor.
6. *Collective responsibility/individual responsibility difference,* in which legislators, of course, share responsibility and governors are open to direct blame.[21]

In many one-party Southern states, governors play a major role in organizing the legislature and selecting its leadership. Where opposition from a competing party is absent, governors tend to have stronger influence among legislators.

It has been difficult for states to maintain a satisfactory balance of power between their governors and legislatures. Although the governor should have full control over administrative personnel, the legislature should be capable of developing its own programs and of evaluating the actions of the governor. On occasion, governors are weak and unable or unwilling to act. In such instances, the legislature must be able to take the initiative and participate actively in policymaking. As we will see in Chapter 6, there has been significant reform of the executive branch since the 1960s. In a sense, the strengthening of gubernatorial power has also bolstered legislative power, and both branches have been able to increase their influence.

LEGISLATIVE OVERSIGHT

With the growth of gubernatorial power and the expansion of state administrative bureaucracies, legislatures have struggled to find ways to check executive authority. Because their attention tends to be focused on immediate policy issues, such as school finance or taxes, legislators find it difficult to deal with the long-range review (oversight) of bureaucrats. For example, the real challenge in budgeting often comes after legislative approval, when allotment procedures and executive transfers can change legislative intent.

Legislative oversight takes many forms.[22] Legislators are constantly being asked by constituents for help in dealing with state agencies. In responding to a particular problem, legislators may be prompted to review in more general terms how an agency is performing. In the budget process, several committees—appropriations, ways and means, and finance—review requests from state agencies, and this allows legislators to examine how well the agencies are performing. After funds have been appropriated and programs have been enacted, legislatures are devoting more time to evaluation. More than forty states have an auditor selected by the legislature to evaluate programs in terms of effectiveness and efficiency. In addition, legislators are increasingly reviewing the ways in which federal funds are spent in their states. With recent cuts in federal grants, this has become an increasingly critical procedure.

Since the mid-1970s a majority of the states have enacted **sunset laws,** which call for the termination of specified executive agencies unless the legislature formally reviews and extends their programs. At one time thirty-six states had enacted such laws, but six states repealed them and six others allowed the laws to lapse into inactivity.[23] Generally the agencies that have been terminated have been minor and had lost their usefulness. Most states also have provisions for legislative review of administrative rules and regulations that have been established by state agencies. Several states now hold special veto sessions after the end of the regular sessions to consider bills vetoed by the governor. States that seldom overrode governors' vetoes in the past now regularly do so.

As in all areas of legislative work, there are questions that need to be addressed regarding the best way for the legislature to act effectively without delegating too much to professional staff and without undermining the morale of administrators. Alan Rosenthal offers the following note of caution:

> The legislature must recognize that in oversight, as in anything else, it cannot do everything. To try to do everything is to wind up doing nothing, or at least nothing well. The legislature will have to pick and choose what to pursue and where to put its energies. Like the executive branch, to whom it relates, the legislature will have to set priorities for itself. Not all constraints of oversight are the same. Not all merit the same attention or the same resources. Not every administrative agency, not every policy, not every program merits review. Not every problem that is uncovered merits a legislative recommendation; not every one has a legislative solution (or perhaps any solution at all).[24]

LOCAL LEGISLATURES: CITIES, COUNTIES, AND TOWNS

If it is dangerous to make generalizations about fifty state legislatures, the pitfalls clearly are multiplied when presenting an overview of *councils* in nearly 20,000 municipalities. Councils vary in size from fifty members in Chicago to nine members in Toledo, Boston, and Pittsburgh. In most cities, council members (or aldermen) devote only part of their time to city business and continue their full-time employment, often as local merchants or, in large cities, as lawyers. Typically, their pay reflects this part-time service and is nominal. Only in the largest cities are council members paid well and do they devote full time to their public employment.

Currently almost all city councils are unicameral, although at the turn of the century many large cities had bicameral councils. At that time it also was common to elect council members by wards. There has been a trend toward at-large elections in all but the largest cities as well as a trend toward nonpartisan elections.

Reformers believe that at-large elections lessen the inclination toward a parochial outlook and logrolling, which are common in cities with ward elections. *Logrolling* refers to the trading of votes among council members to achieve passage of projects of interest to one another. However, as noted earlier, blacks and ethnic minorities are disadvantaged by at-large elections, in which their voting strength is diluted. The typical council member is a man who owns a small business and is only slightly better educated and more affluent than his constituents.

When council members exhibit low levels of professionalization (and this is widespread in large and small cities), it is easy for the mayor or city manager to dominate their decision making. It also is common for city councils to act on behalf of strong local interests such as realtors, builders, or main-street merchants when making city policy. The degree of council participation in decision making is greatly affected by the form of city government (see Chapter 6). Where there is a weak-mayor system or a commission system, the council will have considerable formal authority. In cities with strong mayors or managers, the basic function of council members is often to act as representatives to bring complaints to the attention of city hall. In most cities, councils are passive and seldom act as policy innovators. Their most common role is to oppose rather than to propose policy. Because turnover is high and voter participation low, it is difficult to hold council members accountable by threatening to defeat them in the next election. In most cases, incumbents are re-elected or they retire voluntarily from office. Often they retire before the end of their term, allowing the mayor to appoint a successor, who then has the advantages of incumbency in the next election. In such a situation, the general public is limited in its ability to influence public policy through legislative representatives.

A few cities use a **commission form of government,** in which several (usually three to nine) commissioners, elected at-large, exercise both legislative and executive authority. The commissioners are organized as heads of various city departments (public works, parks, finance), and they also act collectively to pass ordinances and control spending (see Figure 5.2). Often a mayor is selected from among the commissioners, but his or her duties are largely ceremonial.

After its initiation in Galveston, Texas, in 1903, use of the commission plan spread quickly, and by 1917 it was in operation in about 500 cities. But its use has declined significantly in recent years. Only about 3 percent of all cities now have a commission form of government—only two of them (Tulsa and Portland) being cities with population over 250,000. Even Galveston now has a manager form of government.

The commission plan has many disadvantages. Because it does not provide for the separation of powers, it places little control on spending and administration. In most cities it is difficult to attract top-quality persons to serve as commissioners, and thus government business is often in the hands of amateurs. Without a chief executive, it is difficult to pinpoint responsibility. As with county governments, the small size of the commission does not foster debate and criticism, and it encourages a fraternity of tolerance. City commissioners often practice a mutual hands-off policy from one another's functional areas, and each moves in his or her own direction without overall coordination. (Other forms of city government are discussed in Chapter 6.)

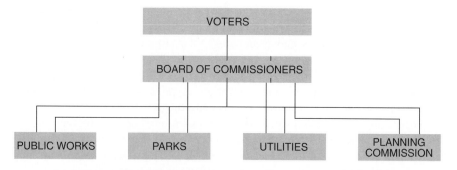

USUALLY SMALL MEMBERSHIP (4–7 MEMBERS). COMMISSIONERS EACH SERVE AS DEPARTMENT HEADS. COMMISSIONERS SIT AS A LEGISLATIVE BODY. OFTEN ONE COMMISSIONER ACTS AS MAYOR (POWER EQUAL TO OTHER COMMISSIONERS).

Figure 5.2   Hypothetical Commission Plan

Traditionally, most counties have been administered by a three- or five-member board of commissioners. However, many counties have moved to council-manager or an executive selected by the council. Currently about 40 percent of counties have boards of commissioners, 38 percent have a manager, and 22 percent have an executive selected by the board of commissioners. Counties are found in all states except Connecticut and Rhode Island (Louisiana calls them "parishes" and Alaska, "boroughs"), although they have never been important in the New England states, where the town remains the basic unit of local government. The size and number of counties vary greatly. Delaware and Hawaii have only 3 counties each, while Texas has 254. San Bernardino County, California, is larger than Vermont and New Hampshire combined. In contrast to Los Angeles, Cook (Chicago), and Harris (Houston) counties—each of which has over 3 million people—there are about 700 rural counties with populations of less than 10,000. Alaska, Arizona, and New Mexico each created a new county in the 1980s. Counties have traditionally performed a wide variety of functions in the areas of health, welfare, education, criminal justice, maintenance of roads, and record keeping.

Counties have been given additional functions in recent years as the administrative units for federal and state programs in the areas of social welfare, education, and crime control. Although rural counties have traditionally been the most important unit of government within their geographical areas, urban counties have been gaining significant authority. In some states, home-rule charters allow counties to perform functions that previously were city responsibilities. These include water supply, library services, sewage disposal, flood control, and management of airports. Counties that are neither urban nor rural—so-called 50-50 areas (they are 50 miles from a metropolitan area and have populations of around 50,000)—are experiencing new demands from affluent families who are moving away from cities yet still want many urban services.

The **town** continues to be the basic form of local government in New England.

In colonial America, a "town" included a village and its surrounding farms. It is here that the fabled town meeting met to levy taxes, determine how money would be spent, and elect the next year's "selectmen." The selectmen acted in a manner similar to county commissioners to oversee the administration of schools, roads, health, and welfare.

As counties were established and municipalities became incorporated, the towns' functions became more limited. Because attendance at town meetings declined, a representative town-meeting plan has been devised whereby the voters choose a large number of citizens (around 100) to attend the town meeting and represent their views. School consolidation also has limited the responsibilities of town governments. In many instances, the administration of local services has been turned over to a town manager.

In a similar fashion, the **township** continues to function as an intermediate form of government in the Middle Atlantic and Midwestern states. In the Midwest, townships were carefully laid out in six-mile squares. Midwest counties were designed so that no one would be more than a day's driving time from the county seat, and the township hall was within a one-hour buggy ride. While some townships continue to use an annual town meeting, many elect trustees to act as legislators as well as administrators. Rural townships have transferred much of their authority (e.g., repair of roads and bridges) to counties. In many urban areas, townships continue only as units for representation on the county board. In a few wealthy, suburban areas (in Pennsylvania and Kansas, for example), townships have gained powers nearly equal to those of cities.

CHANGES IN STATE LEGISLATURES

As noted earlier in this chapter, to receive a high evaluation, legislatures must perform well their basic tasks of representation, administrative oversight, and policy initiation. Because many legislatures perform ineffectively, reformers view legislative change as an urgent matter. Yet there are many barriers to reform. Public awareness of legislatures is very low, and thus few people are concerned about legislative improvement. Often governors are indifferent or hostile to reform, which they believe threatens their power position. Legislatures are usually poorly covered by the press, so that problems are not brought to the public's attention to the degree they are with Congress.

As we will see in Chapter 6, legislative reform lagged behind changes in the executive branch. As governors by the late 1950s gained longer tenure, stronger veto power, and more budget control, legislators continued to be hampered by nineteenth-century limits on the length of sessions, salaries, and the nature of legislative districts. During this period, the Citizens' Conference on State Legislatures described legislatures as "marked by wholesale corruption at worst and mediocrity at best."

Reform in the 1970s centered on institutional and procedural matters. By 1980, forty-three states had instituted annual sessions; pay was increased; staff became professionalized; and legislatures could call themselves into session. By the late 1970s, legislators began to shift their attention to making more efficient use of their time. Several states placed limitations on the number of bills that could be introduced. Interim committees were created to allow consideration of bills before the legislative session. Deadlines were placed on the introduction of bills during legislative sessions. Committees were consolidated and their authority increased, and joint house-senate committees were formed. One of the most significant changes has been increased legislative staffing. In the 1980s, increased attention was given to executive oversight, and legislatures have entered the age of computers and information processing.

The effects of this process of legislative modernization include the following.[25] Legislatures are more independent of the governor and better able to develop policy on their own. Legislators have become more specialized and, with the help of added staff, better able to understand technical problems. As committees and individual legislators have become stronger, the centralization of legislatures, which previously existed around party leaders, has weakened. In many ways, state legislatures have come to resemble the U.S. Congress. This is true in regard to the role of committees, increased staff, longer tenure, independent sources of campaign finance, and in the increased attention directed to constituency service. The good news is that these changes have made legislatures better equipped to make policy and to check gubernatorial power. The bad news is that it has made them more fragmented, more political, and more partisan.[26]

Perhaps the most significant issue in the changing nature of state legislatures is whether they should be considered full-time bodies. On the one hand, some people want to cling to the notion of citizen-legislators who work part-time and remain in close contact with their constituents. In this model there is usually a desire to keep lawmaking at a minimum. On the other hand, most legislatures have increased their time in session in order to deal with the complexities of program oversight and budget making.

Those who support the part-time lawmaker, or citizen-legislator, argue that career legislators lose touch with their constituents when they spend too much time in the capital. As the new breed of legislator spends more time campaigning and eyes higher political office, it is contended that he or she will be more influenced by funds provided by interest groups. A more full-time legislature also makes it less attractive for people in certain occupations, such as law, farming, and business, to run for office. It is suggested that there will be a shift to more legislators who are independently wealthy or retired. At the same time, full-time legislatures are attracting more women and more young people. These people should be freer of the conflicts of interests that have traditionally marked the part-time farmer or businessperson serving in state legislatures.

As we have seen, the "New Federalism" programs and the federal budget deficit have made state legislatures the focal point of action on many domestic policy issues. We can expect this trend to continue in the 1990s. As more demands are placed on legislatures, the amount of "professionalization" will increase and members will have to seek more ways to streamline the legislative process.

KEY TERMS

Advertiser legislators Those who view legislative service as a way to further their careers. Ambitious young lawyers are the most typical.

Baker **v.** *Carr* **(1962)** The Supreme Court decision that ruled for the first time that legislative apportionment is a proper matter for judicial review. Led to widespread reapportionment of state legislatures.

Bicameral legislature A legislature with two chambers; typically a house and senate.

Commission form of government Used in only a few large cities, a type of city government headed by a board of commissioners (five to ten members) rather than by a single mayor or city manager.

Cross-party coalitions Cooperation between Democrats and Republicans in a few states to organize legislative chambers and select leaders from both parties.

Gerrymandering Drawing legislative districts in such a way that one political party or faction has a clear advantage and thus should control a majority of the total seats.

Initiative A procedure whereby citizens can bypass legislatures and propose new statutes or changes in government charters; these proposals are then placed on the ballot for voter approval.

Lawmaker legislators Those who carry the main burden of making policy.

Legislative apportionment The allocation of legislative seats by dividing a state into voting districts that are approximately equal in population. Past failure to reapportion on a regular basis led to malapportioned legislatures in many states.

"Professionalized" state legislature Those legislatures characterized by higher salaries, increased staff support, more flexible procedures, and improved methods of overseeing the executive branch.

Recall A procedure whereby petitions are circulated calling for removal of a public official from office. If a sufficient number of signatures is obtained, an election is held in which voters decide whether or not to keep the official in office.

Referendum A procedure whereby citizens can vote for or against proposals recommended by a legislative body.

Reluctant legislators Those who were pressured to run and find "politics" unpleasant.

Self-starters Candidates who decide to run on their own initiative without strong encouragement from political parties or interest groups.

Spectator legislators Those who find legislative work "interesting" but are passive members.

Sunset laws Laws passed by state legislatures providing that the powers of specified executive agencies will expire after a certain date unless renewed by the legislature.

Town A unit of local government in New England that includes an urban center and its surrounding rural area. Performs functions similar to those of cities and counties in other states.

Township A unit of local government found principally in the Middle Atlantic and Midwestern states. Midwestern townships typically cover 36 square miles and exclude municipal areas. Township responsibilities include law enforcement and maintenance of roads.

Unicameral legislature A legislature with a single chamber or house.

REFERENCES

1. See John Burns, *The Sometime Governments* (New York: Bantam Books, 1971).
2. Rich Jones, "The State Legislatures," in *The Book of the States 1990–91* (Lexington, Ky.: Council of State Governments, 1990), p. 110.
3. Samuel C. Patterson, "State Legislators and the Legislatures" in Virginia Gray, Herbert Jacob, and Robert B. Albritton, eds., *Politics in the American States,* 5th ed. (Glenview, Ill: Scott, Foresman/Little, Brown, 1990), pp. 178–179.
4. James David Barber, *The Lawmakers* (New Haven: Yale University Press, 1965).
5. See Robert B. McKay, "Affirmative Gerrymandering," in Bernard Grofman et al., *Representation and Redistricting Issues* (Lexington, Mass.: Lexington Books, 1982), pp. 91–94, and David C. Saffell, "Affirmative Gerrymandering: Rationale and Application," *State Government,* vol. 56, no.4, (1983), pp. 140–151.
6. V. O. Key, *American State Politics: An Introduction* (New York: Knopf, 1956), pp. 52–84.
7. Morris P. Fiorina, "Divided Government in the States," *PS: Political Science and Politics,* December 1991, p. 648.
8. See Timothy O'Rourke, *The Impact of Reapportionment* (New Brunswick, N.J.: Transaction Books, 1980), and David C. Saffell, "Reapportionmemt and Public Policy: State Legislators' Perspectives," *Policy Studies Journal,* vol. 9, no. 6 (Special #3, 1980–1981).
9. See Charles M. Price, "The Initiative: A Comparative Analysis and Reassessment of a Western Phenomenon," *Western Political Quarterly,* June 1975.
10. Patterson, "State Legislators and Legislatures," pp. 193–194.
11. Jess Unruh, "Unicameralism—The Wave of the Future," in Donald G. Herzberg and Alan Rosenthal, eds., *Strengthening the States: Essays on Legislative Reform* (Garden City, N.Y.: Anchor Books, 1972), p. 87.
12. Jones, "The State Legislatures," p. 111.
13. William J. Keefe and Morris S. Ogul, *The Legislative Process,* 7th ed. (Englewood Cliffs, N.J.: Prentice-Hall, 1989), p. 194.
14. Alan Rosenthel, *Legislative Life* (New York: Harper & Row, 1981), p. 195.
15. See Alan Rosenthal, "A Vanishing Breed," *State Legislatures,* November–December 1989, pp. 30–34.
16. Alan Rosenthal, *Governors and Legislators: Contending Powers* (Washington; D.C.: Congressional Quarterly Press, 1990), pp. 62–64.
17. Frank J. Sorauf and Paul Allen Beck, *Party Politics in America,* 6th ed. (Boston: Little, Brown, 1988), pp. 406–408.
18. See Karen Hansen, "Are Coalitions Really on the Rise?," *State Legislatures,* April 1989, pp. 11–12.
19. Harold E. Hughes, "From the Governor's Chair . . .," in Herzberg and Rosenthal, eds., *Strengthening the States: Essays on Legislative Reform* (Garden City, N.Y.: Anchor Books, 1972), p. 112.
20. Sorauf and Beck, *Party Politics,* p. 105.
21. Rosenthal, *Governors and Legislators,* pp. 52–55.
22. Alan Rosenthal, "Legislative Oversight and the Balance of Power in State Government," *State Government,* vol. 56, no.3 (1983), pp. 93–95.
23. Thad L. Beyle, "The Executive Branch: Organization and Issues, 1988–89," *The Book of the States 1990–91,* p. 78.

24. Rosenthal, "Legislative Oversight," p. 97.
25. See William T. Pound, "Legislatures," in *The Book of the States 1988–89,* p. 79, and Rich Jones, "The State Legislatures," in *The Book of the States 1990–91,* p. 115.
26. Alan Rosenthal, "The New Legislature: Better or Worse and for Whom," *State Legislatures,* July 1986.

CHAPTER 6

GOVERNORS, MAYORS, AND BUREAUCRATS

As noted in the last chapter, executive-branch reform preceded legislative reform in the 1950s and 1960s. State governors emerged with much stronger formal authority, and bureaucracies were streamlined. As more power has been turned over to the states since 1980, governors have been well equipped to respond with effective leadership, and they have become major policymaking forces across the country. A measure of their increased prestige is that in 1988 a large number of governors were serious contenders for presidential and vice presidential nominations. In addition, several members of Congress and cabinet officers gave up their positions in the 1980s and 1990s to run for governor and lieutenant governor.

CHIEF EXECUTIVES: A HISTORICAL OVERVIEW

The history of state government has been marked by an increasing centralization of power in the hands of the chief executives. As the nation became more urbanized and industrialized, demands for services grew, and nineteenth-century government structures were unable to respond to society's complex needs. Governor and mayors were handicapped by constitutions and charters that provided for short terms of office, limits on reelection, the election of many lesser executives, and limits on their authority to appoint and remove administrative officials. When the early state constitutions were written, all government power was distrusted, but executives were particularly suspect because of the colonial experience under King George III. Legislatures dominated early state government—in ten of the original states the legislature chose the governor, and in only one state did the governor have the power to veto. Virginia did not elect its governor until 1851.

During the **Jacksonian era,** the prestige of chief executives was enhanced. Pushed by disclosure of legislative corruption and incompetence, states extended the terms of governors and added the veto power. However, the movement for "popular democracy" brought continuing structural restraints. The long ballot was generally used, and it meant that most state and local administrators were elected, rather than being appointed by the chief executive. Short terms continued to ensure rotation in office, and because of patronage many amateurs were placed in high-level administrative positions. This attitude toward government dominated nineteenth-century thinking, and most of the state constitutions were written during this period.

In the last quarter of the nineteenth century, the reform movement gained momentum in response to widespread corruption in state and local government (see references to urban political machines in Chapter 3). Reformers concluded that partisan political activities were responsible for many of the problems of state and local government. In the early twentieth century, this antipolitical sentiment was translated into policies aimed at limiting the power of political parties. Civil service systems were created to replace patronage; the number of boards and commissions that operated independently from governors and mayors was increased; nonpartisan elections were instituted; and the city-manager plan was created.

Many twentieth-century reforms fall under the heading **administrative efficiency.** While reformers also stressed merit appointments, they called for improved coordination and control of administrative actions to centralize administrative authority and responsibility. Urbanization, the Great Depression, and the growth of federal welfare programs administered by the states placed increasing burdens on state and local governments. In most cases, states were unable to respond to these new demands because of corruption, malapportionment, and weak constitutional powers for governors and legislatures. As a result, they invited an increase in federal authority. Study commissions after World War II called for a reduction in the number of state departments and advocated stronger gubernatorial authority to provide for coordination and management of state government.

Since 1950, gubernatorial powers have continued to increase whenever changes have been made by constitutional conventions or by legislative action. Reapportionment has reduced the influence of rural legislators, who historically have been hostile toward executive authority. Another factor helping to strengthen the role of governors has been the general acceptance of the view that chief executives should maximize their power in the manner of Franklin D. Roosevelt. The presidential model still continues to have a strong influence on people's willingness to support strong executive authority at all levels. Certainly, since the 1930s the executive branch had dominated government affairs in both state capitols and city halls.

Along with increased responsibilities have come higher salaries for governors. In only one state (Arkansas) is the governor's salary less than $50,000. When former Vice President Spiro T. Agnew was governor of Maryland in the 1960s (he later was accused of accepting kickbacks from firms doing business with the state), he was paid $15,000. Still, governors' salaries remain much lower than those of chief executive officers in private business and those of many other state employees. For example, the president of The Ohio State University receives a salary nearly twice as high as the governor's. Even more than deans of law schools and medical schools, university coaches can claim to be the highest-paid state employees. For example, the football coach at the University of Illinois had a 1990 salary of $149,950 plus $35,000 as athletic director and $45,000 for directing a football camp. In addition he had athletic shoe and radio/television contracts. Estimates are that Indiana basketball coach Bob Knight earns $750,000 a year from university and outside sources.

The responsibilities of governors have grown substantially for several reasons. State government activities have become more complex; public expectations about how government should perform have risen; the states' role in intergovernmental relations has grown; and there has been a move for financial restraint. As a result, governors must manage larger bureaucracies, they must deal with local governments that want more money and a federal government that wants to give states less money, and they must contend with more active and professional legislators. Larry Sabato believes that there is an emerging new breed of governors who are "much younger, better educated than ever, and more thoroughly trained for their specific responsibilities."[1]

THE SELECTION AND TENURE OF GOVERNORS

The typical governor is a white male lawyer in his late forties. Like presidents and U.S. senators, governors are usually family men who have served in the military, and in general they present an all-American image. In states with strong party organizations (e.g., Massachusetts and Ohio), there is often a pattern of service in the state legislature and tenure as the assembly speaker or in some statewide elective position such as lieutenant governor. For example, Michael Dukakis served for eight years in the Massachusetts house (1963–1971) and he was nominated for lieutenant governor (1970) before being elected governor in 1975. About 25 percent of governors since 1950 have had experience in the state legislature, and only 10 percent have not held public office before their election. In the South, governors often have in their backgrounds service in judicial or law enforcement posts. Occasionally governors step into office without prior elective government experience. Ronald Reagan, Edmund G. Brown, Jr., and Nelson Rockefeller are examples of governors who had never previously been elected to public office. In each of these exceptional cases, the political newcomer was helped by the weakness of state political parties, by the familiarity of his name, by his family wealth, or by some combination of those factors.

The experience of the late governor Ella Grasso of Connecticut makes a good case study of how to become governor in an urban, industrial, competitive, two-party state. Grasso was the first woman ever to be elected governor (1974, 1978) without succeeding her husband; yet her background of twenty-two years of activity in the Democratic party and election to statewide office in Connecticut are typical of the career pattern for many governors. Currently, there are three female governors—Joan Finney of Kansas, Barbara Roberts of Oregon, and Ann Richards of Texas—all elected in 1990. Diane Feinstein, a former mayor of San Francisco, was narrowly defeated in her bid to become governor of California in 1990, and incumbent Kay Orr lost in Nebraska. Three other women, all Republicans, lost their bids to become governor. In 1989 Virginia lieutenant governor Douglas Wilder became the first black elected governor since Reconstruction.

All but three states (New Hampshire, Rhode Island, and Vermont) now provide a four-year term for their governors. Recently voters in Vermont and Rhode Island rejected proposals to increase their governors' terms to four years, and Arkansas switched to a four-year term in the mid-1980s. In 1789, Connecticut, Massachusetts, New Hampshire, and Rhode Island held gubernatorial elections every year. In 1992, twenty-nine states restricted their governors to no more than two four-year terms. In spite of the longer tenure potential, few governors can expect to remain in office more than eight years, and of all major political positions, governorships are second only to the presidency in their lack of security.

In recent years, it has been common to think of governors as becoming increasingly vulnerable in terms of their chances to succeed themselves in office. Since the electorate wants both increased state services and lower taxes, governors are faced with a dilemma. If they balance the state budget but do not increase services, they may lose in their bid for reelection. If they increase services and raise taxes to pay for them, they again may lose in their bid for reelection. Finally, if they increase services but do not raise adequate revenues, they may be labeled financially irresponsible, which again may cost them the election. For example, first-term Nebraska governor Kay Orr was defeated in 1990 after breaking her pledge not to raise taxes. Her opponent warned voters, "Don't be fooled again."

When the hypothesis of vulnerability was tested by J. Stephen Turett, it was discovered that governors actually have been *less* vulnerable to reelection defeat since 1930.[2] Turett's study indicated that governors are running further ahead of their party's congressional nominees than ever before. In comparing states to determine whether there were particular factors that increased gubernatorial vulnerability, Turett found *no* strong correlation with economic or demographic differences nor with differences in levels of urbanization, unemployment, expenditures, or taxes among the states. On the average, a governor has at least a 70 percent chance of being reelected to a second term. Election losses by governors who had recently raised taxes seemed to peak in the 1960s. Still, most governors remain cautious. Current governors forced to raise taxes can take hope in the example of Ronald Reagan, who as governor requested and received the largest tax increase in California's history.

Political scientist Thad Beyle notes that incumbency has become a stronger factor in electoral success for governors. In the period 1977–1989 eligible incumbents sought reelection 78 percent of the time and were successful in 74 percent of those elections.[3] However, in 1990 six of twenty-three incumbents seeking reelection were defeated (a 74 percent success rate). In comparison, only one incumbent U.S. senator was defeated. There was a swing in control of fourteen governorships from one party to the other, and independents were elected in Alaska and Connecticut. New York governor Mario Cuomo was narrowly reelected with 53 percent of the vote. Economic bad times and abortion rights were the major issues in several elections. In 1991 incumbent governor Buddy Roemer lost in the Louisiana primary, and former Democratic governor Edwin Edwards defeated David Duke in a runoff election that gained national attention. In 1992 Democrats held governorships in twenty-eight states (see Figure 6.1). This includes Vermont, where the Republican governor died in August 1991 and was replaced by the Democratic lieutenant governor.

Governors may gain added security if the trend to hold gubernatorial elections in nonpresidential election years continues. All the states but one (North Dakota) that have switched to four-year terms for governors in this century have scheduled gubernatorial elections in nonpresidential years. Only in eight states do gubernatorial elections occur in presidential years. (In the three states that still have two-year terms, every other gubernatorial election does, of course, occur in a presidential election year.) This procedural change means that gubernatorial elections are becoming more independent of national trends. One effect has been that the proportion of incumbent governors who have been defeated when seeking reelection has declined in the past thirty years.

Governors often resign or retire voluntarily in order to run for federal office. About 25 percent of all senators have been governors, and a substantial number of governors have obtained appointments to the cabinet or other federal administrative positions (e.g., the original Nixon cabinet in 1969 had three former governors). A few governors move on to some other state office, and some receive federal judgeships. Traditionally, governors from large states have been a major source of presidential candidates. Of the first thirty-one men to serve as president (through Franklin D. Roosevelt), thirteen were former governors (three of them had served

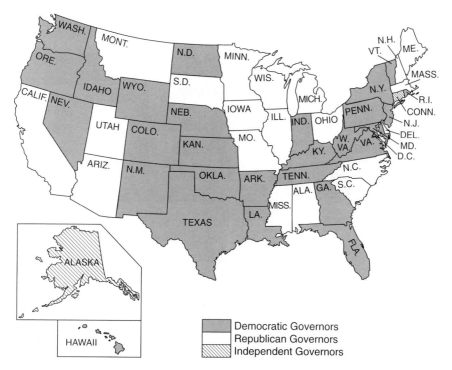

Figure 6.1   Governors for 1992

as governor of Virginia and three as governor of New York). After Roosevelt, no governor was elected president until Jimmy Carter in 1976. Since 1976, there has been a substantial increase in the number of governors who have been serious presidential contenders.

With an increasing number of voters identifying themselves as independents, and with issues often being downplayed in campaigns, the personal characteristics of candidates will continue to play an important role in their reelection success. Looking to the near future, Jewell and Olson offer the following prediction:

> The highly successful gubernatorial candidate of the future is likely to be one who is capable of appealing across party lines, who knows how to make effective use of the media, who has attractive personal qualities—rather than one who has climbed the ladder of political office by winning the support of party leaders and workers. It is not necessarily true that anyone who can afford an expensive television advertising campaign and who hires a good PR firm can win elections, but it is true that use of television and other media is frequently crucial to the success of campaigns. If the voters are relying less on party loyalty than on their perception of candidates, the care and feeding of the candidate's image become highly important.[4]

THE FORMAL POWERS OF GOVERNORS

In a much-cited comparative analysis of governors, Joseph A. Schlesinger studied five major gubernatorial powers to define the strength of governors and then to ob-

tain an overall measure of the relative political impact of governors on the administration of the states.[5] A summary of Schlesinger's analysis of gubernatorial powers,
as updated by Thad Beyle, follows.[6]

Tenure Potential

As noted earlier, governors have traditionally had short terms of office. In ten of the
original thirteen states, the governor was limited to a term of one year. In two other
states the term was two years, and in one state it was three years. States moved first
to two-year terms (by the 1840s), and now forty-seven states have four-year terms.
However, some states prohibit reelection; and in recent years more states have followed the model of the Twenty-second Amendment, prohibiting their governors
from serving more than two consecutive terms. Southern states historically provided short gubernatorial terms. As a general rule, governors with short tenure potential are weakened in their role as policy leaders. A four-year term allows governors
the time to prove themselves—policies enacted during their first two years (e.g., the
creation of a state income tax) can be evaluated by reelection time two years later.
The ability to succeed oneself in office means that the governor will not be a lame
duck who the legislature knows cannot run for reelection. Also, extended tenure allows a governor to attract national attention. The possibility of being able to secure
a federal position through a former governor who has been elected to Congress can
bring extra support from legislators and administrators. Longer tenure also helps
governors in their relations with other states, as they become leaders of interstate
organizations, including the National Governors Association. Governors are relatively equal in tenure potential, since forty-seven of them have four-year terms.
However, only eighteen of the governors with four-year terms are free from restraints on reelection.

The Power of Appointment

Governors are strongest when they alone make appointments. Appointive power di-
minishes when one or two houses of the legislature must approve appointments or
if the appointment is made by a department director. If the position is elective, then
the governor's formal power reaches zero. Thus the use of the long ballot in state
elections and the presence of numerous independent boards and commissions are
factors that tend to weaken governors. Governors who are free to appoint major
state officials can select people whose political views are similar to theirs and who
will feel a sense of obligation to them.

Just as the governor's political power is lessened when the legislature is controlled by the opposition party, it is also adversely affected when the office of lieutenant governor or attorney general is an elective one and a member of the opposition party is elected. Governors need to be able to appoint to top-level posts those
people who share their views and priorities in order to be able to propose a strong
program and put it into action. But even when governors have the power to make
appointments they may be weakened because of the difficulty in getting the best
people to accept state jobs. First-rate people may refuse appointments because of

low pay and the location of some capitals in remote areas. Also, governors may face strong political pressure to appoint certain people.

In addition, governors need strong removal power (which they seldom have) to make the power of appointment truly effective. In many cases governors' removal power is limited because specific causes must be cited or the process requires approval by the legislature. As noted in Chapter 3, court decisions have limited dismissal for purely political reasons. Many governors have pushed for the reduction of patronage. Although they want to make top-level appointments, they do not want to be burdened with naming people to minor positions. As a result, many governors have led movements to broaden civil service programs.

Organizational Power

Along with the ability to make appointments, the governor needs the power to reorganize state administrative agencies and personnel without seeking legislative approval. Specific suggested reforms in this area are as follows:

1. Moving to a four-year term for the governor.
2. Moving to a short ballot, reducing the number of elected statewide officials to three or four—governor, lieutenant governor, attorney general, and possibly auditor.
3. Shifting control of state departments from commissions to a single removable appointee of the governor.
4. Grouping state agencies and departments by consolidation or elimination into five to twenty-five departments that report to the governor.

There has been considerable reorganization of state government. As a result, the number of state administrative agencies has declined by about 15 percent since the early 1960s. However, governors in most states lack strong organizational power. In about half the states the governor can authorize reorganization by executive order, but subject to legislative veto. The legislative veto—provided by forty-two legislatures—is a device by which legislators can reject a specific administrative rule or regulation before it takes effect (without subsequent acceptance or veto by the governor). Because of the Supreme Court's ruling against the legislative veto by Congress in *Immigration and Naturalization Service* v. *Chadha* (1983), its legality at the state level is also in doubt. State government often lacks accountability, because there is not a clear chain of command in the executive branch. There continue to be large numbers of elected officials and independent boards outside the control of the governor.

Governors have strongly supported **reorganization** of state agencies. Consolidation of responsibilities in areas such as environmental protection and transportation improves the delivery of services and increases accountability. For governors, it concentrates authority in their hands by allowing them to appoint the head of new agencies.

Control over the Budget

In the past fifty years, most states have instituted an **executive budget.** This means that the budgets are prepared by the governors and those appointed directly by them. Recent state governors, like recent presidents, have greatly increased the size of their staffs, including a budget director and professional assistants. The budget staff reviews requests for funds from all state agencies and, with the governor, prepares a budget that is then acted upon by the legislature.

Most governors are strong in this area—forty-eight states have adopted the executive budget procedure. Traditionally, budget making was dominated by legislatures, but changes were made during the 1920s and 1930s when states were under great financial pressure. Regarding their control over the budget, in only six states (most in the South) have governors been weakened by having to share responsibility for budget preparation with civil service appointees or with the legislature. Even when they have strong formal powers, most governors find their position significantly weakened because so many budget items are beyond their control. Often more than 50 percent of the budget is earmarked to provide funds for specific purposes (such as gasoline taxes for highways).

Veto Power

As with budgetary powers, most governors can exercise strong control through their authority to veto bills passed by the legislature. The Depression years brought an expansion of this power, allowing many governors to veto *individual items* in appropriate bills. This power of an **item veto,** which is not given to the president, permits governors in forty-seven states to avoid the difficult presidential choice of accepting or rejecting an entire bill. In ten states there is also a *reduction veto* for cutting specific items in appropriations bills without vetoing the line item entirely. Seven states permit the governor to condition approval of a bill with amendments or rewording of the lines. In an extreme example, Governor Tommy Thompson of Wisconsin used the partial veto to eliminate parts of words and save those letters to create new words. The Wisconsin constitution permits the governor to veto "words, parts of words, letters, and digits" in appropriations bills. Thad Beyle notes that the line-item veto and its variants have increased formal conflict between governors and legislatures and that they tilt the balance of power toward the governor.[7] This, in turn, precipitates litigation between the two branches of government and brings in the judiciary to settle disputes.

Typically, the governor's veto must be overridden by at least a three-fifths vote of both houses of the legislature. This means that the governor has to persuade only a small percentage of the legislators in one house to support him on the vote to override a veto. By vetoing particular appropriations items, the governor can control total spending and also influence specific programs being carried out by administrative agencies. Only in North Carolina does the governor lack the authority to veto. In South Carolina the governor must veto a bill within two days following its passage.

Use of the veto has varied greatly among states and among individual governors. For example, the governors of California vetoed 26 percent of all bills presented to them during the period 1927 to 1952. Thomas E. Dewey as governor of New York vetoed about 365 bills each year. As governor of Michigan (1949–1955), Democrat G. Mennen Williams vetoed 25 percent of the bills sent to

Table 6.1   The Institutionalized Powers of the Governorship: 1965–1985

	Range of Scores Possible	1965 Average	1985 Average	Change in Scores (%)
Tenure potential	1–5	3.3	4.1	+.8 (24%)
Appointive powers	0–7	3.6	4.0	+.4 (11%)
Budget-making powers	0–5	4.3	4.6	+.3 (7%)
Legislative budget-changing authority	1–5	1.3	1.2	−.1 (8%)
Veto powers	0–5	4.2	3.6	−.6 (14%)
Party control	1–5	3.8	3.4	−.4 (11%)
Overall scores*	3–32	20.7	21.1	+.4 (1.9%)

SOURCE: Thad L. Beyle, "The Institutionalized Powers of the Governorship: 1965–1985," *Comparative State Politics Newsletter,* February 1988, pp. 28–30. Reprinted with permission.

him by a Republican-dominated legislature. In all states, governors veto an average of about 5 percent of the bills that are passed by legislatures, and about 4 percent of vetoes are overridden by legislatures. The New York legislature achieved the first veto override ever in 1976; only one veto was overridden by the Pennsylvania legislature between 1900 and 1950, and the California legislature did not override a single veto between 1946 and 1976.

Studies published in 1988 and 1990 have updated the Schlesinger material by adding two indices—legislative budget-changing authority and measurement of party control in the legislature.[8] Because these new indices consider political strength, they are less formal than the Schlesinger categories and give a better look at the "real world" in which governors operate. They also give a twenty-year comparison of gubernatorial power. The results in terms of which states have the strongest and weakest gubernatorial power (see Table 6.1) are relatively similar to Schlesinger's and they show overall growth in gubernatorial authority (see Table 6.2). The scores in Table 6.2 are based on a numerical value given by Beyle to each measure of the governor's power as indicated in Table 6.1. The most significant gains in power were in Republican, rural states where governors traditionally had limited control. The results also indicate that governors have lost power in some areas through gains in legislative authority. Governors of urbanized Northern states tend to have the strongest institutionalized power, and Southern governors are weakest.

THE INFORMAL POWERS OF GOVERNORS

Within their own states, the governors of Texas, North Carolina, and South Carolina may be stronger political forces than the governors of Maryland and Massachusetts. In fact, there are no weak governors. In large, industrial states, governors need substantial formal power to manage a giant bureaucracy and to compete for power with mayors of large cities, presidents of giant corporations, and heads of strong labor unions. In two-party, competitive states it is less risky to give governors strong formal powers because of the expected turnover in office. In one-party states, such as Mississippi, substantial formal power could become dictatorial when

Table 6.2   The Institutionalized Powers of the Governorship: 1965–1990, by State

									1965						
Very Weak			Weak			Moderate			Strong				Very Strong		
14	15	16	17	18	19	20	21	22	23	24	25	26	27	28	29
IN	IA	NH	AZ	RI	FL	AR	AL	DE	CO	AK	CA		NY		MD
	VT	ND	MS	SC		MI	CT	IL	GA	HI					
			NC	WI		MT	KS	MN	KY	ID					
			OK			NV	LA	MO	MA	OH					
						NM	ME	NE		TN					
						TX	OR	NJ		UT					
						WV	SD	PA		VA					
								WY		WA					

									1990						
Very Weak			Weak			Moderate			Strong				Very Strong		
14	15	16	17	18	19	20	21	22	23	24	25	26	27	28	29
	RI	TX	NC	NH	AL	IN	AZ	CA	AK	AR	MN	NY	MA		MD
				SC	ME		FL	CO	DE	CT			WV		
				VT	NV		ID	GA	IL	HI					
					NM		KY	MS	IA	KS					
					OK		MO	MT	LA	NE					
								WA	MI	NJ					
								WI	ND	OR					
								WY	OH	TN					
									PA	UT					
									SD						
									VA						

SOURCE: Thad L. Beyle. "Governors," in Virginia Gray, Herbert Jacob, and Robert B. Albritton, eds., *Politics in the American States,* 5th ed. (Glenview, Ill.: Scott, Foresman/Little, Brown, 1990), p. 228. Copyright © 1990 by Virginia Gray, Herbert Jacob, and Robert B. Albritton. Reprinted by permission of HarperCollins Publishers.

controlled by the same party over a long period of time. But lists of formal powers measure only *potential* effectiveness. Governors with strong formal powers may be weakened by hostile legislators, regional tensions within their states, and powerful special-interest groups.

Schlesinger states that "the consequences of formal restraints upon the governor's *tenure* are by no means clear." He notes, for example, that some Southern governors once free from concern about reelection have become much more liberal than their campaign platforms indicated. Others, such as Orval Faubus of Arkansas, have become more conservative (i.e., more segregationalist) as they seek reelection— Faubus was returned to office five times by the voters of Arkansas. Even when limited by not being able to succeed themselves in office, governors with strong personalities have made successful returns to office after a forced absence. George Wallace had his wife, Lurleen, occupy the governor's chair in his absence and was reelected himself in 1970 after four years out of office. In Ohio, James Rhodes was reelected after a four-year absence—Ohio's constitution prohibits governors from serving more than two consecutive terms. Even those governors with four-year terms and no restraints on reelection are seldom elected to more than two terms.

Although the inability to *appoint* top-level officials potentially weakens the governor, there are a variety of means whereby a governor can compensate for this apparent lack of power. If the governor is a dominant figure in the political party, he or she can usually control nominations. A governor who runs strongly at the top of the ticket in the general election can pull other party members along to victory. Clearly this creates as strong a feeling of loyalty and obligation as would an appointment. Even when governors can make appointments, they need to have the authority to remove appointees from office if they are to control subordinates effectively.

Governors may also compensate for their inability to appoint cabinet-level people by controlling the awarding of hundreds of patronage jobs as well as the granting of state contracts. For the governor of New York, such patronage, encompassing many positions, would be a crushing burden. In Mississippi, however, it allows the governor to exercise influence over the legislature, interest groups, and administrators that the formal powers of the office appear to deny.

Sarah McCally Morehouse suggests that it is the *political leadership* of the governor, rather than socioeconomic variables, that most strongly affects state policymaking.[9] Morehouse contends, for example, that executive fragmentation adversely affects the content of public policy. Her findings indicate that governors who can unify state administration by appointing people who share their political viewpoints are better able to put forward and sustain programs calling for higher welfare benefits and more progressive taxes.

Morehouse concludes that the governor's political leadership and formal powers, plus professionalism in the legislature, explain a significant amount of public policy. She places strong emphasis on the governor's ability to exert leadership by building a substantial coalition within the party that can be expected to support policies once elected. The governor's ability as a leader, says Morehouse, is enhanced by the ability to run for reelection, to plan a budget, and to reorganize the state bureaucracy. As we shall see in the next section, the governor's power is also strengthened by the skillful use of informal resources—including the abilities to set the policymaking agenda for the legislature and to coordinate state policy—which support his or her role as a party leader.

As noted in Chapter 1, we need to remember that a state's *political culture* affects the power of the governor. States with moralistic cultures are more willing to grant strong formal powers to their governors than are traditional or individualistic states. This situation stems from the fact that the moralistic style emphasizes the positive role of government to promote the general welfare. When much is expected of government, governors are usually given substantial authority to act as initiators of policy. The moralistic culture is also willing to support a professionalized bureaucracy and to accept the idea of administrative unification under the governor. In contrast, traditional and individualistic cultures seek to limit government intervention and seldom wish to initiate new programs or open new areas of government activity. In particular, the traditional culture is very antibureaucratic, because bureaucracy interferes with the well-established network of informal personal relationships that has developed over several generations. In this informal, personalized environment, a skillful politician, such as Earl K. Long of Louisiana or George Wallace of Alabama, can build a powerful political organization by the use of such resources as patronage, contracts, and publicity.

GUBERNATORIAL ROLES

In a manner similar to (if on a considerably smaller scale than) the president, the governor plays a variety of public roles. Some of these roles are specified in the state constitutions; others have simply evolved. The reader is cautioned that these roles cannot be neatly separated from one another. Authority in one area often overlaps into another.

Chief of State

As chief of state, the governor performs a variety of ceremonial functions. These include dedicating new highways and bridges, attending funerals and weddings, greeting visitors to the state capitol, proclaiming special days or weeks (e.g., Laugh Week), crowning beauty queens, and attending football games. Although much of this activity appears trivial and undoubtedly bores many governors, it does reap political rewards in terms of publicity and image building.

The governor acts as the official spokesperson for the people of the state. As the voice of the people, the governor can speak in highly moralistic terms about the way government should respond to citizen needs. This approach can be effective in the area of civil rights when governors are able to promote social justice by their actions—appointing blacks to office and introducing legislation prohibiting racial discrimination—as well as by their words. For example, in his inaugural speech, Governor Jimmy Carter of Georgia stated, "I say to you quite frankly that the time for racial discrimination is over." Carter went on to appoint blacks to important positions in state government and to place a portrait of Martin Luther King, Jr., in the statehouse. Governors may also use their media access to castigate legislators and push their own partisan programs.

In recent years, governors have acted as economic advocates for their states by luring businesses and manufacturing concerns from other states and encouraging plant investment from foreign corporations. Governor James Rhodes of Ohio, for example, traveled to Germany to encourage Volkswagen to build a plant in his state; he created an economic task force to travel around the country touting the advantages of business relocation in Ohio; and he used the slogan "Profit is not a dirty word in Ohio." Even if Rhodes was not always successful in bringing new business to Ohio (Volkswagen decided to build its plant in Pennsylvania), his personal popularity was enhanced because of these activities. In many respects, governors may have little control over whether or not their states have a "favorable business climate." For example, such factors as strong unions and high wages may cause businesses not to locate in some Northern states.

Governors and the president are constitutionally granted the power to **pardon** prisoners convicted of state and federal criminal offenses—a power that has its origins with the king of England. Before this century, being granted a pardon was about the only way a prisoner could be released prior to completing a full prison sentence. Currently, few people receive either a gubernatorial pardon (the release from the legal consequences of a crime and restoration to the position they enjoyed prior to conviction) or a commutation (a change of sentence or punishment to one that is less severe). Governor John C. Walton of Oklahoma pardoned 698 prisoners in eleven months and was subsequently impeached and convicted in 1923 for taking bribes to give the pardons.[10] More recently, Governor Ray Blanton of Tennessee attempted mass pardons of convicted murderers. He was convicted in 1981 of extortion, conspiracy, and mail fraud in connection with the pardons he had made. Blanton had been pushed out of office several days before his term ended in 1979 to prevent his giving additional pardons.

There has been a strong trend toward the use of full-time boards staffed by correctional experts to make pardon decisions. Other boards are used to grant parole, and judges often employ probation and indeterminate sentencing to soften the impact of the law where circumstances indicate that leniency is in order. Most governors find the pardoning power very bothersome because they are besieged with applications for pardons from friends and relatives of the many inmates of state prisons who believe they got a "bum rap." Particularly when dealing with members of organized crime, there is the added possibility of bribery.

Chief Legislator

Chapter 5 discussed the role of governors as initiators of legislation who set the legislative agenda and manage their programs throughout the lawmaking process. Governors use a variety of formal powers, such as the veto or threat of veto, plus their informal powers as party leader and voice of the people, to influence legislative action. They clearly realize that their degree of legislative success will have a substantial influence on their prospects for reelection.

Governors are able to employ a wide range of legislative strategies. One common technique is to create study commissions composed of private citizens representing both political parties, which are given the task of developing ideas to supplement those of state agencies and the governor's staff. Governors occasionally present grandiose programs for public education or economic development that would require vast expenditures of state funds. If there is strong public support for the programs, adroit governors may be successful in getting the legislature to go to the people seeking additional taxes and thus take credit for the initiation of the program while avoiding blame for higher taxes. Governors may also focus attention on a particular issue by calling the legislature into special session to deal with politically difficult problems. Because many legislatures meet for short sessions, the ability to call members back into session gives governors a means of exerting considerable pressure on reluctant legislators. According to Alan Rosenthal, most governors are concerned about presenting only a few major pieces of legislation each session.[11] Often when a large number of separate proposals is made, legislators have difficulty deciding which have the highest priority and governors risk having major parts of their programs defeated.

As noted in Chapter 5, governors are often weakened because one or both houses of the state legislature are controlled by the opposition party. It should be remembered that even when the governor's party is in the majority, gubernatorial proposals may face strong opposition from ideological factions in the legislature. Because of recent gains in power for the legislature, Rosenthal believes that in most states there is a relatively equal balance between the legislative and executive branches.

Party Chief

In a manner similar to the president, all governors are party leaders—some accept the role reluctantly and few succeed in fully dominating their party. In large part, governors suffer as party leaders because of the decentralized nature of political parties (see Chapter 3), which allows local organizations to act independently of the state party. Governors are also weak because they lack formal means of party control and must rely on a variety of informal resources.

Success in securing passage of his or her program depends largely on the governor's ability as a party leader. The governor's control of patronage can be used to build legislative support and personal loyalty. On the average, state governors make about 400 appointments to state agencies and departments, and they make many other appointments to advisory boards and commissions. Patronage power is especially significant in low-income, job-oriented states, where state positions are highly prized. In addition to jobs, a governor's ability to influence the awarding of contracts and the location of state projects can also be used to reward political friends and punish enemies.

The number of patronage positions has declined significantly since the 1960s, when nearly half of all state jobs were filled by the governor. In some states nearly all state employees are covered by civil service systems. While governors may lose some political power because of this change, many supported the reduction of patronage jobs. The patronage system was difficult to administer, many low-paying jobs were unattractive to party workers, and some party members were disappointed when they did not get the job they wanted. Reform governors used the move to merit systems as a way to build a favorable public image.

Governors can promise campaign support or threaten to oppose party members who refuse to back their party's programs. In some states where the governor plays a major role in the organization of the legislature, he or she can manipulate committee assignments and leadership posts to benefit supporters. In general, if the governor's personal popularity is high, most party members will seek to identify themselves with his or her program. When the governor's personal fortunes drop, party support may quickly erode.

Governors continue to be weakened as party chiefs and chief legislators by divided government in which the opposition party controls a majority of seats in the legislature. In a similar fashion, the inability to appoint top-level cabinet personnel means that the governor must deal with politically ambitious rivals, both within and without the party, who repeatedly oppose policies and point out mistakes.

Commander-in-Chief

Although governors do not command a navy with nuclear-powered submarines or an air force with jet fighters, they do control the **National Guard** (formerly called the state militia) when it is not called into national service by the president. The Constitution provides for a cooperative system in which states appoint officers (the state adjutant general is their commander) and Congress organizes, arms, and finances the Guard. Since 1916, the former militias have been organized as an auxiliary of the regular army subject to substantial national control. As its civilian commander-in-chief, the governor may call the Guard into service for such emergencies as floods, tornadoes, or urban riots. The president may also call the Guard into service, at which time all state jurisdiction ends. Control over the Guard allowed some governors to become involved in foreign affairs by refusing to send their state troops to Central America for training exercises in 1986. In response, Congress passed a bill to prohibit governors from interfering with overseas troop deployment.

The record of the Guard in responding to civil disturbances has ranged from adequate to disastrous. Prior to World War II, the Guard often was used brutally to break up racial disturbances, labor strikes, and prison riots. The most conspicuous failures include the Michigan and Ohio forces. Michigan National Guardsmen, not well trained in dealing with riot situations, were quickly replaced by U.S. Army troops when confronting the Detroit ghetto riot in 1967. In 1970, Ohio National Guardsmen killed four students and injured others in responding to an antiwar demonstration at Kent State University. Because of the growing size and professionalization of the state police or highway patrol, many governors prefer to use them in order-maintenance situations rather than to call out the Guard.

On a more positive note, the Guard has been effective (often invaluable) when dealing with natural disasters. With guardsmen posted on nearly every corner, looting quickly diminished after two days of rioting in Los Angeles in 1992. The Los Angeles police clearly had lost control of the situation.

The way in which governors react to crisis situations may have long-lasting political effects. In most cases, the governor visits the scene of the disaster, offers condolences to the victims and their families, and promises to do everything possible—usually including a request for federal disaster relief funds—to restore the area to its previous condition. On other occasions, more complicated judgments have to be made quickly under high-stress conditions. For example, in 1971, Governor Nelson Rockefeller was faced with a riot at Attica Prison in which convicts had taken control of a courtyard and were holding hostage a group of prison guards and civilians. Rockefeller rejected requests that he visit the prison, and after four days, he ordered state troopers to regain control of the prison. When 200 troopers stormed the prison, thirty-two inmates and eleven hostages were killed. Ten of the hostages died from the troopers' fire. Governor Rockefeller did not run for reelection following the Attica riot (he resigned to become vice president), but continued criticism of his response limited his political effectiveness during the remainder of his term as governor.[12]

Chief Administrator

The governor is responsible for the management of all state administrative agencies. However, governors do not always control their agencies. As we shall see in the following section on administration, governors have traditionally been limited by fragmented administrative systems that undercut their authority as chief executives.

As administrators, governors are weakened by several other factors as well. Unlike the president, governors must contend with department heads who are separately elected and thus largely independent of them. Even the lieutenant governor is elected separately in several states. The results can be embarrassing for the governor. For example, Republican Lieutenant Governor Mike Curb took literally his constitutional duty to act when Democratic Governor Edmund Brown, Jr., left California to campaign for president in 1980. Curb actually made appointments and overturned some of Brown's actions. Many state departments are headed by independent boards and commissions whose members may be just as independent of the governor as elected heads. In addition, governors have increasingly had to deal with the demands of public employee unions. Most states allow collective bargaining, and a few permit strikes by public employees.

To help governors cope with their increasing administrative burdens, states have acted in recent years to increase their formal authority. This has been done by consolidating departments, by giving the governor the ability to appoint more key administrators, by eliminating control by boards and commissions, and by various innovations in budgeting and planning. These are discussed later in this chapter.

Because of the increasing complexity of state government and the ever-broadening responsibilities of their office, governors have surrounded themselves with expanding numbers of *staff personnel* who provide both political and administrative assistance. In large states a governor's staff of perhaps 100 people will include a press secretary, an executive secretary, a legal adviser, a speech writer, a director of the budget, a commissioner of administration, and others assigned by the political party. Staff personnel tend to be young (in their thirties) and politically ambitious. Many are lawyers, and most staff members worked in the governor's campaign or in the campaigns of other candidates in their party. Many staff people have political ambitions of their own.

In addition to serving in an administrative capacity—as budget officers; as liaison with state, local, and federal agencies; as liaison to the state legislature to help manage the governor's legislative program—the governor's staff provides other, more personal services. The staff serves as a reference bureau to provide information and to help shape the governor's position on a wide range of policy issues. Staff members serve as public relations specialists to do such things as write press releases and keep the governor posted on political developments that may affect his or her office. Staff members attend to the task of answering the mail, and they control who has access to the governor. As with the president, the governor must guard against the dangers of an overprotective staff that isolates him or her from the real world beyond the office.

Martha Wagner Weinberg notes that reformers have often suggested that if governors would only adopt modern business management techniques, they would be able to manage public affairs much more effectively.[13] She believes, however, that this assumption overlooks some major differences between governors and private sector chief executives. The governor's management task is much more difficult because the environment in which his or her decisions are made is more complex and less controllable. Moreover, the governor's term is limited, and power must be shared with many groups. Even compared with large private businesses, the operations of states such as New York and California, or even Nebraska, are much more complex in terms of budget, number of personnel, and variety of functions. Unlike private sector managers, governors have only limited control over the hiring and firing of personnel.

In addition, there are differences between managing state government and private enterprise that relate more directly to the political process. Governors must share power with the legislative and judicial branches. Also, they must operate within a federal system in which the national government is supreme.

Of course, governors are constantly aware of how management decisions might affect their future political aspirations. Management functions for the governor and his or her staff include the following:[14]

> Changing or initiating a policy
> Maintaining a policy or a position under pressure
> Setting a tone and keeping morale high
> Mediating disputes among different agencies or among factions within agencies
> Marketing or selling a political or policy issue within the bureaucracy or to the general public
> Recruiting government personnel
> Allocating resources (budgeting)

Federal Systems Officer

Increasingly, governors have become involved as administrators placed in the middle between the federal government and local governments.[15] They lobby for money from Washington and then attempt to have the money spent by local governments in accordance with their plans for state development. In order to accomplish their goals, governors must pressure state legislatures for supporting funds and mediate among cities in order to coordinate state programs.

Despite cutbacks in the 1980s, nearly two-thirds of all state agencies get some federal funds and about one-fourth receive half their funding from Washington. In the past, neither legislators nor governors have had effective control over these federal dollars. However, states increasingly are gaining control over how administrative agencies spend federal funds. About one-third of the states require that all or most federal funds be reapportioned by the legislature. Because of this heavy dependence on Washington, the National Governors Conference has set up an office to make possible full-time lobbying in the nation's capital. The office provides weekly analyses and special reports to governors and their staffs. In addition, nearly thirty states have established their own Washington offices to lobby for specific aid. Keeping up to date with these lobbying activities means that governors must allocate considerable time to travel and staff consultation. Several states have an intergovernmental coordinator who works in the governor's office.

With the increasing emphasis on block grants (see Chapter 2), the role of the governor as federal systems officer has become even more crucial to the welfare of each state. Cities and counties have become more dependent on state officials to determine how federal money is allocated, and state decisions to maintain funding for programs cut by the federal government will also become critical to local governments. Governors most often are cited as the key actors in shaping state responses to the changes brought about by the Reagan administration. For example, Nathan and Doolittle report that when Michael Dukakis replaced Edward King as governor of Massachusetts in 1982, the issue of how to respond to cuts in social programs shifted from *whether* to replace federal aid to *how much* to replace.[16] State responses to Reagan's changes were influenced by the role of political leaders, the fiscal condition of states, and the state political culture. Thus in Arizona, where there is a strong conservative political and fiscal tradition, there was a reluctance to spend money for public service regardless of which political party was in power.

Some existing federal grant programs designate the governor as the chief planning and administrative officer in the state. Governors need to have this authority in order to ensure that federal programs are compatible with state policy goals. As Sarah McCally Morehouse notes, "The major struggle governors have is trying to convince the Congress that they need to be consulted in the planning and execution of federal programs and in convincing the mayors and local officials that they are willing to assume responsibility with respect to urban problems."[17]

STATE ADMINISTRATION

As discussed in Chapter 1, the scope of state government activities has increased greatly in recent years. As a result, state and local payrolls and numbers of employees now far outstrip those of the federal government (see Table 6.3). While there was a drop in federal employment in the early 1980s, overall federal employment increased in the 1980s and state and local employment increased at about the same rate. Note that federal employment declined during the 1970s, while state and local employment increased significantly. This expansion of **bureaucracy** has, of course, placed increasing burdens of responsibility on governors, who historically have been denied strong formal powers as chief administrators. States have responded by giving governors control of budget preparation and by increasing gubernatorial power to appoint and remove officials.

Financial hardships in recent years have placed severe burdens on most state bureaucracies. Budget cuts have led to employee layoffs and staff reductions. In the face of a loss of federal funding and opposition to tax increases, there has been a demand for increased services to deal with problems such as crime, drug abuse, and environmental protection. The recession in the early 1990s increased the workload for various social service agencies, including unemployment offices.[18] In cases such as Michigan, where a new conservative governor was elected in 1990, the administration has used budget shortfalls as an excuse to further its ideological aims of limited government.

As noted earlier in this chapter, governors continue to be limited as administrators by the fragmented nature of state government. Most states failed to develop well-organized administrative structures because of the piecemeal growth of bureaucracy. As new functions were given to the states, the easiest response was to create a new state agency as visible proof to concerned citizens and interest groups that the state was "doing something" about the problem. Under these circum-

Table 6.3 Summary of Public Employment in the United States, Selected Years 1929–1989

Year	NUMBER (THOUSANDS)					ANNUAL PERCENTAGE INCREASE OR DECREASE					PERCENTAGE DISTRIBUTION				
	Total Public Sector	Federal (Civilian)	State and Local	State	Local	Total Public Sector	Federal (Civilian)	State and Local	State	Local	Total Public Sector	Federal (Civilian)	State and Local	State	Local
1929	3,100	600	2,500	600	1,900						100.0%	19.4%	80.6%	19.4%	61.3%
1939	4,200	1,100	3,100	700	2,400	3.1%	6.2%	2.2%	1.6%	2.4%	100.0	26.2	73.8	16.7	57.1
1944	6,537	3,365	3,172	700	2,472	9.3	25.1	0.5	<	0.6	100.0	51.5	48.5	10.7	37.8
1949	6,203	2,047	4,156	1,037	3,119	-1.0	-9.5	5.6	8.2	4.8	100.0	33.0	67.0	16.7	50.3
1952	7,105	2,583	4,521	1,060	3,461	4.6	8.1	2.8	0.7	3.5	100.0	36.4	63.6	14.9	48.7
1954	7,232	2,373	4,859	1,149	3,710	0.9	-4.2	3.7	4.1	3.5	100.0	32.8	67.2	15.9	51.3
1957	8,047	2,439	5,607	1,300	4,307	3.6	0.9	4.9	4.2	5.1	100.0	30.3	69.7	16.2	53.5
1959	8,487	2,399	6,088	1,454	4,634	2.7	-0.8	4.2	5.8	3.7	100.0	28.3	71.7	17.1	54.6
1964	10,064	2,528	7,536	1,873	5,663	3.5	1.1	4.4	5.2	4.1	100.0	25.1	74.9	18.6	56.3
1969	12,685	2,969	9,716	2,614	7,102	4.7	3.3	5.2	6.9	4.6	100.0	23.4	76.6	20.6	56.0
1970	13,028	2,881	10,147	2,755	7,392	2.6	-3.1	4.2	5.1	3.9	100.0	22.1	77.9	21.1	56.7
1971	13,316	2,872	10,444	2,832	7,612	2.3	-0.3	2.8	2.7	2.9	100.0	21.6	78.4	21.3	57.2
1972	13,759	2,795	10,964	2,957	8,007	3.2	-2.8	4.7	4.2	4.9	100.0	20.3	79.7	21.5	58.2
1973	14,139	2,786	11,352	3,013	8,339	2.7	-0.3	3.4	1.9	4.0	100.0	19.7	80.3	21.3	59.0
1974	14,628	2,874	11,754	3,155	8,599	3.3	3.1	3.4	4.5	3.0	100.0	19.6	80.4	21.6	58.8
1975	14,973	2,890	12,084	3,271	8,813	2.3	0.6	2.7	3.5	2.4	100.0	19.3	80.7	21.8	58.9
1976	15,012	2,843	12,169	3,343	8,826	0.3	-1.7	0.7	2.2	0.1	100.0	18.9	81.1	22.3	58.8
1977	15,459	2,848	12,611	3,491	9,120	2.9	0.2	3.5	4.2	3.2	100.0	18.4	81.6	22.6	59.0
1978	15,628	2,885	12,743	3,539	9,204	1.1	1.3	1.0	1.4	0.9	100.0	18.5	81.5	22.6	58.9
1979	15,971	2,869	13,102	3,699	9,403	2.1	-0.6	2.7	4.3	2.1	100.0	18.0	82.0	23.2	58.9
1980	16,213	2,898	13,315	3,753	9,562	1.5	1.0	1.6	1.4	1.7	100.0	17.9	82.1	23.1	59.0
1981	15,968	2,865	13,103	3,726	9,377	-1.5	-1.2	-1.6	-0.7	-2.0	100.0	17.9	82.1	23.3	58.7
1982	15,861	2,848	13,013	3,764	9,249	-0.7	-0.6	-0.7	1.0	-1.4	100.0	18.0	82.0	23.7	58.3
1983	16,034	2,874	13,160	3,816	9,344	1.1	0.9	1.1	1.4	1.0	100.0	17.9	82.1	23.8	58.3
1984	16,436	2,942	13,493	3,898	9,595	2.4	2.3	2.5	2.1	2.6	100.0	17.9	82.1	23.7	58.4
1985	16,690	3,021	13,669	3,984	9,685	1.5	2.6	1.3	2.2	0.9	100.0	18.1	81.9	23.9	58.0
1986	16,933	3,019	13,914	4,068	9,846	1.4	-0.1	1.8	2.1	1.6	100.0	17.8	82.2	24.0	58.1
1987	17,281	3,091	14,191	4,115	10,076	2.0	2.3	2.0	1.1	2.3	100.0	17.9	82.1	23.8	58.3
1988	17,588	3,112	14,476	4,236	10,240	1.7	0.7	2.0	2.9	1.6	100.0	17.7	82.3	24.1	58.2
1989	17,879	3,114	14,765	4,365	10,400	1.7	0.1	2.0	3.0	1.6	100.0	17.4	82.6	24.4	58.2

SOURCE: *Significant Features of Fiscal Federalism 1991*, vol. 2 (Washington, D.C.: Advisory Commission on Intergovernmental Relations, 1991), p. 219.

stances, the duties of each agency were not clearly defined and the jurisdiction of new agencies often overlapped with that of already established agencies. Large cities had similar problems of fragmented organization. However, city reform came earlier than did state reform because of the adoption of strong-mayor–council and council-manager plans at the beginning of this century.

Because of the desire to take politics out of state government, many agencies were placed under the control of boards and commissions that acted independently of the governor. Agencies and departments performing similar tasks were nevertheless separated from one another with no one to serve as a coordinator. Communication between agencies was limited, and it was difficult for the governor or the legislature to know what the agencies were doing or who was responsible for their actions. Mergers were opposed by bureaucrats who sought to protect their jobs and by interest groups that were being aided by agencies they had helped create. At their peak in the 1950s, many states had more than 100 boards, commissions, and departments. There were stories of dead men being appointed to serve on obscure boards. Currently, the state of Ohio, for example, has about 200 boards and commissions. They include the Safety in Skiing Board, the Board of Embalmers and Funeral Directors of Ohio, and the Underground Parking Commission. However, the governor appoints, with senate approval, twenty cabinet-level heads (see Table 6.4) plus the adjutant general. In Ohio, the superintendent of public instruction heads another major department within the executive branch, but he or she is appointed by and serves at the pleasure of the State Board of Education. In all, thirty-eight states have some kind of cabinet system. They range in size from forty-two members in Illinois to four in Wyoming and five in Iowa.

The movement for administrative reform began in the 1890s but did not take hold in state government until after 1920, when administrative reorganization in Illinois under Governor Frank Lowden became known around the country. State

Table 6.4   Major Elective and Appointive Positions in Ohio, 1992

Statewide Elective Positions	County Elective Positions	Governor's Cabinet*	
Governor	Auditor	Adjutant general	Industrial relations
Lieutenant governor	Clerk of courts	Administrative services	Liquor control
	Coroner	Aging	Lottery
Attorney general	Engineer	Agriculture	Mental health
Secretary of state	Prosecuting attorney	Budget and managing	Mental retardation and developmental disabilities
Auditor		Commerce	
Treasurer	Recorder	Development	
	Sheriff	Employment services	Natural resources
	Treasurer	Environmental protection	Rehabilitation and corrections
	Commissioners (3)	Health	Taxation
		Highway safety	Transportation
		Human services	

*Appointed by governor with state senate approval.

commissions on reorganization were appointed in several states, although there were few instances of substantial reform. The basic goal of the early reformers was to reduce the number of agencies and bring them more directly under the control of the governor. There was a general attempt to upgrade the bureaucracy by creating civil service commissions for merit appointment and by developing the executive budget. Following World War II and the report of the **Hoover Commission,** there was a revival of interest in structural organization.

In the 1980s, there was a partial reorganization in most states, aimed at consolidating agencies and centralizing power with the governor. Political scientist Richard C. Elling speaks of the "religion of reorganization" in which twenty-two states completed organizational restructuring from 1965 to 1987.[19]

Because state administration is a highly *politicized* process, these apparently logical goals of centralization have met with strong resistance in virtually every state. Interest groups often prefer separation because of the strong control they have been able to maintain over state agencies. State legislators are able to use separate agencies to their political advantage, and they are inherently suspicious of moves to strengthen the governor. Groups such as physicians are unwilling to have their profession licensed and controlled by people who do not have professional training. The general public prefers to keep "politics" out of government and therefore supports "independent" boards and commissions. Finally, by requiring specific allocation of matching funds to support categorical grants, federal grants-in-aid have encouraged separate agencies.

POLICY IMPLEMENTATION AND BUREAUCRATS

In large part, *policy development* takes place in the legislative, executive, and judicial branches, and it is presented in the form of statutes, executive orders, and court decisions. Of equal importance in the policy process is the **implementation** of these written directives—a task that falls to bureaucrats. Policies must be enforced and carried out, and agencies often prepare instructions to their staff members regarding the execution of policy-development orders that are more detailed than the original directives. Typically, agencies are given little statutory direction. As a result, bureaucrats have wide discretion in the application of the law. Moreover, within particular agencies and departments, "street-level" personnel, such as building inspectors and police officers, are frequently given the discretion to decide how rules will be applied in specific instances. Because of their experience and technical knowledge, career bureaucrats often know how best to deal with problems, and this gives them power as policymakers.

Policy implementation is strongly affected by administrative structure (as noted in the previous section) and by **bureaucratic culture.** The culture (or distinguishing characteristics) of government bureaus is influenced substantially by the process of agency *recruitment.* When recruitment is on a patronage basis (i.e., jobs are dispensed by the party in power), public employees tend to be more concerned about keeping their jobs and keeping their party in office than they are about pursuing policy goals.

In agencies where recruitment is under a **merit system** of civil service, goals are more varied.* Under most merit systems, employees serve for a probationary period after which they cannot be removed except for cause, and they are entitled to a hearing where the reasons for dismissal are discussed. When merit systems were first used in the early twentieth century, their main objective was to eliminate patronage jobs. More recently, their basic goal has been to get the right people for the right job. In agencies that use examinations as a basis for promotion, bureaucrats are often mainly concerned with meeting the formal requirements for promotion and protecting their jobs. As under patronage systems, there is little incentive to be program-oriented. In contrast, some agencies give relatively less emphasis to written examinations and base their promotion decisions mainly on achievement. In such a situation, individuals are more likely to be goal-oriented and innovative. Collective bargaining has made it more difficult to provide merit increases because it stresses seniority.

Budgeting

The type of budget system used by government agencies and departments may encourage greater policy orientation on the part of bureaucrats. **Incremental budgeting**—the traditional system—provides little opportunity for overall review or program evaluation. Budgeting inches ahead from year to year, the starting point each year being last year's budget. Agencies make requests for a few new programs, and they routinely overstate the amount of money they need. Governors make some cuts and legislators cut some more. As a result, old programs are seldom reviewed, little innovation occurs, legislators can point to their efforts to keep spending down, and agencies usually get about what they need to run their programs.

In the 1960s, some states and cities attempted to adopt a **program-planning-budgeting system** (PPBS), in which expenditures are placed together in a comprehensive program package, such as improved environmental quality or the control and reduction of crime. Instead of having to justify specific line items in their budget requests (as in traditional budgeting), under PPBS departments are forced to justify appropriation requests in terms of program objectives. That is, they must link the political ends of their programs to economic means. In some cases, program performance is quantitatively assessed to determine the most effective use of money to attain program goals. Under such a system, there is continuous evaluation and feedback to measure the effectiveness of programs in meeting the needs of the public.

Program budgeting was attempted by several states, but it was abandoned in the 1970s. In part, it failed because states lack good data on program efficiency and impact and they lack personnel skilled in cost-benefit analysis. The process is too

*Although all states have established some form of merit system and most have statewide civil service systems covering two-thirds of all state employees, only about 60 percent of cities over 25,000 have civil service plans. It is difficult to make comparisons among cities because many civil service commissions have only minimal coverage over public employees. Moreover, merit systems may appear similar but in practice operate very differently. For example, New York City and Chicago have similar types of civil service systems, yet Chicago has thousands of patronage positions, whereas New York has a strong merit system.

complicated to have any real chance of success in a highly political environment in which legislators do not want to give up their power base. Still, such attempts have stimulated new data on performance and program evaluation.

In spite of the failure to implement PPBS, the experiments with it have produced some valuable spin-off benefits to budgeting. One of the most publicized has been **zero-based budgeting** (ZBB), in which each department must justify all appropriations items each year. The budget is broken down into units, called decision packages, prepared by managers at each level, which cover every existing proposed activity of each department. This approach encourages greater policy orientation, because out-of-date programs are dropped instead of being continued as existing budget items that are not questioned once they become part of a department's established budget. In some cases, departments rank their programs in order of priority and set performance levels for all programs. Zero-based budgeting has not been widely adopted. It was used in some states (and some private businesses) in the 1970s, but it faced essentially the same barriers as did PPBS. However, where it has been phased in gradually, starting with only a few programs, ZBB can be successful.

Other, more general management innovations have included program evaluation—a follow-up by the legislature on how well programs have worked—and management by objectives (MBO)—a system in which department heads outline the major objectives of their departments for the coming year. Evaluation includes measuring both *efficiency* and *effectiveness.* Whereas efficiency of operation can usually be quantified, effectiveness often involves long-term judgments that are very difficult to make. For example, an evaluation of the effectiveness of vocational training for incarcerated felons requires follow-up studies to determine if they were able to get jobs and avoid criminal behavior after their release from prison.

Recent evaluation suggests (not surprisingly) that budget reforms have been more form than substance. Rather than any "pure" system, most states have developed their own unique budgeting procedures, which are a combination of several models. In practice, this means that incrementalism is still the basic approach in most states, but new concepts, such as cost-benefit analysis and program evaluation, are being implemented.

Although governors play the dominant role in budget formulation, the role of the legislature has increased significantly in the last twenty years. Increased staff, computerized information systems, and better revenue-estimating ability all have helped legislatures review and modify state budgets.[20] In addition, legislatures have taken a role in determining how federal funds will be used by state agencies.

Personnel Practices

The *personnel systems* of agencies also affect their culture and expectations of employee behavior. Some agencies may discourage awarding middle-management positions to outsiders, while others encourage transfers with experience in other types of organizations. When there is a strong preference to promote from within the agency, the bureaucrats who attain supervisory posts tend to be rigid and less open to new ideas than are relative newcomers to the agency.

Personnel practices also include determination of the kinds of people preferred by an agency in its initial recruitment. In New York City, for example, the police historically have favored the Irish in hiring, Italians have dominated the sanitation department, and Jews have been preferred as teachers. There is considerable evidence to indicate that recruitment patterns that stress ethnic backgrounds affect the way in which various clientele groups of the agency are treated. Other agencies may have a preference for graduates of particular colleges.

An agency's culture (and its policy implementation) is influenced by the **professional ideology** of its employees. For example, social workers continue to place a strong emphasis on working with individual clients, whereas reformers contend that group political action is a more effective way to deal with problems of the poor. In addition, professional codes of conduct may serve as a check on the abuse of administrative power.

As in any organization, newly hired employees in government agencies undergo a period of socialization, in which they learn how they are expected to act within the framework of their agency's culture. Those who deviate from established norms will usually encounter difficulty in working with their peers, and they may be denied promotions by their superiors. Although some agencies are program-oriented and encourage innovation, most are conservative in their opposition to change.

Top-level bureaucrats frequently influence policymaking because of their expertise and professionalism. Bureaucrats testify before legislative committees and they meet informally with legislators to help draft legislation. However, their most significant role in the policy process is in implementation. Particularly in large executive establishments, bureaucratic autonomy is increased because chief executives simply cannot know what each agency is doing. Bureaucrats may implement orders in a very formalistic manner without any personal enthusiasm; they may delay implementation by sticking closely to all administrative regulations; or they may refuse outright to follow legislative or executive directions. As a result, reluctant or hostile administrators can create major difficulties for governors and mayors, and they can alter substantially the intention of legislators.

State and local employees increasingly became unionized during the 1970s. One result has been that strikes or slowdowns by city workers have occurred in areas where they previously had been viewed as illegitimate by public employees. While unions have encouraged militancy in demands for higher salaries, they also have reinforced the natural inclination of bureaucrats to support the status quo. Unions seek to ensure that department routines and regulations, particularly in dealing with personnel problems (hiring, grievance procedures, and dismissal), remain unchanged.

Nearly one-third of all state and local employees are members of organizations that engage in **collective bargaining.** Since the mid-1980s about forty states have engaged in some form of negotiations with their employees, but serious collective bargaining is followed only in about half the states. Across the country about 40 percent of state employees are members of an employee organization or union.[21] Unionization is most likely to occur in Northeastern and Great Lakes states, where private sector unions are strongest. In Connecticut and New York, more than 80 percent of state employees are in bargaining units. At the other extreme, there are about a dozen states (all in the South and West) where no state employees are in bargaining units. The most prominent organizations are the National Education Association, the American Federation of Teachers, and the American Federation of State, County, and Municipal Employees, AFL-CIO. Organizational activities have been particularly successful in large cities in recent years. Just over 50 percent of all city firefighters belong to unions, and nearly 30 percent of public hospital workers are unionized. As will be seen in Chapter 8, the demands of public employee unions in New York City played a significant role in the city's financial crisis of 1975–1976. New York City, however, is an unusual case. Evidence across the country suggests that unionization increases wages of state employees about 5 percent and that unionization and merit principles are not incompatible. Although strikes by public employees are illegal in most states, strikes have occurred in many cities, and groups such as firefighters and police officers have "sick-ins" (e.g., cases of the "blue flu") as a means of expressing their demands on city officials. In many cases, state law stipulates that public employee labor disputes must go to arbitration. Both public and private unions faced major obstacles in the 1980s. The firing of striking federal air traffic controllers by the Reagan administration encouraged antiunion sentiment, and the more recent financial crunch has led some public unions to agree to wage concessions in return for more job security.

Privatization

Privatization, "the act of reducing the role of government, or increasing the role of the private sector, in an activity or in the ownership of assets,"[22] has become an increasingly common management technique for states and localities. As explained by E. S. Savas, it can appear in several forms. Perhaps the most familiar is contracting with private firms to perform a service previously done by government employees. This includes managing prisons, providing janitorial services, operating homeless shelters, and collecting taxes. Privatization also includes contracting with not-for-profit agencies to provide a service such as meals-on-wheels, forming neighborhood security patrols, selling off publicly owned businesses, and giving housing vouchers to the poor.

It is argued that privatization will save money, improve services, and reduce the size of government. Proponents believe that competition will force government agencies to become more efficient or they will be eliminated. Opponents contend that the private sector is just as prone to error and corruption as is the public sector. Critics fear a loss of control over the treatment of individuals, violations of civil rights, an escalation of cost, and the dismissal of public employees.

Although the concept of privatization originally was more appealing to conservatives than liberals, it has become a centerpiece for policy innovation by both political parties. Even in Chicago, long dominated by political patronage, Mayor Richard M. Daley has shifted work to private towing companies and janitorial services in some public buildings. Daley notes that "people want services without higher taxes, and they don't care who gives it to them."

Privatization has become more popular as cities face a financial squeeze in the 1990s. If the only alternatives seem to be higher taxes or cuts in services, privatization promises a way to escape from the horns of this dilemma and improve the management of services as well as cut costs.

STATEWIDE ELECTED EXECUTIVE OFFICIALS

Continued use of the long ballot means that most states elect several other state executive officials in addition to the governor. Brief descriptions of these offices and their duties follow.

Lieutenant Governor

The functions of the lieutenant governor are comparable to those of the vice president. Basically, the lieutenant governor acts as presiding officer in the upper house and stands first in line to succeed the governor. In about two-thirds of the states, the lieutenant governor serves on state boards and commissions. In Alaska, Hawaii, and Utah, the lieutenant governor performs the duties normally assigned to secretaries of state. Also in the tradition of the vice president, lieutenant governors have seldom been first-rate politicians capable of being elected governor on their own. An important difference from the national model is that many states have separate elections for governor and lieutenant governor. This means that governors occasionally must deal with politically ambitious lieutenant governors of the opposite party. Twenty-two states now have joint election of the governor and lieutenant governor.

The lieutenant governor of Illinois resigned in the 1980s, citing insufficient responsibilities. In 1982, South Carolina reduced the position to a half-time job. In nearly half the states, the lieutenant governor is not the presiding officer in the state senate. Eight states do not have an office of lieutenant governor, and in Texas the lieutenant governor is selected by the legislature. In states where there is not a lieutenant governor, the secretary of state or senate president stands next in line to succeed the governor. In fifteen states, the lieutenant governor does not normally serve as acting governor when the governor is out of the state. In 1989 the lieutenant governor of Washington resigned after serving for thirty-two years. The previous lieutenant governor in Washington had served for thirty years.

Attorney General

As the state's chief legal officer, the attorney general represents the state in legal disputes and serves as the legal adviser to the governor and other state executive officials. Curiously, in about half the states, the attorney general does not have to be a licensed attorney. Attorneys general are elected in forty-four states, appointed by the governor in five states, chosen by the state legislature in one state, and chosen by the supreme court in one state. When the governor, the legislature, administrative agencies, county attorneys, or city attorneys ask the attorney general for advice regarding an interpretation of state law, the attorney general's opinion generally has the force of law unless challenged in court.

In most states, the attorney general is the second most powerful political figure in state office. His or her power stems in large part from the ability to initiate prosecution in well-publicized criminal and civil cases and from the authority to issue quasi-judicial opinions. In addition, the attorney general's office often serves as a state headquarters for consumer complaints about faulty merchandise or misleading advertising. Recently several attorneys general have taken very active roles in seeking to regulate industries such as insurance and airlines. They also have become involved in some well-publicized battles with governors. For example, the attorney general of Arizona was a leader in the move to impeach Governor Evan Mecham in 1986–1987. In many instances, the attorney general heads the largest law office in the state. This ability to appoint hundreds of young lawyers to serve in state government gives the attorney general a substantial power base should he or she choose to run for governor or senator after those attorneys have moved into private practice around the state. Several attorneys general have gone on to become governors and then well-known national political figures. They include Robert La Follette of Wisconsin, Thomas Dewey of New York, and more recently James Thompson of Illinois.

Secretary of State

The duties of the secretary of state are to keep records—such as the state constitution, constitutional amendments, legislative acts, and mortgages—and to supervise both federal and state elections. They are elected in thirty-eight states and selected either by the governor or the legislature in eleven states; Alaska does not have such a position. As noted earlier, the lieutenant governor performs the duties of the secretary of state in three states. Secretaries of state receive statements of candidacy for public office; they oversee the printing of ballots; and they certify election results. Because secretaries of state are basically record keepers, many reform proposals call for the transfer of these duties to the regular administrative departments. In recent years, several secretaries of state have become governors. These include Jerry Brown, Ella Grasso, and Jay Rockefeller. About twenty secretaries of state have become governor in this century, but many do not have further political ambitions. For example, Thad Eure retired in 1989 as secretary of state of North Carolina after fifty-two years in office.

Auditor and Controller

The auditor's primary duty is to ensure fiscal accountability by making certain that state expenditures have been made as intended by the legislature or in accordance with the state constitution. The auditor's **postaudit** occurs after the expenditure has been made by a state agency. The controller performs a *preaudit,* in which expenditures are approved before they have been made. The preaudit involves an interpretation of legislative intent as well as a determination of the authority of agencies to perform specific functions. Because these can be highly political decisions, reformers suggest that the controller be appointed by the governor.

In contrast to the controller's executive function, the duties of the auditor are more legislative—to check on the actions of executive departments. Here reformers suggest the creation of an office similar to the U.S. controller general, who is appointed by the president with the Senate's approval for a fifteen-year term. The controller general heads the General Accounting Office, which has the power to validate all payments to ensure that they meet with the purposes of congressional appropriations acts and to standardize the accounting systems of government agencies. The controller general can be removed only by impeachment or by joint resolution of Congress.

Treasurer

State treasurers collect taxes, make payments to those furnishing goods and services to the state, and oversee the investment of state funds. However, other state agencies often perform functions similar to those of the treasurer. For example, a liquor-control commission may collect liquor taxes. Again, most reformers recommend the elimination of this office to centralize financial operations under a department of revenue. In their constitutions, the states of Alaska and Hawaii both omit the office of treasurer.

EXECUTIVES IN CITIES

Cities acted somewhat sooner than states to centralize authority and strengthen executive authority. However, many mayors continue to be limited by fragmented local organization. In addition, few mayors develop strong party organizations and must therefore depend on the strength of their personal appeal in providing political leadership. As state and federal funds support more local projects, mayors and local administrators are subjected to increased rules and regulations established by state legislators and by members of Congress.

Being the mayor in most large cities is a perilous job with constant political and economic pressure. Few survive well enough to be successful in running for higher office.* In small towns, mayors are often main-street merchants who lack the ambition to seek higher office. Even if they perform effectively, mayors often have difficulty becoming well known when seeking statewide office.

City executives function as part of four basic forms of government: **weak-mayor–council, strong-mayor–council,** council-manager, and commission (the latter was discussed in Chapter 5).

Weak-Mayor–Council Plan

Until the 1870s, all American cities operated with a weak-mayor–council plan of government. As with early state government, city government structure was strongly affected by skepticism about politicians and about government. At a time when local government performed few functions and city officials were coordinated by party organizations, people were afraid to give substantial power to a single executive.

*Of course, there are exceptions to every generalization. Hubert Humphrey, for example, began his political career as mayor of Minneapolis. Richard J. Daley, as noted in Chapter 3, clearly built a powerful local organization and remained in office over a long period of time. Moreover, Daley presided over a city with numerous boards and commissions, which supposedly fragment power. We need to remember, however, that individuals such as Abe Beame, John V. Lindsay, and Carl Stokes apparently ended their political careers after serving as mayors of large cities. New York City's Mayor Ed Koch failed to win the gubernatorial primary in his state.

In a weak-mayor–council system, the council is both a legislative and an executive body (see Figure 6.2). Council members appoint administrative officials; they make policy; they serve as ex-officio members of boards; and they prepare the budget. The mayor is "weak" because of a lack of effective administrative power. The authority to appoint is restricted, and the authority to remove is often altogether lacking. Often the mayor cannot veto ordinances passed by the city council. In cities with weak mayors, no single person is charged with overall responsibility for government action. Other executive officials are independently elected (there is a long ballot that often is not understood by voters), and a number of boards and commissions are not controlled by the mayor. This system was intended to isolate departments from improper political coercion by the mayor.

Weak-mayor–council plans are the product of a different era in American government. They were never intended to serve large, impersonal, urban communities. Currently, this form of government is found mainly in small cities where the scope of public activities is limited. Minneapolis and Los Angeles are examples of large cities with a weak-mayor–council plan.

Strong-Mayor–Council Plan

Under the strong-mayor–council plan, there is a short ballot. The mayor controls the budget and has broad power to appoint and remove city officials (see Figure 6.3). The council confirms appointments, and it usually controls the appropriations process. The mayor's legal position provides a firm base for political leadership, and the mayor is constantly in the limelight. In most cities the "strong" mayor is, in fact, a compromise between a weak and a very strong system.

This plan is used in most large cities where a complex administrative structure requires firm leadership and direction. Most cities with more than 1 million popula-

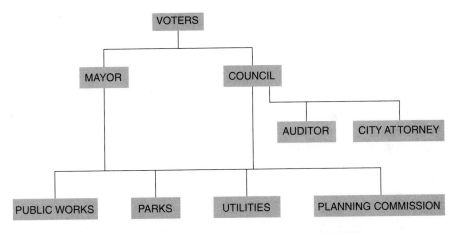

COUNCIL HAS BOTH LEGISLATIVE AND EXECUTIVE AUTHORITY. COUNCIL MUST CONSENT TO MAYOR'S APPOINTMENTS OF DEPARTMENT HEADS. MAYOR'S POWER OF REMOVAL RESTRICTED. COUNCIL HAS PRIMARY CONTROL OVER THE BUDGET.

Figure 6.2   Hypothetical Weak-Mayor–Council Plan

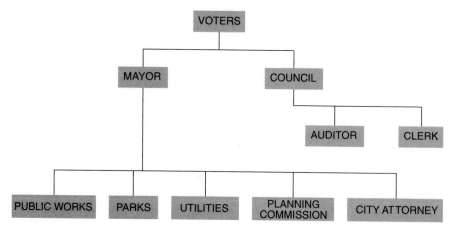

Figure 6.3   **Hypothetical Strong-Mayor–Council Plan**

tion have a strong-mayor–council system. Problems arise when voters expect too much from the mayor and find it easy to blame that individual for whatever goes wrong in the city. Often, those politicians who are effective campaigners lack the administrative skills to manage the day-to-day affairs of a large city. To offset this shortcoming of the system, several cities with strong mayors, including New York City, have established the position of **chief administrative officer** (CAO). Appointed by the mayor, this professional person is given broad authority to manage the financial affairs of the city. In some cities the CAO is a permanent position that carries over from one administration to another. In other cases, it is subject to appointment by the mayor.[23] In New York the mayor selects several CAOs or deputy mayors.

Council-Manager Plan

The council-manager plan originated early in the twentieth century as part of the Progressive movement. Reformers sought to eliminate corruption from city hall by removing administration from partisan politics. Their answer was to replace the mayor with a professional administrator appointed by the council. Among the early city reformers was Richard S. Childs, who founded the national short-ballot organization in 1909. A short ballot implied consolidation of elected offices, and from this followed Childs's manager plan to provide professional or "businesslike" administration. In many cases, plans calling for a **city manager** were accompanied by the initiation of nonpartisan elections.

By 1920, there were 158 cities with managers. The plan has continued to grow in popularity, and there are now more than 3,000 cities, as well as some counties, with managers. This represents about 40 percent of all cities. A majority of all medium-size cities (25,000–250,000) have a council-manager form of government.

Large cities with managers include Kansas City and Cincinnati plus many Sunbelt cities such as San Diego, Phoenix, San Antonio, Memphis, and Miami Metro.

In most cases there is a small council, elected at large, which hires a manager (see Figure 6.4). In the past, managers were often civil engineers. Now they are likely to be people trained in public administration. The manager serves at the pleasure of the council in a relationship similar to that of a superintendent of schools and the board of education. Usually, a mayor is selected from among the council members to perform ceremonial duties. In a few cities, a mayor is popularly elected and shares power with the manager.

Although managers are not supposed to be policy innovators, typically they are involved in presenting proposals to council members and working for their adoption. Increasingly managers see a policymaking role for themselves, and patterns of liberal or conservative policy solutions can be associated with particular managers.[24] The duties of most managers include preparing the city budget, supervising the hiring and firing of city personnel, and negotiating with labor unions. Managers are expert advisers, providing information to city councils.

Much of the political science literature suggests that managers are most likely to be found in cities whose population is predominantly white, Protestant, white collar, middle class, college educated, growing, and mobile. But Thomas R. Dye and Susan A. MacManus, in testing these assumptions, found that the presence of a city manager is only weakly related to population size, economic class, race, religion, and the age of the city.[25] The best indicator of a manager form of government was ethnicity, or the percentage of foreign-born residents in a city. The lower the percentage of foreign-born, the greater the likelihood of a city having a manager. Dye and MacManus did discover that managers are likely to be found in newer, fast-growing cities with mobile populations. This description fits many suburban

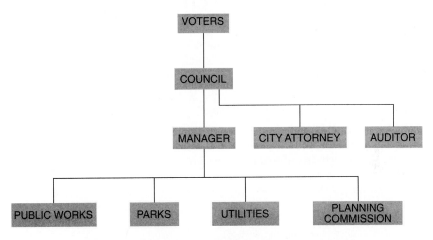

USUALLY SMALL COUNCIL (5–7 MEMBERS). OFTEN NONPARTISAN ELECTIONS.
COUNCIL MEMBERS MAKE POLICY AND OVERSEE CITY ADMINISTRATION.
FULL-TIME PROFESSIONAL MANAGER. BUDGET PREPARED BY THE MANAGER.
MAYOR USUALLY HAS ONLY CEREMONIAL POWER.

Figure 6.4   Hypothetical Council-Manager Plan

communities, and it is there that continuing support for creating council-manager forms of government is to be found. For example, most of the commuter suburbs of Westchester County, New York, have managers.

In general, medium-size cities in the Northeast and Midwest tend to have strong mayors, while Sunbelt cities have managers. In growth areas of the South and Southwest, planning for streets and water lines are priorities, and the council-manager plan seems to work well. In the Northeast and Midwest, the priority is on responding to a variety of racial and ethnic groups, and the strong-mayor–council system has worked well in those circumstances.

Although some reformers have overstated the impact of the manager system (in particular, they fail to understand that "politics" cannot be eliminated and that the struggle for power will not disappear once partisan labels are removed), it has provided efficient, accountable government in many cities. Weaknesses stem from the nature of individual managers—it is difficult to attract competent, experienced people, and the manager must maintain a middle-of-the-road position in which he or she avoids, on the one hand, setting policy and, on the other hand, simply running errands for the council.

Some managers have had a tendency to become very closely identified with business and professional interests in their community. Because of this perceived bias, organized labor in many cities has opposed the creation of a manager plan. There has also been opposition from blacks and other minorities who believe their interests will be better served in nonreformed cities where the mayor's office may be more responsive to citizen demands. Also cities with managers may lack effective political leadership because of the weak position of the mayor.

THE ROLE OF CITY MAYORS

Most mayors lack strong formal authority, even when operating under a strong-mayor system. When big-city mayors must contend with a weak-mayor system, many of them simply cease to function as chief executives. The following exchange between Mayor Samuel Yorty of Los Angeles and Senator Abraham Ribicoff of Connecticut during a congressional hearing in 1966 makes it abundantly clear that the mayor's authority was nearly nonexistent.

SENATOR RIBICOFF: As I listened to your testimony, Mayor Yorty, I have made some notes. This morning you have really waived authority and responsibility in the following areas: schools, welfare, transportation, employment, health, and housing, which leaves you as the head of the city basically with a ceremonial function, police, and recreation.
MAYOR YORTY: That is right, and fire.
SENATOR RIBICOFF: And fire.
MAYOR YORTY: Yes.
SENATOR RIBICOFF: Collecting sewage?
MAYOR YORTY: Sanitation; that is right.
SENATOR RIBICOFF: In other words, basically you lack jurisdiction, authority, responsibility for what makes a city move?
MAYOR YORTY: That is exactly it.[26]

Because the powers of mayors are often weak and the problems of big cities—crime, drugs, homelessness—seem to defy solutions, many cities have been viewed as ungovernable. More recent financial cutbacks by the federal government and the states have placed additional burdens on city administrations. In the accompanying reading for this chapter, political commentators Germond and Witcover wonder why anyone would want to be mayor.

Mayors, like governors and presidents, play a variety of roles. As the ceremonial head of the city, the mayor greets distinguished visitors to the city, attends endless rounds of dinners, and issues proclamations. These activities help give mayors visibility, and they build up political goodwill. As chief administrators, mayors oversee the work of city employees and prepare an executive budget. They are limited in this function, however, by the presence of independent boards and commissions and other officials who are independently elected. As chief legislators, mayors often exercise strong control over the agenda considered by the council, and they may veto ordinances passed by the council. Increasingly, mayors act as chief city ambassador, devoting a great deal of time to meetings at the state capital and in Washington. Many cities have full-time lobbyists in Washington, and others act through the United States Conference of Mayors and the National League of Cities.

The ways in which mayors carry out their formal duties depend in large part on their style of leadership. At one extreme is the *passive caretaker and policy mediator.* Mayors of this sort take very little initiative, preferring to have private groups agree on projects, which they may endorse. These mayors make little effort to influence policy. Their basic concern is to maintain city services and make as few waves as possible. In some instances, the caretaker mayor may excel at ceremonial duties—cutting ribbons, welcoming conventions—and thus improve the image of the city. At the other extreme is the *policy innovator and champion.* Mayors of this sort want to exert strong leadership over their councils and the entire city. For example, Mayor Fiorello La Guardia of New York City (1933–1945) believed that "*his* policies should prevail in *every* area of government activity." Of course, some activist mayors may not be able to accomplish much in the way of substantive policy change. Douglas Yates cites the example of John Lindsay, who as mayor of New York City in the 1960s was a crusader for change but accomplished only a limited amount.[27] The *opportunistic policy broker* style of mayor stands between these two extremes. While these mayors do not wish to dominate all city activities, neither do they wish to handle only housekeeping responsibilities. Richard J. Daley of Chicago is described as a classic broker politician who chose from policy proposals put forth by individuals outside city hall. It was, however, only Mayor Daley's "seal of approval" that could put the proposals into operation.

The power of mayors, even more than the power of the president, rests in their ability to persuade through the use of public relations approaches, the mass media, and bargaining among various urban interests. If mayors are effective as persuaders, they can overcome many of the handicaps of weak formal authority—as did Richard Lee of New Haven, Connecticut. In a classic study of political power, Lee was described as "not [being at] the peak of a pyramid but rather at the center of intersecting circles."[28] He rarely commanded. He negotiated, cajoled, exhorted, beguiled, charmed, pressed, appealed, reasoned, promised, insisted, demanded,

Why Would Anyone Want to Be Mayor?

SAN DIEGO—The natural question that occurs to anyone attending the 59th annual meeting of the U.S. Conference of Mayors is why in the world anyone would want to be a mayor in the first place.

The catalog of problems confronting major cities seems both endless and disheartening: crime, drugs, homelessness, AIDS, struggling schools, inadequate health care, decaying housing, collapsing infrastructures. And the mayors are dealing with them with few weapons in their arsenals.

Their financial crises have become routine. Although Bridgeport, Conn., may be the first large city to declare bankruptcy, dozens of others are papering over near collapses with fiscal gimmicks, deep cuts in services and staff and—in more cases than not this year—tax increases. The flow of money from the federal government and states has been cut radically in a decade of Republican Administrations in Washington.

Unsurprisingly, the major cities are also in danger of being the prime losers from the 1990 federal census. The new estimates of the population show the undercount was greatest in communities with large numbers of minority citizens—enough so that, for example, Atlanta Mayor Maynard Jackson says the undercount would cost him more than $40 million a year in federal aid. But there is no assurance Commerce Secretary Robert A. Mosbacher will certify the revised figures by the deadline for such action next month. [Secretary Mosbacher did not approve adjustment of the census.]

National politicians seem to have a horror of being identified with mayors whose principal constituents often are an underclass of blacks and Hispanics, many of them welfare recipients who consume tax money that white middle-class voters increasingly resent spending on them. Although President Bush spent a recent weekend making speeches and playing golf in California within an hour of the gathering of mayors, he didn't show up here.

Bush is by no means the first President of either party to skip the Mayors Conference. But most Administrations have at least dispatched a few Cabinet officials who deal with urban problems to make a show of concern. But not even Housing Secretary Jack F. Kemp, who has shown a genuine interest in city problems, turned up for this one.

The brush-off was bipartisan, however. The only Democratic presidential candidate, declared or de facto, who appeared was former Sen. Paul E. Tsongas of Massachusetts, perhaps the longest-odds bet in the potential field today and, as such, a man in search of opportunities to deliver his message that the Democratics must build a better relationship with business.

The President's willingness to ignore the cities is no surprise. He was elected by the white middle class, and he has no reason to expect his support in the underclass to be any more substantial next year. The much-advertised Republican Party attempt to broaden its base by reaching out to more black voters has been exposed as empty rhetoric.

But no one would accuse Democratic congressional leaders of falling all over themselves to help the cities, either. And if they imagine that they would have those comfortable majorities in the Senate and House without the overwhelming Democratic votes in the cities, they are very much mistaken.

To some degree, the federal government's attitude can be attributed to its own fiscal situation. The deficits that have accumulated in the past decade leave little room for any fresh attacks on urban problems, particularly during a recession. But it is also unquestionably true that Democrats—with a few exceptions—don't relish being identified with the mayors and their tax-consuming constituencies.

Voicing a demand for new job-producing federal spending, Boston Mayor Raymond L. Flynn, the incoming president of the conference, put it this way: "Washington's policy, for Democrats and Republicans alike, has been to close their eyes and pretend that people aren't out of work, aren't in danger of losing their homes and aren't worried about providing for their families. But mayors can't run away and hide, because the people who need jobs, the people who can't make ends meet, the people who can't send their kids to college—they are our neighbors, and they are in trouble. Of course, some people say that the recession has bottomed out. But when you're 30 feet in a ditch and you climb up 5 feet, you're still deep in the hole, and you still need a rope or a ladder to help you pull out of it."

Some of the more politically astute mayors also recognize, however, that they may be compounding their practical problems if they engage in constant complaints against the federal government and continue to emphasize the vexing travail of the underclass.

Mayor Richard M. Daley of Chicago, for example, has established a reputation for reaching out to minorities in his city. But Daley says that the Mayors Conference would be politically wiser to put more emphasis on middle-class concerns such as education. Improving the public schools, the Chicago mayor points out accurately, can do more than any other single thing to hold the middle class in cities.

Even if the nation's mayors are guilty, however, of some strategic failures, the distance at which they are being held is clearly a symptom of the "I'm all right, Jack" disdain in the American electorate for social programs that are largely geared to the poor and any return to an expanded role for the federal government.

To some degree, the mayors' problems may also be a reflection of the resurgent racial resentment in the electorate.

In theory, the government in Washington is supposed to play a balancing role in American society by providing at least a minimum social opportunity for those of its citizens who have been put at a competitive disadvantage for one reason or another.

That isn't happening, and it is one of the reasons you have to wonder why anyone wants to be a mayor.

SOURCE: Jack W. Germond and Jules Witcover, *National Journal*, June 22, 1991, p. 1582. Reprinted by permission.

even threatened; but he most needed support from other leaders who simply could not be commanded. Because the mayor did not dare command, he had to bargain.

Although it is difficult to generalize about the backgrounds and attitudes of mayors, case studies have discovered historical patterns in selected cities. In Chicago, for example, most mayors since 1930 have been Catholic, and all have risen through the ranks of the local party organization. In San Francisco and St. Louis, local businesspeople with outgoing personalities have most often been elected mayor. In the past thirty years, the office of mayor seldom has been a steppingstone to higher political office. Former mayors such as Carl Stokes (Cleveland) and John Lindsay (New York) have simply built up too many political liabilities. In many cases, mayors have not even been able to secure their party's nomination for statewide office.

Minority mayors constitute an increasingly large category of individuals who, while they have different styles of leadership, face similar problems. Since 1980, blacks have served as mayors of many of the nation's largest cities—Detroit, Philadelphia, Chicago, Los Angeles, Atlanta, Baltimore, Seattle, New Orleans, Memphis, and New York. Hispanics have been mayors of San Antonio, Miami, and Denver. There have been women mayors in San Francisco, San Diego, Houston, and Dallas. In most cases, blacks have been elected because they received virtually 100 percent of the black vote. Once in office, they need to work with the predominantly white business community in order to further economic development for blacks. Some black mayors find it difficult to maintain an effective balance between catering to their black electoral constituency and forging alliances with upper-class white bankers and merchants. Another problem is that mayoral races between black and white candidates tend to polarize racial issues in a city. Studies show that while minority mayors may have special problems, they have increased the number of blacks and women working for the city.[29]

In this chapter, the fragmented nature of state and local government has been stressed repeatedly. Governors and mayors have been given little formal authority as chief administrators, and government agencies have developed in a haphazard manner. The following chapter deals with an equally fragmented system—state and local courts. Once again, much of the twentieth-century history of state court systems can be written in terms of attempts to unify and make manageable a structure based on nineteenth-century needs and attitudes.

KEY TERMS

Administrative efficiency An early-twentieth-century reform goal to be achieved through merit appointments and better control and coordination of administrative departments.

Bureaucracy The administrative system of government agencies, which carries on day-to-day decision making by the use of standardized procedures.

Bureaucratic culture The social and procedural factors that distinguish particular government agencies or departments.

Chief administrative officer An adviser to mayors who is usually responsible for budgeting and personnel.

City manager A professional administrator, appointed by the city council, whose responsibilities include personnel management and the preparation of a city budget. Performs the administrative tasks typically assigned to a mayor.

Collective bargaining Negotiating the terms of employment between labor and management.

Executive budget State budget prepared by the governor and his or her appointees.

Hoover Commission Study of the federal executive branch conducted in 1949; it recommended the consolidation of many federal agencies.

Implementation The carrying out of public policies by bureaucrats. In government, it is marked by widespread discretion on the part of individual administrators.

Incremental budgeting Basing the current budget largely on last year's budget.

Item veto Allows the governor to veto (return unsigned a legislative proposal or indicate points of disagreement) objectionable parts of bills without rejecting bills in their entirety.

Jacksonian era Beginning with the election of Andrew Jackson as president in 1828, a period marked by an increase in democratic procedures, including universal manhood suffrage, direct election of public officials, short terms of office, and the spoils system.

Merit system Making appointments to public office on the basis of the ability to perform assigned tasks. This system uses scores on competitive examinations as the basis for hiring and promoting.

National Guard A volunteer armed force commanded by state governors. The Guard may be called into federal service at any time by the president. Formerly called the militia.

Pardon The power of governors to release people from punishment after they have been convicted of a crime.

Postaudit A check by the state auditor to see if state agencies have spent money as intended by the legislature. *Preaudits* are performed by the controller to approve administrative expenditures before they are made.

Privatization Turning over the management of public services to the private sector. Includes contracting out, using vouchers, and selling off public enterprises.

Professional ideology Codes of conduct, based on membership in professional associations, which influence the behavior of public officials.

Program-planning-budgeting system A budget technique in which government agencies must justify specific requests for appropriations in terms of how well particular programs are achieving their intended goals.

Reorganization Changes in administrative structure that often consolidate departments and promote more centralized control of bureaucracy.

Strong-mayor–council A system of local government in which the mayor exercises broad administrative authority. Found in most large cities.

Weak-mayor–council A system of local government in which the mayor has limited administrative authority (particularly concerning the budget and personnel) and the council performs both legislative and executive duties.

Zero-based budgeting A technique that breaks down each government agency into its individual functions and analyzes each function annually. Thus each agency's budget starts at zero and builds in programs only if they can be justified each year by the agency.

REFERENCES

1. Larry Sabato, *Goodbye to Good-Time Charlie,* 2d ed. (Washington, D.C.: Congressional Quarterly Press, 1983), p. 52. For an examination of how governors perceive them-

selves, see Thad L. Beyle and Lynn R. Muchmore, eds., *Being Governor* (Durham, N.C.: Duke University Press, 1983).

2. J. Stephen Turett, "The Vulnerability of American Governors, 1900–1969," *Midwest Journal of Political Science,* February 1971.

3. Thad L. Beyle, "The Governors," in *The Book of the States 1990–91* (Lexington, Ky.: Council of State Governments, 1990), p. 50.

4. Malcolm E. Jewell and David M. Olson, *American State Political Parties and Elections,* 3d ed. (Chicago: Dorsey Press, 1988), p. 289.

5. Joseph A. Schlesinger, "The Politics of the Executive," in Herbert Jacob and Kenneth N. Vines, eds., *Politics in the American States,* 2d ed. (Boston: Little, Brown, 1971), pp. 222–234.

6. Thad L. Beyle, "Governors," in Virginia Gray, Herbert Jacob, and Robert B. Albritton, eds., *Politics in the American States,* 5th ed. (Glenview, Ill.: Scott, Foresman/Little, Brown, 1990), pp. 217–230.

7. Beyle, "The Governors," p. 54.

8. Thad L. Beyle, "The Institutionalized Powers of the Governorship: 1965–1985," *Comparative State Politics Newsletter,* February 1988, pp. 23–29; and Beyle, "The Governors," pp. 227–230.

9. Sarah McCally Morehouse, "The Governor as Political Leader," in Herbert Jacob and Kenneth N. Vines, eds., *Politics in the American States,* 3d ed. (Boston: Little, Brown, 1976), p. 239.

10. Charles R. Adrian, *State and Local Governments,* 4th ed. (New York: McGraw-Hill, 1976), p. 237.

11. Alan Rosenthal, *Governors and Legislatures: Contending Powers* (Washington, D.C.: Congressional Quarterly Press, 1990), p. 97.

12. See Tom Wicker, *A Time to Die* (New York: Quadrangle, 1975).

13. Martha Wagner Weinberg, *Managing the State* (Cambridge, Mass.: MIT Press, 1977), pp. 6, 21–23.

14. *Ibid.,* p. 24.

15. Sarah McCally Morehouse, *State Politics, Parties and Policy* (New York: Holt, Rinehart and Winston, 1981), p. 224.

16. Richard P. Nathan, Fred C. Doolittle, et al., eds., *Reagan and the States* (Princeton, N.J.: Princeton University Press, 1987), pp. 109–110.

17. Morehouse, *State Politics,* p. 227.

18. Richard C. Elling, "Bureaucracy," in Gray, Jacob, and Albritton, eds., *Politics in the American States,* pp. 288–289.

19. *Ibid.,* p. 298.

20. Rosenthal, *Governors and Legislatures,* pp. 140–141.

21. Elling, "Bureaucracy," pp. 307–308.

22. E. S. Savas, *Privatization: The Key to Better Government* (Chatham, N.J.: Chatham House, 1987), p. 3.

23. Bernard H. Ross, Myron A. Levine, and Murray S. Stedman, *Urban Politics,* 4th ed. (Itasca, Ill.: F. E. Peacock, 1991), pp. 97–98.

24. David N. Ammons and Charldean Newell, "City Managers Don't Make Policy: A Lie, Let's Face It," *National Civic Review,* March/April 1988, pp. 124–132.

25. Thomas R. Dye and Susan A. MacManus, "Predicting City Government Structure," *American Journal of Political Science,* May 1976, p. 260.

26. Quoted in Jay S. Goodman, *The Dynamics of Urban Government and Politics* (New York: Macmillan, 1975), p. 315.

27. Douglas Yates, *The Ungovernable City* (Cambridge, Mass.: MIT Press, 1977).

28. Robert A. Dahl, *Who Governs? Democracy and Power in an American City* (New Haven, Conn.: Yale University Press, 1961), p. 204.

29. See Peter K. Eisinger, "Black Mayors and the Policy of Racial Advancement," in William C. McReedy, ed., *Culture, Ethnicity, and Identity* (New York: Academic Press, 1983), pp. 95–109, and Grace Hall Saltzstein, "Female Mayors and Women in Municipal Jobs," *American Journal of Political Science,* February 1986, pp. 128–139.

CHAPTER 7

COURTS, POLICE, AND CORRECTIONS

The state courts deal with those issues that most directly affect people's everyday lives. Most criminal cases are decided in state courts. Virtually all cases dealing with domestic relations—divorce, adoption, child custody—are heard by state courts. Questions of property ownership, contracts, zoning, wills and estates, and automobile accidents all originate in state courts.

The legal system of the United States is complicated by a federal structure that permits a variety of laws and courts, rather than specifying a unified plan. Throughout the country, state law is the basic law. In the United States, federal law is drafted for specific purposes and **common law** is interpreted individually by each state.* In such a situation, both state and federal courts are bound by state law unless a state statute has been superseded by federal law or is in conflict with the Constitution.

The system is made even more complex by the dual nature of state and federal courts. Unlike many other federal systems, in the United States both the states and the federal government have a complete set of trial and appellate courts. Although federal courts are concerned only with cases that raise federal issues (i.e., involve the interpretation of federal laws or the U.S. Constitution), the jurisdiction of state and federal courts occasionally overlaps. In some civil suits this gives plaintiffs the choice of initiating action in a state or federal court, and in some criminal cases it means the defendant may be tried in both state and federal courts. State courts are inferior to federal courts in the sense that decisions of state supreme courts can be reviewed and overturned by the U.S. Supreme Court. However, the Supreme Court annually reviews only a handful of the thousands of state court decisions.

Although there have been significant organizational reforms in state court systems in the past twenty years, the judicial branch clearly has not been changed as much as the legislative and executive branches. As we will see in this chapter, current issues being addressed include reduction of delay, selection of judges, the role of women and minorities in the courts, and alternative resolutions to disputes.

STATE COURT ORGANIZATION

The historical development of state court systems is strikingly similar to the development of state and local bureaucracy as discussed in Chapter 6. In the nineteenth century, the forces of urbanization and industrialization created a myriad of social and economic problems. Crowded cities led to increases in crime and juvenile delinquency and to the breakup of families. Landlord-tenant relations caused conflicts that were resolved by lawsuits. Questions of employer liability for personal injury and property damage opened new areas in the law. The use of automobiles created traffic law problems; and, of course, accident claims placed a heavy burden on city courts.

---

*Common law is judge-made law that originated in England from decisions shaped according to existing custom. Decisions were reapplied in similar situations and, over a period of time, became common to the nation. English common law formed the basis of legal proceedings in the American states—except in Louisiana, where French legal traditions were used—and it has been preserved over the years. Common law also serves as the basis for much federal constitutional and statutory law.

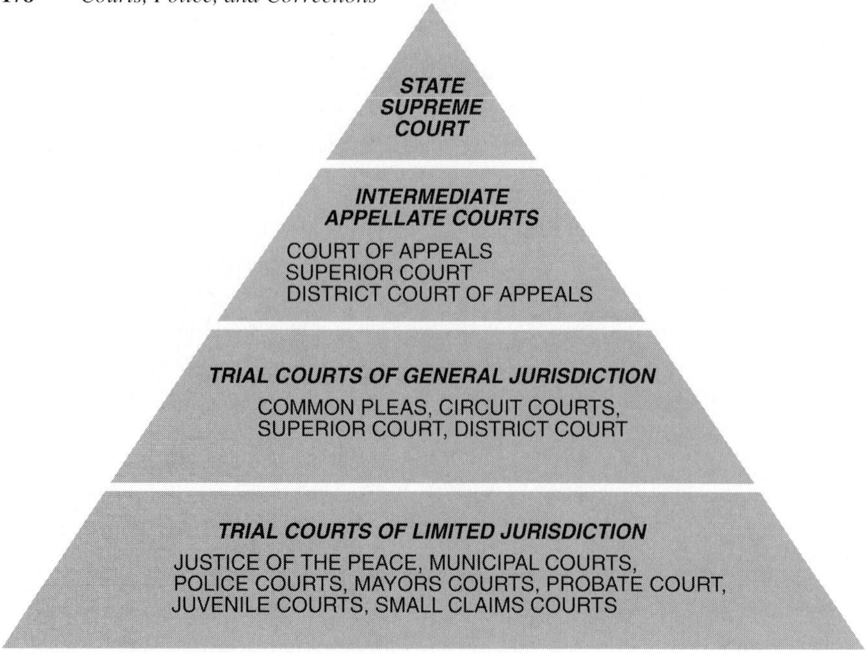

STATE
SUPREME
COURT

INTERMEDIATE
APPELLATE COURTS
COURT OF APPEALS
SUPERIOR COURT
DISTRICT COURT OF APPEALS

TRIAL COURTS OF GENERAL JURISDICTION
COMMON PLEAS, CIRCUIT COURTS,
SUPERIOR COURT, DISTRICT COURT

TRIAL COURTS OF LIMITED JURISDICTION
JUSTICE OF THE PEACE, MUNICIPAL COURTS,
POLICE COURTS, MAYORS COURTS, PROBATE COURT,
JUVENILE COURTS, SMALL CLAIMS COURTS

Figure 7.1   Basic Structure of State Court Systems

The response of many states was to create new courts, just as new boards and commissions were added to cope with regulatory problems. As with the bureaucracy, courts expanded in an unplanned manner. Their jurisdiction often overlapped, and each court acted independently of others.* New courts included those for juvenile and family relations, small claims, and traffic. Each court had its own rules of procedure, and the nature of decisions varied among courts with similar jurisdiction. As with state administrative structures, much of the history of twentieth-century court organization can be written in terms of reform attempts to unify and streamline complex state court systems.

Although the names of particular courts vary from state to state, a basic three- or four-tier division of courts can be identified in each of the fifty states: trial courts of limited jurisdiction, trial courts of general jurisdiction, and appellate courts (see Figure 7.1).

Courts of limited jurisdiction typically handle only cases dealing with certain subject matter (for example, traffic offenses), or they are limited to hearing less serious criminal and civil cases. Municipal courts, for example, often hear only criminal misdemeanor cases where the punishment is a fine or a jail sentence of less than six months. They hear civil suits where there is a limit of perhaps $500 in damages being sought. When a case is appealed from these courts, a new trial is held *(trial de novo)* without reference to the first proceeding.

*A 1931 study found there were 556 independent courts in Chicago, of which 505 were justice of the peace courts. Cited in Henry R. Glick and Kenneth N. Vines, *State Court Systems* (Englewood Cliffs, N.J.: Prentice-Hall, 1973), p. 25. In such a situation, court costs, reputation of judges, and speed of securing a decision were considered in deciding which court to use. Justices of the peace competed for business and would often trade favorable decisions for continued use of their courts.

At the bottom rung of **trial courts,** many states have abolished justices of the peace and courts presided over by mayors and magistrates. These have been replaced by county or municipal courts. Justices of the peace settled local traffic law violations, issued warrants for arrest and search, and performed marriages. In some states, they did not receive a base salary but were paid a percentage of fines collected. This led to the classic "kangaroo court," in which the justice and local police officers cooperated in the profitable business of setting speed traps and sharing the fines. Mayors' courts have operated in a fashion similar to justices of the peace, with many small-town mayors meting out "justice" in a very personal manner.

In most towns of moderate size, municipal judges perform the functions previously reserved for justices of the peace. These judges are reasonably well paid and are trained as lawyers. In addition to deciding civil and criminal cases (whose procedures are described below in the section on "Trial Court Procedures"), municipal courts also conduct preliminary hearings in felony cases (serious crimes) to determine if there is sufficient evidence to hold an accused person for trial in a higher court. Large cities have created vast networks of specialized courts to handle such matters as traffic offenses, juvenile delinquency, and drunkenness.

Courts of general jurisdiction handle all civil and criminal cases that involve the interpretation of state law. Typically such courts are established at the county level. These are courts of original jurisdiction, from which decisions may be appealed to higher courts. However, as with courts of limited jurisdiction, few decisions are appealed, and thus for most litigants these are, in fact, courts of first and last resort.

Intermediate **courts of appeal** are found in thirty-seven states. Some states have one appellate court; in other states there are several regional appellate courts. Even where these intermediate courts do exist, cases will often proceed directly from the trial court to the *state supreme court* . Appellate courts have at least three members, and supreme courts have between five and nine members, with seven being the most common number. Appellate courts serve as a check on errors of fact or law that may have arisen in trial courts. Unlike the U.S. Supreme Court, which has broad discretion in accepting or rejecting petitions for review, most state appellate courts must accept virtually all cases appealed to them.

Also in contrast to the U.S. Supreme Court, there are relatively few dissents among judges in state supreme court decisions. Several factors help explain this apparent lack of conflict. First, legal tradition supports unanimity in order to present clear policy guidelines. Second, appellate courts often assign one judge to research the case and write the opinion. In such circumstances, the other judges are likely to concur, since they have not paid close attention to the case. Moreover, because of the nature of their interaction in a small group setting, there is a need to maintain congenial personal relations. Finally, in contrast to legislators, judges are more likely to be drawn from a homogeneous upper-class or middle-class background, which means they tend to share similar perspectives on many legal issues. In the mid-1980s ten states did not have a woman appellate judge, and in thirty-one states there were not any black appellate judges.[1]

REFORM OF STATE COURTS

The structure of state courts can have an important political impact on a variety of groups. Particularly in urban areas, courts have massive backlogs of cases, a situation that directly influences the administration of justice. In the past thirty years, the number of cases filed and disposed of has increased by 1,000 percent. Because they are unable to make *bail* (money or credit deposited with the court to get an arrested person temporarily released on the assurance that he or she will appear for trial), large numbers of people charged with crimes, but assumed innocent until proved guilty, are forced to spend months in county jails waiting for their cases to appear on the court calendar. Forced to exist in overcrowded, outdated facilities, many prisoners have suffered physical hardships, and a variety of suits have been initiated by civil liberties groups to force improvements in jail conditions. These same groups have protested against the bail system, which forces indigents to await trial in jail, and they have complained vigorously about judicial sentencing practices in which different penalties, ranging from probation to several years in prison, are given to individuals who have committed similar offenses. The backlog of cases has also led to the widespread use of **plea bargaining** (discussed in the following section), in which the accused are encouraged to plead guilty to lesser charges in return for the promise of leniency in sentencing. As a result, seemingly routine court decisions have had serious cumulative effects on the administration of criminal justice.

The variety of courts operating under different rules of procedure within a single county results in confusion and unequal application of the law. The quality of "justice" may depend largely on how successful attorneys are in steering cases to courts presided over by friendly judges. Trial judges function independently of one another, and there are few effective controls that can be applied to them by appellate courts.

Faced with such a situation, reformers have called for an integrated system in which the number of separate courts would be greatly reduced and the problem of overlapping jurisdiction eliminated. Reformers would place all judges under the general supervision of the chief justice of their state in order to ensure uniform practices and standards of conduct. As will be seen later in this chapter, reformers would also like to eliminate the use of judgeships as political patronage.

Structural reform includes both the **consolidation of courts** and the **centralization of courts.** Only a few states have consolidated their court system into a single set of courts that handle all trial court litigation. Most continue to have a number of specialized courts with their own procedures. For example, Indiana has eleven kinds of trial courts. States have been more successful in centralizing or unifying their court system under an administrative judge who controls workloads, makes staff assignments, and determines budgets. Increasingly (twenty-nine states), states are assuming all or most of the funding of court systems. Only a few states, such as Hawaii, have consolidated *and* centralized their courts. At the other extreme, the court systems in Indiana and Massachusetts are nonconsolidated and decentralized. Most states fall in the middle in both areas, and centralization and consolidation do not necessarily coincide.[2]

Reform is difficult to accomplish because traditional court practices benefit groups, such as lawyers and political parties, that have substantial political influence. Opposition also comes from legislators and judges who believe their existing power would be diminished by the elimination of the current maze of courts. However, since 1978 all states have had a court administration office, and some states monitor courts and shift judges to respond to case loads across the state.

Judicial reform has stressed better access to the courts. Many people are effectively denied access because of legal costs. Many states do not require public defender systems statewide. Even when they exist, public defender offices are often underfunded, and budgets for paying court-appointed counsel were cut in the 1980s. Most researchers conclude that public defenders are more effective than court-appointed attorneys, who may have little criminal court experience. In general, however, defending the poor is not a high priority for state and local governments.[3] The United States is the only Western democracy in which civil litigants are not guaranteed legal counsel. Access is also limited by language difficulties, particularly for Spanish-speaking Americans. Racial and ethnic minorities face an additional psychological barrier. The courts, controlled by white men in black robes, present a fearful image. If access is improved, it will, of course, increase the case loads of courts that are already crowded.

A means of helping to resolve disputes without overburdening the courts is to use alternatives to the formal structure. A recent trend has been to increase the use of mediation and arbitration, especially to deal with domestic relations cases. Many of these programs have been developed at neighborhood justice centers that operate without recognition by the regular courts. Some states have hire-a-judge programs in which litigants in civil disputes can hire a retired judge to hear their case.

TRIAL COURT PROCEDURES

A popular view of the administration of justice is that of the classic adversary system in which the attorney (say, Perry Mason) battles valiantly on behalf of his or her clients. There is always a jury, a narrow-minded prosecutor, and a white-haired judge who wields even control as the attorneys take turns objecting to the irrelevant, immaterial, and leading questions of their worthy opponent. In such a setting, justice always triumphs as the defendant is exonerated and the guilty person is dramatically exposed. In fact, however, most legal issues are settled without a trial when the defendant pleads guilty and the judge issues a sentence.

Only about 10 percent of all criminal cases come to trial. Most are settled in pretrial negotiations among the defendant, the prosecutor, and the judge. Plea bargaining is a common practice because it appears to benefit each of the interested parties. *Defendants* plead guilty because they receive a reduction of charge (e.g., from aggravated murder to manslaughter); a reduction in length of sentence; a promise of probation; or some combination of these agreements that results in softening the potential damage of the original charge. *Prosecutors* seek to avoid time-consuming trials, and they also wish to keep their conviction rates high. In some cases, the prosecutor may have obtained evidence illegally or may wish to protect informants by keeping them from taking the witness stand; he or she is therefore willing to trade a trial with its doubtful outcome for the sure thing of a guilty plea to a reduced charge. Attorneys for both sides like pretrial settlements because they can control the flow of information. Witnesses are not questioned and they are not subject to the strict rules of trial procedure. *Judges*, concerned with avoiding delay and backlogs, encourage plea bargaining as a speedy way to dispose of cases. The *police* benefit because they do not have to appear in court as witnesses during their off-duty hours. Plea bargaining also helps the police "clear" cases and therefore bolsters their image as successful crime fighters. This was acknowledged as a judicial fact of life by the U.S. Supreme Court in *Santobello* v. *New York* (1971). While the *Santobello* decision recognizes the need for plea bargaining, it also requires that bargains be kept and that judges make sure that defendants understand the agreements.

Plea bargaining is a quick and efficient means of disposing of legal disputes. Given the existing structure of the courts and the limited number of judges, the legal system in most states would rapidly break down if even half the criminal defendants pleaded not guilty and demanded a jury trial. At the present time, many defendants are convinced that they will be in for a rough time if they do not cooperate with the police and plead guilty rather than having their cases come to trial.

Plea bargaining has been going on for more than 100 years, and it is not a technique that developed in response to a heavy criminal workload in big cities. In fact, evidence suggests that heavy workloads do not cause plea bargaining.[4] Plea bargaining is widespread in rural counties that have low crime rates, and in some cities with heavy case loads it is used relatively little. Researchers suggest that the use of plea bargaining is closely tied to the closeness of interaction among members of the courtroom work group—judges, lawyers, and prosecutors.[5] Since these officials often work closely together for a year or more, close personal relations develop and they seek more informal solutions for cases. Pretrial settlements in civil cases are a product of the same circumstances that lead to plea bargaining in criminal cases. In both situations settlement reduces uncertainty. It allows the court to dispose of cases more quickly, and all members of the work group benefit.

In spite of its appealing characteristics, plea bargaining has many disturbing consequences. In plea bargaining, the procedures are invisible and informal. Records are not kept of conversations, and decisions seldom are reviewed by higher courts to determine if the defendant really was guilty as charged. There is a strong potential for coercion as the prosecutor pressures the defendant. Illegally obtained evidence that might be held inadmissible in a court is never questioned. Often the unsuspecting defendant is simply advised by his or her court-appointed attorney to plead guilty, thereby saving the attorney time and allowing him or her to collect an easy fee.

Given the broad criticism of plea bargaining, it is not surprising that there have been calls to abolish it. Indeed, some state and local governments have experimented with strict limits on plea bargaining. However, most have reinstated it rather quickly. As noted earlier, close-knit courtroom work groups encourage plea bargaining, and in most cases it is clear that the defendant is guilty. Several states and the federal government have passed new laws requiring mandatory minimum sentencing for certain crimes. This would eliminate plea bargaining in those instances. However, prosecutors often refuse to charge defendants with crimes that require a mandatory sentence because it limits their power to bargain.

In civil cases, there is typically an even greater delay than in criminal cases. In urban areas it may be several years before a case comes to trial. Trial court delay may be caused by a variety of factors. These include lax continuance policies that allow lawyers to control the pace of litigation, lack of adequate case monitoring by the court system, and lack of commitment by judges to control their dockets.[6] Delay is a major factor leading to out-of-court settlements, in which the two parties agree to a financial resolution of their dispute. Many civil suits involve personal injury in which the plaintiff has accumulated substantial medical bills. Because of the pressure of medical and legal expenses, plaintiffs may choose to settle before a trial date arrives. The defendant (often an insurance company) can usually better afford the costs incurred in delay but may wish to settle privately, being aware of exorbitant awards made by juries in cases where physical injury has resulted in the permanent loss of sight or limb.

When the full range of legal procedures is employed, the following patterns in civil and criminal cases can be identified as common among the states.

Civil Disputes

The procedure in a **civil dispute** is as follows:

1. The plaintiff (the complainant, the one who brings suit) approaches a lawyer, who requests the clerk of the proper court to issue a *writ of summons*. This writ, delivered by a sheriff, directs the defendant to appear in court to answer the plaintiff's charges. Failure to appear will result in the defendant losing the judgment by default.

2. Once the summons is delivered, the plaintiff files a *complaint* stating his or her cause of action and establishing that the court has jurisdiction and can provide a remedy in his or her dispute. The complaint is filed with the clerk of courts, who then has a copy delivered to the defendant along with a notice that the complaint is to be answered by a certain date. The defendant may admit to the charges, deny some or all of the charges, or argue that the charges do not raise a sufficient legal issue for the case to come to court. The judge will rule on the defendant's response and, unless he or she has admitted guilt, will allow the defendant to file a more detailed answer. This process of charge and response and possible countercharge by the defendant may continue for an extended period of time. When all complaints are answered and all pleadings filed, the issue is "joined" and the attorneys prepare for trial.

3. *Preliminary motions* are made and the case then lies dormant for several months (or years) as the trial date approaches. During the delay, negotiation takes place in an attempt to settle the dispute out of court. More than two-thirds of the cases filed never get beyond the preliminary stages, and in fact many cases are filed with no intention of pushing them to trial. Because lawyers in many civil cases are compensated on a contingency basis (they receive from 25 to 40 percent of the award), they push for out-of-court settlements to be sure of receiving some payment and to save the time and effort of going to trial. Shortly before the trial date, **pretrial conferences** are held in which the judge meets with attorneys for each side in an attempt to clarify and simplify the issues.

4. If a settlement cannot be reached privately, the case goes to *trial.* The parties have a constitutional right to a jury trial in controversies exceeding $20. Often the jury trial is waived, although plaintiffs in personal injury cases may prefer a jury rather than having the case heard by a judge, who they believe will be less generous. The judge or jury will decide which party was legally at fault and will also determine the amount of damages to be awarded. It is possible to appeal the verdict to a higher court.

Criminal Disputes

The procedure in a **criminal dispute** is as follows:

1. Before any arrests are made, the police must secure a **warrant.** A magistrate issues the warrant directing a search or the apprehension of a suspect, having received a sworn statement that there is probable cause to believe that a crime has been committed by a particular person at a given time and place. If the warrant authorizes a search, it must state clearly the place to be searched and the material to be seized.
2. Following his or her arrest, the defendant is brought before a magistrate (often a municipal judge) for a *preliminary hearing.* The purpose of this hearing is to determine if the prosecution has sufficient evidence to hold the accused and, if so, to set bail.
3. The prosecutor proceeds to determine the strength of his or her case. In many states, the prosecutor (district attorney) simply files a statement (the "information") with the appropriate court, which *indicts* or formally accuses a person of the commission of a crime. In other states, the prosecutor presents evidence that a serious crime has been committed to a **grand jury.*** If the grand jury finds sufficient reason to believe the accused committed the crime for which he or she is charged, it will return a "true bill" that indicts the accused, who then is bound over for trial.
4. When both the defendant and the prosecutor are ready for trial, the defendant is brought to court for **arraignment.** The charges are read and a plea of guilty or not guilty is entered. A plea of no contest *(nolo contendere)* is treated essentially the same as a guilty plea.
5. At the *trial* stage, the defendant in most states may waive the right to a jury trial and have the case heard by a judge. If the defendant is found guilty by a judge or jury, it is the judge who determines the sentence. In most states, judges are given broad discretion between minimum and maximum penalties for specific crimes. Of course, the defendant may appeal a guilty verdict.

Juries

Juries have been mentioned in the discussion of both civil and criminal disputes, and a few words of explanation are in order. A group of potential jury persons (a *venire*) is selected by lot, usually from voting lists. These people are called into

---

*The *grand jury* is a body of twelve to twenty-five members whose purposes are inquisitorial and accusatorial. It is contrasted with a *petit jury,* usually of twelve persons, which determines guilt or innocence. The grand jury meets in secret and decides by a majority vote. On occasion, it may conduct its own investigations into official misconduct. The grand jury has the power to subpoena witnesses and records and to compel testimony under oath. It usually follows the dictates of the prosecutor. Because grand juries are expensive and time-consuming, they have been abolished in many states.

court as jury cases arise and are examined regarding their qualifications to return an impartial verdict in the case at hand.

In spite of the importance attached to the jury system, it is not employed as often as one might expect. In some jurisdictions, as many as 90 percent of all people charged with criminal offenses plead guilty. Of those going to trial, roughly half opt to have their cases heard by a judge. Although the Constitution guarantees the right to a jury trial in criminal and civil cases, fewer than 10 percent nationwide of those charged with a criminal offense demand a jury trial. Juries are not required for all cases, and typically criminal misdemeanors and various civil actions—divorce, small claims, landlord-tenant disputes—are heard by judges alone. Juvenile defendants are not automatically guaranteed jury trials.

Compared with judge-tried cases, jury trials are longer, cost more, and involve more people. Most research indicates that judge and jury decisions are remarkably similar. A major study of the American jury system found that judges agreed with jury verdicts 80 percent of the time. When there was disagreement, the jury tended to be more lenient than the judge and more willing to consider a social, as opposed to a strictly legal, definition of guilt.[7] Despite the decline in its use, the jury remains a basic protection of citizens against the overreach of official power.

THE IMPACT OF SUPREME COURT DECISIONS ON THE STATES

Criminal procedures in state trial courts and state criminal statutes have been directly affected by a series of Supreme Court decisions beginning in the early 1960s. The activist Warren Court overturned a number of state court decisions, ruling that the constitutional rights of criminal defendants had not been adequately protected by state officials. In the course of these decisions, the Supreme Court nationalized (i.e., made applicable as limits on state officials) provisions of the Fourth, Fifth, Sixth, and Eighth amendments to the U.S. Constitution. A brief review of some leading decisions since 1960 follows.

In *Mapp* v. *Ohio* (1961), the Supreme Court ruled that the Fourth Amendment (which guarantees freedom from illegal search and seizure) extends to state as well as federal officials. In other words, the police could no longer seize evidence illegally (i.e., without a proper search warrant) and then have that material introduced during a trial to support the prosecutor's case. In **Miranda v. Arizona (1966),** the Court ruled that when state officials take individuals into custody, they must warn them that they have the right to remain silent (Fifth Amendment), that anything they say may be held against them (Fifth Amendment), that they have the right to an attorney (Sixth Amendment), and that if they cannot afford an attorney one will be provided for them. In both *Mapp* and *Miranda,* the Court overruled state convictions on the grounds that the defendants had been denied equal protection of the law as guaranteed by the Fourteenth Amendment. Although the U.S. Supreme Court has not directly overturned its rulings in *Mapp* or *Miranda,* since the mid-1980s it has created exceptions that clearly weaken these rules and permit greater flexibility by state and local law enforcement officers. For example, *Mapp* has been weakened by the concept that if the police act in "good faith" and later discover a warrant is defective, the evidence seized still can be used in court. Regarding *Miranda,* the Court has adopted a "public safety" exception that allows rules to be bypassed if they might delay immediate recovery of a dangerous weapon. In 1991 the Court held that a coerced confession introduced at trial does not necessarily overturn a conviction. Even as the Court chipped away at *Mapp* and *Miranda,* it also reaffirmed and expanded some *Miranda* provisions in its 1990–1991 term.

In *Gideon* v. *Wainwright* (1963) the Supreme Court held that states must provide free legal counsel to indigent defendants accused of felonies. Later, in *Argersinger* v. *Hamlin* (1972), the Court extended the right to court-appointed counsel to include those charged with misdemeanors so long as they faced the possibility of imprisonment. Before the *Gideon* decision, most states already provided free legal counsel to poor defendants. However, these two decisions have placed considerable financial burdens on state and local governments to provide lawyers in criminal cases. By 1968, four-fifths of all defendants in New York City were provided with free lawyers. Two systems for providing counsel to indigent defendants have been used by local governments: assigned counsel from among lawyers in private practice, and public defenders who are paid salaries by public or quasi-public agencies to handle the defense of poor people. In many cities, neighborhood legal-assistance offices, funded by grants from the federal government, provide a third type of counsel to indigents.

The Supreme Court has also ruled that juvenile defendants have a right to legal counsel. *In re Gault* (1967) extended essentially the same basic rights to defendants in juvenile court—right to counsel, right to confront and cross-examine witnesses, privilege against self-incrimination, right to appeal—as are provided adults in the regular court system.

Occasionally a Supreme Court decision will affect the administration of justice in virtually every state, necessitating a revision of criminal statutes across the country. This has occurred in the areas of capital punishment and abortion. In *Furman* v. *Georgia* (1972) a badly divided Court (5 to 4) overruled the imposition of the death penalty in Georgia, declaring that it constituted cruel and unusual punishment in violation of the Eighth and Fourteenth amendments. Since 1972, most states have rewritten their capital punishment statutes in an attempt to institute the death penalty within limits acceptable to the Court. In 1976, the Court upheld capital punishment in Georgia, Florida, and Texas, where statutes allow the judge or jury to set the death penalty after considering mitigating factors. At the same time, the Court struck down mandatory death penalty statutes in North Carolina and Louisiana. In 1977, the Court ruled that capital punishment could not be imposed for the crime of rape. The Court has held that opponents of the death penalty can be excluded from trial juries in capital cases. In general, the Court has deferred to state legislative decisions and ruled in favor of state capital punishment procedures since the 1980s. For example, in 1987 it upheld the death penalty in Georgia, even though statistics showed that blacks were much more likely to be executed than whites. In 1989 the justices agreed that the Eighth Amendment does not bar absolutely the execution of murderers with mental deficiencies or the execution of sixteen- and seventeen-year-old murderers. In both opinions Justice Sandra Day O'Connor cast critical votes with the 5-to-4 majority. In 1991 the Court set limits on the number of petitions that could be filed by death row inmates, hoping to speed up the process of execution.

In *Roe* v. *Wade* (1973) the Supreme Court overturned a Texas statute that made it a felony for anyone to destroy a fetus except "on medical advice for the purpose of saving the life of the mother." Since the Texas statute was typical of those in effect in most states, statutes have been rewritten to allow state control of abortions *after* the third month of pregnancy. Then, in 1977, the Court ruled that state and local governments could choose whether or not to finance abortions for nontherapeutic reasons under Medicaid. In 1980, the Court upheld a congressional ban on federal payments through Medicaid for abortion even to those women for whom the procedure is medically indicated. In one of its most significant abortion decisions since 1973, the Court in *Webster* v. *Reproductive Health Services* (1989) upheld several provisions of a Missouri statute that limited abortion rights. Stopping just short of overturning *Roe* v. *Wade,* the majority in *Webster* sustained provisions making it "unlawful for any public facility to be used for the purpose of performing or assisting an abortion not necessary to save the life of the mother" and "unlawful for any public employee . . . to perform or assist in an abortion not necessary to save the life of the mother." In 1990 the Court upheld a Minnesota law requiring teenage girls to notify both parents or get judicial permission before having an abortion. In 1991 the Court ruled 5 to 4 against abortion counseling in federally funded clinics. This decision raised serious First Amendment expression issues as well as privacy issues.

In 1982, in *Plyler* v. *Doe,* the Supreme Court ruled that alien children's right to "equal protection" under the Fourteenth Amendment encompasses the right to the same education as that offered to all other children by the state of Texas (a 1975 Texas law had empowered local school districts to bar aliens from public schools or to charge them tuition). The Dallas Independent School System had until the decision refused to admit illegal aliens, and the Houston system had charged tuition of $162 a month. Texas as a whole had provided free public education to alien children since 1980, when a federal district court ruled against the 1975 law. In 1981–1982, the number of illegal aliens enrolled in Texas schools was estimated to be from 20,000 to 30,000. Texas estimated that it would cost the state $100 million a year to educate them and argued that the Court's ruling might encourage other aliens to enroll. For the five-person majority, Justice Brennan argued that, although the Court had held that education is not a fundamental right, the Texas law should be subjected to substantial scrutiny because it "imposes a lifetime hardship on a discrete class of children not accountable for their disabling status." Writing for the minority, Chief Justice Burger noted that the equal protection clause "is not an all-encompassing equalizer designed to eradicate every distinction for which persons are not responsible. . . . The Constitution does not provide a cure for every social ill, nor does it vest judges with a mandate to try to remedy every social problem."

Three cases involving the use of juries illustrate the Court's willingness to allow state experimentation with unorthodox practices in criminal procedures. In *Williams* v. *Florida* (1970), the Court upheld the conviction of a criminal defendant in Florida who was tried by a six-person jury as allowed under Florida law in all cases except capital offenses. In *Apodaca* v. *Oregon* (1972), the Court upheld the conviction of a defendant when the jury had voted 10 to 2, the minimum margin necessary under Oregon law, that he was guilty. In 1981, the Court upheld camera coverage of trials in Florida, and since that time most states have permitted television coverage of court proceedings.

With the addition of a clear conservative majority since 1986, the Supreme Court has become increasingly deferential to the states. As we have seen, the Court has been willing to accept state experimentation in the areas of criminal procedures, the death penalty, and abortion. A curious aspect of this approach by the Supreme Court can be seen in *Cruzan* v. *Missouri* (1990), and so-called right-to-die case. In a 5-to-4 opinion the Court upheld the right of a state to establish procedures by which people can express their desire not to be kept alive by artificial means. The majority agreed with the state of Missouri's argument that Nancy Cruzan's parents had not shown clear evidence of their daughter's wishes. In a concurring opinion Justice O'Connor noted that "the more challenging task of crafting appropriate procedures for safeguarding incompetent's liberty interests is entrusted to the laboratory of the states."

The *Cruzan* and *Webster* decisions give states the opportunity to demonstrate how well they can deal with controversial issues and shape public policy.[8] At the same time, this passive role by the U.S. Supreme Court allows losers to pursue their objectives in other forums.[9] For example, Nancy Cruzan's parents brought additional evidence of her desire not to remain in a comatose state to another trial court hearing, and subsequently the feeding tubes were withdrawn. Once abortion became a state legislative issue, prochoice activists gained strength in several states.

JUDICIAL SELECTION

The way in which state court systems function is influenced strongly by the quality of judicial personnel. In turn, the type of judge presiding in courtrooms across the country is influenced by the ways in which judges are selected. Judicial selection is a highly political process that affects very directly the interests of the most powerful partisan forces in states and communities. Political parties use judgeships as a source of patronage. Lawyers and their bar associations are very much involved in the selection process. Not only are the judgeships themselves prized positions, but judges are able to spread the patronage further by assigning counsel in criminal cases, by naming administrators of estates where a will does not exist, and by appointing numerous minor court officials.

Several selection systems are currently used by the fifty states—election, appointment by governors, appointment by legislatures, merit plans, and various combinations of these basic plans (see Table 7.1). Several states use one system for trial judges and another for appellate judges. Trial judges are more likely to be elected than are appellate judges.

Election continues to be the most popular way of selecting judges. Judges are on the ballot along with a variety of other officials, and parties participate by endorsing candidates and managing nominations. Even when nonpartisan systems are used, parties often play a dominant role. In Ohio, for example, judges are chosen in

Table 7.1 Initial Judicial Selection in the States: Appellate and Major Trial Courts

Partisan Election	Appointment by Legislature	Gubernatorial Appointment	Nonpartisan Election	Merit Plan
Alabama	Connecticut	Delaware	Arizona	Alaska
Arkansas	Rhode Island	Hawaii	California	Arizona
Illinois	South Carolina	Maine	Florida	California
Indiana	Virginia	Massachusetts	Georgia	Colorado
Mississippi		New Hampshire	Idaho	Connecticut
Missouri		New Jersey	Kentucky	Florida
New Mexico		New York	Louisiana	Hawaii
New York		Rhode Island	Michigan	Indiana
North Carolina		Vermont	Minnesota	Iowa
Pennsylvania			Montana	Kansas
Tennessee			Nevada	Maryland
Texas			North Dakota	Missouri
West Virginia			Ohio	Nebraska
			Oklahoma	Oklahoma
			Oregon	South Dakota
			South Dakota	Tennessee
			Washington	Utah
			Wisconsin	Vermont
				Wyoming

SOURCE: *The Book of the States 1990–91* (Lexington, Ky: Council of State Governments, 1990), pp. 210–212.

nonpartisan general elections, but partisan primaries are conducted in which judges' party affiliations are clearly stated. Partisan election (election by party label) is most likely to occur in the South. In most cases judicial elections are nearly invisible to voters. They get the lowest voter turnouts of all types of elections.

In many instances, judges resign before their term of office expires. This allows the governor to make an interim appointment. Typically, incumbent judges stand an excellent chance of being reelected. In addition to low turnout, often there are no opposition candidates in judicial elections.

In nine states, the governor *appoints* some judges in a manner similar to the presidential selection of federal judges. Usually the legislature confirms the appointment, and a strong role is played by interest groups to influence nominations. In a few states, the legislature appoints judges. In those cases, the governor often plays a major role in controlling the legislature's choices.

Most states adopting new plans of judicial selection since the 1930s have chosen some form of *merit system.* These plans are based on a selection process first instituted by California in 1934 and made popular by Missouri. The goal of merit plans is to remove judicial selection from the influence of partisan politics and to select judges on the basis of ability, in large part as determined by lawyers and sitting judges.

The **Missouri Plan** operates as follows. Whenever a judicial vacancy arises, the governor appoints an individual from a list of acceptable names submitted by a commission. There are three commissions in Missouri to nominate judges for three types of courts. The commissions are composed of lawyers, ordinary citizens, and a sitting judge. The lawyers are elected by all the lawyers in the court's district; the lay citizens are appointed by the governor; and the judge is the presiding judge of the court of appeal in that area. After a judge has served for a period of time, his or her name appears on the ballot and the voters check yes or no. If the vote is no, the selection process begins again. If the vote is yes, the judge's name will appear on future ballots, again without an opponent, and the voters will decide if they wish the judge to remain in office.

Most studies indicate that merit plans do *not* produce judges who differ substantially from those who are elected or appointed. They have not had better legal qualifications nor have they decided cases in a noticeably different manner from judges selected by other methods. In the most comprehensive review of the Missouri Plan, the authors note that "governors have used their appointments to reward friends or past political supporters and have implemented the plan very largely from a personal and political viewpoint."[10] Under this plan, only one judge has been given a no vote by the citizens of Missouri. Turnout usually is low in retention elections, and few judges have been voted out of office in states with merit plans. In California, no judge had been voted out of office since the plan was implemented in 1934 until chief justice Rose Elizabeth Bird and two justices were overwhelmingly denied reconfirmation in 1986. Merit systems do not remove partisan considerations from the judiciary, nor do they make judicial elections different from elections for other public offices.

Regardless of the method of selection, partisan politics plays a major role in the selection of judges. Even in Missouri, governors have appointed most judges from their own party. In nonpartisan elections, parties are usually active in primary elections, and they are often directly involved in general elections. Interest groups are active participants in every selection plan. Governors tend to draw a high percentage of their appointments from current and past members of the state legislature. Under both partisan and merit systems, judges seem equally objective and equally attuned to popular sentiment in their states. Although most judicial reform proposals call for a merit system, only nineteen states have adopted one, and in several of those states some judges continue to be elected.

We have seen that in practice judges selected by merit plans enjoy a lifetime of service, although they are subject to periodic approval at the polls. Unlike federal judges, few state judges are given life tenure in a single appointment. For appellate courts, the typical length of a term is five to twelve years. Generally, terms of trial judges are shorter, averaging four to eight years. Long terms are believed to be beneficial because they help ensure judicial independence.

As we would expect, most state judges are white men. As recently as 1985 twelve states did not have any black trial judges.[11] Although all states had at least one woman trial judge in 1985, seventeen states did not have any women appellate judges and thirty-three states did not have any black appellate judges. Of course, some states such as Vermont have very few black residents. The highest percentage of black appellate judges was in Virginia and South Carolina, where judges are selected by the legislature. Washington was the only state with a majority (54 percent) of women appellate judges. All judges in Washington are elected on nonpartisan ballots. As the percentage of women and black lawyers increases and political organizations make special efforts to diversify the bench, we can expect the number of black and female judges to increase.

Discipline and Removal of Judges

All state judges serve for at least four years. Terms range up to fourteen years (in New York). In Rhode Island, judges have life appointments, and in a few states appointment is to age seventy. Only in rare instances have judges been removed, or even disciplined, during their term in office. Most states have constitutional provisions for impeachment, but the process (which involves securing valid signatures on petitions and holding trials) is time-consuming and very expensive. Few judges have been impeached and removed from office. Seven states permit judicial recall; but even fewer judges have been recalled than have been impeached.

Not only are these traditional means of removal time-consuming and costly, they also are often perceived as overly harsh penalties for the alleged offenses. As a result, judges with serious problems frequently escape removal because voters or legislatures are reluctant to take such drastic action. Occasionally judges resign when threatened with impeachment.

A more practical solution to dealing with problems of judicial incompetence or unethical behavior has been the creation of judicial tenure commissions composed of lawyers, judges, and citizens. They investigate complaints, hold hearings, and impose penalties ranging from temporary suspension to removal. Over thirty states have judicial commissions. Most are patterned after the California Commission of Judicial Qualifications, which was created in 1961. The California commission has nine members (five judges appointed by the state supreme court, two lawyers selected by the state bar association, and two citizens appointed by the governor and approved by the senate) and receives over 300 complaints a year. If it believes a judge has acted unprofessionally, the commission issues a report to the state supreme court, which can discipline or remove an offending judge. In many instances judges have resigned while under investigation.

THE POLICYMAKING ROLE OF STATE COURTS

Court decisions are important in the study of state government because they do much more than decide narrow legal issues between two parties.[12] Decisions of state courts significantly affect the nature of public policy in a variety of ways. For example, court decisions concerning environmental protection have important economic as well as ecological consequences; decisions regarding legislative apportionment or the eligibility of a governor to run for reelection directly affect the success of political parties; decisions reviewing the constitutionality of state statutes covering such matters as abortion and capital punishment literally involve questions of life and death for the state's citizens; decisions interpreting rights of criminal defendants may allow convicted felons to be freed; decisions concerning state tax policies affect the distribution of individual wealth and they may also affect the type of education made available in the state's schools and colleges.

In a few celebrated cases, state courts make policy by deciding issues not previously considered by the judicial system. Innovative decisions are more likely to come from appellate courts than from trial courts.[13] This is so because appellate judges have broader powers and jurisdiction than trial judges, and they are less limited by the status quo. The written opinions of state appellate judges are often cited by judges in other states, and this of course broadens their policymaking impact.

Innovative decisions, in which major policy implications derive from a single case, clearly are exceptional. More often, judicial policy is made by a series of decisions in apparently routine cases. Over a period of time, for example, decisions regarding sentencing of criminals may affect conditions in jails and, more fundamentally, may influence the rate of crime. Decisions may have a ripple effect as interested parties become aware of the kinds of decisions being handed down by certain courts. In this respect, environmentalists may be encouraged by court decisions to concentrate on litigation rather than on legislative lobbying or media appeals to achieve their goals.

The nature of court decisions (and therefore the nature of court policymaking) is affected by the personal characteristics of judges and by the type of selection plan employed. One study found that Democratic and Republican judges decided cases in ways that correspond with their political party's position on certain issues.[14] For example, Democrats were more likely to vote for the defense in criminal cases; for labor unions in labor-management cases; and for tenants in landlord-tenant cases. In states where judges are appointed, their voting behavior typically does not follow closely the established positions of political parties. In other states, such as Michigan, the selection is highly partisan and judges' decisions tend to run parallel to party lines.

THE ROLE OF THE POLICE

Although this chapter has concentrated on the courts as a focal point in the administration of justice, we should be careful not to underestimate the role of the police. The police are a significant factor in the criminal justice system. In most instances they have unusually broad **discretionary authority** in the performance of their job. It is the police officers—working alone or in pairs, with little direct supervision from police administrators—who most often make arrests, which set in motion the series of events leading to indictment, sentencing, and incarceration. About one-half of all crimes are not reported to the police, and of those that are reported only about one-fourth are solved by arrest. Within police departments it is the officers on patrol, rather than their superior officers, who exercise the greatest discretion in the performance of their duty. James Q. Wilson notes that police discretion is inevitable, "partly because it is impossible to observe every public infraction, partly because many laws require interpretation before they can be applied at all, partly because the police can sometimes get information about serious crimes by overlooking minor crimes, and partly because the police believe that public opinion would not tolerate a policy of full enforcement of all laws all the time."[15]

In the United States, the management of police forces is overwhelmingly the responsibility of local governments. The FBI is not a national police force. The number of federal law enforcement personnel (about 60,000) is dwarfed by that of state and local law enforcement personnel (about 500,000). Of the more than 20,000 law enforcement units in the United States, about 80 percent of the personnel are local, 15 percent are state, and 5 percent are federal. New York City has about 27,000 sworn police officers, and the FBI has about 10,000 special agents. Typically, police costs comprise about 15 percent of city expenditures. Curiously, there are more police than social workers in the United States and more police employees than U.S. postal workers.[16]

Every state has a law enforcement agency known as the *state police,* the state highway patrol, or, as in Texas, the Rangers. In a quarter of the states, the responsibility of this central police force is limited to highway duties. In the other states, law enforcement responsibilities include aiding local police in making arrests and controlling riots.

Traditionally, the *county sheriff* has been a central figure in American law enforcement. In addition to making arrests, the sheriff maintains the county jail and serves summonses and warrants. In every state except Rhode Island, which does not have counties, the sheriff is elected. While sheriffs continue to play a major role in rural counties, *municipal police forces* have assumed most of the sheriff's law enforcement duties in urban areas. In this brief look at the police, the focus is on urban departments.

In his study of police behavior in eight communities, James Q. Wilson identified three basic styles of operation.[17] In the **watchman style,** police are poorly paid, are locally recruited, and receive minimal initial training. This style emphasizes maintenance of order in public places, rather than law enforcement. The police ignore a certain amount of minor violations and often do not interfere in private disputes, particularly in black neighborhoods. In performing their duty, police officers tend to judge people by "what they deserve." Such a style was characteristic of nineteenth-century police departments.

The **legalistic style** is usually found in cities where police were previously corrupt. Police organization stresses formal, hierarchical authority in which officers are constantly evaluated. There is an emphasis on technical efficiency in which all officers on patrol are under some pressure to produce arrests. In such circumstances, many traffic tickets are issued, juveniles are detained and arrested, and there are substantial numbers of arrests for misdemeanors. Because so many arrests are made, there are inevitable charges, especially by minority groups, of police "harassment."

The **service style** is most often found in homogeneous middle-class communities. Here police seek to protect a well-established public order against occasional threats. Serious matters—burglaries, robberies, assaults—are taken seriously. Minor infractions, particularly when juveniles are involved, are handled more informally. Police are courteous, well-paid, and well-trained. In many cities a kind of evolutionary development can be identified, beginning with the traditional watchman style and moving to a service style.

During most of this century, reformers have advocated higher educational standards for police, and they have worked to free police departments from local political control. There also has been a general acceptance of the idea that the police officer's behavior (as in television shows) should be cool and detached. In the face of these traditional goals, citizens' groups have been pushing for changes in standards to allow police departments to become more representative of their community; they have advocated more accountability through elected officials; and they have called for the police to be more "human" and personally involved in the performance of their job.[18] In response to criticism from citizens and from a series of presidential commissions in the late 1960s, police departments have created community-relations units, but they have strongly opposed the establishment of civilian review boards. An amateur videotape of the beating of a black man by Los Angeles police in 1991 led to renewed concern about police brutality and racism, and, as noted earlier, the trial of the police officers was followed by rioting.

Major questions remain concerning the organization of police departments and their control. While it has been assumed that the major function of police is to prevent crime and apprehend criminals (law enforcement), in fact most calls received by the police concern such matters as medical emergencies and family quarrels (service and order maintenance). Because police perform a variety of functions most of the time, it is important not to *replace* training for law enforcement with training for community service. Rather, police need to be trained for a complex role in which they are both "cops" and "social workers."

Earlier we examined how the police are controlled by constitutional and legal restraints—these include limits on conducting searches and questioning suspects. Police are also controlled by internal discipline and by the types of recruitment and training procedures that law enforcement departments follow. Unfortunately, training is a low-priority item in most departments across the country. Police corruption is a widespread problem that has been very difficult for many departments to correct. Some believe that it often starts with the notion that police are entitled to free meals and cut-rate prices and then moves to accepting money or favors for failing to make certain kinds of arrests or for destroying evidence and to appropriating confiscated items (e.g., drugs) for personal use.

It should be realized that the police are only the most visible part of a very fragmented system of criminal justice. The police cannot fairly be expected to prevent crime, nor should they be blamed for increased crime. For the system to be successful in working toward the goals of crime prevention and reduction, police, prosecutors, judges, and corrections administrators must work together more effectively. The tasks of the criminal justice system are complicated by the fact that criminal activity is strongly influenced by socioeconomic factors—urbanization, loss of community, poverty, racial discrimination, drug abuse—over which the actors in the system have little, if any, control.

CORRECTIONAL FACILITIES

Since 1960 violent crimes and burglaries reported to the police have increased over 300 percent, and the prison population is up 150 percent. In 1990 all crime rose 1 percent, but there was an 11 percent increase in violent crimes. There were 2,262 murders, 3,126 rapes, and 147,123 auto thefts reported in New York City in 1990 (that is about 400 car thefts each day). New York City ranked tenth among the country's twenty-five largest cities in murders per capita. Washington, D.C., was first with 77.8 homicides for every 100,000 residents. Not surprisingly, most crime occurs in cities and suburbs, and rural states have the lowest crime rates (see Table 7.2). Increases are blamed on the fact that children of the baby-boom generation are growing up—most crimes are committed by men between the ages of fifteen and thirty—on drug abuse, and on poverty.

The Sentencing Project reported that the U.S. prison population reached 1 million in 1990. Because this reflects the number of people in prison or jail on a given day, it grossly underestimates the number of people jailed during a year. That figure is about 9 million. In 1990, 426 of every 100,000 U.S. residents were imprisoned. For black males the rate was 3,109 per 100,000. South Africa had the world's

Table 7.2   Crime Rate, per 100,000 Population 1989

1. District of Columbia	10,293.4	28. Delaware	4,865.2
2. Florida	8,804.5	29. Alaska	4,779.9
3. Arizona	8,059.7	30. Ohio	4,733.2
4. Texas	7,926.9	31. Alabama	4,627.8
5. Georgia	7,073.1	32. Arkansas	4,555.7
6. California	6,763.4	33. Tennessee	4,513.6
7. Washington	6,593.8	34. Indiana	4,440.0
8. New Mexico	6,573.8	35. Minnesota	4,383.2
9. New York	6,293.2	36. Virginia	4,211.4
10. Nevada	6,271.7	37. Wisconsin	4,164.8
11. Hawaii	6,270.4	38. Nebraska	4,091.6
12. Louisiana	6,241.3	39. Vermont	4,088.5
13. Oregon	6,161.1	40. Iowa	4,081.4
14. Colorado	6,039.4	41. Montana	3,997.5
15. Michigan	5,968.3	42. Idaho	3,931.0
UNITED STATES	5,741.0	43. Wyoming	3,889.1
16. Utah	5,682.1	44. New Hampshire	3,596.2
17. Illinois	5,639.2	45. Maine	3,583.6
18. South Carolina	5,619.2	46. Mississippi	3,515.3
19. Maryland	5,562.6	47. Pennsylvania	3,360.4
20. Oklahoma	5,502.6	48. Kentucky	3,317.1
21. Connecticut	5,270.0	49. South Dakota	2,685.2
22. New Jersey	5,269.4	50. North Dakota	2,560.9
23. North Carolina	5,253.8	51. West Virginia	2,362.8
24. Rhode Island	5,224.8		
25. Massachusetts	5,136.0		
26. Missouri	5,127.1		
27. Kansas	4,982.8		

SOURCE: Edith Horner, ed., *Almanac of the Fifty States* (Palo Alto, Calif.: Information Publications, 1991), p. 436. Reprinted with permission.

second-highest incarceration rate, with 333 people imprisoned per 100,000, and its rate for black males was 729 per 100,000. Rates of incarceration in European countries range from 35 to 120 per 100,000 residents. The rate was 268 per 100,000 in the Soviet Union in 1990.

Those imprisoned in the mid-1980s in the United States had the following characteristics:[19]

- Over four-fifths were repeat offenders.
- Two-thirds were serving a sentence for a violent crime (i.e., murder, robbery, and assault).
- About 13 percent were first-time offenders in for a violent crime.
- More than a third (35 percent) were under the influence of a drug at the time of their offense.
- More than half (54 percent) were under the influence of drugs and/or alcohol at the time of their offense.
- 62.3 percent used drugs on a regular basis prior to incarceration.
- 95.6 percent were male.
- 49.7 percent were white, and 46.9 percent were black.
- 12.6 percent were Hispanic.
- 72.4 percent were between the ages of eighteen and thirty-four.
- 61.6 percent had fewer than twelve years of education.

Increases in the number of people on probation have placed additional financial burdens on states. Over 2 million Americans are on **probation**—supervised community living for those found guilty of a crime. Several states have eliminated **parole** for prisoners—releasing convicted offenders after they serve a period of confinement as long as certain conditions are met—and with more mandatory sentencing the number of people on parole is declining.

Even though violent crime has increased, the overall U.S. crime rate fell about 3 percent in the 1980s. At the same time the prison population doubled. This apparent inconsistency is explained by the facts that people committing violent crimes are more likely to be sentenced to prison than those committing nonviolent crimes (robbery compared with burglary) and that there has been a change in sentencing policy. Until recently, most sentencing was "indetermine"—that is, there were broad ranges of sentences (two to ten years) and parole boards would decide when prisoners were "ready" to be released.[20] In the 1980s **determinate sentencing** became more common; exact sentence times were specified for various crimes. In addition, "good time"—time off a sentence for good behavior—has been eliminated in many instances. Some state legislatures imposed mandatory sentences for particular kinds of crime. By 1990 forty-six states had laws requiring prison sentences for certain criminal offenses. These laws, together with tougher penalties for drug violations, have contributed to the great increase in prison inmates.

The policy changes were in response to public concern about getting tough with criminals. In addition, there was wide criticism of indeterminate sentencing, which often resulted in relatively short sentences for many people who committed serious crimes. Indeterminate sentencing was connected to the idea of prison rehabilitation—a concept that was losing support among academics and corrections officials.

There are about 4,600 state and local detention and correctional facilities. Total state prison populations in the late 1980s ranged from 76,000 in California and 44,000 in New York to 466 in North Dakota and 811 in Vermont. California's annual corrections budget is about $2 billion, and corrections is one of the most rapidly expanding state expenditures. The accompanying reading describes how Minnesota, Missouri, and Michigan have pioneered some cost-saving alternatives to traditional imprisonment.

Currently there is a major construction program under way in many states. New prisons are being built because of overcrowded conditions in most existing facilities and because so many prisons are at least fifty years old. Nevada, South Carolina, and Louisiana have the largest number of prisoners relative to their populations (see Table. 7.3); North Dakota, Minnesota, West Virginia, and New Hamp-

Table 7.3   Incarceration Rate, 1989*

1.	District of Columbia	1,129	28.	Indiana	218
2.	Nevada	473	29.	Wyoming	217
3.	South Carolina	419	30.	Tennessee	213
4.	Louisiana	395	31.	Illinois	211
5.	Alaska	363	32.	Connecticut	194
6.	Oklahoma	355	33.	New Mexico	186
7.	Arizona	354	34.	Idaho	181
8.	Delaware	344	35.	South Dakota	178
9.	Michigan	342	36.	Pennsylvania	176
10.	Alabama	329	37.	Montana	169
11.	Maryland	325	38.	Rhode Island	147
12.	Florida	311	39.	Washington	144
13.	Georgia	302	40.	Nebraska	144
14.	Mississippi	294	41.	Hawaii	143
15.	California	286	42.	Wisconsin	139
16.	New York	285	43.	Utah	137
17.	Ohio	279	44.	Iowa	126
	UNITED STATES	274	45.	Massachusetts	123
18.	Missouri	269	46.	Maine	116
19.	Virginia	265	47.	Vermont	108
20.	Arkansas	261	48.	New Hampshire	104
21.	North Carolina	252	49.	West Virginia	83
22.	New Jersey	251	50.	Minnesota	71
23.	Texas	239	51.	North Dakota	61
24.	Oregon	237			
25.	Kansas	223			
26.	Kentucky	222			
27.	Colorado	220			

*The number of prisoners sentenced to more than one year, per 100,000 residents

SOURCE: Edith Horner, ed., *Almanac of the Fifty States* (Palo Alto, Calif.: Information Publications, 1991), p. 437. Reprinted with permission.

The Costly Penal System

The premise behind all this expense, of course, is that throwing men and women behind bars, regardless of the nature and severity of their crimes, will make our streets safer and allow little old ladies to sleep better at night. Unfortunately, our prison-building binge has not had that effect.

Look at Michigan. It has added about 15,000 prison beds in the past six years in one of the U.S.'s most resolute prison-building programs. "We've been building prisons since 1984," says Bob Brown, Michigan's prison commissioner from September 1984 until last month. "The purpose of building all the additional prisons was to lower the crime rate. But the crime rate hasn't gone down."

For states financing a never-ending parade of bad guys to their prisons, alternatives to incarceration for nonviolent crimes appear to be the way of the future. The list of possibilities—which can be used individually or in a variety of combinations—is long and growing. These include house arrest, with or without electronic monitoring, intensive supervision by parole officers, community service and halfway houses.

The advantages are obvious: The alternatives cost less than traditional incarceration. A year in prison in a number of states runs $20,000 per inmate or more. By contrast, intensive supervision by a parole officer—with random urine tests and daily meetings—costs a small fraction of that.

What's more, when criminals are kept out of jail, they can help compensate their victims and often are able to hold down jobs to support themselves and their families.

One of the states that has pioneered alternatives to incarceration is Minnesota. As far back as 1973—when most states weren't even thinking of prisons as an important budgetary issue—it was advancing cost-effective ideas in penology.

Indeed, Minnesota boasts one of the lowest rates of incarceration in the country, currently 73 inmates per 100,000 people. True, Minnesota doesn't have the crime problems of New York or California. But crime rates often have little to do with incarceration rates. Crimes occur at about the same frequency in Virginia as in Minnesota, for instance. But a prevailing attitude that bad guys should be locked up has placed Virginia's incarceration rate at over three times that of Minnesota.

More important, the techniques used in Minnesota are applicable in any state. "The question really is this," says Orville Pung, the state's corrections department commissioner, "Are you going to use prison space for offenders who ought to be in the Mayo Clinic or in local hospitals? If we had decided to stop the polio problem by building more iron lungs, we'd have a hell of a lot of people in iron lungs today. It's the same thing with prisons. Just building more prisons is not the most efficient way to address the problem of crime."

One of the keys to Minnesota's success is its Sentencing Guidelines Commission, which directs the state's judges through the thicket of potential sentences for various crimes by concentrating on two factors: The severity of the offense and the criminal history of the offender. The commission accents putting nonviolent offenders into various local corrections programs, often forcing them to pay restitution and perform community service.

A more recent convert to prison alternatives is Missouri. About three years ago, the state became concerned about its fast-growing prison population. "We were projecting a growth over the next seven or eight years that was almost going to double our population to nearly 30,000," says Gail Hughes, deputy director of Missouri's department of corrections and a 38-year veteran of the system. "We said we can't tolerate this. These are precious dollars that should be aimed toward highways, education. So, we began planning toward managing the population."

One big improvement in Missouri: "We found that technical parole violators were coming into our prisons in droves," says Hughes. "These were individuals on parole who were caught with alcohol, or dirty urine, or who left supervision. We found that when they went back, they stayed an average of 14 months; this seemed like an awful long time. So, we developed some intensive programs, started to keep them in for 90 days, and saved 11 months of bed space per prisoner. We call the program 'recycling.'"

The state now has 200 beds devoted to that program, and is quickly adding more. Consider the savings. Even at a cheap per-diem rate of $29, each recycled prisoner saves the state almost $10,000. Multiply that by the 800 individuals who can use the 200 available beds in a year, and you have a savings of $8 million. Happily, the state has seen absolutely no change in its crime rate from placing these people on the streets that much sooner.

"We're here to produce an economic product," says Hughes. "The real goal of corrections is not to spend money, but to produce a good product at a reasonable cost to society."

Statistics make it clear that alternative solutions cut costs dramatically. In Missouri, a maximum-custody cell costs the state $33.71 a day; minimum custody, $25.44; and house arrest, $15.35 less 25% that offenders contribute from their earnings in mandatory work programs.

The Missouri legislature wanted proof that the various alternatives genuinely worked. "Three years ago," says Hughes, "we targeted July 30, 1990, as the date that our [prison] population would take a downward turn. Well, through the first half of 1990, our population grew. We had a big increase in January, and it scared the hell out of us. But come July, for the first time in 10 years, our population dropped. By two."

As the year progressed, the downward trend accelerated. It now seems clear that the Missouri state legislature is convinced.

Typically, however, state legislators resist such logic in favor of building more slammers. Just a few years ago, for example, the state of Washington's corrections system was the envy of the nation. Washington regarded prison space as an expensive, scarce resource with only one purpose. "Prisons are for punishment," explains Chase Riveland, the straight-talking head of the state's prison system. "Nonviolent offenders should not go to prison. Violent offenders should get more time."

Those convicted of nonviolent crimes were shuttled to community-based alternatives to prison, a truly sensible idea. But in 1989, in an effort to address public dismay over the drug epidemic, the state legislature passed a get-tough law that mandated prison sentences for malefactors involved in drug-related offenses. Now, of the 8,500 people in the state's prisons, over 1,500 are there for nonviolent drug-related crimes.

Result: Washington's prisons are chock-full—and the state is in the process of adding one major facility and three prison camps. The legislature is now considering spending $100,000 to study whether something should be done to get these people out of prison and into community-based treatment programs. Though Riveland is quick to point out that Washington's prison system is still in far better shape than most states', he is not happy about this recent turn of events. Says he: "We lost our way."

Will other states take note? Most likely they will be forced to when they realize that they are hocking their education programs to build prison cells. Even Michigan is beginning to turn in the direction of Minnesota and Missouri. "We're moving toward alternatives," says Brown. "But it's not being done because people believe philosophically in those alternatives. Rather, it's being accepted just for cost-cutting reasons. Prison building is bringing us to our fiscal knees."

SOURCE: *Financial World,* May 28, 1991, pp. 54–55. Reprinted with permission.

shire have the fewest. Note that the rate of imprisonment in the District of Columbia is eighteen times greater than in North Dakota. The crime rate per capita is relatively similar to the incarceration rate (see Table 7.2), although it is far from a perfect correlation. For example, South Carolina ranks third in incarceration and eighteenth in crime rate. This reflects a greater willingness of Southern officials to put people in jail.

The highest rates of imprisonment (from 50 to 100 percent higher than other regions) and the lowest levels of spending per inmate are in the South. The imprisonment rate is lowest in the Plains states and in New England. The discussion of political culture in Chapter 1 helps explain these geographical differences in crime rates and rates of imprisonment. The authoritarian aspects of traditional political cultures in the South have led to oppression of the poor by the elite, and there have been historically high rates of violence. In the moralistic cultures of New England and the upper Midwest, individuals are treated more equally and government power is used more humanely.[21] In the 1980s, about three-fourths of all the death sentences imposed were in the South. There were 150 executions in the United States from 1976, when the Supreme Court upheld the use of the death penalty, through 1991. Crime rates tend to be highest in Western states, but their incarceration rates are relatively low. Drug trafficking helps account for the high crime rate in Florida.

Not surprisingly, the nation's jails have become increasingly crowded. Although citizens want tougher policies enacted, they seldom wish to pay more taxes to support jails. Overcrowding and inadequate facilities have led to widespread violence. Twenty-one prisoners died in Louisiana jails in 1980, mostly from suicides and fires. One of the most violent prison riots in history occurred in 1980, when inmates of the New Mexico State Penitentiary killed thirty-three fellow prisoners. In the first twenty months following that riot, six inmates and two guards were killed in that prison. Five inmates were killed in a 1991 prison uprising in Montana.

Since the 1970s federal district court judges increasingly have stepped in to manage state prisons in response to lawsuits concerning overcrowded, unsanitary, dangerous conditions. By 1990, forty-five states had been issued federal court orders or litigation was in progress. Typically federal judges name a special master to represent them in managing prison conditions.

Many state prison systems are so overcrowded that emergency release programs have been put into effect. Increasingly states have been using alternative punishments to save money and relieve crowded conditions. These include intensive supervision or probation, community service, house arrest, electronic monitoring, and boot camps. Boot camps are designed for young first offenders. They are a highly structured military environment with drills and physical training and are followed by supervised releases.

As noted by Timothy H. Matthews, the biggest issue in corrections in recent years has been privatization.[22] Privatization encompasses many trends, ranging from contracting with private companies for some prison services (e.g., drug treatment) to authorizing private construction and operation of jails and prisons. The latter represents a dramatic departure from traditional experience and raises concern among civil libertarians regarding treatment of prisoners (remember that nearly two-thirds of the states are under court orders to correct miserable conditions in their prisons). Advocates point to speed and flexibility in private construction, as well as costs that are estimated to be 20 to 40 percent lower.[23]

Another developing trend is the aging of prison populations. As the baby-boom generation gets older, there are more older criminals. In addition, fewer paroles and tougher sentencing laws mean that prisoners stay in jail longer. Elderly inmates present a variety of problems, including chronic poor health and attacks by more aggressive younger prisoners. Few prison officials know how to run homes for the aged.

The philosophy of **rehabilitation** has dominated prison management in this century. Rehabilitation stresses education and vocational training aimed at altering the behavior of inmates after they are released. However, almost all studies show that rehabilitative efforts have no appreciable effect on future criminal behavior. A majority of prisoners will commit crimes after they are released and they will return to prison.

Since prison specialists cannot agree on goals—to rehabilitate prisoners, deter crime, or simply punish offenders by keeping them locked up—it is virtually impossible to measure the effectiveness of imprisonment. And if effectiveness cannot be measured, then it is difficult to hold any group accountable for the crime rate.

Reform is resisted by "get tough" legislators, judges, prison guards, and prison administrators. Frederick M. Wirt suggests that state prison systems go through cycles in which "prison riots over living conditions generate public attention, the governor appoints a committee to investigate and recommend, the recommendations are announced publicly, but thereafter the media and the public ignore what happens to the suggestions—which is usually not much."[24]

KEY TERMS

Arraignment The stage in a criminal proceeding in which the defendant is brought before a judge to hear the formal charges and to enter a plea of guilty or not guilty.

Centralization of courts Control of state courts under an administrative judge, who assigns cases and manages workloads for a more efficient system of justice.

Civil disputes Legal disputes in which the parties are private citizens.

Common law Law that has developed from a series of decisions by judges in similar situations. In the United States, there is no federal common law, but common law exists within state judicial systems. American common law originated in England, and it forms the basis of legal procedures in all states except Louisiana.

Consolidation of courts The process of streamlining court systems into a single set of trial courts.

Courts of appeal Those courts that review the proceedings of trial courts to determine if significant legal errors have occurred.

Criminal disputes Legal disputes in which the state prosecutes people accused of violating criminal codes. Criminal law includes felonies (serious crimes for which the penalty is imprisonment) and misdemeanors (less serious offenses for which the maximum penalty is a fine or short jail sentence).

Determinate sentencing The imposition of exact sentences for specific crimes; in *indeterminate sentencing,* by contrast, the length of the sentence can vary greatly.

Discretionary authority The freedom of administrative officials, including police officers, to make decisions on their own judgment without close legislative scrutiny.

Grand jury A body of twelve to twenty-five people that considers evidence brought by a prosecutor concerning the commission of a serious crime. Grand juries do not determine guilt or innocence; they determine only whether a matter should go to trial.

Legalistic style A style of police operation that is characterized by a concern for technical efficiency. The police force is formally organized and there is strong pressure on officers to make arrests.

***Miranda* v. *Arizona* (1966)** A major Supreme Court decision defining the rights of criminal defendants.

Missouri Plan A method of selecting judges in which the governor makes an appointment from a list of three names prepared by a commission. After the judges have served for a period of time, their names appear on the ballot unopposed for the voters to retain or remove them on the basis of their record.

Parole Supervised freedom granted to convicted criminals after they have served time in prison.

Plea bargaining An arrangement between the prosecutor and the defendant in which the defendant agrees to plead guilty if the prosecutor will reduce the charges and recommend a lighter sentence.

Pretrial conference A meeting between the judge and attorneys in civil cases to clarify the issues about to come to trial and to determine if the conflict can be settled out of court.

Probation Supervised community living for convicted criminal offenders who must meet certain conditions of behavior.

Rehabilitation A prison policy that stresses vocational and educational training of inmates to prepare them for productive lives when they are released.

Service style A style of police operation that is characterized by a concern to treat serious threats to the peace seriously but to handle minor violations more informally. Police officers are courteous, well-paid, and well-trained in service-style forces. Often found in affluent suburbs.

Trial courts Courts that conduct examinations of the facts presented by plaintiffs and defendants to resolve criminal and civil conflicts. This is the first step in the process of trial and appeal. In criminal cases, the state is always the plaintiff, initiating the legal proceedings.

Warrant A judicial order authorizing a law enforcement official to make an arrest, seizure, or search. To secure the warrant, the law enforcement official must swear that he or she has probable cause to believe a crime has been committed by a specific person.

Watchman style A style of police operation that is characterized by a concern to maintain order, rather than closely enforce laws. Watchman-style police forces are marked by low pay, local recruitment, and minimal initial training.

REFERENCES

1. Herbert Jacob, "Courts: The Least Visible Branch," in Virginia Gray, Herbert Jacob, and Robert B. Albritton, eds., *Politics in the American States,* 5th ed. (Glenview, Ill.: Scott, Foresman/Little, Brown, 1990), pp. 263–264.
2. *Ibid.*
3. Henry R. Glick, *Courts, Politics, and Justice,* 2d ed. (New York: McGraw-Hill, 1988), p. 193.
4. *Ibid.,* p. 186.

5. See James Eisenstein and Herbert Jacob, *Felony Justice* (Boston: Little, Brown, 1977).

6. Erick B. Low, "State of the Judiciary," in *The Book of the States 1988–89* (Lexington, Ky.: Council of State Governments, 1988), p. 149.

7. Harry Kalven and Hans Zeizel, *The American Jury* (Boston: Little, Brown, 1966).

8. Elder Witt, "On Issues of State Power, the Supreme Court Seems to Be of Two Minds," *Governing,* October 1990, p. 64.

9. Neil Skeme, "The Supreme Court's Passive Policy Role," *Congressional Quarterly Weekly Report,* March 23, 1991, p. 778.

10. Richard A. Watson and Ronald G. Downing, *The Politics of Bench and Bar: Judicial Selection Under the Missouri Nonpartisan Court Plan* (New York: Wiley, 1969), pp. 338–339.

11. Jacob, "Courts," pp. 263–264.

12. See Herbert Jacob, *Justice in America,* 4th ed. (Boston: Little, Brown, 1984), Chapter 3.

13. Glick, *Courts, Politics, and Justice,* pp. 225–226.

14. Stuart Nagel, "Political Party Affiliation and Judges' Decisions," *American Political Science Review,* 1961, pp. 843–860.

15. James Q. Wilson, *Varieties of Police Behavior* (New York: Atheneum, 1973), p. 7.

16. Wesley G. Skogan, "Crime and Punishment," in Gray, Jacob, and Albritton, eds., *Politics in the American States,* 5th ed., pp. 379–380.

17. Wilson, *Varieties of Police Behavior,* Chapters 5–7.

18. Patrick V. Murphy, "The Development of the Urban Police," *Current History,* June 1976, pp. 247–248.

19. Timothy H. Matthews, "Issues in Corrections," in *The Book of the States 1988–89,* p. 394.

20. Skogan, "Crime and Punishment," pp. 387–390.

21. Frederick M. Wirt, "Institutionalization: Prison and School Policies," in Virginia Gray, Herbert Jacob, and Kenneth N. Vines, eds., *Politics in the American States,* 4th ed. (Boston: Little, Brown, 1983), p. 294.

22. Matthews, "Issues in Corrections," p. 397.

23. E. S. Savas, *Privatization: The Key to Better Government* (Chatham, N.J.: Chatham House, 1987), pp. 186–187.

24. Wirt, "Institutionalization," pp. 301–302.

CHAPTER 8

FINANCING STATE AND LOCAL GOVERNMENT

STATE AND LOCAL EXPENDITURES AND TAXES

As the responsibilities of state and local governments have grown, their expenditures have increased nearly fourfold since 1972. Per capita state and local government expenditures doubled in the 1980s. In 1989 states spent $2.11 billion per capita and local governments spent $2.14 billion per capita.[1] Expenditures have grown because of several factors. States have greatly increased their share of funding for programs such as education and welfare that previously were largely funded by local governments. Urbanization and population growth have placed increasing demands on state and local governments for additional services. Wage increases, **inflation,** and expanding pension plans have all put pressure on state and local governments to raise more revenue. As noted in Chapter 2, cuts in federal grants-in-aid in the early 1980s, followed by only modest increases, have substantially increased the financial burden of state and local governments. Federal aid as a percentage of state and local outlays dropped from a high of 26.5 percent in 1978 to 17.3 percent in 1989. (See Table 2.1, p. 43.)

As noted in Chapter 2, states and localities entered the 1990s in the midst of a financial crisis. In addition to the reduction in federal aid noted above, economic recession, a strong public aversion to raising taxes, and strong pressure to spend more money to deal with such matters as health care, crime, education, and federal regulations have precipitated the crisis. In addition, the Federal Tax Reform Act of 1986 eliminated many deductions of state taxes on federal returns and made it more difficult for many states to forecast revenue. Cities have had extra burdens of dealing with social problems and complying with federal and state mandates. State spending for prisons and Medicaid rose rapidly in the 1970s and 1980s. Total expenditures were tempered by a downturn in school enrollments and a great reduction in the institutionalization of the mentally ill. In the 1990s school enrollments are expected to increase, as is the number of people eligible for Medicaid.

Despite promises by governors and legislators not to raise taxes, a majority of states have done so in the 1990s. In addition, employees have been laid off and budgets have been slashed. *The New York Times* reported that cities and states are trying to tax "everything that moves." California's sales tax extends to snacks and bottled water, New York is taxing dating services, and Arkansas is taxing used-car sales.[2] Fees have been increased for everything from copies of birth certificates to fire code violations. Facing a deficit equal to nearly half the state's annual budget, Governor Lowell Weicker of Connecticut persuaded the state legislature to establish an income tax and reduce its high sales tax. Nine states missed their July 1, 1991, deadline for approving budgets, and Maine and Connecticut stopped some services intermittently. From 1988 through 1991 more than two-thirds of all cities raised fees and charges every year, and 40 percent increased property taxes each year. Financial problems have been less severe in the Midwest and South.

State and local spending on a per capita basis varies greatly among states and regions. As Table 8.1 shows, it is highest in the Pacific states and lowest in the South Central states. Table 8.1 also indicates the effort state and local governments make relative to personal income. As noted in Chapter 1, there are marked differences between neighboring Vermont (strong effort) and New Hampshire (very

Table 8.1   State and Local Government Expenditures, 1988
(millions of dollars)

STATE	GENERAL REVENUE						
			Per capita				Per $1,000 Personal Income
		From Federal	Total		Taxes		
	Total	Government	Amount	Rank	Total	Rank	
U.S.	**727,161**	**117,602**	**2,958**	**(X)**	**1,772**	**(X)**	**179**
New England:							
Maine	3,584	730	2,974	22	1,832	16	197
New Hampshire	2,590	381	2,387	41	1,472	36	123
Vermont	1,765	353	3,168	13	1,862	14	207
Massachusetts	19,651	3,376	3,337	10	2,160	7	160
Rhode Island	3,051	588	3,072	16	1,841	15	182
Connecticut	10,801	1,521	3,341	9	2,280	4	145
Middle Atlantic:							
New York	79,239	12,514	4,425	4	2,934	3	229
New Jersey	26,405	3,765	3,420	8	2,217	6	155
Pennsylvania	31,851	5,389	2,654	31	1,627	26	163
East North Central:							
Ohio	28,224	4,754	2,600	36	1,569	28	167
Indiana	13,456	2,169	2,422	40	1,441	38	162
Illinois	31,673	4,869	2,727	28	1,782	19	155
Michigan	28,708	4,559	3,107	14	1,884	13	188
Wisconsin	14,642	2,379	3,016	19	1,889	12	194
West North Central:							
Minnesota	15,556	2,463	3,612	5	2,088	9	217
Iowa	8,033	1,248	2,834	24	1,660	24	193
Missouri	11,439	1,813	2,225	50	1,372	41	144
North Dakota	2,003	442	3,003	20	1,436	39	234
South Dakota	1,834	430	2,572	37	1,322	44	202
Nebraska	4,440	704	2,772	26	1,557	29	188
Kansas	6,869	918	2,753	27	1,676	23	175
South Atlantic:							
Delaware	2,259	320	3,422	7	1,820	17	194
Maryland	14,912	2,277	3,226	12	2,093	8	166
District of Columbia	3,980	1,495	6,450	2	3,339	2	302
Virginia	15,941	2,317	2,650	33	1,687	21	150
West Virginia	4,314	1,011	2,300	46	1,212	48	196
North Carolina	15,385	2,481	2,371	42	1,482	34	166
South Carolina	8,221	1,471	2,369	43	1,337	42	183
Georgia	17,069	2,931	2,691	30	1,491	33	176
Florida	32,073	3,776	2,600	35	1,524	31	157
East South Central:							
Kentucky	8,654	1,807	2,322	45	1,271	45	181
Tennessee	11,237	2,307	2,296	47	1,242	47	165
Alabama	9,654	2,113	2,354	44	1,142	49	183
Mississippi	5,940	1,399	2,267	48	1,088	51	204

Table 8.1   State and Local Government Expenditures, 1988 (Millions of dollars)
(Continued)

STATE	GENERAL REVENUE						
		From Federal Government	Per capita				Per $1,000 Personal Income
	Total		Total		Taxes		
			Amount	Rank	Total	Rank	
West South Central:							
Arkansas	4,801	1,028	2,004	51	1,113	50	164
Louisiana	11,611	2,143	2,634	34	1,329	43	214
Oklahoma	8,096	1,317	2,497	39	1,403	40	187
Texas	42,518	6,000	2,525	38	1,495	32	173
Mountain:							
Montana	2,463	581	3,060	18	1,538	30	238
Idaho	2,263	456	2,256	49	1,260	46	178
Wyoming	2,248	453	4,692	3	2,046	10	345
Colorado	9,758	1,368	2,956	23	1,686	22	180
New Mexico	4,627	721	3,070	17	1,472	35	246
Arizona	9,456	1,161	2,710	29	1,690	20	181
Utah	4,484	888	2,653	32	1,460	37	218
Nevada	2,964	385	2,813	25	1,655	25	161
Pacific:							
Washington	13,937	2,441	2,999	21	1,783	18	182
Oregon	8,502	1,665	3,072	15	1,602	27	206
California	93,902	14,551	3,316	11	1,948	11	177
Alaska	6,281	801	11,986	1	3,605	1	628
Hawaii	3,801	575	3,461	6	2,259	5	207

SOURCE: *Statistical Abstract of the United States 1991* (Washington, D.C.: U.S. Bureau of the Census, 1991), p. 286.

weak effort) as well as Wyoming (very strong) and Idaho (very weak). In general, the moralistic states in the West and in the northern Plains make strong efforts, while the traditional-individualistic states of Ohio, Indiana, and Illinois rank below the national average.

LIMITS ON THE ABILITY TO RAISE MONEY

In their attempts to raise revenue, state and local governments are limited by a number of factors. Most fundamentally, they are affected by the level of wealth and personal income within their boundaries. Unless they increase tax rates to unbearable levels, poor states and communities simply cannot raise sufficient revenue to provide services comparable to those in more affluent areas. Moreover, when states or cities do raise taxes, they risk causing an exodus of business, industry, and middle-class residents to regions where taxes are lower. New York City, with an 8¼ percent combined state-local sales tax plus a high income tax, is clearly at a disadvantage when compared with the federal government, which taxes Scarsdale residents as well as those in Harlem. In addition to a state's economic environment, other factors such as changes in federal taxation and political pressures, including interest groups and campaign promises, present barriers to tax increases.

State and local governments also encounter *constitutional* limits on taxation. The U.S. Constitution prohibits interference with federal operations by states through taxation, and it protects interstate commerce from direct taxation or undue interference by the states. It also prohibits states from taxing exports and imports without consent of Congress. In practice, state tax policy has not been strongly limited by provisions of the Constitution. At the same time, state constitutions seriously restrict state taxing authority by exempting certain kinds of property and by defining the kinds of taxes that may be used. Often the state's ability to borrow is limited by constitutional provisions, and in some states, such as California, extraordinary legislative majorities are required to approve both taxation and expenditure measures. If a state wishes to levy a new tax, it can, of course, amend its constitution. However, as was noted in Chapter 1, the process of amendment in most states is time-consuming and the chances of success are limited.

The most serious constitutional limitations are placed on cities. Local governments have only those powers of taxation that state constitutions have granted them. State constitutions prescribe what taxes cities may impose; they often establish the amount of taxation; they specify procedures of tax administration; and they outline the purposes for which specific tax revenues may be used. The only exceptions are in a few states where constitutions contain *home-rule* clauses giving cities a general grant of power to levy taxes. More broadly, home rule allows cities to draft or change their charters and manage their own affairs within the framework of the state constitution.

Taxing policy is affected by competition among the states. Some states may be reluctant to raise taxes, fearing that it will discourage business activity. On the other hand, states are quick to follow the lead of pioneers—such as Wisconsin, which instituted the income tax in 1911, and Iowa, which introduced a tax on cigarettes in 1921. The use of particular kinds of taxes at different levels of government has been strongly influenced by a pattern in which the national government has largely preempted the use of an income tax, state governments have made the broadest use of the sales tax, and local governments have been left with the property tax.

When a state wishes to obtain more revenue through taxation, several alternatives are available.[3] Least visible (and least objectionable) are administrative adjustments to existing tax structures. For example, a state can narrow the brackets in its income tax schedules. As another means of diffusing public opposition, a state may earmark receipts from a tax for a particular service, such as welfare or education. It may also increase user charges for such things as licenses and university tuition. If a new tax is created, legislators can announce that it is replacing an existing tax.

TYPES OF REVENUE

Faced with the mounting cost of expanded public services, governments at all levels have been increasing taxes in the 1990s. Since 1960, thirteen states have established an income tax and eleven states have begun to collect a general sales tax (see Figure 8.1). As a result, states now have more balanced tax systems than in the past, and they now raise substantially more money than do cities. Whereas in 1963 states and cities raised about the same amount of tax revenue, currently states raise about $1.50 for each $1 collected by local governments. This difference is due in large part to greater use of the state income tax, which is more responsive to economic growth. Cities have made increasing use of a personal income tax, and both cities and counties have used the sales tax to bolster revenues. State and local governments collect about one-third of all taxes in the United States. As noted earlier, states and localities have been very active in the 1990s raising taxes and user fees.

The General Property Tax

For local governments, the general **property tax** continues to be the major source of revenue. Property tax was the main source of state revenue in the 1920s. During the Depression, states turned that revenue source over to local governments as they adopted sales taxes. At present, few states levy any general property tax. Administration of the property tax is usually by the county treasurer. The process includes assessment of property values, determination of tax rates (millage), tax computation, and tax collection. A mill is one-thousandth of a dollar. Thus if a house is assessed at $60,000 and the mill rate is 30, the tax will be $1,800 ($60,000 × .030).

The property tax has been broadly criticized. The most common allegations against it include the following: It is difficult to administer; property is often not assessed fairly or equally; much property is exempt from taxation; property is no longer an effective way to gauge wealth; revenues raised do not correspond well to overall changes in the economy; the tax is regressive; and the tax penalizes homeowners who improve their property.

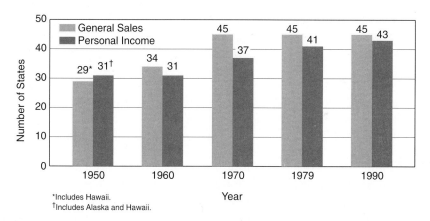

Figure 8.1   Number of States with General Sales and/or Personal Income Taxes

SOURCE: *Significant Features of Fiscal Federalism, 1978-79* (Washington, D.C.: Advisory Commission on Intergovernmental Relations, 1979), p. 51; updated by author.

Property-tax administration is inefficient because assessors, who often have little training, have difficulty determining the value of property that varies from residential to commercial and industrial. Moreover, assessors are under intense pressure to give favorable valuations to influential persons. Wide differences may exist in rates of assessment among cities in the same state. **Boards of equalization** exist within each taxing district to review and equalize rates of taxation. However, these boards seldom have sufficient staff, nor are they given strong statutory authority. Legislators realize that most citizens do not want tax equalization—many fear higher tax bills.

In many cities, nearly 25 percent of all property is tax-exempt. In Boston, the proportion is as high as 50 percent; in New York City, it is 35 percent. In large part, tax-exempt property is owned by the government or by religious organizations. Another cause of revenue loss is that wealth in the form of personal property and intangible goods—for example, stocks and bonds—is seldom taxed effectively. Most often the true value of this sort of wealth is vastly underestimated or not reported at all by taxpayers.

Economists are critical of the property tax because it is sluggish in responding to changes in the general economy. When prices are rising, property-tax revenues remain stable because assessors are slow to make reevaluations. Even when administrative changes are made, there is a considerable delay before government units receive the additional funds. The opposite case also is true. When the economy is faltering, tax rates remain inflexible, thus placing severe strain on taxpayers. Although the most extreme situation occurred during the 1930s, many large cities today face the problem of what to do with hundreds of abandoned houses and apartments that are no longer producing tax revenue.

A longstanding criticism of the property tax is that it is a **regressive tax**—that is, the burden of taxation falls most heavily on those least able to pay. At the opposite pole is the **progressive tax**—for example, the federal income tax, whose graduated scale provides higher rates of taxation for those with higher incomes. The property tax is thought to be regressive because it is believed that landlords pass tax increases along to their tenants. Also, it is assumed that high-income groups possess wealth in the form of personal property and intangible goods that are unlikely to be taxed. In many jurisdictions, small properties tend to be assessed at rates higher than large properties.

More recently, economists have come to believe that the property tax may be less regressive than they once supposed. In most cases, landlords are not able to pass the cost of all taxes along to their renters. When permanent income is considered, some economists believe the property tax is neutral, taking nearly equal proportions from the rich and poor. The use of circuit breakers and homestead credit (discussed below) has helped reduce the regressiveness of property taxes. Some economists conclude that the property tax should be reassessed more often and more accurately. They recommend income-support payments and property-tax postponement for households with low incomes. They believe that defects in property-tax administration can be remedied and that the tax is not regressive.[4]

An additional problem with the property tax is that it is the basic source of revenues used to finance public schools. As discussed in Chapter 9, this produces substantial differences in the amount of money available to finance education in different school districts. Nevertheless, the Supreme Court has upheld the existing system of school financing, ruling that the combination of state aid and local property tax does not violate the constitutional rights of those living in less wealthy districts. Across the country, local governments pay over 50 percent of the costs of public education, and slightly more than half the revenue collected in local property tax is used to support public schools.

Recently, states have taken several actions to help reduce the burden of property taxes on those least able to pay. As of 1989, thirty-four states partially shielded homeowners and renters from property taxes by using state-financed **circuit breakers** (in 1972 only thirteen states had established circuit breakers). Circuit breakers limit the percentage of a homeowner's income that can be taken in property taxes. The device is most popular in the Midwest, where property taxes are high, and least popular in the Southeast, where property taxes are low. Many states classify property to give tax breaks to all homeowners or just senior citizens (*homestead credit*), farmers, and businesses. The number of states giving homestead credit increased from twelve in 1965 to forty-seven in 1989. Whereas only two states gave farmers preferential assessment in 1959, the number increased to forty-nine by the mid-1980s.

In spite of its many shortcomings, the property tax will continue to provide a major proportion of revenue to local governments. Local governments simply do not have any alternatives capable of producing sufficient revenue to replace the property tax. Because property owners benefit most directly from many local government services, it is argued that they should contribute the majority of the financial support for police and fire protection, street maintenance, sewage disposal, and other municipal services. Many defects of the property tax—poorly trained assessors, duplicate assessments of the same property, unequal appraisal of property—can be remedied by more efficient administration. Local governments have moved to diversify their tax base by using other taxes. States, of course, rely heavily on other sources of revenue.

The General Sales Tax

Currently, only five states—Alaska, Delaware, Montana, New Hampshire, and Oregon—do *not* have a general **sales tax.** All states have a tax on cigarettes, liquor, and gasoline. The sales tax was first used by Mississippi in 1932, and twenty-two more states enacted sales taxes during the Depression. Today it is the largest single source of revenue for states. However, as shown in Figure 8.2, income from sales taxes has been decreasing as a percentage of overall state tax collections. The percentage of state revenue from general sales tax ranges from nearly 60 percent in Washington to 21 percent in New York. States without an income tax make heavy use of the sales tax. For example, Nevada derives 85 percent of state revenues from sales and excise taxes. Most states collect a sales tax of about 4 percent, and local governments in twenty-eight states "piggyback" on state sales taxes with an added percentage of their own.

Merchants object to the added administrative work involved in collecting sales taxes, and in some cases they fear that business will be lost when purchasers go out

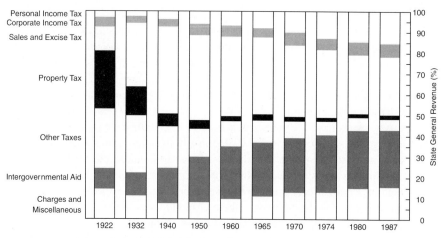

Figure 8.2   Sources of State Revenue, 1922–1987

SOURCE: Bingham, Hawkins, and Hebert, *The Politics of Raising State and Local Revenue* (Praeger Publishers, New York, and imprint of Greenwood Publishing Group, Inc., 1978), p. 7. Copyright © 1978 by Praeger Publishers. Reprinted in Gray, Jacob, and Albritton, *Politics in the American States,* 5th ed. (Scott Foresman/Little Brown). Reprinted with permission.

of state. To counteract this problem, states may impose a "use tax" on purchases made outside their taxing jurisdiction by their residents. However, it is very difficult to monitor out-of-state purchases and to collect the tax.

Like the property tax, the sales tax is criticized for being regressive, in that everyone pays the same rate of taxation. In addition, the poor must spend a higher percentage of their income for food, clothing, and fuel than do the rich, and this increases the regressiveness of the tax. Some states have acted to lessen the regressive effects of the sales tax by exempting from taxation such items as food and drugs. Recently a few states have given tax exemptions for residential heating. Other than a reduction in the rate of taxation, there is little that can be done to offset the impact of inflation on those paying sales tax.

The sales tax is attractive to state and local governments because it is easy to administer and substantial amounts of money are collected. It is relatively painless for the consumer, who often considers the tax a part of the selling price of a purchase. Moreover, governments find it reasonably easy to increase the tax rate by an additional percentage point without incurring the wrath of taxpayers. Indeed, one of the major problems with the property tax is that owners receive an annual or semi-annual bill that vividly reminds them of the burden imposed by the tax. In addition, increases in property tax rates must be approved in popular referenda, and overburdened taxpayers will often defeat bond issues even when it means cutbacks in public school programs.

Income Tax

Forty-three states employ a tax on individual earned income and forty-five levy a corporate income tax. Wisconsin pioneered the first state **income tax** in 1911. Cities or counties in fourteen states use an income tax, but only a few cities in some states use the tax, whereas hundreds of cities in Ohio and Pennsylvania have an income tax. For many years, the federal government had largely preempted the field by its use of a fairly heavy personal income tax. Faced with increasingly serious financial problems, many cities and states in the late 1950s began for the first time to employ a withholding system to collect income tax in a manner similar to that of the federal government.

Rates of state income taxes are typically much lower than are rates of federal income taxes. In three states, the tax rate is a fixed percentage regardless of the income level. Three other states assess a flat percentage based on the federal tax owed. Also, although most state income taxes are graduated—that is, the rate of taxation increases as income increases—the rate of increase is much less for states than it is in federal tax schedules. In addition, state tax plans typically include generous exemptions and deductions. Nevertheless, the income tax is considered to be the most progressive state tax. Oregon, which does not have a sales tax, makes the heaviest use of the income tax (65 percent of its state revenue).

Taxes on the income or profits of corporations produce about one-third as much revenue for the states as does the personal income tax. However, substantial use of this tax is concentrated in a few states—California, Massachusetts, New York, Pennsylvania, and Wisconsin. Only five states do not have a corporate income tax. Many large, industrial states levy only a token corporate income tax, and some do not use one at all. This reflects the fear of interstate competition luring business and industry to relocate with the promise of low taxes.

Excise and Severance Taxes

As noted earlier, all states place an **excise tax** on cigarettes, liquor, and gasoline. The rate of tax on cigarettes in 1990 ranged from .02 cent a pack in North Carolina to 41 cents a pack in Texas. These large state variations have led to cigarette bootlegging. States also collect fees from automobile and driver's licenses and from licenses issued for the sale of liquor. The liquor business is so profitable that several states control its sale exclusively through state-owned stores.

A variety of other taxes are levied—on admissions to entertainment events, inheritance, stock transfers, gifts, and parimutuel betting. In states that have valuable natural resources—such as coal, oil, natural gas, and timber—a **severance tax** is often levied on their extraction and removal. About two-thirds of states employ some form of severance tax. However, only a few states account for most of the severance tax revenue. In Alaska, North Dakota, Montana, New Mexico, and Wyoming, severance taxes account for more than 25 percent of all state tax revenue. Alaska receives nearly two-thirds of its state revenue from severance taxes. As we would expect, fluctuating prices for oil, natural gas, and coal have a strong effect on severance tax revenues. The significant drop in severance revenue in the mid-1980s had a disastrous impact on the economies of Alaska, Wyoming, Oklahoma, Texas, and Louisiana.

Other Revenue Sources

State and local governments also receive money from assorted fees and special service charges. For example, California receives more than $50 million a year from hunting fees, and some small states, such as Idaho, also receive relatively large amounts of money from these fees. Other licensing fees, court costs, fines, and money from parking meters add significantly to city revenue. Some cities run their own utilities (gas and electric), which may be quite profitable. As noted in Chapter 2, intergovernmental grants constituted an increasingly large percentage of state and local revenues in the 1960s and 1970s, but have declined in importance since the early 1980s (see Table 2.1, p. 42). Twenty-nine states plus the District of Columbia have lotteries. On the average, lotteries provide 2.2 percent of state general-fund expenditures. The percentage of state expenditures paid for by lottery proceeds ranges from 0.7 percent in Kansas and Colorado to 7.6 percent in Florida.[5] Per person ticket expenditures average about $100 a year in states with lotteries. Administrative costs are high, there is the possibility of fraud, and it is argued that lotteries are regressive because low-income groups are most likely to buy lottery tickets. Moreover, they have not produced as much revenue as expected. Nevertheless, states have become increasingly interested in gambling revenues. Only four states—Hawaii, Indiana, North Dakota, and Utah—do not permit any form of gambling. Nevada receives about 50 percent of its state revenues form gambling taxes. New Jersey became the second state to sanction casino gambling, and that has prompted several other states, including South Dakota, to follow suit. In the accompanying reading, *New York Times* columnist William Safire criticizes states for their willingness to seek a quick financial fix through gambling promotions.

Tax Revolts—Proposition 13

In 1966–1976, property taxes more than doubled in over half the states. In the 1970s, public opinion polls showed the property tax to be the most unpopular of all taxes (see Table 8.2). As early as 1972, voters in Washington state approved a referendum limiting the property tax to 1 percent of assessed value. That limit, however, did not apply to schools and certain other public projects. Many states failed to respond to public outcries against increasing taxes. In California, real estate values doubled during the period 1973 to 1978. Moreover, efficient local assessment and frequent turnover in housing led to skyrocketing property tax bills.

In that state, Howard Jarvis began a campaign in the early 1960s to place a tax-reduction measure—(ultimately **Proposition 13**)—on the ballot. California's tradition of using the initiative process obviously helped Proposition 13. In addition, Howard Jarvis was an especially effective campaigner who was generously financed by the real estate industry. With a $7 billion surplus, the state's threat to cut services was not an effective counterargument. Although labor, teachers, public employees, the League of Women Voters, and most elected officials urged a no vote on Proposition 13, it passed in 1978 with nearly 70 percent support in a high-turnout election.[6] The proposition had two main provisions:

- It generally limited property taxes to 1 percent of market value based on 1975 values, and provided for updating annually after that with increases of no more than 2 percent per year. However, any change of ownership or new construction on the property triggers reappraisal—and higher taxes—based on current value.
- It prohibited the state from raising any state taxes to make up for lost revenue unless the new taxes are approved by a two-thirds vote of the legislature.

**Table 8.2   Which Do You Think Is the Worst Tax—That Is, the Least Fair?
(percent of U.S. public)**

	May 1986	May 1985	May 1984	May 1983	May 1982	Sept 1981	May 1980	May 1979	May 1977	April 1974	March 1972
Federal income tax	37	38	36	35	36	36	36	37	28	30	19
Local property tax	28	24	29	26	30	33	25	27	33	28	45
State sales tax	17	16	15	13	14	14	19	15	17	20	13
State income tax	8	10	10	11	11	9	10	8	11	10	13
Don't know	10	12	10	15	9	9	10	13	11	14	11

SOURCE: *Significant Features of Fiscal Federalism 1987* (Washington, D.C.: Advisory Commission on Intergovernmental Relations, 1987), p. 111.

The initial impact of Proposition 13 in California was positive. Property-tax bills declined significantly but because of the state's budget surplus, most public services remained about the same. Problems began to emerge in the early 1980s when the surplus disappeared and continue to plague the state.[7] Like other states, California was affected by the national recession and the reduction of federal aid. As a result, there were cuts in many state departments and communities began to impose user fees for many services. Since two-thirds of the reduction in property taxes was in commercial property (including agriculture), residential homeowners did not benefit as greatly as some had anticipated. California has relied more heavily on sales and income tax, and this has shifted government power from the local level to the state.

Under Proposition 13, property-tax assessments were rolled back to 1975 levels and limits were placed on tax increases as long as property remained in the same hands. However, when property is sold, it is reassessed at the new value. Because property values have increased greatly since 1975, new property owners may pay taxes as much as ten times higher than those people owning similar houses that are still protected by Proposition 13. In 1992 the Supreme Court upheld this unique system that assesses property according to purchase price, not market value.

The initial success of Proposition 13 led to a flurry of tax-cutting activity in more than half the states in 1978–1980. During this tax revolt, eighteen states approved limitations on taxes and expenditures. A dozen more considered limitations and rejected them. The most extreme limits were approved in Massachusetts, Minnesota, and Idaho. As a result of the passage of Proposition 2 ½, Boston lost about 75 percent of its property-tax revenue. By the late 1980s, Massachusetts faced severe financial problems and support for Governor Michael Dukakis plummeted. Hansen notes that, in general, states with a tradition of using the initiative process were the ones most successful in reducing taxes. As a result of reform efforts, public attitudes regarding property taxes have improved since the early 1970s.

In the early 1980s, the pattern of cutting taxes was reversed as states came under increasing financial pressure because of inflation, recession, and cuts in federal spending. As noted, most states increased taxes in 1982 and 1983. Thus the burden of taxation was shifted; property taxes remained stable while sales, excise, gasoline, and user taxes were increased. According to one post–Proposition 13 survey, California residents believe that cuts were made in the wrong places—education instead of the bureaucracy.[8] Still, most said they would vote for it again. California voters in 1980 rejected a constitutional amendment to limit state income

Shame of the States

In Deadwood, S.D., where in 1876 Wild Bill Hickok was shot in the back during a poker game while holding a hand of aces and eights, gambling was re-introduced in 1989. Despite a betting limit of $5, the amount wagered by tourists and other suckers in the once-moribund town has already passed a third of a billion dollars.

That's only for openers. South Dakota's state lottery, reaching for the youth market, has also invested in video games, the modern equivalent of state-sponsored slot machines. West Virginia is experimenting with video machines at racetracks.

New York and Connecticut up the ante with telephone off-track betting, likely to spread to faxes and computer modems for hacker-touts. And liberal Iowa, on the pretense of reviving interest in the less savory elements of its history, has launched river-boat gambling on the Mississippi—retaining 20 percent of casino winnings, which long-time gamblers grumble is too much vigorish.

All this means that Americans at the state level are deciding that gambling is good—not just a tolerable evil, but a positive value. Gambling has become a goal of public policy.

Only a few years ago, proponents of state lotteries were claiming that state control would channel the profits of an unstoppable human frailty toward good ends. Why let numbers racketeers and Mafia casino operators bilk the public, their argument went—why not steer those ill-gotten gains into public schools?

The answer is spreading like a poison through state and local governments: immoral means have never led to moral ends. We are no longer skimming the profits from a criminal activity: we are putting the full force of government into the promotion of moral corruption.

What am I, some kind of stiff? Is a friendly game of gin rummy at a penny a point to be frowned upon, or a church social that raises its costs at a bingo game to be condemned, or a privately owned gambling yacht catering to rich drunks cause for conservative concern?

I'm a libertarian. If people want to titillate themselves with a game of chance, or delude themselves into thinking they can beat the odds, that's their private business. I just do not think it should be the public business.

Gambling promotion has become a key to state budget-balancing. Card-carrying right-wingers are not supposed to mind taxing the poor, but really soaking the poor—as this excessively

taxes. Ohio voters in the mid-1980s defeated a move to reduce their state income tax rates. With the cutbacks in federal aid since 1981, the pattern has been for states to *increase* tax rates. There was some sign of tax cuts in the mid-1980s, but the Federal Tax Reform Act of 1986 has placed more financial pressure on state and local governments, and the pattern of tax *increases* continues into the 1990s.

A Comparison of State Taxes

As shown in Table 8.1, per capita tax levels vary greatly among the states. While Wyoming had a tax level nearly double the national average in 1988, New regressive taxation does—sticks in my craw.

Why? Because it is wrong for the state to exploit the weakness of its citizens. It is the most unfair and painful form of "painless" taxation. The money isn't coming from a few big bookies and croupiers, but from the pockets of millions.

And gambling taxation feeds on itself. We cannot give up the state income from betting, say legislators who feel guilty about pretending that gambling is good, because the states have become dependent on the money, or because other states will use casinos to lure their tourism. They have become as hooked on gambling as a source of revenue as any compulsive gambler betting the milk money.

Here's what you can do to stop the explosion of government-sponsored gambling:

Tell your local television anchor you've had it with media hype of gambling. Features of giggling lottery winners or hoo-hahing over million-dollar jackpots is cheap-shot journalism; show us some people impoverished by gambling, or expose the cost of the state bureaucracy pushing it.

Apply truth-in-advertising to state-sponsored slots, lotteries and video games. Display prominently the odds against winning; state the number of losers for every winner. Demand stations make free equal time available for anti-gambling messages.

Demand that gubernatorial gamesters stop using their "take" for advertising. The old numbers racket was never permitted mass-market advertising; the creation of fresh demand for gambling by a public agency is against the public interest.

Tell your kids that gamblers are life's losers. Private gambling, like prostitution, should not be illegal, but it should not be treated as a value. And to make the state hustling of gambling profits the basis for state education is like shooting Marshal Hickok in the back.

Hampshire's level was substantially below the national average. The states of the South have the lowest taxes per capita. During this century, relative rates of taxation have remained remarkably stable among the states. However, the gap between the top and bottom states has narrowed somewhat because of increasing urbanization and affluence in the South. The urbanized, industrial states of the Northeast and Midwest have great private wealth, which when taxed at even a moderate rate can produce substantial revenue. These same states also tend to place a heavy emphasis on the income tax. States that use the income tax more than the sales tax or other taxes are also more likely to levy the heaviest taxes and thus collect the most revenue.

Although per capita taxes tend to be high in wealthy states (New York, California, and Massachusetts), there are several exceptions to this rule. West Virginia, which ranks low in median family income, has high per capita taxes. Other states with above-average wealth, such as Indiana, rank very low in per capita taxes. This leads to a consideration of **tax burden** as related to income. Economists refer to tax burden as a measure of how tax systems affect taxpayers' incomes. States such as Oregon and Minnesota that rely heavily on more progressive taxes (income) have high tax burdens, and the burden falls more heavily on those with middle and upper incomes. Some states, such as Vermont, tax their residents at a high rate even though personal income is low. In those cases economists speak about a strong *tax effort*. In very wealthy states, such as Connecticut, a great deal of money can be raised without taking a large percentage of personal income. Thus the tax burden is high in Vermont, relatively low in Connecticut (although it will increase with the new state income tax), and very low in New Hampshire. Some states such as Alabama and Mississippi are so poor that even though their tax rates are low, the tax burden is still relatively high. Because different states rely more heavily on some kinds of taxes than others, per capita rankings and tax burdens can be somewhat misleading. For example, there appears to be a very heavy tax burden on Wyoming residents. Because much of their revenue is raised by severance taxes, the actual payment of the tax is made by out-of-state consumers of Wyoming resources.

As discussed in Chapter 2, poorer states are aided by the system of federal grants-in-aid, which distributes proportionately more money to them than to rich states. Other financial differences between rich and poor states include the fact that public services in low-income states (particularly in the South) tend to be centralized with the state government. In the richer states (especially in the Northeast), local governments raise a greater proportion of revenue and provide more services than do state governments. In turn, this means that the property tax (collected by local governments) is a more important source of revenue in rich states than in poor states.

BORROWING AND DEBT POLICIES

When tax revenue is insufficient to meet general operating costs or when state and local governments wish to finance major capital programs such as highways or schools, money must be borrowed. Although borrowing to meet current expenses is discouraged, long-term borrowing for permanent improvements is standard procedure. Because of unsound financial management in the nineteenth century, state constitutions place narrow limits on borrowing. Limits are placed on the amount of debt that can be incurred, and borrowing decisions are most often made by the voters in referenda, rather than by legislators.

State indebtedness declined in the late 1980s, but it has increased in the 1990s. New York and California faced large budget deficits in 1991, but like all states except Vermont, their constitutions require balanced budgets. Older cities in the

Northeast tend to have more debt than other cities because of the variety of services they provide and their deteriorating financial base. State debt occurs because capital spending (e.g., building and repairing bridges) necessitates borrowing. States and cities are rated by private agencies, and if they have low ratings (based on their financial condition) they must pay higher rates of interest. Debt also exists because states form government corporations to finance public works projects, and these corporations can borrow money in excess of state constitutional limits.

A part of state and local debt is in the form of short-term bank loans and tax-anticipation warrants, which are paid out of current revenue. To pay for capital improvements such as a school building or a convention center, governments issue bonds. **General-obligation bonds** are backed by the full faith and credit of the issuing government. In approving this kind of bond, usually by a referendum, the community agrees to increase taxes to pay the interest and ultimately retire the bond. **Revenue bonds** are supported by the income from some self-liquidating project such as a toll road. In most cases, voter approval is not needed to issue revenue bonds, and they can often be used to extend the total debt beyond constitutionally allowable limits. As with general-obligation bonds, interest on revenue bonds is exempt from federal taxation. Since revenue bonds are somewhat more risky than general-obligation bonds, they usually pay a higher rate of interest. Local governments, too, have been issuing revenue bonds for such things as civic centers and industrial development. This means that both cities and states are borrowing more short-term money at relatively high interest rates.

Although the financial crisis in New York City temporarily depressed the bond market when it was feared that the city might default, state and local bonds are generally most attractive to wealthy investors. Their popularity results from government policy in which the interest income on state and municipal bonds is exempt from federal taxation. The volume of municipal bonds dropped markedly after passage of the Tax Reform Act of 1986. However, 1991 was the second highest bond year ever.[9] Interest rates declined on tax-exempt bonds, prompting cities to issue bonds to pay for schools, roads, and hospitals. Individual demand increased and Congress may ease some of the 1986 tax code regulations. In *South Carolina* v. *Baker* (1988), the U.S. Supreme Court held that there is no constitutional requirement that municipal bonds be tax-free. However, Congress is not likely to eliminate the exemption completely. Generally speaking, cities put their financial houses in order in the 1980s by cutting services, raising taxes, and improving financial management. However, they have suffered cuts in federal grants-in-aid and the elimination of revenue sharing, and financial pressures have grown in the 1990s.

The best means of repayment is to issue **serial bonds,** in which a certain portion matures each year and is retired from current income. In the past, governments created a "sinking fund" in which they set aside a given amount of money each year to provide sufficient funds when the bonds matured. In many cases, however, governments dipped into the sinking fund for other purposes or tax revenues dropped and the extra money was not available once current operating expenses were met.

KEY TERMS

Boards of equalization Boards that act to review tax computations within each taxing district to ensure that properties of equal value are taxed at the same rates.

Circuit breaker A device that places a limit on the amount of a homeowner's income that can be taken in property taxes.

Excise tax A tax levied on the manufacture, transportation, sale, or consumption of goods. States often levy such a tax on liquor and tobacco.

General-obligation bonds Bonds issued by state or local governments that are backed by the full faith and credit of the issuing body. The community increases taxes to pay the interest on the bonds.

Income tax Tax levied on individual and corporate income received from profits, salaries, rents, interest, and dividends.

Inflation In economics, an increase in available currency, which causes a rise in prices.

Progressive tax A graduated tax whose rates increase as the ability to pay increases. Most income tax rates are graduated.

Property tax A tax levied by local governments through the county. It involves the assessment of property values (homes and businesses), determination of tax rates, tax computation, and tax collection.

Proposition 13 An initiative passed in California in 1978 that substantially cut property taxes and made it more difficult to increase them.

Regressive tax A tax in which low-income groups pay proportionally more than high-income groups. The property tax and sales tax are generally considered to be regressive.

Revenue bonds Bonds supported from the income earned by such projects as toll roads and bridges.

Sales tax A tax levied by state and local government on the purchase of commodities. Rates vary from 2 to 6 percent, and usually the tax is limited to retail sales.

Serial bonds Bonds that mature in part each year, with that portion retired from current income. As a result, the issuing body is not faced with the problem of having to pay off the entire bond obligation at one time.

Severance tax A tax levied on the extraction of scarce natural resources, such as timber, oil, coal, and natural gas.

Tax burden The amount of taxes paid as a percentage of personal income. In poor states, moderately high tax rates will create a heavy tax burden on residents.

REFERENCES

1. *Significant Features of Fiscal Federalism 1991,* vol. 2 (Washington, D.C.: Advisory Commission on Intergovernmental Relations, 1991), p. 82.
2. Michael de Courcy Hinds, "States and Cities Fight Recession with New Taxes," *The New York Times,* July 27, 1991, pp. 1 and 8.
3. Susan B. Hansen, "The Politics of State Taxing and Spending," in Virginia Gray, Herbert Jacob, and Robert B. Albritton, eds., *Politics in the American States,* 5th ed. (Glenview, Ill.: Scott, Foresman/Little, Brown, 1990), pp. 355–356.
4. See Henry J. Aaron, *Who Pays the Property Tax? A New View* (Washington, D.C.: Brookings Institution, 1976); and J. Richard Aronson and John L. Hilley, *Financing State*

and *Local Governments,* 4th ed. (Washington, D.C.: Brookings Institution, 1986), Chapter 7.

5. "Lottery Dollars," *Governing,* March 1991, pp. 52–53.
6. Hansen, "The Politics of State Taxing," p. 364.
7. See Jerry Hagstrom and Neal R. Peirce, "The Quake That Didn't Quit," *National Journal,* May 25, 1988, pp. 1413–1416.
8. See Paul Richter and Terry Schwadron, eds., *California and the American Tax Revolt: Proposition 13 Five Years Later* (Berkeley: University of California Press, 1984).
9. John Cranford, "Mini Bond Forecast: Sunny . . . for Now," *Governing,* June 1992, p. 69.

CHAPTER 9

STATE POLICYMAK-ING: CONFLICT AND ACCOMMODATION

In the preceding chapters such matters as political and structural factors in state and local government, intergovernmental relations, the nature of party organization and competition, the role of interest groups, the organization and operation of legislatures, formal and informal powers of governors, the structure of court systems, and the administration of justice have been considered. In this chapter and in Chapter 10 we will focus on an analysis of the **policies** that are produced by public officials acting within this political and structural system.

In making policy, state and local governments act as producers of goods and services demanded by various groups within their jurisdictions. As noted in Chapter 1, state and local governments administer most of the nation's domestic programs, and their expenditures account for nearly two-thirds of all government purchases of goods and services in the United States. However, as the discussion of federalism in Chapter 2 indicated, most state and local programs are supported by federal grants. To receive federal funds, state and local officials must adhere to a host of federally established rules and regulations. As a result, even after recent federal cutbacks, public programs are usually joint ventures carried out by at least two or three levels of government. This chapter examines five areas of policymaking: welfare, education, civil rights, highways, and housing. Chapter 10 discusses growth and environmental protection.

State and local policymakers have had to operate in a difficult environment since the early 1980s. At the same time that federal aid was reduced (if we exclude AFDC and Medicaid, federal aid fell by one-third in the 1980s), states and cities have been pressured to spend more money for health care, crime control, infrastructure repair, and education. Moreover, federal mandates now account for about 60 percent of many state budgets. These problems are compounded by the Bush administration's very limited domestic agenda. In the first three years of his administration (until the Los Angeles riots and the 1992 campaign), Bush focused his attention on international problems—the Gulf War, arms control, changes in Eastern Europe, an attempted coup in the Soviet Union—with which he had much more success than he had in dealing with crime, rising medical costs, poverty in the United States, and a sluggish economy.

As we shall see, in each area of policymaking, governments have been pressured to reduce expenditures on the one hand yet provide higher-quality services at the same time. This has been particularly true in education. The public seems to want to have its cake and eat it too: At the same time that financial cuts are being made, there is criticism of the job being done by the schools.

STATE AND LOCAL POLICYMAKING

This book has analyzed throughout how socioeconomic, political, and cultural factors influence the structure of state and local government and the nature of public policy. In this chapter, the particular concern is to describe different policies among the states and to seek to understand why these differences exist. In the social sciences, it is always dangerous to speak of having discovered *the cause* of a particular kind of behavior. Although B follows A, a third factor, C, may influence the relationship between A and B or, in other situations, B may not follow A. As a result, the best that can be hoped for is to identify certain **causal patterns,** in which various social and political factors appear to be interrelated.

Chapter 1 discussed the relationship between the level of economic development in the states and government structure and policy. Thomas R. Dye, in his study of the effects of economic development, discovered a positive relationship between expenditures for education, health, and welfare and high levels of economic development. At the same time, Dye discovered a weak relationship between political factors (voter participation, interparty competition, legislative apportionment) and the enactment of public policy.[1]

Chapter 1 also cautioned against accepting economic development (or any other one measure) as a single-factor explanation of policymaking. Economic influences may vary in importance over a period of time; they may differ in their impact on various areas of policymaking; and they may not have an equal impact at all levels of government. In addition, it was noted in Chapter 3 that economic factors are of less influence in reformed cities than in cities with nonreformed government structures. Although it remains true that the richest states (California and New York) tend to provide the highest levels of service in education and welfare, some rich states have low levels of service, whereas some relatively poor states have a tradition that supports certain policy areas.

Clearly, socioeconomic factors do have an influence on state and local policymaking. Political factors such as interparty competition and voter turnout are positively related to state expenditures for welfare and education. Of course, high levels of political participation and party competition are associated with wealthy states where the people are also well educated. States with high levels of legislative and judicial professionalism (high salaries and sufficient staff assistance) tend to devote substantial resources to supporting social welfare programs. Policymaking also is influenced by the quality of political leadership. Governors such as Huey Long in Louisiana and Robert La Follette in Wisconsin were able to overcome major barriers and redirect state policy.

Political culture and established traditions are also influences on policymaking. For example, the moralistic political culture of the states of the upper Midwest has influenced the legislatures of those states to enact a series of progressive programs in the areas of welfare, education, and environmental protection. States with traditional political cultures generally provide low levels of public services. Yet Oklahoma, which would be classified as traditional, has provided generous welfare support to its citizens. Oklahoma suffered severe economic hardship during the Depression and in 1933 created a sales tax whose revenue was earmarked for public welfare programs.

Tradition also affects the degree to which public services are provided by state or local government. At the extremes, the New England states have a long history of **localism,** while Southern states have a strong tradition of **centralism.**[2] The New England states historically have stressed local decision making through the town meeting and local financing of public projects. In the South, the destruction of local services by the Civil War forced the states to finance many programs, such as public education, that typically are administered locally in other parts of the country.

Although Southern state governments have been relatively inactive, this tradition has strengthened the role of their governors by giving them control over areas of policymaking that many states leave to local governments.

The effects of localism and centralism can be clearly seen in state education policy. In New England, where public schools were first established, most financing comes from local governments. In the South, which did not begin to operate effective public school systems until after the Civil War, there has been centralized control of policymaking as well as financing. As a result, state legislatures in the South have established teacher salaries and have set policy in regard to such matters as Bible reading and racial segregation in public schools. A similar pattern exists for public welfare expenditures. In most Southern states, the share paid by local governments is very small—often less than 1 percent of the total. In the New England and North Central states, the percentage paid by local governments is sometimes greater than the state share.

Given the political setting in which policymaking occurs, it is important to remember that decisions are made in an atmosphere of *conflict and accommodation.* There is opposition to virtually every policy proposal, and agreement is reached only after bargains have been struck and compromises have been agreed on. As noted in Chapters 5 and 6, government structure has been established specifically to delay decision making. Thus reformers confront opposition in the form of structural barriers (legislative committees, executive boards, and commissions) as well as barriers placed by those opposed to their proposals for reasons of practicality or political expediency.

The four stages in the policymaking process need to be kept in mind as each policy area is examined. First is *policy development.* Once problems are identified, they need to get on the public agenda, and means must be developed to deal with them. Problems may be identified by a variety of sources, including elected public officials, bureaucrats, public opinion, the media, and political parties. Basic questions to be addressed include whether anything should be done by government about a social problem, and if so, what level of government should respond.[3] The second stage is *policy adoption* or enactment. How much money should be spent and how the money should be raised are basic questions for legislators at this stage. While very poor states cannot afford to do much, they may make a greater effort in some areas than rich states. The third stage is *implementation.* How should the services be delivered? Are bureaucrats following the wishes of legislators and the governor? The fourth stage is *evaluation.* How well did government perform its functions?

WELFARE POLICIES

No other area of policymaking illustrates better than welfare the interrelationships among levels of government in the United States. Welfare policies, including such programs as Social Security, food stamps, Workers' Compensation, Aid for Families with Dependent Children, and housing, emerge from a maze of some 20 congressional committees, 50 state legislatures, and 1,500 county welfare departments. General assistance is available in forty states for those who do not qualify for federal welfare programs. But eligibility standards and benefits vary greatly among the states.

Attempts to measure the number of people in the United States who are poor are complicated by defining poverty in absolute terms or as relative deprivation. That is, are people poor when their incomes fall below a certain level or are they poor when measured against an acceptable standard of living of others in their community. The most widely accepted standard is the poverty line, established by the Bureau of the Census. This represents what a family of four needs to spend for an "austere" standard of living (the amount was $13,359 in 1990). Many conservatives criticize the measurement because it excludes cash benefits, such as food stamps, and they argue that it exaggerates the rate of poverty. Others argue that the figures underestimate poverty because the original threshold, developed in the 1960s, has not been fundamentally reevaluated and does not take into consideration the increased percentage of income that goes for child care.[4]

In 1960 about 40 million Americans (22.2 percent of the population) were defined as poor. The figure declined to 24.5 million (11.4 percent) in 1978. As Figure 9.1 shows, the number of poor people rose in the early 1980s and remained stable. The number of poor increased by 2.1 million from 1988 to 1990. The poverty rate for blacks in 1990 was 31.9 percent and it was 26.2 percent for Hispanics (see Figure 9.2).

Before 1930, neither the states nor the federal government had enacted significant welfare programs. Welfare was largely a local responsibility, and benefits var-

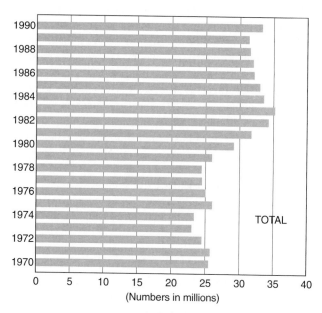

Figure 9.1   Number of Americans Living Below the Poverty Level

SOURCE: U.S. Bureau of the Census, as reported in *The New York Times,* September 27, 1991, p. A–11.

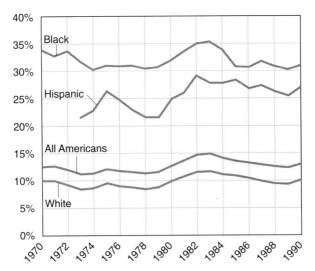

Figure 9.2 Percentage of Americans Living Below the Poverty Level

SOURCE: U.S. Bureau of the Census, as reported in *The New York Times,* Semptember 27, 1991, p. A–11.

ied greatly even within the same state. Although Wisconsin enacted the first state aid to the blind in 1907, as late as 1934 only twenty-four states had followed this lead and created similar aid-to-the-blind programs. At the same time, only twenty-eight states had established programs to aid the aged.

American welfare policy changed dramatically with the passage of the Social Security Act of 1935. This landmark legislation established several federal programs; it provided incentive to states to formulate their own welfare programs; and it encouraged uniformity in welfare programs across the country. The Social Security Act established a national social insurance plan under the headings Old Age, Survivors', Disability, and Health Insurance. Among its twenty major titles, the act also provided federai grants to assist the states in creating programs to aid the blind, aged, and disabled, as well as dependent children. Social Security programs are funded through compulsory payroll taxes and administered by the federal government. The other welfare programs are jointly funded from federal, state, and local general revenues. These programs require annual appropriations, and they are administered in large part by state and local officials. Since the creation of Supplemental Security Income (SSI) benefits in 1972, the federal government has set national minimum standards of assistance and eligibility for persons previously covered by Old Age Assistance, Aid to the Blind, and Aid to the Permanently and Totally Disabled.

To be eligible for assistance under federally initiated programs, persons must fit into a particular category, such as blind or disabled. General assistance, for those not covered by categorical federal programs, is provided by the states. They, in turn, rely heavily on local governments to finance and administer general welfare programs. As a result, these programs vary greatly from state to state in terms of eligibility and levels of benefits.

In 1965, the Social Security program added Medicare to provide basic medical services to persons receiving aid under any of the four primary federal categorical assistance programs. Also in 1965, the **Medicaid** program was created, under which states finance medical care for poor people who do not qualify for Medicare. By 1973, Medicaid had become the largest single item in state welfare budgets, and it is the largest federal grant program. **Aid to Families with Dependent Children (AFDC)** recipients are automatically eligible for Medicaid, and states can provide Medicaid coverage to other individuals if they wish. Like AFDC, Medicaid benefits vary greatly among the states. Medicaid has been the fastest-growing state expense in recent years, increasing by 18 percent in 1990 and nearly doubling in total cost in the 1980s. Costs are up as a result of a general increase in medical expenses, an increase in federal mandates for expanded coverage, and an increasingly elderly U.S. population. Medicaid took 3 percent of state spending in 1970; by 1990, it was up to 12 percent. The federal government sets guidelines and pays 56 percent of the costs, on the average, of the program. The federal share ranges from 50 percent in several states to 80 percent in Mississippi. Although all AFDC recipients are eligible for Medicaid, they receive only about one-fourth of Medicaid expenditures. Because Medicaid pays about 45 percent of *all* nursing home costs (Medicare pays 2 percent), the elderly account for about 40 percent of Medicaid expenditures.

Under the Reagan administration, changes in AFDC eligibility reduced the number of families entitled to receive Medicaid benefits. Federal legislation in 1981 also gave states more control over Medicaid, and it provided for reduction of federal matching funds for states that failed to control hospital and doctor costs. The states responded by making strong efforts to preserve or even expand Medicaid services. This was in contrast to federal cuts in AFDC, which were not offset as well by the states. Medicaid received stronger political backing than AFDC because nearly two-thirds of Medicaid spending is for the elderly and disabled and the medical profession supports it. Moreover, the general population perceives it as a joint federal-state program rather than exclusively federal.[5]

AFDC is the largest and most controversial of the federally assisted welfare programs. The federal government pays about 55 percent of total AFDC spending. Each month about 12 million people in 4 million families receive AFDC benefits. Of the recipients, half are black, half are white, and about three-fourths live in metropolitan areas. Under a complex formula, states are reimbursed by the federal government up to a maximum amount. Originally AFDC benefits were intended to provide aid to children whose father was not in the home, but they have been extended to cover families in which an able-bodied male is present. If the states wish to provide aid above the federal maximum, they must finance that part of the program from their own funds. Because of this discretion, payments vary greatly among the states. AFDC recipients in California receive over five times as much money as do recipients in Mississippi (see Table 9.1). In California, which gained 6.1 million people in the 1980s, including 35 percent of all legal immigrants to the United States, Governor Pete Wilson set off a debate by saying that the state must reduce the "magnetic effect" of its generous welfare payments by limiting migration.

AFDC spending more than tripled in the 1960s when court decisions required states to cover families who met federal eligibility requirements. Expenditures

peaked in 1976 and declined until the mid-1980s as the Reagan administration re-duced the number of beneficiaries by 8 percent. Enrollment increased moderately in the late 1980s. **Food stamps,** a federally funded program, made up part of the loss in AFDC benefits, which did not keep pace with inflation in the 1980s. Food stamp expenditures in 1990 were about $15 billion, compared with $17.5 billion for AFDC. All AFDC recipients are eligible for food stamps. Because the amount of food stamps is based on family size and income and is uniform across the country, the program tends to reduce differences in welfare benefits among the states.

Prior to 1988, there was an optional program (AFDC-UP) in twenty-seven states in which two-parent families could qualify for welfare if the "principal wage earner" was unemployed. In 1988, in the first major revision of the welfare system in fifty-three years, all states were required by the Family Support Act to provide such benefits. It was argued that AFDC encouraged fathers to leave home and that the new program would lead to greater family stability. Congress also enacted the first mandate ever requiring welfare parents with children over three years old to participate in a new Job Opportunities and Basic Skills (JOBS) program offering education, training, and work activities ranging from high school to community jobs. JOBS participants will receive transportation and child-care help. States also are required to step up child support collections by setting standardized formulas for the amount of payment. In 1988, twenty-eight states had mandatory "workfare" programs, but only nine were statewide. States are required to provide transitional child care and Medicaid for twelve months after a participant leaves AFDC to take a job. Here and elsewhere, state governments are caught in a crossfire of increased federal mandates, more recipients, and increasing budget deficits.[6]

AFDC payments per recipient tend to be highest in wealthy states such as New York, Connecticut, and Michigan (see Table 9.1). These states also tend to make the greatest welfare effort as a percentage of state personal income. There are, of course, some exceptions: Relatively rich states such as Ohio and Indiana make only modest welfare efforts. Vermont, a poor state, makes a strong welfare effort. In general, Southern and Rocky Mountain states rank at the bottom. Since they are poor states, this increases the gap in absolute dollars between welfare benefits in the South and in the North. While New Mexico and Wyoming devote less than 10 per-cent of their state budgets to welfare, New York and Michigan spend nearly 30 per-cent of their budgets on welfare. Neighboring states often provide contrasting views of welfare effort. For example, the high-effort states of California and Vermont are bordered by Arizona and New Hampshire, which make only minimal efforts to pro-vide welfare benefits.

Forty-four states also provide "general assistance" for people who do not quali-fy for AFDC, Medicaid, or other federal welfare programs. Most recipients are single people and childless couples who are not elderly and not disabled. While some states provide long-term benefits, others give only emergency relief. Due to state budget deficits and the public perception that many able-bodied people get help, nearly one-third of the states cut their general assistance budgets in the early 1990s. Such cuts have increased costs for other state services, such as shelters for the homeless.

There are several explanations as to *why* welfare effort varies so greatly across the country. As in other areas of policymaking, Thomas Dye concludes that eco-

Table 9.1   AFDC Benefits

DIVISION AND STATE OR OTHER AREA	RECIPIENTS (1,000)			PAYMENTS FOR YEAR (MILLIONS OF DOLLARS)			AVERAGE MONTHLY PAYMENT PER FAMILY	
	1980	1988	1989	1980	1988	1989	1988	1989
Total	**11,101**	**10,898**	**11,183**	**12,475**	**16,827**	**17,466**	**$374**	**$383**
U.S.	10,923	10,707	10,987	12,409	16,754	17,388	(NA)	388
N. Eng.	**647**	**467**	**505**	**910**	**1,012**	**1,098**	**501**	**524**
ME	58	49	53	60	80	90	375	408
NH	24	12	15	27	22	26	408	417
VT	24	19	21	32	40	43	476	500
MA	348	239	256	510	566	600	545	559
RI	54	41	44	72	82	88	455	483
CT	140	106	117	209	221	252	491	534
Mid. Atl.	**2,216**	**1,806**	**1,779**	**2,954**	**3,382**	**3,330**	**453**	**451**
NY	1,110	986	964	1,623	2,180	2,146	536	530
NJ	469	297	308	560	451	441	357	357
PA	637	524	508	771	751	743	352	356
E. No. Cent.	**2,419**	**2,307**	**2,274**	**2,838**	**3,491**	**3,459**	**366**	**373**
OH	572	633	623	561	801	837	297	314
IN	170	148	149	139	166	163	263	263
IL	691	640	623	722	801	789	309	320
MI	753	637	641	1,063	1,227	1,223	480	480
WI	232	249	237	353	495	447	472	461
W. No. Cent.	**614**	**611**	**619**	**697**	**907**	**925**	**361**	**368**
MN	146	163	164	207	342	343	520	523
IA	111	99	97	144	152	149	349	360
MO	216	202	207	182	215	223	263	272
ND	13	15	16	16	22	24	355	366
SD	19	19	19	19	21	22	271	271
NE	38	41	41	42	56	57	323	333
KS	72	73	77	87	99	107	339	349
So. Atl.	**1,463**	**1,386**	**1,471**	**1,125**	**1,531**	**1,640**	**259**	**267**
DE	34	19	21	32	24	26	270	283
MD	220	176	181	214	253	272	336	356
DC	82	49	47	92	76	79	347	363
VA	176	147	150	160	169	169	258	260
WV	80	109	109	60	108	109	242	253
NC	202	196	216	154	212	225	243	238
SC	156	109	105	72	90	93	189	208
GA	234	262	285	138	276	295	258	261
FL	279	319	356	203	324	371	241	253
E. So. Cent.	**704**	**656**	**686**	**366**	**423**	**454**	**152**	**160**
KY	175	154	171	136	146	161	209	223
TN	174	193	207	85	130	146	158	170
AL	178	130	130	84	62	61	114	114
MS	176	179	178	61	86	85	119	118

Table 9.1   AFDC Benefits (*Continued*)

DIVISION AND STATE OR OTHER AREA	RECIPIENTS (1,000)			PAYMENTS FOR YEAR (MILLIONS OF DOLLARS)			AVERAGE MONTHLY PAYMENT PER FAMILY	
	1980	1988	1989	1980	1988	1989	1988	1989
W. So. Cent.	**716**	**979**	**1,038**	**401**	**707**	**743**	**183**	**183**
AR	85	70	71	51	54	55	191	193
LA	219	277	281	124	183	186	167	167
OK	92	103	105	92	121	125	281	288
TX	320	529	581	134	350	377	169	168
Mt.	**302**	**381**	**407**	**274**	**450**	**477**	**291**	**293**
MT	20	28	32	19	41	40	363	356
ID	20	17	16	24	19	19	249	251
WY	7	14	14	9	19	19	304	307
CO	81	98	100	81	127	133	318	324
NM	56	59	60	42	55	55	225	225
AZ	60	103	117	40	107	122	268	271
UT	44	43	45	48	61	64	344	352
NV	14	20	23	11	21	25	273	277
Pac.	**1,843**	**2,115**	**2,208**	**2,844**	**4,850**	**5,263**	**562**	**589**
WA	173	217	225	251	405	424	444	449
OR	94	88	87	147	131	139	349	361
CA	1,498	1,749	1,833	2,328	4,177	4,553	590	620
AK	16	19	19	27	54	55	599	619
HI	61	43	44	91	82	92	506	546
PR	170	183	189	60	68	72	101	102
GU	5	4	4	3	3	3	216	228
VI	3	3	3	2	2	3	195	280

SOURCE: *Statistical Abstract of the United States 1991* (Washington, D.C.: U.S. Bureau of the Census, 1991), p. 373.

nomic resources largely determine spending levels for welfare and that income is the single most important determinant of levels of welfare benefits.[7] But Dye admits that political factors such as party competition and voter participation have some independent, liberalizing effect on increasing welfare benefits. Sarah McCally Morehouse believes that the quality of party leadership, the strength of the governor's formal powers, and legislative professionalism are most significant in explaining welfare policy.[8] She notes that the states with the greatest need (i.e., the highest percentage of families below the poverty line) are the least generous in welfare payments even as a ratio of per capita income.

According to Robert Albritton, income is not a strong indicator of welfare effort. He sees state population size as the major determining factor in welfare effort. Albritton suggests that in states with large urban areas, "the size of the pool of persons eligible for welfare assistance appears to have a dynamic effect in determining the proportion of the population admitted to welfare assistance categories."[9] Perhaps this is a function of more effective organization and political pressure than is found in smaller, rural states. Others have noted that all but five of the top twenty states in AFDC benefit levels have moralistic cultures, while sixteen of the bottom twenty have traditional cultures. Benefit levels, as opposed to welfare effort, are closely tied to economic resources, which are more plentiful in moralistic states.

Differences in welfare payments among the states are diminishing as poor states make a greater effort to provide benefits to more people and as the federal government moves to standardize welfare payments and eligibility. The federal food stamp program also reduces disparities in welfare among the states because the federal government pays the cost of all food stamp benefits and splits the administrative costs evenly with the states.

EDUCATION POLICIES

The history of public education in the United States dates from 1647, when Massachusetts towns were required to establish schools. The Northwest Ordinance of 1787 provided that one-sixteenth of each section be set aside for a school. Connecticut in 1850 was the first state to mandate free education. Mississippi in 1910 was the last. The Morrill Act of 1862 provided land grants to the states to establish universities that emphasized agriculture and engineering and later commerce and business. In 1870, the University of Michigan established a policy of accepting all students who graduate from public schools accredited by the university. By 1900, most states had compulsory attendance laws and most had created the position of state education officer. It was not until the Elementary and Secondary Education Act of 1965 that Congress approved the first general federal intervention in local education, providing over $1.3 billion for special education programs and support of education for minority-group students.

Today, states spend more money on education than on any other single function. When compared with welfare, federal financial assistance to education (about 6 percent of the total public expenditures for education) is low and federal rules and regulations are less complex. Since World War II, the American educational system has faced a series of crises regarding such matters as why Johnny can't read, sex education, religion in the schools, the new math, racial balance, student rights, sources of financing, and community control. It is somewhat comforting to realize that many of these same issues—racial equality, finances, popular control, and moral purpose—were equally controversial more than 100 years ago.

The basic government unit for America's schools continues to be the local school district, whose board members levy taxes and hire the superintendent and teachers. Although other units of government have multiplied in this century, school districts have been reduced in number—through *consolidations*—from about 126,000 in 1932 to about 14,000 in 1991.* Between 1950 and 1980, nearly three of every four school districts in the United States were eliminated through consolidation. Those supporting consolidation argue that it is more economical to have one large school rather than several small schools and that children attending

*As an extreme example, in 1905 Philadelphia had 43 elected school boards with 559 board members. As late as the mid-1960s, Kansas, Minnesota, Nebraska, Pennsylvania, and South Dakota each had more than 2,000 school districts. See Frederick M. Wirt and Michael W. Kirst, *The Political Web of American Schools* (Boston: Little, Brown, 1972).

larger, better-equipped schools, whose teachers are better paid, will receive superior educational instruction.

In opposition to this trend, there has been a movement to *decentralize* school administration. The debate has been particularly strident in large cities, where ethnic and racial minorities contend that community control is necessary in order to ensure that the educational and social needs of inner-city children are met. In the late 1960s, in a highly politicized atmosphere, the state legislature divided New York City schools into thirty administrative districts.

Schools in all but three states are organized in local school districts. Nearly 75 percent of all school board members are popularly elected, most on nonpartisan ballots, and incumbents are seldom defeated. School boards appoint a superintendent, whose relationship to the school board is similar to the relationship between the city manager and council in a small city. However, the superintendent typically dominates policy decisions to a greater extent than a city manager, and council members typically have more experience than do school board members. In most instances there is little conflict between the board and the superintendent regarding school policy.

Many states also have elected county school boards, and all states except Wisconsin have a state board of education. The state board sets overall requirements for the state, including minimum standards for graduation. It also distributes state **foundation money** as determined by the state legislature. In most states, members of the state board of education are appointed by the governor. The superintendent of education is separately elected in eleven states, down from twenty-two states in 1965. Despite attempts to insulate state boards from political pressure, governors often control their budgets and influence boards to do their bidding. As governors increasingly make education a policy issue, legislators and boards often follow the governor's lead. Morehouse notes that when governors are assertive in educational policy, states are more likely to spend more money on education.[10]

Public dissatisfaction with the schools has grown significantly in the past decade. Declining enrollments have affected schools in most larger cities. High school dropout rates have been alarmingly high (see Figure 9.3). For example, the dropout rate for blacks and Hispanics in California is more than 40 percent. Buildings have been closed and teachers laid off. Vandalism has increased, as have physical attacks on teachers. Some teachers have gone on strike as more states allow collective bargaining. Many good teachers experience burnout after a few years on the job, and most new teachers come from the bottom quarter of college graduates. Public response to school problems has centered on minimum-competency testing of students and teachers. By 1990 all but three states had taken some action to mandate minimum-competency testing. While the original emphasis focused on high school graduation, it was later broadened to identify student needs at lower levels.

Average statewide teacher salaries in 1989 ranged from $20,500 in South Dakota to $41,700 in Alaska. The second-highest-paying state was Connecticut at $37,300. Many states have been concerned about raising salaries to attract better teachers, and some have moved to merit systems to encourage good people to stay in education. All states certify teachers, and about twenty-five have created or are

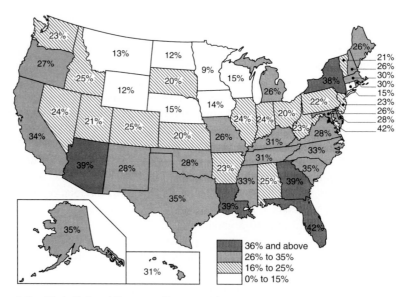

Figure 9.3   High School Dropout Rates, 1988

SOURCE: *The Chronicle of Higher Education,* August 28, 1991, p. 5.

seriously considering statewide teacher tests. Some states have begun internship programs for new teachers. In this regard, Tennessee is in the forefront, with a four-step classification for teachers: apprentice, professional, senior, and distinguished senior teacher.

On the average, state governments currently provide about 50 percent of the costs of public schools, the share of local governments averages 44 percent across the country, and the federal government's share is 6 percent. In 1920 the state share was 16.5 percent, the local share was 83 percent, and the federal government's share was 0.3 percent. In the 1980s, the trend was toward increasing the state share, as both the local and the federal share have declined. The state share now exceeds 60 percent in about twenty states. The pattern of state-local expenditures varies greatly among the states. At the extremes, Hawaii finances public education almost entirely from state funds, while in New Hampshire the state's share is about 5 percent. In general, political culture is the strongest indicator of centralization.[11] The traditional Southern states have a history of centralized control of education. In contrast, the moralistic states of the upper Midwest have stressed local control and financing of schools. But funding in most states has become more centralized because of political pressure from special-interest groups, stronger interest by the governor, and the passage of tax limitation measures such as Proposition 13.

As we would expect, there is a wide range in educational expenditures among the states (see Tables 9.2 and 9.3). At the top, the average per pupil expenditure in New Jersey was about $7,500 per year in 1989. At the bottom, it was less than $3,000 in five states. Most Southern states rank very low in per pupil expenditures, whereas Eastern states (New York, New Jersey, Delaware, Maryland, Vermont,

Connecticut, Rhode Island, and Pennsylvania) rank high. In general, state wealth is the clearest indicator of educational expenditures. The wealthier the state, the more it spends for education. However, educational expenditures are relatively low in California, Ohio, and Indiana, although they have above-average wealth. Such factors as urbanization and party competition do not significantly affect the levels of spending. Educational effort tends to be high in states such as Wisconsin and Oregon, which have strong Progressive traditions. Note that Wyoming ranks second in expenditures per capita for education even though it is thirty-seventh in per capita personal income.

Although President Reagan made quality of education a major issue in the 1984 presidential campaign, the percentage of federal funding for elementary and secondary education declined in the 1980s as the administration continued to stress that education is a state and local government responsibility. President Reagan en-

Table 9.2   Expenditures for Public Schools, Per Capita, 1989

1.	Alaska	$1,664	28.	Iowa	722
2.	Wyoming	1,152	29.	Nevada	713
3.	Connecticut	1,026	30.	Utah	703
4.	New Jersey	1,006	31.	West Virginia	695
5.	New York	991	32.	Ohio	691
6.	Washington	897	33.	Indiana	687
7.	Vermont	873	34.	Florida	687
8.	Maine	850	35.	New Hampshire	685
9.	District of Columbia	838	36.	Illinois	668
10.	Arizona	830	37.	Idaho	657
11.	Montana	827	38.	South Carolina	653
12.	Minnesota	826	39.	North Dakota	640
13.	New Mexico	809	40.	North Carolina	639
14.	Texas	806	41.	Nebraska	628
15.	Maryland	803	42.	Hawaii	625
16.	Virginia	799	43.	South Dakota	619
17.	Oregon	794	44.	Kentucky	614
18.	Wisconsin	792	45.	Missouri	611
19.	Michigan	792	46.	Oklahoma	606
20.	Colorado	787	47.	Louisiana	605
21.	Delaware	782	48.	Mississippi	586
22.	Pennsylvania	772	49.	Tennessee	551
23.	Kansas	762	50.	Alabama	541
	UNITED STATES	757	51.	Arkansas	516
24.	Massachusetts	750			
25.	Rhode Island	748			
26.	Georgia	738			
27.	California	729			

SOURCE: Edith Horner, ed., *Almanac of the Fifty States* (Palo Alto, Calif.: Information Publications, 1991), p. 432. Reprinted with permission.

Table 9.3   Expenditures for Public Schools, Per Pupil, 1989

1. New Jersey	$7,571	28. Ohio	4,138
2. New York	7,338	29. California	4,075
3. Connecticut	7,199	30. New Mexico	4,034
4. Alaska	7,134	31. Hawaii	4,034
5. Rhode Island	5,939	32. Nevada	3,974
6. District of Columbia	5,827	33. Arizona	3,904
7. Massachusetts	5,818	34. West Virginia	3,879
8. Pennsylvania	5,621	35. North Carolina	3,872
9. Delaware	5,506	36. Indiana	3,858
10. Wyoming	5,462	37. Texas	3,842
11. Maryland	5,391	38. Missouri	3,838
12. Wisconsin	5,117	39. Nebraska	3,732
13. Vermont	5,057	40. Kentucky	3,655
14. Maine	4,845	41. South Carolina	3,465
15. Oregon	4,818	42. North Dakota	3,447
16. Virginia	4,744	43. Louisiana	3,352
17. Colorado	4,633	44. South Dakota	3,329
18. Minnesota	4,577	45. Tennessee	3,305
19. Michigan	4,576	46. Oklahoma	3,212
20. Illinois	4,513	47. Idaho	2,946
UNITED STATES	4,509	48. Alabama	2,915
21. Florida	4,487	49. Mississippi	2,846
22. Kansas	4,404	50. Arkansas	2,698
23. Washington	4,339	51. Utah	2,574
24. New Hampshire	4,334		
25. Iowa	4,289		
26. Montana	4,259		
27. Georgia	4,143		

SOURCE: Edith Horner, ed., *Almanac of the Fifty States* (Palo Alto, Calif.: Information Publications, 1991), p. 433. Reprinted with permission.

tered office committed to abolishing the Department of Education. From 1980 to 1985, federal aid to higher education decreased slightly, while aid to elementary and secondary education increased about 10 percent. The major change was that twenty-nine categorical grants were merged into the elementary and secondary education block grant for fiscal 1982. In the short run, the block grant reduced funds available to local school districts, but this cut came at a time when state aid was increasing. The net effect was that some urban districts that had been receiving federal desegregation aid lost funds, but other districts gained under new state distribution formulas.[12] President Reagan supported merit pay for teachers and competency testing of students. He also supported such proposals as tax deductions and vouchers to assist parents whose children attend private schools. Vouchers are government grants that would allow parents to "shop around" and, if they wished, use the grant to pay part of the costs at private schools. (Tax deductions are discussed in the next section.)

After talking in the 1988 presidential campaign about his wish to become "the education president," George Bush announced a proposal in 1991 that called for "a revolution in American education." Major components included (1) incentives to states and localities to promote freedom of choice among public and private schools; (2) development of 535 new schools with one-time congressional grants of $1 million to each school; (3) state assessment of students in grades 4, 8, and 12 in five core subjects; (4) incentive pay to teachers who teach well or in challenging situations; (5) certification of nontraditionally trained teachers; (6) voluntary nationwide examinations in core subjects; and (7) requests that business develop a set of job-related skill standards. No congressional action was taken in 1991 on the Bush proposal.

Freedom of choice has been strongly supported by Presidents Reagan and Bush. Under the Bush plan, states and localities would be encouraged to change their rules so that parents could apply tax dollars to send their children to public or private schools. At the same time Congress would be asked to permit federal aid to go to children in private and parochial schools. Unlike past proposals, the Bush plan has received support from educators and leaders of teachers' unions. The accompanying reading maintains that Republicans have framed a new argument for reform, using federal funds as incentives, not subsidies. Although federal control would be limited, federal influence over education would grow.

Of course, there have been many education reforms. Following the publication of *A Nation at Risk* by the National Commission on Excellence in Education in 1983, nearly all states had tightened curriculum requirements by 1988, most required minimum grade-point averages of new teachers, many states enacted merit pay, virtually all increased salaries, and new standardized tests were developed for teachers and students. With all this reform, little improvement was evident in the educational process. SAT verbal scores fell to a record low in 1991 and SAT mathematics scores declined for the first time since 1980. In part, this occurred because most reforms transferred power away from local school boards to state boards of education, and teachers had little involvement in the process.

After years of incremental reform, it has become clear to many people that more radical change is needed.[13] Two examples of radical change in the 1980s came in Minnesota, which instituted a plan to give families a choice of crossing district lines into neighboring towns to find a school for their children, and in Kentucky, where the state supreme court held that the legislature had violated the state constitution by not providing an "efficient system of public schools." In response, the legislature went beyond the court's opinion to raise taxes, channel funds to poor districts, and overhaul the state education department. Education policymaking has become increasingly politicized, with governors now playing the major role. Interest groups, including the National Education Association, the American Federation of Teachers, and the National Congress of Parents and Teachers, are strong advocates for education in virtually all states.

In response to the growing demand for higher education, state support for colleges and universities has expanded greatly since World War II. In 1947, about half of all college students were enrolled in state institutions. By 1968, the figure had risen to 71 percent, and by 1990 to over 80 percent. Increased student demand has

Bush Is Reshaping the Schools Debate

The goals of President Bush's education initiative, announced in mid-April, are certainly ambitious. Among them: At least 90 per cent of all Americans will graduate from high school. Every American adult will be literate. Every U.S. school will be free from drugs and violence. And American students will lead the world in mathematics and science.

The Bush Administration's most ambitious goal is not on the list, however. It is to demonstrate that the federal government can solve problems without spending a lot of money or creating vast new bureaucracies. That goes far beyond simply answering the charge that the Administration has no domestic agenda. It means formulating an entirely new approach to governance—relying on innovation and incentives instead of taxing and spending. A "New Paradigm," so to speak.

The traditional party debate in this country is between more government and less government. By advocating less government, Republicans have usually put themselves in the position of defending the status quo—that the problems facing the country are not serious or that the government cannot solve them. By advocating more government, Democrats have usually put themselves in the position of raising taxes and "throwing money at problems." Neither of these positions is widely supported anymore.

Republicans are attempting to frame a different debate, one between new ideas and old ideas. They want the GOP to be the party that comes up with interesting and provocative ideas about how to use government. They want Democrats to be the party that de-

fends the status quo. On the education issue, that is exactly what each party is doing.

In announcing his plan, Bush said, "If we want America to remain a leader, a force for good in the world, we must lead the way in educational innovation." The innovative part of the President's initiative is the creation of 535 experimental schools, at least one in each congressional district, to serve as national models of excellence. These "high-performance" laboratory schools would be underwritten partly by the federal government and partly by a business-led nonprofit corporation.

The Administration is also proposing incentives for educational improvement. These include voluntary national tests to determine whether students and schools meet new national standards of achievement. Another proposal encourages state and local school districts to allow parents to send their children to any public or private school they want. Federal money earmarked for disadvantaged students would follow the students to the schools of their choice. In effect, public and private schools would be encouraged to compete for students. "Dollars will follow the child," Education Secretary Lamar Alexander announced.

But "dollar bills don't educate students," Bush was saying at the same time. The Administration wants to use federal funds as incentives, not as subsidies. It describes the initiative as "a long-term strategy, not a federal program." The plan would cost the government about $820 million, a small part of the Education Department's budget of $27.1 billion for 1992. The details of administering the plan would be left to states and local communities. "People who want Washington to solve their educational problems are missing the point," the President said. "What happens here in Washington won't matter half as much as what happens in each school, each local community and, yes, in each home."

So on the one hand, the Administration is proposing limited government spending and limited federal control. On the other hand, it is looking for a substantial enlargement of federal influence over education.

Albert Shanker, president of the American Federation of Teachers, called the plan "a turning point in the federal role." He explained, "This is the very first time the President of the United States has said the federal government had a major role in improving elementary and secondary education."

Congressional Democrats are worried that the plan could undermine the public school system. They are concerned that subsidies for parochial schools could violate the constitutional separation between church and state. They complain that the President should have provided more money for existing programs. And they are determined to protect the popular Chapter 1 program that channels money to schools with disadvantaged students.

All of which leaves the Democrats in the position of protecting the status quo and defending the special interests. That's what it sounded like when Sen. Edward M. Kennedy, D-Mass., chair-

man of the Labor and Human Resources Committee, warned that the President's initiative could become "a death sentence for public schools struggling to serve disadvantaged students."

Democrats are nervous because, according to a recent ABC News-*Washington Post* survey, the voters rate the two parties about equal when it comes to improving education. Democrats have enjoyed a long-standing advantage on the education issue, and they expected to use Bush's 1988 campaign pledge—"I intend to be the Education President"—against him in the campaign next year. What will they do now?

They will complain that the President's plan consists of nothing but recycled Democratic ideas. The Democrats are perfectly capable of recycling their own ideas, which they did when they rushed an alternative, and more expensive, proposal through the Labor and Human Resources Committee on a party-line vote.

The Democrats will also complain, as House Majority Leader Richard A. Gephardt, D-Mo., did, that the Administration's proposal "falls short" of the "radical reform" needed to improve the nation's educational system. Gephardt added, "Had the Founding Fathers adopted this definition of revolutionary change, America would still be part of England."

In other words, the Democrats will fight back with everything they have— sour grapes and sound bites.

SOURCE: William Schneider, *National Journal,* April 27, 1991, p. 1026. Reprinted by permission.

meant expanded facilities on existing campuses, the creation of new colleges, and a tremendous increase in the number of community colleges. This, of course, has resulted in vast expenditures of state funds. In several states, expansion in the 1960s was followed by declining enrollments in the 1970s and by legislative cutbacks in funding for higher education. Since the 1980s, college enrollment has been inching ahead, while vocational and technical schools have had substantial increases.

State funds account for about half the income of public colleges. The other half is divided almost evenly between student fees and federal grants. Appropriations per student vary greatly among the states. It is difficult to discern any geographical or regional pattern, although the Northeastern states rank very low in appropriations per student for higher education. Socioeconomic and political factors also have little correlation to appropriations per student. In terms of willingness to allocate funds for higher education, most Southern states have placed a high priority on higher education in recent years. However, because of the low level of personal income, these states are unable to raise the tax revenues needed for high dollar levels of funding for higher education. Well-established private institutions continue to dominate in the Northeast, although Massachusetts made a determined effort to upgrade its state system of higher education until beset by serious financial problems in the late 1980s. Most states make some form of aid available to private colleges; only three states—Arizona, Nevada, and Wyoming—do not. (Those states have few private colleges.) Among the more generous states, New York and Illinois have gift programs for students attending private colleges and they also make per capita payments to private colleges. Pennsylvania's gift and loan program extends to students who attend private colleges out of state. Most states restrict payments to in-state students. Increasingly, states have developed innovative plans to help parents finance their children's college education. For example, several states allow families to purchase tax-exempt bonds for college savings, and a few offer prepaid-tuition plans that allow parents to pay a set sum of money, years in advance, for their children's education.

The quality of public institutions of higher learning has improved significantly during the past fifty years. The University of California (at Berkeley and Los Angeles) and the state-supported Big Ten universities stand on an equal footing with the best private institutions. Several states have established "centers of excellence" at their major universities, and special funds have been created to lure eminent scholars to public universities. The state of California led the way in creating an integrated state system of universities, four-year colleges, and two-year community colleges. Other states, such as Wisconsin and New York, have followed the California model in expanding and unifying their colleges and universities. In California and Florida, more than one-half of all undergraduates are enrolled in public community colleges. California's community college system has 107 campuses.

Unlike the administration of elementary and secondary schools, state control of colleges is much more diverse.[14] In some states, such as Wisconsin, there is a single board for all universities; in other states, such as Illinois, there are several university systems and several boards. In most cases board members are appointed by the governor, although they are publicly elected in a few states. States with several boards usually have a coordinating panel to review operations of all universities.

Often there is considerable political conflict among state universities competing for public funds. Faced with serious budget problems, nearly half the states cut their higher-education expenditures in 1991. It was the first time in the last thirty-three years that states appropriated less money for higher education than they had the year before.[15] The largest decrease for the period 1990–1991 was 28 percent in Massachusetts, and the largest increase for the two-year period was 31 percent in Nevada. States spent about $40.1 billion for higher education in 1991.

Community colleges also offer strong competition for appropriations. While total spending for higher education increased 3 percent in 1990–1991, state support for community colleges was up 13 percent. Community colleges are popular with legislators because they are relatively inexpensive and their emphasis on vocational education is appealing to the practical-minded. The recent increase in enrollment of these schools has been much greater than in universities and four-year colleges.

THE SCHOOLS AND THE COURTS

In several states, legal action has challenged the way in which schools are financed. Because of the heavy reliance on the local property tax and the resultant inequities in per pupil expenditures among school districts in the same state, some have charged that students from poor districts are being denied equal protection of the law as guaranteed by the Fourteenth Amendment. In one such suit, the supreme court of California agreed with the plaintiffs and ordered that action be taken to equalize school expenditures throughout the state (*Serrano* v. *Priest*, 1971). Several other state supreme courts have subsequently handed down similar decisions regarding school financing in their states. When based on *state* constitutional guarantees, these decisions require significant changes in patterns of state aid to education.

A *national* right to equalized funding for education was denied by the United States Supreme Court in *San Antonio Independent School District* v. *Rodriguez* (1973). This opinion overturned a federal district court ruling that had held that the Texas system of school finance violated the equal protection clause because it discriminated against less wealthy districts. In the San Antonio area, the most affluent school district spent nearly twice as much per year, per pupil, as did the poorest district. In upholding the Texas school finance system, the Court argued that education is not a fundamental right protected by the Constitution. In spite of this ruling, other state supreme court decisions (as noted above) remain in effect regarding equalization of educational funds throughout the state.

Other areas in which the Supreme Court has had a significant impact on state educational policy involve racial integration, state aid to parochial schools, and religious practices in public schools. School integration and the subsequent issues of busing and segregated private schools are discussed in the following section on civil rights.

Since the 1950s, the Supreme Court has made some very controversial rulings dealing with interpretations of the First Amendment's establishment of religion and free exercise of religion clauses. These decisions have effected significant changes in state and local educational policies. The Court's record in maintaining a **wall of**

separation between church and state has been mixed. While it has ruled against state-ordered prayers, a moment of silence for meditation, and Bible reading in public schools, it has allowed such actions as providing secular textbooks and bus transportation to students attending parochial schools.

In 1987, the Court overruled a Louisiana statute that forbade "the teaching of the theory of evolution in public schools unless accompanied by instruction in 'creation science.'" The majority held that the primary purpose of the Creationism Act was to endorse a particular religious doctrine. The Court permitted a program in Minnesota in which parents are allowed a state income tax deduction for school expenses, up to a certain amount, to send their children to public or private schools. Expenses include books, tuition, and transportation. Obviously, this plan benefits those who choose to send their children to private schools, of which 95 percent are religiously affiliated in Minnesota. The Court has upheld state grants to church-related colleges, but it has overruled a plan in Pennsylvania to use state funds to pay teachers' salaries in parochial schools. In distinguishing between aid to parochial schools and aid to church-related colleges, the Court argued that college students are less impressionable than elementary school students and that the church-related colleges reviewed did not attempt to indoctrinate students with religious beliefs. In a 1986 opinion, the Court unanimously upheld assistance under a state of Washington vocational rehabilitation program to a blind person studying at a Christian college and seeking to become a pastor, missionary, or youth director. In 1990 the Court upheld a federal law that requires public high schools to allow student religious and political clubs to meet in school buildings on the same basis as other extracurricular groups.

Several recent decisions affect the ways in which the rights of students are defined. For example, in 1984 the Court ruled that public schools that open their facilities to student meetings must allow student-run religious services to take place. In *New Jersey* v. *T.L.O.* (1985) the Court held that although the Fourth Amendment (prohibiting unreasonable searches and seizures) applies to school officials, they need not have a warrant to search student lockers or purses. What is required, said the Court, is that officials have "reasonable cause" to conduct a search.

The most widely publicized decisions of the Supreme Court in the 1970s concerned the issue of affirmative action as it affected university admissions practices. In *Regents of the University of California* v. *Bakke* (1978), the Court ruled 5 to 4 against a rigid preference system in which the University of California at Davis had reserved 16 percent of the places in its first-year medical school class for minority applicants. However, the Court also ruled 5 to 4 that admissions programs that consider race to remedy past discrimination are not necessarily unconstitutional. As a result, universities and colleges could continue to use affirmative action admissions programs so long as they avoided fixed quotas.

CIVIL RIGHTS POLICY

Unlike the other topics discussed in this chapter, civil rights is not a separate, well-defined area of policymaking. Rather, civil rights policies become significant as they relate to other policy areas such as welfare, education, and housing. In the period since 1960, civil rights has been the most explosive issue facing city governments. In response to pressure from federal courts and Congress, state and local officials have enacted a variety of laws aimed at protecting the civil rights of black Americans, Hispanics, and other racial and ethnic minorities.

As discussed in Chapter 2, the American federal system has protected segregationist policies under the banner of states' rights. Federalism permits considerable state and local independence, and it allowed the states to discriminate by law prior to the 1960s. Although the most conspicuous segregation occurred in the South, public education and housing policies have supported segregation throughout the country.

Prior to the enactment of the **Civil Rights Act of 1964,** many Northern states had passed legislation aimed at prohibiting racial discrimination. New York passed the first state antidiscrimination law regarding private employment in 1945. By 1966, thirty-three states had similar laws concerning fair employment practices, and thirty-five states had approved legislation forbidding discrimination in public accommodations. In 1957, New York City passed a fair-housing ordinance that provided a set of procedures progressing from complaints to court sanctions to ensure compliance. When Congress passed open-housing legislation in 1968, twenty-two states already had similar laws. Still, in 1954, seventeen Southern and border states plus the District of Columbia required segregation by race in public schools. Four other states (Arizona, Kansas, New Mexico, and Wyoming) gave local school boards the option of instituting segregation.

State civil rights policy has been strongly influenced by federal court decisions and acts of Congress. In 1954 (*Brown* v. *Board of Education of Topeka, Kansas*), the Supreme Court first ruled against racial segregation in public schools. There was widespread resistance to the *Brown* decision, and few schools in the South had been integrated by the mid-1960s. Yet by 1970, public schools in the South had become more integrated than schools in the North. Now more than 50 percent of blacks in the North attend schools that are 95 to 100 percent black, whereas only about 20 percent of blacks in the South attend schools that are overwhelmingly black. Federal troops were used in the South to enforce desegregation rulings and some federal grants to states and communities have been withheld because of continued racial discrimination. More significantly, however, there has been a voluntary acceptance by many Southerners of equal rights for black Americans.

The Civil Rights Act of 1964 makes it unlawful to discriminate against or segregate people on the basis of race, color, religion, or national origin in any place of public accommodation. The law also provides that employers (or labor unions) of more than twenty-five people cannot discriminate in employment because of race, color, religion, sex, or national origin. To help ensure integration, the law states that financial assistance will be terminated if states refuse to comply with federal desegregation orders. All school districts in the seventeen states that by law maintained segregated schools in 1954 were required to submit desegregation plans in order to continue to receive federal grants.

In large part, Southern schools in large cities have become integrated as a consequence of court-ordered *busing*. Where school systems were segregated by law (**de jure segregation**) before 1954 (as in Charlotte, North Carolina, and Louisville, Kentucky), the constitutionality of court-ordered busing plans has been upheld by the Supreme Court. The Court did not, however, approve a plan for metropolitan Detroit that involved busing children from inner-city schools to suburban schools. There it ruled in 1974 that racial segregation in area suburbs is the result of residential patterns (**de facto segregation**) and not the product of actions taken by public officials. However, in 1979 the Court upheld broad busing plans in Columbus and Dayton, Ohio.

The courts have upheld busing plans for Northern cities, such as Boston and Detroit, when suburbs are not involved. These plans, and those in the South, have been strongly criticized, and resistance in some cases has been violent. Opponents charge that busing encourages the flight of whites to the suburbs. Sociologist James Coleman, whose famous report in 1966 predicted that "integrated schools should be expected to have a positive effect on Negro achievement," has rejected busing on the grounds that it is counterproductive to achieving lasting integration. Coleman has been particularly concerned about the flight of whites from cities to suburbs.[16] In *Missouri* v. *Jenkins* (1990) the Supreme Court held that a federal district judge had the authority to order a local school board to raise taxes to pay for a school desegregation plan. This case involved a long-running battle in Kansas City, Missouri.

The Reagan administration was unwilling to support court-ordered busing, and it reduced federal funds that finance desegregation. Civil rights advocates charge that there was a "new leniency" in enforcement of *Brown* by the Department of Justice under Reagan. Rather than bringing suit in federal courts, justice officials preferred voluntary measures adopted in negotiated consent decrees, and they stressed the magnet-school concept to attain an acceptable racial mix.[17] The Bush administration has been criticized for opposing civil rights legislation that it charged would establish racial quotas and for nominating conservative federal judges, including Clarence Thomas to the Supreme Court. In 1991 the president and congressional Democrats agreed to a compromise civil rights bill that reversed several Supreme Court decisions that had made it difficult to bring job discrimination suits. The bill expands the rights of job discrimination victims, including victims of sexual harassment, to sue and collect damages.

Debate continues on the question of whether integration improves the academic achievement of black children. Both the NAACP and the National Urban League have strongly supported busing, in the belief that integrated schools improve the learning situation for black children. Other black educators argue that busing is a subtle way of maintaining black dependency on whites. While academics continue to offer conflicting opinions on the reasons for white flight and educational achievement in integrated schools, the American people have registered overwhelming opposition to busing. Some also pose the question of whether efforts to desegregate may instead lead to greater racial imbalance and isolation. They speak of a "tipping point" when blacks exceed 30 percent of the population in schools and housing projects and whites begin to flee their neighborhoods.[18]

Federal court orders and acts of Congress have also affected discrimination in state and local housing policy. The Civil Rights Act of 1968 prohibits discrimination on the basis of color, race, religion, or national origin in selling and renting property. The act exempts small apartments and people selling their own homes without the use of a real estate agent. However, discrimination in advertising for any dwelling is prohibited. In *Hills* v. *Gautreaux* (1976), the Supreme Court ordered the federal government to subsidize low-income housing in the Chicago suburbs in order to alleviate racial segregation in inner-city housing. The Court found the Department of Housing and Urban Development (HUD) guilty of segregative practices by confining most public housing projects to black neighborhoods and by imposing quotas on the few white housing projects to ensure that the black population never exceeded 7 percent.

Despite the ruling in *Gautreaux*, there has not been much dispersal of low-income housing in suburban areas. This is because local governments retain strong control over zoning and other land use. In order to be successful in court, proponents of low-income housing must prove that there was a "discriminatory intent" to segregate housing. In addition, there has been little federal financial support for low-income housing since the 1980s. Although more blacks have moved to suburbs since 1970, most live in suburban neighborhoods that are predominantly black.[19]

The nation's large cities have had to bear the brunt of racial conflict. Increasingly, black Americans have become urban residents—over 80 percent of all blacks live in cities (see Table 9.4). Urban blacks face interrelated problems of poor housing, inadequate education, lack of health-care facilities, and high levels of crime—in addition to overt racial discrimination. The frustrations of black Americans led to violence in many cities during the late 1960s. The most destructive outbreaks were in Watts (Los Angeles) and Detroit. During the Watts riot in 1965, over 200 buildings were destroyed by fire and thirty-four people were killed. In 1967, during a week of rioting in Detroit, 1,300 buildings were destroyed when an area of 14 square miles was gutted by fire. As noted in Chapter 4, urban rioting occurred in 1980 and 1989 in Miami and in Los Angeles in 1992. New York City has had a series of black-white conflicts in the 1990s, including clashes between blacks and Jews in 1991 in the Crown Heights section of Brooklyn.

Because discrimination has economic, social, and psychological consequences (increased feelings of alienation and frustration), there cannot be a simple solution to such a complex problem. Until 1992 racial protest had moderated significantly since the late 1960s. Among various reasons that might be cited for this "cooling off" of American cities are such positive factors as substantial gains in education and an expanded black middle class. In addition, blacks have been elected mayor in several major cities (Atlanta, Chicago, Cleveland, Detroit, Memphis, New York, Los Angeles, Gary, Philadelphia, and Newark), and many blacks hold positions on city councils. The estimated number of black elected city and county officials in the United States increased from 719 in 1970 to about 5,000 in 1991. In the quarter century since *Brown* v. *Board of Education,* significant changes have occurred to better relations between blacks and whites in America. However, the 1992 riots in Los Angeles showed how fragile race relations are in most large cities, where housing and job opportunities for blacks often have become worse since 1980.

Table 9.4   U.S. Cities with Black Populations of 150,000 or Greater, 1990

Black Rank	Overall Rank	City, State	Total Population (thousands)	Black Population (thousands)	Percent Black
1	1	New York, NY	7,322.6	2,102.5	29
2	3	Chicago, IL	2,783.7	1,087.7	39
3	7	Detroit, MI	1,028.0	777.9	76
4	5	Philadelphia, PA	1,585.6	631.9	40
5	2	Los Angeles, CA	3,485.4	487.7	14
6	4	Houston, TX	1,630.6	458.0	28
7	13	Baltimore, MD	736.0	435.8	59
8	19	Washington, DC	606.9	399.6	66
9	18	Memphis, TN	610.3	334.7	55
10	25	New Orleans, LA	496.9	307.7	62
11	8	Dallas, TX	1,006.9	297.0	30
12	36	Atlanta, GA	394.0	264.3	67
13	24	Cleveland, OH	505.6	235.4	47
14	17	Milwaukee, WI	628.1	191.3	31
15	34	St. Louis, MO	396.7	188.4	48
16	60	Birmingham, AL	266.0	168.3	63
17	12	Indianapolis, IN	742.0	165.6	22
18	15	Jacksonville, FL	673.0	163.9	24
19	39	Oakland, CA	372.2	163.3	44
20	56	Newark, NJ	275.2	160.9	59

SOURCE: U.S Bureau of the Census, 1991.

TRANSPORTATION POLICIES

Although it has been an area of intense political conflict, highway policy has not generated the kinds of emotional responses from the public that have resulted from welfare, education, and civil rights policies. Still, state and local governments spend more on highways than on anything else except education and welfare. Decisions regarding highways are highly politicized because of their potential patronage and because they affect such matters as business location and suburban residence patterns.

Since the early days of the automobile, responsibility for road building has become more centralized within states. However, counties and townships maintain about 80 percent of all rural roads. Most states have developed a system of highway classification under which rural and urban roads are divided into primary, secondary, and local categories. The category sets responsibility for maintenance and construction, and it also determines which level of government—state, county, township, city—will finance the work. In many instances, local interests have sought to have roads classified as state highways in order to improve service and shift the tax burden away from local sources.

When highway expenditures are compared among the states, low levels of industrialization and urbanization are found to be directly related to high per capita highway expenditures. Alaska, Wyoming, North Dakota, South Dakota, and Montana have the highest levels of per capita spending for highways. At the other extreme, small Eastern states such as Rhode Island, New Jersey, Connecticut, and Massachusetts allocate less than 7 percent of state expenditures to highways. Curiously, California ranks fiftieth among the states in per capita expenditures for highways. Geographical area and sparse populations contribute to higher levels of highway expenditures in rural states, where total budgets are relatively low and there are considerable distances between cities. Moreover, it is politically easier to build roads in the country than in the city, where costs are higher and there is likely to be extended debate over location. As a proportion of overall state spending, transportation expenditures have declined significantly since 1970. This is due largely to increases in spending for social welfare programs, rather than to cuts in transportation budgets. However, the inability to increase transportation expenditures has led to a deteriorating **infrastructure** of roads, bridges, and sewage systems.[20]

States have received federal aid for highways since the Federal Aid Road Act of 1919. Under the direction of the Bureau of Public Roads, plans for highways were to be approved by the federal government and each state was required to have a highway department. During the 1920s, the highway aid program was by far the largest federal program of grants to states. During the Depression, the National Industrial Recovery Act directed that one-fourth of federal grants to the states could be used on extensions of highways into or through incorporated municipalities. Another one-fourth of the funds could be used for secondary roads. Although these policies were aimed at providing jobs for the unemployed, they also had the effect of improving highways and laying the groundwork for later federal programs.

The **Federal Highway Act of 1944** established for the first time the idea of a system of interstate highways designed to connect major cities and industrial areas. The Bureau of Public Roads was given authority to supervise highway classification and route selection. Uniformity was established in such matters as construction and engineering specifications and weight limits for highway users. However, no federal funds were allocated for these highways until 1952. The 1956 Federal Highway Act represented the beginning of a strong federal commitment to financing interstate highways. Congress changed the proportion of federal funding from 50 percent to 90 percent. The 1956 act set 1972 as the target date for completion of the system. By 1991, after spending $100 billion in the biggest public works project in world history, the 44,328-mile interstate system was virtually complete. Although the interstate system constitutes only 2 percent of the nation's total road surface, it carries more than 20 percent of the total traffic.

After nearly a year of consideration, Congress in 1991 approved a $151 billion transportation bill. The measure designates $119 billion to highways and $31.5 billion to mass transportation over six years, with most of the money coming from taxes on motor vehicles. The federal share of transportation programs was set at 80 percent. This nearly doubles the rate of funding for mass transit and it also gives state and local governments more flexibility to divert highway funds to mass transit. The Bush administration wanted to spend about $10 billion a year for a 155,000-mile national highway system—a nationwide network of interstate highways and other major routes—but the amount was reduced to about $6 billion a year. The secretary of commerce stated that as many as 4 million new construction jobs could be created over the life of the bill. The bill also includes funds for technological innovations such as high-speed trains that ride on magnetic cushions, "smart" cars, and highways equipped with computers designed to speed the flow of traffic; it also mandates several safety features, including airbags for both the driver and front-seat passenger beginning with 1998 car models.

Until 1991, Congress had acted in a modest way to support **urban mass transit.** Federal spending for mass transit began in 1961 and states in the Northeast began to make significant expenditures for mass transit in the 1960s.[21] The Urban Mass Transportation Act of 1964 encouraged research and planning for mass transportation, and it also provided for the relocation of people whose dwellings were taken over to make room for mass transit systems.* The creation of the Department of Transportation in 1966 represented a victory for supporters of mass transportation because it placed the Federal Highway Administration and the Urban Mass Transportation Administration in an equal position in the organizational hierarchy within the cabinet-level department. A major barrier to the development of urban mass transit systems has been that the use of the Highway Trust Fund (federal revenue received through highway-user taxes) has been authorized only for highway construction and maintenance. In a similar manner, states generally earmark revenue from gasoline taxes and license fees for use on highways only. In 1973, Congress for the first time authorized a portion of the Highway Trust Fund to be allocated to support public transportation in urban areas.

President Reagan opposed spending federal money for mass transit, arguing that it should be a local responsibility. Federal funding for mass transit dropped from $4.6 billion in 1981 to $3.2 billion in 1991. The transportation bill submitted to Congress by President Bush would have increased highway spending by 40 percent and given only a token increase to mass transit. Moreover, it would have given states little flexibility to allocate federal funds for mass transit. As noted, the bill President Bush signed in 1991 gave a big increase to mass transit, and it continues federal subsidies to big-city transportation programs.[22]

The system of federal grants has encouraged greater development of mass transit since the mid-1970s. For example, federal highway grants are prohibited to states where comprehensive urban transportation plans have not been developed. In several cities, citizen-action groups have been successful in blocking proposed freeways that would have damaged historic neighborhoods. Still, mass transit systems in most cities are woefully inadequate. Only ten cities—Atlanta, Baltimore, Boston, Chicago, Cleveland, Miami, New York, Philadelphia, San Francisco, and Washington, D.C.—have rapid transit systems that include subways or trains. Fewer than half the states have money for mass transit, and eight states (largely in the Northeast) account for nearly 90 percent of all government outlays for mass transit.[23] Public transit ridership declined between 1945 and 1975. Although it has risen since 1975, it is still below 1945 levels. Eighty-six percent of all passenger

---

*The power of *eminent domain,* inherent in all governments, allows the takeover of private property, provided that it is taken for a public purpose and adequate compensation is awarded. Without this authority, state and local governments would be unable to initiate such actions as highway relocation and slum clearance.

miles in the United States are traveled in automobiles, 12 percent in airplanes, and 2 percent in all forms of mass transit. The new systems in Miami and Atlanta have attracted far fewer riders than planned. Even under the best of conditions, rapid transit systems are extremely expensive. Several states, including California, Florida, and Texas, are investigating the possibility of establishing high-speed rail service between major cities.

In making decisions to reallocate money from highways to mass transit, legislators are confronted by a potent array of interest groups that support continued highway expansion. Road builders, oil and gasoline companies, tire makers, motel owners, automobile clubs, truckers, and automobile manufacturers all have a direct economic interest in highway development. In many states, highway construction provides the greatest single source of patronage to political parties, allowing them to award contracts and jobs. As a result, state legislators face intense pressure when making decisions regarding such matters as highway location, rights-of-way, construction policies, and weight limits. The mass transit versus highways debate also brings out classic urban-rural political divisions in states.

By the mid-1980s, forty states had created comprehensive departments of transportation. These departments have operated with a great deal of independence from either legislative or gubernatorial control. Their independence stems largely from the support of powerful interest groups plus their unique financial position. Their funds come from earmarked state gasoline taxes (the state tax on gasoline must, by law, be used to support highways, airports, and state police) and from the federal Highway Trust Fund. State departments of transportation are also responsible for overseeing rail and air transportation plus mass transit.

Road construction has had a powerful influence on urban development. Historically, rural transportation was given priority over urban transportation. With the advent of the interstate highway program, cities now confront new problems. Interstate highways in metropolitan areas have removed taxable property from city tax rolls, cut off and isolated ghetto neighborhoods, and made it easier for suburbanites to commute downtown to work. New edge cities have sprung up at the intersection of interstate highways.[24] At the same time, rural residents living away from interstate highways have become more isolated than they were 50 years ago, when most small towns had rail-passenger and bus service.

HOUSING AND COMMUNITY DEVELOPMENT

The state role in housing and community development has been increasing since the early 1970s. In the past, states left the problem of housing assistance largely to the federal government. Their role was limited to regulating construction and building conditions and to protecting against racial discrimination. More recently, states have created mortgage lending programs and housing finance agencies to raise funds for housing by issuing tax-exempt bonds. Housing finance agencies use the proceeds from bond issues to finance home mortgage loans for those unable to buy a home, for rental housing development (where federal support has nearly ended), and for home improvement loans.

Although much poor housing exists and more people are homeless than at any time since the Great Depression, overall the quality of housing in the United States has been improving since World War II. This means that substantially fewer people are living in dilapidated or overcrowded housing. However, the cost of housing has increased to the point that about 60 percent of poor families spend over 50 percent of their income on housing. The high cost of urban and suburban housing also creates big problems for those with moderate incomes. Still, most substandard housing is located outside metropolitan areas.

Federal programs began in 1934 with the creation of the Federal Housing Administration. FHA programs, initiated after World War II, provide insured mortgages and financing that has strongly promoted home ownership. In many instances, however, it is bankers and middle-class suburban residents who have benefited most from these federal programs. By making it easier for white, middle-class families to buy a house in the suburbs, federal policies have contributed to the deterioration of central cities. As noted in the section on civil rights, federal programs have also been designed to perpetuate racial segregation in urban housing.

The Department of Housing and Urban Development, created in 1965, administers a wide range of programs, including housing assistance, community planning and development, and fair housing and equal opportunity. HUD also directed the Model Cities Program, which emphasized the integration and coordination of housing and urban development programs with federal transportation, education, economic opportunity, and crime control programs. The hundreds of participating cities in the Model Cities Program submitted long-range proposals regarding urban planning and also gave evidence of significant citizen participation in the planning process. Following the passage of the Housing and Community Development Act of 1974, the Model Cities Program ceased to exist as a separate entity. This act placed a variety of categorical housing programs into a revenue-sharing block grant to be distributed to state and local governments to help eliminate slums, increase low-cost housing, and preserve property with special value. **Community development block grants** (CDBGs) are awarded according to a formula that includes population, level of poverty, and condition of existing housing. Cities over 50,000 population are automatically eligible for funds. The money may be used for some public services other than public housing. The 1974 legislation also had a rent supplement section that encouraged builders to construct apartments for low- and middle-income renters. Local communities do not have to provide matching funds, but they must prepare a comprehensive plan for meeting housing needs. Seventy percent of funds go to cities and the rest to state-administered small towns and rural areas.

The Reagan administration shifted aid from new construction in favor of aid for low-income residents in existing housing.[25] This shift was under way during the Carter administration, and the result has been a substantial reduction in new or rehabilitated low-income housing since the 1980s. Relatively few states have responded to federal cuts by increasing their housing assistance.

Funds for CDBGs were reduced in the 1980s, but cities were given more control over how the funds could be spent. The number of new subsidized housing units dropped from 16,000 per year in 1981 to 2,000 in 1987. When George Bush became president, a major scandal in HUD was unfolding. It was alleged that under Secretary Samuel Pierce the Department of Housing and Urban Development lost about $4 billion in the 1980s because of fraud and poor management. Pierce's replacement in the Bush administration, Jack Kemp, set about restoring confidence in HUD, but there has been little change in the number of new federally funded housing units in the 1990s.

Housing programs administered independently by cities include rent control and urban homesteading. New York City continues to administer its World War II rent control program. The purpose of the program was to ensure a supply of housing that the poor could afford. In recent years, however, more than 30,000 apartment units have been abandoned annually in New York City. In large part, this is because landlords cannot raise rents enough to cover their costs, and because there has been a steady decline in the city's population. **Urban homesteading** programs allow the purchase of abandoned dwellings at a low cost or nominal fee. The buyer agrees to restore the building and live in it for several years. Such programs, tried in Philadelphia, Baltimore, Boston, and Wilmington, remain experimental.

Many state and local governments have worked with the Department of Housing and Urban Development to provide broad-based community development in urban areas. HUD's Urban Development Action Grant program and its Neighborhood Strategy Area program have been the core of state programs attempting to attract private investment in designated urban areas. In some large cities, whole neighborhoods have deteriorated and only a concerted public-private effort can revive them. For example, the Woodlawn area in Chicago lost 41 percent of its population during the 1960s, and the city tore down more than 400 of its buildings. One congressional district in New York City lost one-third of its population in the 1970s. Detroit lost about 200,000 people (14 percent of its population) in the 1980s.

Several well-intentioned but poorly executed housing programs in the 1960s and 1970s have created much skepticism regarding government housing programs. Federal urban renewal (1949–1974) spent billions of dollars to improve inner-city neighborhoods. While they helped some business leaders, urban renewal programs often destroyed a sense of community and had the effect of removing blacks from their neighborhoods. An unintended effect of urban homesteading (or of other programs where middle-class people purchase deteriorating property) has been that poor people are displaced as property values increase. When young professionals move into inner-city neighborhoods, the relocation of poor people can become a major problem. Small businesses that depend heavily on local trade may also be adversely affected. Most major cities witnessed a continuing decline during this period. Public housing projects in the 1950s and 1960s also were major failures. The poor typically were segregated into a few designated areas in large cities and placed together in high-rise apartment buildings. Vandalism and crime were rampant.

There have also been some unsuccessful attempts to relocate people in so-called new towns. In 1968–1974, several new towns were started on the outskirts of cities, but none was successful. The area was to provide moderate-income housing in suburban areas and help manage urban sprawl. High building costs, bad management, rising energy costs, and lack of public interest doomed some very ambitious programs. "New towns in-town" met a similar fate. Here the idea was to attract middle-class people back to inner-city neighborhoods by building new housing and renovating some existing structures. As with new towns in suburbs, they were envisioned as partially self-contained areas with their own shops and schools. No new town in-town was ever successfully implemented.

Long-range planning commissions exist in all urban areas to consider such matters as housing, education, transportation, and pollution control. Much of the impetus has come from directives that require planning in order for cities to receive many federal grants. In addition, the federal government has provided financing for urban renewal and slum clearance. In Chapter 10 we will confront more directly the problems of metropolitan growth and its impact on the environment.

KEY TERMS

Aid to Families with Dependent Children (AFDC) A program of public assistance for children who need financial support and are living with one parent or relative, or whose father is unable to work. AFDC is financed by the federal government, with additional state contributions, and is administered by the states.

Causal patterns Evidence evidence suggesting that various social, economic, and political factors are interrelated. While finding the single cause of an occurrence is often very difficult, causal patterns require less supporting evidence.

Centralism A pattern in which the administration and funding of most government functions are done by the state government, rather than by local governments. This pattern is predominant in the South.

Civil Rights Act of 1964 Major federal legislation that included provisions to bar discrimination in public facilities, such as hotels and restaurants.

Community development block grants Part of 1974 legislation to provide funds to cities for redevelopment.

De facto segregation The existence of racially segregated facilities caused by neighborhood racial patterns. Predominantly white and black neighborhoods lead to racially segregated schools. Found in many large cities in the North.

De jure segregation The existence of racially segregated facilities as required by law.

Federal Highway Act of 1944 Legislation that created the idea of the interstate highway system and gave new authority to the Bureau of Public Roads to set national standards for highways.

Food stamps A program administered by the Department of Agriculture through state and local welfare agencies, which determine eligibility and issue stamps to be exchanged for food at retail stores.

Foundation money State programs to provide financial aid to local schools based, in part, on need. States try to equalize funds by giving proportionally more aid to poor districts than to rich districts.

Infrastructure A support system of roads, bridges, and sewage systems.

Localism A pattern in which the administration and funding of most government functions occur at the local level (city or town), rather than in the state capital. This pattern predominates in the New England states.

Medicaid A joint federal-state program to provide medical services, including nursing home care, to certain low-income people. *Medicare* is a federal health insurance plan for the elderly and the disabled. Both were established in 1965.

Policies The decisions reached by governments; policymaking is the process by which those decisions are reached.

Urban homesteading A program that allows the purchase of abandoned city dwellings at a nominal cost if the buyer agrees to improve the property and to live in it for a given period of time.

Urban mass transit Train, subway, bus, or ferry transportation in large cities.

Wall of separation An imaginary line between church and state. Although the courts have limited state support of religious activities, they have allowed such practices as state aid to church-related colleges and state purchase of secular textbooks for parochial schools.

REFERENCES

1. Thomas R. Dye, *Understanding Public Policy,* 6th ed. (Englewood Cliffs, N.J.: Prentice-Hall, 1987), Chapter 11.
2. Daniel J. Elazar, *American Federalism: A View from the States,* 2d ed. (New York: Crowell, 1972), p. 200.
3. See Frederick M. Wirt, "Institutionalization: Prison and School Policies," in Virginia Gray, Herbert Jacob, and Kenneth N. Vines, eds., *Politics in the American States,* 4th ed. (Boston: Little, Brown, 1983), p. 288.
4. Jason DeParle, "Poverty Rate Rose Sharply Last Year as Incomes Slipped," *The New York Times,* September 27, 1991, pp. 1 & 11A.
5. Richard P. Nathan, Fred C. Doolittle, et al., eds., *Reagan and the States* (Princeton, N.J.: Princeton University Press, 1987), p. 76.
6. See *Intergovernmental Perspective,* Spring 1991 (special issue on welfare reform).
7. Thomas R. Dye, *Politics in States and Communities,* 6th ed. (Englewood Cliffs, N.J.: Prentice-Hall, 1988), pp. 476–477.
8. Sarah McCally Morehouse, *State Politics, Parties and Policy* (New York: Holt, Rinehart and Winston, 1981), p. 363.
9. Robert B. Albritton, "Social Services: Health and Welfare," in Virginia Gray, Herbert Jacob, and Robert B. Albritton, eds., *Politics in the American States,* 5th ed. (Glenview, Ill.: Scott, Foresman/Little, Brown, 1990), p. 430.
10. Morehouse, *State Politics,* p. 395.
11. Frederick M. Wirt, "Does Control Follow the Dollar? School Policy, State-Local Linkages, and Political Culture," *Publius,* vol. 10 (1980), pp. 69–88.
12. Nathan, Doolittle, et al., *Reagan and the States,* p. 85.
13. Edward B. Fiske, "Starting Over," *New York Times Education Supplement,* Fall 1989, pp. 34–35.
14. Frederick Wirt and Samuel Gove, "Education," in Gray, Jacob, and Albritton, eds., *Politics in the American States,* 5th ed., p. 471.
15. Scott Jaschik, "State Funds for Higher Education Drop in Year," *Chronicle of Higher Education,* November 6, 1991, p. 1.
16. James S. Coleman, *Equality of Educational Opportunity* (Washington, D.C.: U.S. Government Printing Office, 1966). Coleman's later findings are reported in *The New York Times,* June 7, 1975, p. 25.
17. Lucius J. Barker and Twiley W. Barker, Jr., *Civil Liberties and the Constitution,* 5th ed. (Englewood Cliffs, N.J.: Prentice-Hall, 1986), p. 363.
18. Michael W. Giles et al., "White Flight and Percent Black: The Tipping Point Re-Examined," *Social Science Quarterly,* June 1975, pp. 85–92.
19. Gary A. Tobin, "Housing Segregation in the 1980s," in Gary A. Tobin, ed., *Divided*

Neighborhoods: Changing Patterns of Racial Segregation (Washington, D.C.: Urban Affairs Annual Reviews, 1987), p. 11. Also see *African Americans in the 1990s* (Washington, D.C.: Population Reference Bureau, 1991); and David Dent, "The New Black Suburbs," *New York Times Magazine* (June 14, 1992), pp. 18–25.

20. See Robert S. Freidman, "The Politics of Transportation," in Gray, Jacob, and Albritton, eds., *Politics in the American States,* 5th ed., p. 557.
21. Neal R. Peirce, "A Policy Paved with Good Intentions," *National Journal* (July 20, 1991), p. 1819.
22. John H. Cushman, Jr., "Lawmakers Near $151 Billion Pact on Transport Bill," *The New York Times*, November 26, 1991, p. A-10.
23. Friedman, "The Politics of Transportation," p. 542.
24. Joel Garreau, *Edge City: Life on the New Frontier* (New York: Doubleday, 1991).
25. Nathan, Doolittle, et al., *Reagan and the States,* p. 93.

CHAPTER 10

METROPOLITAN GROWTH AND THE ENVIRONMENT

Most community development has taken place in a haphazard manner with little public concern for long-range planning. In many cases, public policy in the form of zoning and the creation of planning commissions has come only *after* uncontrolled development has done serious damage to the environment. The result is that cities face overwhelming problems of air, water, and noise pollution; little space is available for recreation; residential and industrial areas are not sufficiently separated from each other; and the visitor to most cities is greeted by a familiar scene comprising a seemingly endless string of neon signs, franchise restaurants, and motels.

URBAN SPRAWL

As people have moved farther away from the central city, **urban sprawl** has created a maze of government units over which there is little or no coordination or control by a central authority. The New York City metropolitan area, for example, extends over more than twenty counties in three states and includes more than 18 million people. The Chicago metropolitan area contains over 1,100 government units. Phoenix in 1940 had a population of 65,000 within a 10-square-mile area. Currently it has a population of about 1 million in a 386-square-mile area. In addition, suburban sprawl has led to the expansion of Tempe, Mesa, Scottsdale, Paradise Valley, and other new Arizona cities.

The *fragmentation* of metropolitan government makes it extremely difficult to establish responsibility for metropolitan area policy. In addition, public services suffer because small units are unable to provide many specialized services; there is duplication of services when many governments independently operate facilities such as sewage-disposal and water plants; and it is difficult to deal with the many problems—pollution, mass transit, crime, traffic congestion—that extend over several community boundary lines. While affluent suburbs can spend vast sums of money for education, central cities face a declining tax base and an increasing demand for services. At the same time, many suburban governments need to spend relatively little money for crime control or public health. However, there are many middle-class suburbs that increasingly must deal with social and economic problems similar to those confronting central cities.

As noted in Chapter 1, by 1980 about three-fourths of all Americans lived in **metropolitan areas.** In 1990 there were 284 metropolitan areas in the United States. This was a substantial increase from the 212 metropolitan areas identified by the Bureau of the Census in 1960 and the 243 identified in 1970. About 42 percent of the nation's growth in the 1980s was in the fifteen largest consolidated metropolitan areas (see Table 10.1). More than one in three Americans lives in one of these fifteen areas. Much of the growth, even in Sunbelt areas such as Phoenix, was on the fringes where housing is less expensive. Overall in the 1980s metropolitan areas grew by 11.6 percent, while nonmetropolitan population growth was 3.9 percent.

Table 10.1   The Fifteen Largest Metropolitan Areas, 1980–1990

Consolidated Metropolitan Area	1980	1990	Change
New York City	17,539,532	18,087,251	+ 3.1%
Los Angeles-Anaheim-Riverside	11,497,349	14,531,529	+26.4
Chicago-Gary-Lake County	7,937,290	8,065,633	+ 1.6
San Francisco-Oakland-San Jose	5,367,900	6,253,311	+16.5
Philadelphia-Wilmington-Trenton	5,680,509	5,899,345	+ 3.9
Detroit-Ann Arbor	4,752,764	4,665,236	− 1.8
Boston-Lawrence-Salem	3,971,792	4,171,643	+ 5.0
Washington-Maryland-Virginia	3,250,921	3,923,574	+20.7
Dallas-Fort Worth	2,930,568	3,885,415	+32.6
Houston-Galveston-Brazoria	3,099,942	3,711,043	+19.7
Miami-Fort Lauderdale	2,643,766	3,192,582	+20.8
Atlanta	2,138,136	2,833,511	+32.5
Cleveland-Akron-Lorain	2,834,062	2,759,823	− 2.6
Seattle-Tacoma	2,093,285	2,559,164	+22.3
San Diego	1,861,846	2,498,016	+34.2

SOURCE: U.S. Census Bureau, 1991.

LIFE IN SUBURBS AND CITIES

Since the 1920s, Americans have become an increasingly suburban people. More now live in suburbs than in central cities. As noted in Chapter 9, movement to suburbs has been accelerated by better transportation systems and by federal programs that have assisted middle-class purchasers of housing. In many instances, business and industry have moved to more modern facilities in the suburbs and employees have followed. Shopping centers, schools, and hospitals have added to the attractiveness of suburban living. An increasing trend since the 1980s has been the expansion of **satellite cities** on the fringes of metropolitan areas.[1] Although cities such as West Palm Beach (Miami), Scottsdale (Phoenix), and White Plains (New York) are related to the central city, they are employment centers in their own right and often have downtowns and cultural complexes that are quite separate from the core city. Residents of these satellites may have little direct contact with the central city.

There have been both push and pull effects regarding patterns of residence. While suburbs have "pulled" residents out of cities with their promise of a better life, residents of central cities have also been "pushed out" because of a variety of city problems. Migrants from large cities most often mention crime as their major reason for leaving. Rundown schools, drugs, pollution, high taxes, and the rising cost of living are other factors that push people to the suburbs. As the percentage of blacks and Hispanics increases in central cities, a clear undercurrent of racism also influences whites to flee to predominantly white suburbs. In large cities, people also sense a loss of community feeling and often find it difficult to participate in government decision making.

It is a mistake to think of all suburbs as white, upper-class, bedroom communities surrounding central cities. Only about one-third of all suburbs are accurately described as residential or *dormitory*. The other two-thirds are *employing* and *mixed* suburbs, which combine dormitory and employment functions. In addition, suburbs range from being working class in character to being enclaves for wealthy exurbanites far removed from the central city.

When middle-class families and industry leave, the city's tax base shrinks, and this at a time when welfare, police, and public health expenses are increasing. Yet great *private wealth* remains in the nation's largest cities. Ira Sharkansky describes an "irony of urban wealth" in which there is "the juxtaposition of enormous wealth in the private sector with apparent poverty in the public sector."[2] Urban wealth, says Sharkansky, attracts the untrained and unsuccessful who seek a better way of life. Unlike the early twentieth-century immigrants, today's urban poor find few jobs for unskilled workers, and union control of apprenticeship programs makes it difficult to acquire trade skills. In addition, young blacks are particularly frustrated and alienated when they encounter a substantial gap between real and anticipated social and economic gains.

Contrary to much of the criticism of life in American cities, Edward C. Banfield believes that the problems of cities have been exaggerated and not viewed in the proper perspective. According to Banfield, urban residents have never had it so good.[3] He suggests, for example, that housing and education are substantially better in cities than in rural areas. Among urban residents, only a few are confronted directly with problems of crime, disease, and poor housing. Banfield believes that the urban crisis is largely psychological—individuals are frustrated by the expectations of material gain (created in part by promises of political parties and politicians to solve social problems through government action)—and does not reflect the objective conditions of city life.

Banfield's ideas have been vigorously attacked by those who believe that the problems of cities are growing and that the plight of the urban poor is worse than ever. In particular, Banfield's critics point to the effects of racial discrimination as compounding the problems of the urban poor.

But there is increasing evidence to indicate that life in urban areas has actually improved. In cities such as Boston and Baltimore, middle-class people have returned to live in the city and new shopping areas such as Boston's Quincy Market are flourishing. The Society Hill–Market Street East area in Philadelphia is another example of a successful renewal effort. Downtowns are being preserved in virtually all cities. This is in contrast to the mid-1960s, when some 1,600 federally supported urban renewal projects in 800 cities often were bulldozing historic neighborhoods .[4] Federal tax laws now encourage preservation, and cities are putting a priority on downtown development. Unfortunately, as upscale renovation has lured white suburbanites back to inner cities, the increased costs have driven blacks and Hispanics to other urban neighborhoods.

Cities and their suburbs exist in a state of natural hostility. Most fundamentally, there is a substantial difference in life styles between residents of the two areas. Although it would be very misleading to picture Grosse Pointe, Beverly Hills, Shaker Heights, and Scarsdale as "typical" suburbs, suburbanites in Northern and

Western states are better educated, have higher incomes, and are more likely to hold white-collar jobs than are central-city dwellers. In suburbia, life centers around single-family units and there is a strong emphasis on local schools.

As noted in Chapter 9, most large cities have experienced significant white flight during the past two decades, resulting in increasing concentration of Hispanics and blacks in inner cities while suburbs remain overwhelmingly white. Zoning laws, high prices, and open discrimination in the sale of suburban houses to nonwhites combine to restrict suburban housing to whites and a few affluent blacks. Overwhelmingly, black Americans are likely to live in metropolitan areas. According to the 1990 census, 84 percent of blacks, compared with 76 percent of whites, lived in metropolitan areas. Although the number of blacks living in suburbs has increased substantially in the past twenty years, only 25 percent of blacks live in suburbs, compared with 50 percent of whites.[5]

In addition to socioeconomic differences, *political differences* between central cities and suburbs can be identified. From our understanding of socioeconomic factors and their relationship to party identification (see Chapter 3), we would expect cities to be strongly Democratic and suburbs to be strongly Republican. In fact, cities, with their concentrations of union members, ethnic minorities, and blacks, historically have supported the Democratic party in national and local elections. New York City has cast a majority of its votes for every Democratic presidential candidate since Thomas Jefferson. Since 1970 Cleveland, Indianapolis, Minneapolis, San Diego, Toledo, and Salt Lake City have been among the few large cities with Republican mayors. In contrast, suburban voters typically elect Republicans to positions in local government and the state legislature.

Again, there is a need to guard against broad generalizations. There are industrial, working-class, and black suburbs whose voters are predominantly Democratic. As working-class people move to suburbs, they may retain their traditional ethnic labor ties as well as their support of the Democratic party. Social research indicates that suburban residence itself does not affect voting behavior. Nevertheless, many suburbs continue to maintain their WASP characteristics and their Republican allegiance. In general, suburban populations have higher levels of income, occupation, and education than do central-city populations. This is so because in many suburbs the cost of housing is beyond the financial capabilities of *any* middle-class person. Moreover, when people belonging to ethnic minorities move to suburbs, their motivation often is to escape what they regard as urban problems—for example, increases in crime and inferior schools. As noted earlier, both of these problems have strong racial overtones. A result is that white ethnic minorities tend to become more conservative politically (indeed, this also occurs if they remain living in their city neighborhoods) and thus are more likely to identify with the Republican party.

In the days of political machines, urban voters were overwhelmingly Democratic. The Republican commitment to limited government and a dependence on local government appealed to small-town America. However, Sorauf and Beck suggest that since the 1960s, urban-rural divisions between the two major parties have become less visible. These authors conclude that two points are clear regarding urbanism and party loyalty:

First, what differences there are along or within urban-rural lines are largely socioeconomic, and as those SES differences in American party loyalties decline, so too will the urban-rural ones. Second, though a case can indeed be made that there are genuinely urban or rural or small-city interests in American politics, they never have stamped themselves on party loyalties.[6]

THE POLITICS OF METROPOLITAN CONSOLIDATION

Differences in the political, social, and economic composition of cities and suburbs have a direct effect on public policy. As noted earlier, many of the most pressing problems for cities—air pollution, crime, mass transit, welfare, and public health—have little relevance to suburban politicians, whose constituents seek few services beyond schools. For example, Charles R. Adrian reported that in the Milwaukee metropolitan area in the early 1970s, the central city spent 54 percent of its property-tax revenue on schools, the closest suburbs spent 76 percent, and the outer ring of suburbs spent 92 percent.[7] In part, these differences in percentage of spending exist because older areas have already completed large capital expenditures (buildings) while newer suburbs must build to keep up with increasing population.

City-suburban differences also have a major impact on the fate of proposals for consolidation of metropolitan governments. In most instances, consolidation plans are opposed by both city and suburban officials, who seek to maintain the political independence of their community and the political control of their party. Of the two groups, those in suburbs have been the most opposed to unification. However, the support of residents of central cities has also waned. With population of the central cities declining, metropolitan government would come to mean control by white, middle-class, Protestant suburbanites. The liberal coalitions of labor and blacks that control many city governments would stand to lose considerable power if their political strength were diluted in a metropolitan area. In Cleveland, for example, during the period 1933–1959, voters defeated ten referenda to create various forms of metropolitan government. Over the years, black support declined from 79 percent in 1933 to 29 percent in 1959. White voter support also declined over time, but the fall-off was less dramatic.

Those in favor of **consolidation** are most likely to be business and professional people whose perspective is similar to that of early twentieth-century urban reformers. These groups fear that as the central cities are abandoned by the middle class, the poor and less well educated will gain undue political influence. They also believe that metropolitan government would be more efficient because it could achieve the economies of large-scale operations and provide improved public services.

Blacks and labor leaders usually oppose consolidation for reasons that are more political, social, and psychological than economic. They contend that the existence of many local governments helps increase citizen *access* to decision making, which produces a greater sense of community and personal effectiveness in dealing with smaller units of government. In such a situation, a variety of groups have the opportunity to make their views heard and to affect public policy. White, upper-class suburbanites support **fragmentation** because it allows them to isolate themselves from the problems of cities and to maintain school assignments based strictly on place of residence.

PLANS FOR METROPOLITAN CONSOLIDATION

Because opposition to consolidation is so widespread and is based on so many different rationales, it is not surprising that proposals to establish metropolitan governments have failed in nearly 75 percent of the times they have been brought before the voters. However, a metropolitan area need not make the move from extreme fragmentation to rigid consolidation in one giant step. There are several intermediate options available, such as annexation, special districts, and councils of government. Although there will be opposition to any form of unification, annexation usually has not encountered the same intensity of opposition as has the more extreme city-county consolidation.

Annexation

The most common method of government integration is by **annexation,** in which cities incorporate adjacent land into their municipal boundaries. About one in three communities of more than 2,500 population annex more territory each year. Procedures for annexation are established by state law and often require an affirmative vote by the residents of the central city and of the area proposed to be annexed. In only a few states—Arizona, Missouri, North Carolina, Oklahoma, Texas, Tennessee, and Virginia—may land be annexed by action of the city alone or by judicial procedures. In Texas, some home-rule charters (in Dallas, Fort Worth, Houston, and San Antonio) allow annexation by action of the city council without any voter approval. As one would expect, the most significant annexation in recent years has occurred in these states. Oklahoma City, for example, has annexed more than 500 square miles of territory since 1959.* In 1966, Tulsa added 116.8 square miles in a single annexation.

Total annexations in the 1980s averaged 250,000 people annually, down from about 300,000 annually in the 1970s.[8] Average land area annexed remained about the same—800 square miles annually. Large annexations in the 1980s included Portland, Oregon, which added 52,900 people, and Durham, North Carolina, which annexed 26,000 people, or an amount equal to one-fourth its 1980 population. Denver added 43 square miles, yet lost population in the decade because most of

---

*The largest city in area is Jacksonville, Florida, where city-county consolidation in 1967 gave it an area of 760 square miles. Since 1950, Houston has annexed land to grow from 160 to 572 square miles, and Phoenix has grown from 17.1 square miles in 1950 to 386 square miles. When city-county consolidations are *not* considered, Oklahoma City, with 574 square miles, is the largest city in land area. Los Angeles has 466 square miles. In contrast, older Eastern cities are quite small; Boston has 47 square miles, Pittsburgh 55 square miles.

the land annexed was for the construction of a new airport. Cities in Texas, North Carolina, and California accounted for over one-third the total number of people annexed in the 1980s. Cities in North Carolina were the most active. All seventy cities with more than 5,000 residents added land, and all but two increased population. Cities in nine states—Delaware, Hawaii, Maine, Massachusetts, New Hampshire, New Jersey, Pennsylvania, Rhode Island, and Vermont—either did not annex any territory or annexed less than one square mile in the 1980s.

Some new suburban cities are incorporated with very large populations. West Valley City, Utah, with 72,000 people, was the largest new city in the 1980s. Other large incorporations were Santa Clarita, California (66,730), and Mission Viejo, California (50,000). In a few cases cities detach property from their boundaries. For example, Oklahoma City detached 30 square miles during the 1980s and is still **overbounded**—that is, large amounts of virtually uninhabited land remain within the corporation.

Annexation is viewed as a means by which metropolitan areas can eliminate some conflicts of authority, avoid duplication of services, and promote more orderly growth. In some cases, cities annex land undergoing development in order to control that development or protect the environment. In Oklahoma cities have the power to keep nearby land unincorporated and thus available for annexation. Opposition comes from suburbanites who fear higher taxes and wish to remain independent of the central city. In some cases, cities may simply add to their problems by annexing areas that lack a strong tax base and are in need of costly services such as roads, water, and sewers. Often these fringe areas have not imposed any zoning laws, and thus they present special problems of development to city administrators.

Many large cities—such as Boston, Chicago, Detroit, Minneapolis, and Pittsburgh—have become encircled by incorporated areas and have been unable to expand their boundaries. For them, annexation presents no solution to their metropolitan problems. In the Los Angeles area, for example, Beverly Hills continues to resist the annexation efforts of Los Angeles, which completely encircles that affluent suburb (see Figure 10.1). Los Angeles annexed land from 1910 to 1919 to expand its territory fourfold. Pittsburgh is surrounded by nearly 200 municipalities, and there are nearly 100 municipalities in St. Louis County. Although some central cities are able to coerce annexation by withholding services such as water to independent suburbs, cities in most states cannot force annexation against the wishes of suburban residents. In addition, many of the largest metropolitan areas, including New York City, Philadelphia, Chicago, and St. Louis, extend into two or more states, and of course no central city can annex land outside its state's boundaries. There are many metropolitan areas that cross state lines and five (Detroit, San Diego, El Paso, Brownsville, and Laredo) whose boundaries adjoin urban areas outside the United States. Many large Eastern cities reached their present size through annexations in the nineteenth century.[9] For example, Philadelphia expanded from 2 square miles to its current size of 136 square miles by aggressive annexation in 1854. New York City consolidated with Brooklyn in 1898 and added 240 square miles of territory.

Thomas R. Dye found that annexation efforts have been most successful when

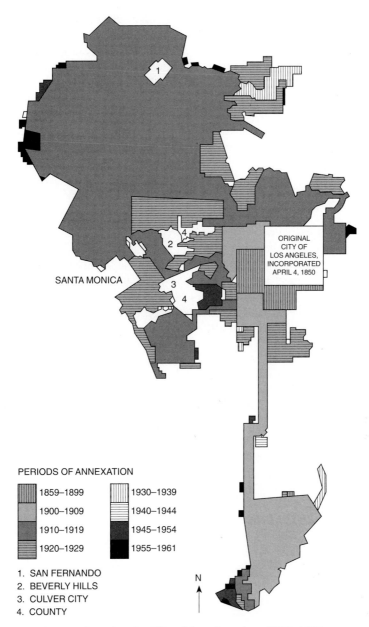

PERIODS OF ANNEXATION

- 1859–1899
- 1900–1909
- 1910–1919
- 1920–1929
- 1930–1939
- 1940–1944
- 1945–1954
- 1955–1961

1. SAN FERNANDO
2. BEVERLY HILLS
3. CULVER CITY
4. COUNTY

N

SANTA MONICA

ORIGINAL
CITY OF
LOS ANGELES,
INCORPORATED
APRIL 4, 1850

Figure 10.1   Annexations by the City of Los Angeles, 1859–1963

SOURCE: Winston W. Crouch and Beatrice Dinerman, *Southern Metropolis* (Berkeley and Los Angeles: University of California Press, 1963), p. 161. Copyright © 1963 by the Regents of the University of California. Reprinted by permission of the University of California Press.

the central city has a substantial proportion of middle-class residents.[10] Where there is less "social-class distance" between city and suburban residents, suburbanites have less fear of unification. Dye's data suggest that cities with managers are more likely to be successful in annexation than are cities with mayor-council systems of government. Managers tend to put suburbanites at ease, indicating to them that the influence of partisan politics has been lessened in the city. Size and age have only a limited effect on annexation, with success being slightly greater in smaller urbanized areas and in newer areas. Curiously, Dye found that the ease or difficulty of legal procedures was not a clear indication of the degree of success in annexation.

Special Districts

A relatively inoffensive way of providing services on a metropolitan-wide or inter-municipal level is to create a special district government to provide a single service. **Special districts** are appealing because they are superimposed on the existing structure of government and leave municipal boundaries untouched. As a result, suburbs receive the services they need without losing their independence. Special districts also have the advantage of bypassing taxation or debt limitations imposed on local units by state law. About half of all existing special districts have been created for fire protection, soil conservation, water, and drainage. Others provide sewer, recreation, housing, and mosquito-control services. Since 1942, the number of special districts has grown from 8,000 to about 30,000 (although school districts may be classified as special districts, they are considered separately by the Bureau of the Census). Recently there has been a significant increase in the number of special districts on the fringes of metropolitan areas. Often these special districts provide a variety of services to suburban residents and become a kind of junior city.[11] Later the area may be annexed by the central city.

Special districts are established under state law and usually require voter approval. In most states, they are governed by a small board, which has taxing and bonding authority. Board members are most often chosen indirectly, rather than being elected directly by popular vote.

In spite of their wide appeal, special districts have many problems. Governing boards have low voter visibility, and in most cases there is little citizen access to their decision making. One result is that contractors and others doing business with special districts (lawyers, bankers, real estate agents) often operate behind the scenes to their own economic advantage. Special districts are frequently established to meet short-range goals. Once created, they lessen the likelihood that long-range planning will be accomplished to meet problems at their most fundamental levels. Because special districts perform only a single function, coordination of government services is made more difficult and district administrators often view public policy from the narrow perspective of what benefits them without considering the overall needs of their community. Special districts usually encompass only a few municipalities within a metropolitan area, so they cannot be viewed as a suitable substitute for metropolitan government.

Councils of Government (COGs)

Nearly 600 **councils of government** (COGs) have come into being since the first one was created in Detroit in 1954. COGs are voluntary regional associations of local governments in a metropolitan area that are concerned about a broad range of problems, such as water supply, transportation, sewers, and airports. Each local government is represented in the COG by its own elected officials. Members of COGs meet to discuss problems, exchange information, and make policy proposals. COGs usually conceive comprehensive plans for metropolitan development.

In 1967, the Twin Cities Metropolitan Council was created to act as a planning, coordinating, and review agency for Minneapolis and St. Paul. Although the council is not a metropolitan government, it does oversee sewers, highways, transit, parks, and airports in a seven-county area that includes 320 separate but overlapping government units, of which 133 are incorporated. The council supervises metropolitan public policymaking through its control of the capital budgets of the operating agencies that provide metropolitan services. Because of its broad authority and taxing power, the Twin Cities Metropolitan Council differs from most councils of government. Although it does not operate public services, it has the power to overrule municipalities, counties, and special districts in its area. John J. Harrigan, a Twin Cities resident, notes: "By the 1980s the Metropolitan Council had attained extensive authority to set areawide policies for issues of metropolitan significance, and it had considerable power to overrule municipalities, counties, special districts, and metropolitan agencies that acted contrary to the council's policies."[12]

The most ambitious regional authority is the Metropolitan Service District (MSD) for Portland, Oregon, which has authority in land use, transportation, air and water quality, and cultural activities. It also runs the Portland Zoo. The MSD originated from a federal planning grant in the mid-1970s. A sixty-five-member citizens' committee studied proposals for regional government and recommended the plan to the Oregon legislature with the provision that it be submitted to area voters. As in the Twin Cities, the Portland COG had existed for several years before the new government was approved by Portland area voters and the Oregon legislature in the late 1970s. The MSD has a paid, elected executive officer and twelve elected council members. The council members are "community activists" who serve part time without a salary. Each represents a district of about 80,000 people. Regional government created by popular vote succeeded in Portland but failed in Tampa, Denver, and Rochester, which had similar federal grants. Its success in Portland was due in large part to Oregon's strong tradition of citizen participation.

Councils of government have been formed in all metropolitan areas to serve as a focal point to help bring local officials together, particularly for the purpose of coordinating federal grants. Indeed, many are federally mandated and funded. The federal government's Model Cities Act of 1966 required cities and counties to clear grant applications with COGs or regional planning agencies. As a result, COGs grew from 35 in 1965 to 352 by 1972. COGs are not governments because they can only make recommendations and hope for voluntary compliance by member governments. Their weaknesses include a tendency to concentrate on less controversial physical problems, such as sewers and water supply, and to avoid more controversial socioeconomic problems, such as racism and poverty. Also their authority is very limited, since they can seldom compel participation or compliance with decisions. Since COGs are voluntary organizations, members can withdraw if they wish. Most are understaffed and few have independent sources of revenue. This means they are dependent on federal grants. Because of federal cutbacks, many COGs were disbanded in the 1980s.[13] In general, they have not solved many problems and they have not effectively increased metropolitan cooperation.

Functional Consolidation

In several places, the county has taken over a variety of public services by entering into contractual arrangements with local governments, a process known as **functional consolidation.** For example, Erie County in New York (Buffalo area) provides health, hospital, library, and welfare services to communities throughout the county. Nassau County (suburban Long Island, New York) pursues a program of providing services, including police protection, to towns and villages that have a strong tradition of home rule. Los Angeles County also provides a variety of services to the hundreds of communities in an area that includes nearly 10 million residents. Large cities also may provide services to neighboring communities. For example, more than a dozen suburbs contract with Chicago for their water supply. The permanent transfer of functions, usually to counties but occasionally to special districts, has limited potential because fewer than half the states permit transfers and often voter approval is required.

City-County Consolidation

The most serious attempts at establishing metropolitan government in the United States have come in the form of consolidating city and county governments. Although proposals have been introduced in many cities, **city-county consolidation** has been successful in only a few large metropolitan areas—Nashville, Miami, Jacksonville, Lexington, and Indianapolis. Voters in Oakland, St. Louis, Portland, Pittsburgh, Memphis, Albuquerque, and Tampa have rejected city-county consolidation referenda. Compared with the other methods of integration, consolidation minimizes more completely the duplication of services and makes possible metropolitan-wide planning and administration. In each instance where such a proposal has been adopted, however, some public services continue to be administered by local units of government whose identities have remained intact. Because many metropolitan areas extend beyond a single county, city-county consolidation offers few possibilities to the nation's largest cities.

In the nineteenth and early twentieth centuries, state legislatures mandated city-county consolidation in New Orleans (1805), Boston, Philadelphia, San Francisco, New York, Denver, and Honolulu. More recently, state-mandated consolidation was achieved in Indianapolis (1969). The merger of one or more municipalities with a county has occurred in twenty-one communities where the population is more than 10,000. There are three city-county consolidations in Alaska and Louisiana, two in Massachusetts and Montana, and one each in ten other states.[14]

Only one consolidation was achieved in the 1980s. All cases where consolidation has been achieved by a voter referendum have been in the South and West. Five were approved in the 1970s—four in the West. Except in Miami, no referendum has been successful in a city with a population greater than 250,000. In Kentucky in 1982, voters in Louisville and in Jefferson County rejected a city-county consolidation by a margin of only 1,400 out of a total of 175,000 votes cast. Over forty cities operate independently of any county and perform both city and county functions; all of them are in Virginia except Baltimore, St. Louis, and Washington, D.C.

In most cases, proponents of consolidation have been successful only after long battles in which ultimate victory was achieved with the help of unusual political circumstances. Prior political corruption has helped in gaining approval of reform proposals, and in one instance (Indianapolis) city-county consolidation was enacted by the state legislature without voter approval.

A proposal to consolidate Nashville and Davidson County was first defeated by county voters in 1958. During the 1950s, residents in unincorporated areas around Nashville requested improved schools, sewers, and fire and police protection, and the lack of sanitary sewers in the county became a major health problem. Nevertheless, the proposal to consolidate failed in 1958 because of opposition from suburban residents. In response, the city of Nashville began a very aggressive program of annexation under the direction of Mayor Ben West.

In 1962, metropolitan government was strongly supported by suburban forces as a means of eliminating harassment by the city and getting rid of Mayor West. Again, the proposal received newspaper support and was endorsed by various good-government groups. The mayor and city officials opposed consolidation. In large part, the city's behavior toward its suburbs and the unpopularity of Mayor West resulted in approval of consolidation in 1962. Although defeated as an economy-efficiency proposal in 1958, consolidation won as a political issue four years later.

Voters in Jacksonville and Duval County approved a consolidation plan in 1967 after annexation plans had failed in 1963 and 1964. The vote was aided by 1966–1967 grand jury charges of corruption and graft in local government and the indictment of ten city and county officials. In addition, city-county schools lost their accreditation in 1965. Blacks and labor leaders joined the usual good-government groups in supporting a plan which closely resembled that of Nashville. The plan was approved by a 2-to-1 majority.

In 1969, Indianapolis became the first Northern city to become part of a city-county consolidation. It is significant that approval came by state legislative action without a popular vote by the residents of Marion County. UNIGOV (as the consolidation is named) operates under a single mayor and a twenty-nine-member council. To a large extent, its creation was made possible because of Republican control of the appropriate state legislative committees and the political leadership of Richard Lugar, the Republican mayor of Indianapolis and currently Indiana's senior U.S. senator. Approval of UNIGOV also was aided by the preservation of most suburban and county offices as well as special service and taxing districts within the county. The large council provides representation for a wide range of groups within Marion County. Republicans have controlled UNIGOV, winning all mayoral elections and often electing at least twenty members of the council.

Many existing governments have remained separate under UNIGOV. School districts continued to maintain their boundaries, and the county, suburban cities, and special districts continue to elect officials and operate as legal entities. Thus the degree of unification is less than that under most other city-county consolidations.

Metropolitan federation is a type of consolidation that meets the desire of local governments to maintain their identity within a metropolitan area. A federal relationship is established between cities and a metropolitan government similar to the relationship between the states and the national government. Proponents argue that such a system provides economic benefits of efficiency and economy as well as political benefits of allowing access to local decision making.

In the United States, the consolidation of Miami and Dade County most closely resembles metropolitan federation. The Dade County "Metro" plan is not a federation because Miami and twenty-seven suburban cities in the county are not represented directly on the board of commissioners. Elsewhere, such a system operates in Toronto, Winnipeg, Berlin, and London. The Toronto plan was approved in 1954 by action of the province of Ontario, not the local voters. The metropolitan government in Toronto is responsible for services involving roads, police, transit, and school buildings. It is financed by tax assessments that are collected by the local governments. Seats on the metropolitan council are awarded on a basis of equality between cities and suburbs, rather than on a strict population basis.

In Miami after World War II, residents were confronted with a host of problems stemming from accelerated growth. In 1957 the voters of Dade County approved a metropolitan form of government.[15] Approval came by a slim margin with only 26 percent of those eligible registered to vote. The proposal was supported by the Miami business community, the newspapers, and such good-government groups as the League of Women Voters. Opposition came chiefly from various local public officials and from the wealthier suburbs, such as Surfside and Miami Beach. In metropolitan Miami the usual opponents of unification—organized labor, political parties, and minority groups—all lacked effective organization. As in Jacksonville, the electorate comprised a large percentage of newcomers to the community. Such a situation is unlikely to exist in any of the older cities of the Midwest or Northeast.

Under a federal-type structure, the twenty-eight cities in the metropolitan Dade County area have kept control of many local functions, including garbage pickup, street maintenance, and police and fire protection. The metropolitan government controls such areawide services as transit and welfare. The plan included the establishment of a council-manager form of government for the county. Eight commissioners are elected at large but represent geographical districts. A ninth commissioner, elected at large and representing the entire county, is designated mayor. But the power of the mayor is weak because of the authority of the county manager. As the population of the area has grown to over 3 million, the metropolitan government's responsibilities have increased, because local units have asked the county to take over local functions. Evidence that all has not gone smoothly can be seen in the strong division among commissioners and in the attempt by several of the wealthier suburbs to secede from the metropolitan unit.

The failure of city-county consolidation plans to be approved in Northern cities is due mainly to the fact that consolidation would shift power toward the

Republican party. In many metropolitan counties, suburban residents outnumber those in the central city, and they thus have the potential to control government under a consolidation plan. Edward C. Banfield noted some years ago that in addition to consequences for political parties, metropolitan government "would mean the transfer of power over central cities from the largely lower-class Negro and Catholic elements who live there to the largely middle-class white and Protestant elements who live in the suburbs."[16] Most residents of metropolitan areas are reasonably satisfied with the existing structural arrangements and they do not wish to give up their independent units of government.

PLANNING

Most nineteenth-century cities in the Midwest and West were "new towns." As such, the layout of streets, the location of parks, and the placement of businesses were planned in detail. However, as city populations rapidly expanded, growth was largely unplanned. Thus by the 1880s, many large cities were crowded, dirty, and unhealthy. The same reform movement that brought changes to the structure and operation of city government (see Chapter 3) also reinstituted planning as a way to beautify cities. Their results in cities such as Chicago were very impressive.

Planners created master plans for the overall development of cities to serve as guides to government officials and private business. In recent years, comprehensive planning has gone beyond earlier concern for a set of maps and land-use guidelines. Planners now consider such matters as population projections, transportation, and sociocultural patterns. Although these plans are not legally binding on communities, most cities take them seriously. Planning has been extended to a metropolitan-wide basis because of federal requirements if the area is to receive funding for such projects as airports, housing, recreation, and transportation.

A major tool to promote orderly growth has been **zoning.** Zoning ordinances divide a community into districts (residential, industrial, light industrial, commercial, recreational) and prescribe the uses that can be made of the land in each zone. Such ordinances are enforced by a building inspector, and a zoning board is created to make exceptions to rules or amend their provisions. In many cities, zoning ordinances have been enacted too late, after commercial and industrial establishments have already misused the land. Zoning ordinances that prescribe the height of buildings or the amount of land necessary for home construction have the effect of keeping minority groups out of upper-class suburbs. Since New York City adopted the first zoning ordinance in 1916, all major cities except Houston have enacted some form of zoning.

There have been over 10,000 state court zoning decisions since the Supreme Court first declared zoning constitutional in 1926. Until recently, most rulings have supported zoning ordinances. Since the late 1960s, exclusionary zoning in suburbs has been under strong attack by civil rights groups, such as the NAACP. These interest groups have been successful in having several zoning ordinances struck down. In one of the most significant state court opinions to date, the New Jersey supreme court ruled in 1975 that all zoning regulations in Mount Laurel were invalid because they failed to provide a range of density levels and building types, including those appropriate for low- and middle-income families. The New Jersey court used the "fair share" concept regarding the location of multifamily housing as well as of houses on small lots within the semisuburban community of Mount Laurel.

However, in 1977 the Supreme Court ruled that communities are not required to alter zoning laws to provide housing for low-income families. The case involved Arlington Heights, a Chicago suburb, and its refusal to rezone a vacant property surrounded by single-family homes to permit construction of a federally subsidized townhouse development. In supporting the Arlington Heights board of trustees, the Court reasoned that predominantly white communities do not have to make special allowances for integration unless there is proof of purposeful racial discrimination. Thus a zoning ordinance was upheld even though it resulted in a racially disproportionate impact. As noted in Chapter 9, low-income housing has not been widely dispersed in American cities.

Although it usually supports zoning laws, the U.S. Supreme Court has overturned zoning that has the effect of taking property without compensation. For example, Los Angeles County prohibited a church from constructing buildings on a recently flooded campground. In a 1987 opinion the Supreme Court held that the county would have to pay compensation if the church was denied reasonable use of its property.

Zoning has also been used to limit growth and to control subdivision by determining how developers will lay out lots, streets, and sewers, and make arrangements for the commercial and industrial use of land. It also has been used to limit the location of pornographic bookstores and X-rated movie theaters.

POLLUTION AND LAND-USE POLICY

Given the general nature of state policymaking, it should not be surprising that environmental regulations represent the results of bargaining among diverse economic and social interests within the states. Only since the late 1960s have environmental groups been successful in bringing their concerns to the public and to state officials. Although not all states have acted with equal effectiveness, remarkable legislative action has been achieved in several states, and there is clear evidence of improved environmental quality in many parts of the country. Since the mid-1980s, there has been a marked increase in state activity.

Historically, states acted under their *police power* to combat pollution. In large part, their response was to enact laws aimed at protecting public health and curbing nuisances. Typically, authority for development and enforcement of environmental controls was delegated to local governments. As a result, by the 1960s many states did not have any comprehensive planning agency, and the administration of antipollution programs rested with departments of health. Air pollution generally was ignored, with only modest efforts made to control water pollution.

The federal government began to pass significant antipollution legislation in the mid-1960s. By the early 1970s, all states had enacted some water- and air-pollution legislation, and many had reorganized their health departments to include pollution control programs. Nearly half the states now require environmental impact statements for private projects that may have an effect on the environment, and twelve currently have environmental protection agencies modeled on the federal EPA.

Expenditures of the U.S. Environmental Protection Agency (EPA) have declined by one-third from 1981 levels. State governments are spending about $7 billion on the environment each year, but their share of total spending is declining. The result is that city and county spending has increased greatly, and it will nearly double by the year 2000.[17] Federal funds have declined but the mandates continue, putting additional strain on state and local governments. As seen in Table 10.2, annual environmental spending per capita ranges from $267 in Wyoming to $6.76 in Texas. In general, the worst spending efforts are made by Southern states.

In recent years, *acid rain* has become a particularly difficult problem. Tall smokestacks in the Midwest send particulates high into the atmosphere. These particulates are carried by winds and eventually fall as rain in states such as New York, Massachusetts, and Vermont. Lakes, rivers, and forests in those states are being adversely affected by the acidity of the rain. Scientists believe that sulfur dioxide is killing aquatic life in hundreds of lakes in the Northeast. Yet financially hard-pressed Midwestern states are reluctant to spend the money needed to alleviate a problem that does not affect them directly. The most far-reaching section of the 1990 Clean Air Act deals with acid rain. It will require industry to reduce sulfur dioxide emissions by 10 million tons by the year 2000. The burden will fall most heavily on utilities in Indiana, Illinois, and Ohio that use high-sulfur coal.

Every state is faced with the problem of how to deal with hazardous waste. This refers to toxic, corrosive, flammable, or reactive wastes generated in industrial production. The Resource Conservation and Recovery Act of 1976 (RCRA) established the first comprehensive federal regulatory program for controlling hazardous waste, and it provided grants and technical assistance to help states manage this problem. As in other areas of environmental control, states are given latitude to design their own programs, but they must conform to minimum federal standards. Superfund legislation passed in 1980 gives the federal government the right to intervene to clean up hazardous waste sites and spills. In general, states that generate the greatest amount of hazardous waste have had the most extensive regulation. The existence of a single state environmental agency and a professional legislature also correlates positively with more extensive regulation.[18] Difficulties exist even for the best-intentioned states because of the enormity of the problem and the fear of driving industry out of the state by enacting strict regulation.

A great deal of public attention was directed to the problem of **hazardous waste** when the federal government was forced to purchase all the property in Times Beach, Missouri, where dioxin dumping had contaminated the town. Early in the Reagan administration, the director of the EPA and the head of its Superfund were forced to resign in the face of charges that the agency had not effectively enforced antipollution laws. In 1986, Congress reauthorized the EPA program to clean up toxic dumps. The 1986 law requires states to certify that they have adequate means of disposing of hazardous waste. Because states generate hazardous waste and are owners of facilities that receive hazardous waste, they are held liable under federal law for cleanup costs that have become very expensive.[19]

Table 10.2 Environmental Spending State by State, 1988

State	Total Expenditures	Rank	Per Capita	Rank
Alabama	64,906,954	29	15.82	42
Alaska	131,684,237	15	251.31	2
Arizona	46,612,900	37	13.36	45
Arkansas	44,188,570	39	18.45	39
California	1,486,124,000	1	52.49	8
Colorado	76,150,000	26	23.07	33
Connecticut	61,996,000	30	19.18	37
Delaware	33,170,000	45	50.26	9
Florida	465,591,276	3	37.75	13
Georgia	93,344,466	23	14.72	44
Hawaii	27,832,208	48	25.35	29
Idaho	61,440,400	31	61.26	6
Illinois	392,844,000	4	33.83	18
Indiana	51,580,177	34	9.50	49
Iowa	88,065,353	24	31.07	22
Kansas	47,817,000	36	19.17	38
Kentucky	120,289,400	19	32.28	21
Louisiana	193,835,955	10	43.97	11
Maine	39,332,000	41	32.64	19
Maryland	150,091,393	14	32.47	20
Massachusetts	237,936,245	7	40.40	12
Michigan	221,424,840	9	23.96	32
Minnesota	126,236,105	17	29.31	28
Mississippi	54,153,592	33	20.67	35
Missouri	106,300,846	21	20.68	34
Montana	69,559,793	28	86.41	3
Nebraska	27,988,000	47	17.47	40
Nevada	36,487,054	42	34.62	16
New Hampshire	33,588,000	44	30.96	23
New Jersey	523,874,000	2	67.85	4
New Mexico	44,782,182	38	29.72	27
New York	236,484,000	8	13.20	46
North Carolina	96,942,764	22	14.94	43
North Dakota	32,524,000	46	48.76	10
Ohio	125,669,234	18	11.58	48
Oklahoma	40,868,619	40	12.61	47
Oregon	186,438,200	11	67.38	5
Pennsylvania	288,766,000	5	24.06	31
Rhode Island	35,878,756	43	36.13	15
South Carolina	71,124,250	27	20.50	36
South Dakota	21,264,000	49	29.82	26
Tennessee	81,180,056	25	16.58	41
Texas	113,769,559	20	6.76	50
Utah	51,419,000	35	30.43	24
Vermont	20,222,111	50	36.31	14
Virginia	152,149,051	13	25.29	30
Washington	246,873,000	6	53.11	7
West Virginia	56,189,209	32	29.95	25
Wisconsin	167,779,368	12	34.56	17
Wyoming	128,050,724	16	267.33	1

SOURCE: "Cleaning Up," *Governing,* April 1991, p. 38. Copyright 1992, *Governing* magazines. Information from Council of State Governments. Reprinted with permission.

Before passage of the federal Clean Air Act of 1963, only nine states had air-pollution control regulations. By 1970, all states had established rules for controlling the sources of air pollution. The act was amended in 1970 and 1977. After years of deadlock, and nearly a year and a half after President Bush introduced legislation to rewrite the nation's main antipollution law, the Clean Air Act was amended in 1990. As amended, this is the most comprehensive environmental legislation ever passed by Congress. Its provisions include sections to reduce urban smog, cut automobile exhaust, control toxic chemicals in the air, and limit the effects of acid rain.

As amended in 1977, the Clean Water Act provided a comprehensive approach to water management by establishing water-quality standards, stream classifications, a pollution discharge permit system, grants for the construction of waste-water treatment facilities, and encouragement of state water-quality management. In 1987, Congress authorized $18 billion to state and local governments through 1994 for construction of sewage-treatment facilities and $2 billion for other forms of water-pollution control. The reauthorization was passed over a presidential veto. The Reagan administration thought the program was too expensive and, more fundamentally, it argued that sewage treatment should be a state and local concern.

State and local governments spend about $15 billion a year to dispose of garbage. More than 70 percent of garbage is buried in 5,500 active landfills across the country.[20] These rapidly are filling up and few new ones have been approved. Cities and counties face irate citizens who don't want landfills in their neighborhoods, and many states face pressure to stop trash coming in from out of state. Most cities have initiated recycling programs, and other conservation measures have been undertaken to reduce the volume of material going to landfills. The dilemma is that some items such as plastic-coated paper cups are not biodegradable in the short run—and they cannot be recycled.

Although Congress has defeated proposed comprehensive land-use legislation, it has enacted bills to protect wetlands, prime farmlands, and coastal and historic areas. The Bush administration has been criticized by environmentalists for giving in to pressure from developers and the oil industry in 1991 to propose action that could reduce by tens of millions of acres wetlands previously protected from development. There has been even more action among the states, which are the nation's primary agents of land-management control. In Hawaii, for example, state **land-use plans** are administered by the State Land Use Commission. In Florida, an Environmental Land and Water Management Act was passed that defines "areas of critical State concern" and "developments of regional impact," allowing the state substantial authority in areas outside the boundaries of local governments. Soon after approval of the state act, Florida voters passed a $240 million bond issue for the purchase of environmentally endangered lands.

In California, a strong "Save Our Coast" movement culminated in 1972 voter approval of a referendum mandating orderly coastline planning and development. In the face of opposition from utilities, oil companies, and building trade unions, the California legislature in 1976 approved the long-range master plan presented by the statewide Coastal Zone Conservation Commission. The master plan's proposals include guaranteed public access to the entire 1,100-mile coastline, requirements that new structures leave ocean views unobstructed, and the preservation of wet-lands. The commission is given jurisdiction over practically all new construction along the coast.

The San Francisco Bay Conservation and Development Commission (BCDC) represents a successful metropolitan approach to environmental planning that liter-ally saved the bay. It also illustrates how citizen groups can be effectively orga-nized for action. Since its creation, the BCDC has denied building permits request-ed by powerful interests, and it has slowed the development of shoreland. More than a century ago, San Francisco Bay's water surface was over 700 square miles; by 1970, it had been reduced to 400 square miles. The accompanying reading dis-cusses the water crisis in California and related environmental problems. Ironically, when residents of the Los Angeles area reduced their water consumption in the summer of 1991, water rates were increased. A cooler, wetter summer in 1991 pro-duced a temporary surplus of water in some parts of southern California, but did not solve more fundamental problems.

Many states have taken leadership roles in environmental policy. For example, Arizona is at the forefront in water-pollution control, requiring that any water dis-charged into the ground must be clean enough to drink. California's South Coast Air Quality Management District has specified 123 pollution control measures for the Los Angeles area.[21] New York regulates the installation of new chemical and petroleum storage tanks.

States have also acted to protect the environment by providing public *open spaces.* Between 1950 and 1970, acreage in state park systems increased over 80 percent while attendance increased over 300 percent. Attendance continued to grow in the 1980s, but there were cutbacks in funding, and park acreage has remained virtually the same. The result is overcrowded conditions at many parks, with pro-jections of even greater use in the future. In response, fees have been increased, some services have been dropped, and a few parks have set limits on the daily num-ber of visitors. In 1989, California led the nation with 72.5 million visitors to its state parks. Ohio was second with 72.1 million visitors. Alaska, with more than 3 million acres, has by far the most area in state parks. California has about 1 million acres in state parks; Illinois is third; Florida fourth; and New Jersey, the nation's forty-sixth largest state, is a surprising fifth. State park acreage often seems unrelat-ed to state land area. For example, Maryland, the nation's forty-second largest state, has 283,000 acres of state parks, while Oregon, the nation's tenth largest state, has 90,000 acres.

TO GROW OR NOT TO GROW

In recent years, an increasing number of scientists (led by such well-known figures as biologist Paul Ehrlich) and a few politicians have called for a national program of little or no growth. They argue that projected growth rates for population, indus-trial and food production, use of resources, and levels of pollution spell disaster for the United States and for other countries.

Opponents of **no-growth** represent diverse interests. In general, the industrial and business communities oppose any policy that would limit their profits. At the same time, those representing minority groups contend that there is no guarantee that a no-growth policy would help redistribute goods and services from the rich to the poor. It is argued that despite declining birth rates, the U.S. population will continue to increase for the next twenty years, and that these newcomers must be provided with homes and jobs. Thus many liberals find themselves caught between supporting the environmentalists and a policy of no-growth or supporting minorities who seek economic growth as a means of achieving social progress.

As with most socioeconomic-political problems, the most promising solutions to the question of economic growth appear to rest in a middle ground. The issue should not be simplified to growth versus no-growth. Rather it is a question of the nature of growth, its location, and the use of its outputs. A realistic policy (i.e., one capable of gaining broad political support) should aim at accommodating and managing growth through such measures as regional planning agencies and zoning ordinances that permit growth, but at a controlled rate.

A large part of the problems associated with growth is that it is not evenly distributed. Metropolitan sprawl continues, and medium-size cities become large cities with the accompanying problems of pollution, congestion, and crime. Kirkpatrick Sale argues that the "ideal" size for cities is a population between 50,000 and 100,000.[22] Currently about one-fourth of the American people live in cities that size. Medium-size cities have better educational, health, and recreational facilities than either large cities or rural areas. They provide public services efficiently and are more economically stable than large cities. Politically, they provide numerous opportunities for participation and involvement.

If, as Sale believes, cities in the 50,000–100,000 range function best and are the best places to live, then the question is: Should governments act to limit growth and redistribute population? If so, what strategies should be followed? Many European countries (Britain, France, Italy, Holland, Belgium, and Sweden) have complex plans to limit urban growth. As noted earlier, some American cities (Petaluma, California; Boca Raton, Florida; Ramapo, New York; and Mount Laurel, New Jersey) have enacted laws prohibiting growth. Developer Andres Duany suggests building small towns on freeways 30 or 40 miles away from large cities and having them contain enough businesses that most residents would not have to commute. He and his partner have dozens of projects in the works. Their new-old-town ideas call for creating a sense of community with relatively high density and walkable environments.[23]

Among various California communities seeking to limit growth, Petaluma has gained special attention. In 1976, the Supreme Court declined to review a decision of the United States Circuit Court in San Francisco upholding Petaluma's growth plan. The plan—described as an "absurd and tragic obstacle to home construction" by construction-industry associations—imposes a limit of about 500 residential units per year. The Court decision has been criticized also for its alleged restrictions on the "right of mobility" of American citizens. Proponents characterized the plan as a "reasonable, well-balanced" proposal for growth.

5-Year Drought Is Only the Latest Trouble in Paradise

Californians yet again have cause to ponder the consequences of the profligacy, recklessness and greed that have long dulled the California dream of hope, renewal and optimism. In what the historian Kevin Starr has called "the intensified pursuit of human happiness" that marks the energetic history of California, insult after insult has been inflicted on this earthly paradise. The great Gold Rush left the mountains scarred like a battlefield. Lumbermen denuded the magnificent stands of redwood to the point that the few remaining trees are tourist curiosities. Automobiles have exhausted the air of Southern California. And now, it seems, the water is nearly all gone.

It did not have to be this way. For four dry years, water officials gambled that the rain and snow would resume soon, treating drought as a temporary inconvenience. To maintain near-normal deliveries, they drew down reservoirs to dangerously low levels. Even as drought tightened its grip in 1990, California farmers racked up record receipts and income. California remained the nation's second largest grower of rice, a monsoon crop that can be grown here only with cheap subsidized water and Federal crop supports. And there seemed plenty of water for Angelenos to fill their pools and wash their sidewalks.

Only now, well into the fifth dry year, when it may be too late, has concerted reaction set in with panicky attempts to conserve water and find additional sources. A few days ago, the Napa Valley wine town of St. Helena, with only a 125-day supply left in its reservoir, imposed rationing for the first time in history. In the San Joaquin Valley, the city of Merced adopted an odd-even outdoor watering rule on Monday, the same day the State Water Project cut off supplies to all farmers. Cities throughout Southern California last week were preparing rationing plans.

The state government's response so far has been hesitant and confused. The Water Resources Control Board twice set dates to impose statewide restrictions and twice postponed them amid doubts about its authority, ultimately deferring to Gov. Pete Wilson, who has appointed a special water panel to make emergency recommendations by Friday. His short-term options are limited, the long-term ones painful.

Few places on earth offer a more improbable setting for vast industrialized cities and prosperous farms than this mostly desertified state. Even as the American settlement of the Pacific frontier was gathering momentum a century and a half ago, a United States naval officer, Lieut. Henry Augustus Wise, pronounced California's future bleak. "Under no contingency," he wrote in 1849, "does the natural face of Upper California appear susceptible of supporting a very large population; the country is hilly and mountainous; great dryness prevails during the summers, and occasionally excessive droughts parch up the soil for periods of 12 or 18 months."

With great disdain for such negativism, Californians rearranged the environment to get the water they needed. Dams and reservoirs snatched water from the snows of the Sierra of Northern California and funneled it into thick aortas, the mighty aqueducts that course through the deserts, making rich farms out of the malarial bogs of the Central Valley and sprouting powerful cities where none were naturally meant to be. Not even mountains stood in the way of the engineers. Huge pumps, like throbbing heart muscles, throw the water over the Tehachapi Mountains and down into that arid tract known as the Los Angeles Basin, land of car washes, swimming pools and now home to 15 million. The result is perhaps the most problematic and vulnerable urban conglomeration in America today, threatened by the twin terrors of earthquake and drought.

"There is something disturbing about this corner of America, a sinister suggestion of transience," wrote the British author J. B. Priestly. "There is a quality, hostile to men in the very earth and air here. As if we were not meant to make our homes in this oddly enervating sunshine." He went on: "California will be a silent desert again. It is all as impermanent and brittle as a reel of film."

That may or not be true. But the means by which the water problem is solved will speak volumes about whether California, in its maturity, will learn from its youth or repeat its mistakes.

"In Iowa there is a humility about the farmer's reliance on nature—he embraces nature and allows himself to be embraced by its generosity," J. S. Holliday, historian of California's rambunctious Gold Rush past, said in an interview. "But here there is an entirely different attitude. The miners brought the attitude that nature had to be cracked open, that nature is a bounteous force from which we will take

whatever we can get however we can get it. We were so flagrant, so arrogant, so profligate."

Already, history is repeating itself. Five years of water profligacy in the face of drought have taken an environmental toll. According to the Natural Resources Defense Council in San Francisco, striped bass counts in the Sacramento Delta and San Francisco Bay are at their lowest levels in history, and numerous birds, sea animals and plants have become candidates for the endangered species list because reduced fresh water flows to estuarine waters have raised salinity.

But the solution that is so obvious to conservationists—to change the outdated system of water rights and impose new incentives for more efficient agriculture—may not be the most politically feasible outcome. It is sobering to realize that even if every household in California, population 30 million, cut its annual water use by 25 percent that would reduce overall use by only 2 percent; agriculture consumes 85 percent of all available water.

"It is an empty exercise to put cities through elaborate conservation exercises," argues William L. Kahrl, author of *Water and Power,* the definitive chronicle of California's water wars. "That picks the course that causes the maximum inconvenience to the largest number of people, rather than looking at the reality of the deliveries. The lesson is they are very likely going to say: 'I don't care about the Sacramento Delta. That's a long way away. Give me more water.' "

Southern California, with the bulk of the population and political power, has long coveted the water of the north. The largest new potential for water would come from building the long-de-

layed peripheral canal that would channel more water to the south from the
Sacramento Delta, water that would
otherwise flow into San Francisco Bay.
Talk about tapping the rivers of rural
far-northern California has also been
revived, a course that would please the
farmers as much as urban leaders, but
that would rearrange the environment
even more than it has been.

"I do not have any thought of giving up water—it's a matter of how we
get it," said Carl Boronkay, the general
manager of the Metropolitan Water
District of Southern California. His is
the largest and most politically powerful of the state's 2,000 water districts,
supplying half the water used by 15
million people in the fast-growing region from Ventura to the Mexican border. Mr. Boronkay talks of taking water
away from rice farmers, of voluntary
transfers between regions—easier said

than done because water cannot be
transferred like money between ac-
counts. Reclamation, rationing and conservation are fine, he said, but "we need
wet water."

The water crisis gives Californians
one more reason to contemplate the
state's failure to prepare for uncertainty
and for growth that seems as inevitable
as it is unwanted. Schools, social programs, freeways, bridges, prisons—
none has kept pace with the exploding
population. "There are a full raft of
problems we have failed adequately to
plan for," said Bill Bradley, author of
the forthcoming book *The United
States of California.* "California is the
quintessence of the American dream,"
he said. "Its history has been based on
betting on the prospect of things going
one's way. There is a lot of strength in
being optimistic. But the down side is
what we are confronting now."

SOURCE: Robert Reinhold, *The New York Times,* February 10, 1991 p. E-3. Copyright © 1991 by
the New York Times Company. Reprinted by permission.

As an affluent country, the United States has both the financial ability and the
technical expertise to limit sources of pollution and manage the use of land. At the
same time, consideration must be given to the less developed segments of the society, which have not shared equally in the nation's wealth. For them, a policy of no-
growth holds real danger. Protection of the environment and provision for the general welfare of all people need not be contradictory goals. In the United States both
can be accomplished if a policy of managed growth is maintained.

KEY TERMS

Annexation The process by which cities incorporate adjacent land into their municipal
    boundaries.
City-county consolidation The process by which a large city and the county in which it is
    located merge into one government unit. UNIGOV, the consolidation of Indianapolis
    and Marion County, is an example of such a plan. The goal is to improve the coordina-
    tion of government functions within a metropolitan area.

Consolidation In metropolitan areas, the uniting of separate, independent government units into a larger, central government.

Councils of government Voluntary regional organizations in which government officials in metropolitan areas get together largely to help coordinate federal programs in their area.

Fragmentation The situation existing in most metropolitan areas, in which there are a large number of small, separate government units.

Functional consolidation A type of limited consolidation in which a large unit of government (typically a county) performs specific services for local governments on a contract basis.

Hazardous waste Materials ranging from low-level radioactive waste to very toxic chemicals that seriously endanger public health and well-being.

Land-use plans Comprehensive public plans to control the use of land by protecting scenic and recreation areas and limiting pollution.

Metropolitan areas Large cities and their surrounding suburbs, which are integrated socially and economically. As defined by the Bureau of the Census, a "standard metropolitan statistical area" includes each county, or group of contiguous counties, containing a city having at least 50,000 population.

Metropolitan federation A plan for metropolitan areas based on the principle of federalism as it applies to national-state relations in the United States. There is a central metropolitan government to provide some areawide services, while local governments continue to provide other limited services. It is used in Toronto, Canada, and on a modified basis in Dade County (Miami), Florida.

No-growth Public policy to restrict severely population and economic growth because of projected scarcities of natural resources.

Overbounded A condition that occurs when cities have large tracts of virtually uninhabited land within their corporate limits.

Satellite cities Independent suburbs located on the fringes of metropolitan areas.

Special districts Units of local government created to perform a single service, such as water supply, fire protection, or soil conservation.

Urban sprawl Uncoordinated residential and commercial growth spreading outward from cities.

Zoning The division of a city or other government unit into districts to regulate the use of land according to residential, industrial, recreational, or commercial classification.

REFERENCES

1. Edward B. Fiske, "U.S. Says Most of Growth in 80's Was in Major Metropolitan Areas," *The New York Times,* February 21, 1991, p. A-12. Also see Joel Garreau, *Edge City: Life on the New Frontier* (Garden City, N.Y.: Doubleday, 1991).
2. Ira Sharkansky, *The Maligned States* (New York: McGraw-Hill, 1972), p. 137.
3. Edward C. Banfield, *The Unheavenly City Revisited* (Boston: Little, Brown, 1974), pp. 1–24.
4. "Spiffing Up the Urban Heritage," *Time,* November 23, 1987, p. 75.
5. *African Americans in the 1990s* (Washington, D.C.: Population Reference Bureau, 1991), p. 8
6. Frank J. Sorauf and Paul Allen Beck, *Party Politics in America,* 6th ed. (Glenview, Ill.: Scott, Foresman, 1988), p. 180.
7. Charles R. Adrian, *State and Local Governments,* 4th ed. (New York: McGraw-Hill, 1976), p. 208.

8. Joel C. Miller, "Municipal Annexation and Boundary Changes 1980–1987," in *The Municipal Yearbook 1990* (Washington, D.C.: International City Management Association, 1990), p. 75.

9. Bernard H. Ross, Myron A. Levine, and Murray S. Stedman, *Urban Politics,* 4th ed. (Itasca, Ill.: F. E. Peacock, 1991), p. 300.

10. Thomas R. Dye, "Urban Political Integration: Conditions Associated with Annexation in American Cities," *Midwest Journal of Political Science,* November 1964, pp. 430–446.

11. Ross et al., *Urban Politics,* p. 298. Also see John C. Bollens, *Special District Government in the United States* (Westport, Conn.: Greenwood Press, 1957).

12. John J. Harrigan, *Politics and Policy in States and Communities,* 4th ed. (New York: HarperCollins, 1991), p. 178.

13. *Ibid.,* p. 296.

14. Victor S. DeSantis, "County Government: A Century of Change," in *The Municipal Yearbook 1989* (Washington, D.C.: International City Management Association, 1989), p. 57.

15. See Edward Sofen, *The Miami Metropolitan Experiment,* 2d ed. (Garden City, N.Y.: Doubleday, 1966).

16. Edward C. Banfield, "The Politics of Metropolitan Area Reorganization," *Midwest Journal of Political Science,* May 1957, p. 77.

17. "Cleaning Up," *Governing,* April 1991, p. 38.

18. Ann O'M. Bowman and Richard C. Kearney, *The Resurgence of the States* (Englewood Cliffs, N.J.: Prentice-Hall, 1986), p. 226.

19. See Rosemary O'Leary, "Will Hazardous Waste Cleanup Costs Cripple Our State and Local Governments?" *State and Local Government Review,* Spring 1990, pp. 84–89.

20. William L. Rathje, "Once and Future Landfills," *National Geographic,* May 1991, p. 118.

21. "Cleaning Up," p. 43.

22. Kirkpatrick Sale, "The Polis Perplexity: An Inquiry into the Size of Cities," *Working Papers,* January–February 1978, pp. 64–77.

23. Garreau, *Edge City,* pp. 249–250.

APPENDIX

State Statistics

State or Other Jurisdiction	LAND AREA In Square Miles	LAND AREA Rank in Nation	POPULATION Size	POPULATION Rank in Nation	POPULATION Percent Change 1970 to 1980	Density per Square Mile	No. of Representatives in Congress	Capital	Population	Rank in State	Largest City	Population
Alabama	50,767	28	3,893,888	22	13.1	76.7	7	Montgomery	177,857	3	Birmingham	284,413
Alaska	570,833	1	401,851	50	32.8	0.7	1	Juneau	19,528	3	Anchorage	174,431
Arizona	113,508	6	2,718,215	29	53.1	23.9	5	Phoenix	789,704	1	Phoenix	789,704
Arkansas	52,078	27	2,286,435	33	18.9	43.9	4	Little Rock	158,461	1	Little Rock	158,461
California	156,299	3	23,667,902	1	18.5	151.4	45	Sacramento	275,741	7	Los Angeles	2,966,850
Colorado	103,595	8	2,889,964	28	30.8	27.9	6	Denver	492,365	1	Denver	492,365
Connecticut	4,872	48	3,107,576	25	2.5	637.8	6	Hartford	136,392	2	Bridgeport	142,546
Delaware	1,932	49	594,338	47	8.4	307.6	1	Dover	23,512	3	Wilmington	70,195
Florida	54,153	26	9,746,324	7	43.5	180.0	19	Tallahassee	81,548	11	Jacksonville	540,920
Georgia	58,056	21	5,463,105	13	19.1	94.1	10	Atlanta	425,022	1	Atlanta	425,022
Hawaii	6,425	47	964,691	39	25.3	150.1	2	Honolulu	762,874	1	Honolulu	762,874
Idaho	82,412	11	943,935	41	32.4	11.5	2	Boise	102,451	2	Boise	102,451
Illinois	55,645	24	11,426,518	5	2.8	205.3	22	Springfield	99,637	4	Chicago	3,005,072
Indiana	33,932	38	5,490,224	12	5.7	152.8	10	Indianapolis	700,807	1	Indianapolis	700,807
Iowa	55,965	23	2,913,808	27	3.1	52.1	6	Des Moines	191,003	1	Des Moines	191,003
Kansas	81,778	13	2,363,679	32	5.1	28.9	5	Topeka	115,266	3	Wichita	279,272
Kentucky	39,669	37	3,660,777	23	13.7	92.3	7	Frankfort	25,973	9	Louisville	298,451
Louisiana	44,521	33	4,205,900	19	15.4	94.5	8	Baton Rouge	219,419	2	New Orleans	557,515
Maine	30,995	39	1,124,660	38	13.2	36.3	2	Augusta	21,819	6	Portland	61,572
Maryland	9,837	42	4,216,975	18	7.5	428.7	8	Annapolis	31,740	5	Baltimore	786,775
Massachusetts	7,824	45	5,737,037	11	0.8	733.3	11	Boston	562,994	1	Boston	562,994
Michigan	56,954	22	9,262,078	8	4.3	162.6	18	Lansing	130,414	5	Detroit	1,203,339
Minnesota	79,548	14	4,075,970	21	7.1	51.2	8	St. Paul	270,230	2	Minneapolis	370,951
Mississippi	47,233	31	2,520,638	31	13.7	53.4	5	Jackson	202,895	1	Jackson	202,895
Missouri	68,945	18	4,916,686	15	5.1	71.3	9	Jefferson City	33,619	12	St. Louis	453,085
Montana	145,388	4	786,690	44	13.3	5.4	2	Helena	23,938	5	Billings	66,798
Nebraska	76,644	15	1,569,825	35	5.7	20.5	3	Lincoln	171,932	2	Omaha	314,255
Nevada	109,894	7	800,493	43	63.8	7.3	2	Carson City	32,022	5	Las Vegas	164,674
New Hampshire	8,993	44	920,610	42	24.8	102.4	2	Concord	30,400	3	Manchester	90,936
New Jersey	7,468	46	7,364,823	9	2.7	986.2	14	Trenton	92,124	5	Newark	329,248

State							Capital			Largest City	
New Mexico	121,335	5	1,302,894	37	28.1	10.7	3	Santa Fe	48,953	2	Albuquerque	331,767
New York	47,377	30	17,558,072	2	-3.7	370.6	34	Albany	101,727	6	New York	7,071,639
North Carolina	48,843	29	5,881,766	10	15.7	120.4	11	Raleigh	150,255	3	Charlotte	314,447
North Dakota	69,300	17	652,717	46	5.7	9.4	1	Bismarck	44,485	2	Fargo	61,383
Ohio	41,004	35	10,797,630	6	1.3	263.3	21	Columbus	564,871	2	Cleveland	573,822
Oklahoma	68,655	19	3,025,290	26	18.2	44.1	6	Oklahoma City	403,213	1	Oklahoma City	403,213
Oregon	96,184	10	2,632,105	30	25.9	27.4	5	Salem	89,233	3	Portland	366,383
Pennsylvania	44,888	32	11,863,895	4	0.5	264.3	23	Harrisburg	53,264	10	Philadelphia	1,688,210
Rhode Island	1,055	50	947,154	40	-0.3	987.8	2	Providence	156,804	1	Providence	156,804
South Carolina	30,203	40	3,121,820	24	20.5	103.4	6	Columbia	101,208	1	Columbia	101,208
South Dakota	75,952	16	690,768	45	3.7	9.1	1	Pierre	11,973	9	Sioux Falls	81,343
Tennessee	41,155	34	4,591,120	17	16.9	111.6	9	Nashville	455,651	2	Memphis	646,356
Texas	262,017	2	14,229,191	3	27.1	54.3	27	Austin	345,496	6	Houston	1,595,138
Utah	82,073	12	1,461,037	37	37.9	17.8	3	Salt Lake City	163,033	1	Salt Lake City	163,033
Vermont	9,273	43	511,456	48	15.0	55.2	1	Montpelier	8,241	5	Burlington	37,712
Virginia	39,704	36	5,346,818	14	14.9	134.7	10	Richmond	219,214	3	Norfolk	266,979
Washington	66,511	20	4,132,156	20	21.1	62.1	8	Olympia	27,447	15	Seattle	493,846
West Virginia	24,119	41	1,949,644	34	11.8	80.8	4	Charleston	63,968	1	Charleston	63,968
Wisconsin	54,426	25	4,705,767	16	6.5	86.5	9	Madison	170,616	2	Milwaukee	636,212
Wyoming	96,989	9	469,557	49	41.3	4.8	1	Cheyene	47,283	2	Casper	51,016
Dist. of Columbia	63		638,333		-15.6	10,132.3	1		3,075			3,075
American Samoa	76		32,395		18.9	419.0		Pago Pago	3,075		Pago Pago	3,075
Federated States of Micronesia	271		73,160		...	...		Kolonia, Ponape	5,549		Moen, Truk	10,351
Guam	209		105,816		24.7	506.3	1	Agana	896		Tamuning	8,862
Marshall Islands	70		31,042		34.9	443.5		Majuro	8,667	1	Majuro	8,667
No. Mariana Is.	184		16,780		74.1	91.1		Saipan	14,549		Saipan	14,549
Puerto Rico	3,421		3,187,570		17.9	931.8	1	San Juan	424,600	1	San Juan	424,600
Republic of Belan	192		12,177		8.1	63.4		Koror	6,222		Koror	6,222
U.S. Virgin Islands	132		95,591		54.6	724.2	1	Charlotte Amalle, St. Thomas	11,842		Charlotte Amalle, St. Thomas	11,842

SOURCE: The Book of the States 1990–91 (Lexington, Ky.: Council of State Governments, 1990), pp. 579–580. © 1990–91 The Council of State Governments; reprinted with permission from The Book of the States.

Historical Data on the States

State or Other Jurisdiction	Source of State Lands	Date Organized as Territory	Date Admitted to Union	Chronological Order of Admission to Union
Alabama	Mississippi Territory, 1798(a)	March 3, 1817	Dec. 14, 1819	22
Alaska	Purchased from Russia, 1867	Aug. 24, 1912	Jan. 3, 1959	49
Arizona	Ceded by Mexico, 1848(b)	Feb. 24, 1863	Feb. 14, 1912	48
Arkansas	Louisiana Purchase, 1803	March 2, 1819	June 15, 1836	25
California	Ceded by Mexico, 1848	(c)	Sept. 9, 1850	31
Colorado	Louisiana Purchase, 1803(d)	Feb. 28, 1861	Aug. 1, 1876	38
Connecticut	Fundamental Orders, Jan. 14, 1638; Royal charter, April 23, 1662(e)	. . .	Jan. 9, 1788(f)	5
Delaware	Swedish charter, 1638; English charter, 1683(e)	. . .	Dec. 7, 1787(f)	1
Florida	Ceded by Spain, 1819	March 30, 1822	March 3, 1845	27
Georgia	Charter, 1732, from George II to Trustees for Establishing the Colony of Georgia(e)	. . .	Jan. 2, 1788(f)	4
Hawaii	Annexed, 1898	June 14, 1900	Aug. 21, 1959	50
Idaho	Treaty with Britain, 1846	March 4, 1863	July 3, 1890	43
Illinois	Northwest Territory, 1787	Feb. 3, 1809	Dec. 3,1818	21
Indiana	Northwest Territory, 1787	May 7, 1800	Dec. 11, 1816	19
Iowa	Louisiana Purchase, 1803	June 12, 1838	Dec. 28, 1846	29
Kansas	Louisiana Purchase, 1803(d)	May 30, 1854	Jan. 29, 1861	34
Kentucky	Part of Virginia until admitted as state	(c)	June 1, 1792	15
Louisiana	Louisiana Purchase, 1803(g)	March 26, 1804	April 30, 1812	18
Maine	Part of Massachusetts until admitted as state	(c)	March 15, 1820	23
Maryland	Charter, 1632, from Charles I to Calvert(e)	. . .	April 28, 1788(f)	7
Massachusetts	Charter to Massachusetts Bay Company, 1629(e)	. . .	Feb. 6, 1788(f)	6
Michigan	Northwest Territory, 1787	Jan. 11, 1805	Jan. 26, 1837	26
Minnesota	Northwest Territory, 1787(h)	March 3, 1849	May 11, 1858	32

State	Source	Organized as Territory	Entered Union	Order
Mississippi	Mississippi Territory(i)	April 7, 1798	Dec. 10, 1817	20
Missouri	Louisiana Purchase, 1803	June 4, 1812	Aug. 10, 1821	24
Montana	Louisiana Purchase, 1803(j)	May 26, 1864	Nov. 8, 1889	41
Nebraska	Louisiana Purchase, 1803	May 30, 1854	March 1, 1867	37
Nevada	Ceded by Mexico, 1848	March 2, 1861	Oct. 31, 1864	36
New Hampshire	Grants from Council for New England, 1622 and 1629; made Royal province, 1679(e)	· · ·	June 21, 1788(f)	9
New Jersey	Dutch settlement, 1618; English charter, 1664(e)	· · ·	Dec. 18, 1787(f)	3
New Mexico	Ceded by Mexico, 1848(b)	Sept. 9, 1850	Jan. 6, 1912	47
New York	Dutch settlement, 1623; English control, 1664(e)	· · ·	July 26, 1788(f)	11
North Carolina	Charter, 1663, from Charles II(e)	· · ·	Nov. 21, 1789(f)	12
North Dakota	Louisiana Purchase, 1803(k)	March 2, 1861	Nov. 2, 1889	39
Ohio	Northwest Territory, 1787	May 7, 1800	March 1, 1803	17
Oklahoma	Louisiana Purchase, 1803	May 2, 1890	Nov. 16, 1907	46
Oregon	Settlement and treaty with Britain, 1846	Aug. 14, 1848	Feb. 14, 1859	33
Pennsylvania	Grant from Charles II to William Penn, 1681(e)	· · ·	Dec. 12, 1787(f)	2
Rhode Island	Charter, 1663, from Charles II(e)	· · ·	May 29, 1790(f)	13
South Carolina	Charter, 1663, from Charles II(e)	· · ·	May 23, 1788(f)	8
South Dakota	Louisiana Purchase, 1803	March 2, 1861	Nov. 2, 1889	40
Tennessee	Part of North Carolina until land ceded to U.S. in 1789	June 8, 1790(l)	June 1, 1796	16
Texas	Republic of Texas, 1845	(c)	Dec. 29, 1845	28
Utah	Ceded by Mexico, 1848	Sept. 9, 1850	Jan. 4, 1896	45
Vermont	From lands of New Hampshire and New York	(c)	March 4, 1791	14
Virginia	Charter, 1609, from James I to London Company(e)	· · ·	June 25, 1788(f)	10
Washington	Oregon Territory, 1848	March 2, 1853	Nov. 11, 1889	42
West Virginia	Part of Virginia until admitted as state	(c)	June 20, 1863	35
Wisconsin	Northwest Territory, 1787	April 20, 1836	May 29, 1848	30
Wyoming	Louisiana Purchase, 1803(d,j)	July 25, 1868	July 10, 1890	44

Continued

Historical Data on the States (*Continued*)

State or Other Jurisdiction	Source of State Lands	Date Organized as Territory	Date Admitted to Union	Chronological Order of Admission to Union
Dist. of Columbia	Maryland(m)	...	...	...
American Samoa	------Became a territory, 1990------			
Federated States of Micronesia	...	May 10, 1979	...	...
Guam	Ceded by Spain, 1898	Aug. 1, 1950	...	...
Marshall Islands	...	May 1, 1979	...	...
No. Mariana Is.	...	March 24, 1976	...	...
Puerto Rico	Ceded by Spain, 1898	...	July 25, 1952(n)	...
Republic of Belau	...	Jan. 1, 1981	...	...
U.S. Virgin Islands	------Purchased from Denmark, March 31, 1917------			

(a) By the Treaty of Paris, 1783, England gave up claim to the 13 original Colonies, and to all land within an area extending along the present Canadian border to the Lake of the Woods, down the Mississippi River to the 31st parallel, east to the Chattahoochie, down that river to the mouth of the Flint, east to the source of the St. Mary's, down that river to the ocean. The major part of Alabama was acquired by the Treaty of Paris, and the lower portion from Spain in 1813.

(b) Portion of land obtained by Gadsden Purchase, 1853.

(c) No territorial status before admission to Union.

(d) Portion of land ceded by Mexico, 1848.

(e) One of the original 13 Colonies.

(f) Date of ratification of U.S. Constitution.

(g) West Feliciana District (Baton Rouge) acquired from Spain, 1810; added to Louisiana, 1812.

(h) Portion of land obtained by Louisiana Purchase, 1803.

(i) See footnote (a). The lower portion of Mississippi also was acquired from Spain in 1813.

(j) Portion of land obtained from Oregon Territory, 1848.

(k) The northern portion of the Red River Valley was acquired by treaty with Great Britain in 1818.

(l) Date Southwest Territory (identical boundary as Tennessee's) was created.

(m) Area was originally 100 square miles, taken from Virginia and Maryland. Virginia's portion south of the Potomac was given back to that state in 1846. Site chosen in 1790, city incorporated 1802.

(n) On this date, Puerto Rico became a self-governing commonwealth by compact approved by the U.S. Congress and the voters of Puerto Rico as provided in U.S. Public Law 600 of 1950.

SOURCE: *The Book of the States 1990–91* (Lexington, Ky.: Council of State Governments, 1990), pp. 577–78. © 1990–91 The Council of State Governments; reprinted with permission from *The Book of the States*.

Federally Owned Land, 1987		High School Graduates, 1980*		People Completing Four or More Years of College, 1980*	
1. Alaska	87.1%	1. Alaska	82.5	1. District of Columbia	27.5
2. Nevada	85.1	2. Utah	80.0	2. Colorado	23.0
3. Idaho	63.7	3. Colorado	78.6	3. Alaska	21.1
4. Utah	63.6	4. Wyoming	77.9	4. Connecticut	20.7
5. Wyoming	49.5	5. Washington	77.6	5. Maryland	20.4
6. Oregon	48.7	6. Oregon	75.6	6. Hawaii	20.3
7. California	46.4	7. Nevada	75.5	7. Massachusetts	20.0
8. Arizona	43.1	8. Montana	74.4	8. Utah	19.9
9. Colorado	36.2	9. Hawaii	73.8	9. California	19.6
10. New Mexico	31.3	10. Idaho	73.7	10. Virginia	19.1
UNITED STATES	31.9	11. California	73.5	11. Washington	19.0
11. Montana	30.3	12. Nebraska	73.4	12. Vermont	19.0
12. Washington	29.2	13. Kansas	73.3	13. New Jersey	18.3
13. District of Columbia	28.0	14. Minnesota	73.1	14. New Hampshire	18.2
14. Hawaii	16.4	15. Arizona	72.4	15. Oregon	17.9
15. New Hampshire	12.8	16. New Hampshire	72.3	16. New York	17.9
16. Florida	12.4	17. Massachusetts	72.2	17. New Mexico	17.6
17. Arkansas	9.9	18. Iowa	71.1	18. Montana	17.5
18. Virginia	9.7	19. Vermont	71.0	19. Delaware	17.5
19. Michigan	9.7	20. Connecticut	70.3	20. Minnesota	17.4
20. West Virginia	7.6	21. Wisconsin	69.6	21. Arizona	17.4
21. Tennessee	7.0	22. New Mexico	68.9	22. Wyoming	17.2
22. North Carolina	7.0	23. Maine	68.7	23. Kansas	17.0
23. Minnesota	6.8	24. Delaware	68.6	24. Texas	16.9
24. South Carolina	6.0	25. Michigan	68.0	25. Illinois	16.2
25. South Dakota	5.6	26. South Dakota	67.9	UNITED STATES	16.2
26. Mississippi	5.5	27. New Jersey	67.4	26. Idaho	15.8
27. Kentucky	5.5	28. Maryland	67.4	27. Nebraska	15.5
28. Vermont	5.4	29. District of Columbia	67.1	28. Rhode Island	15.4
29. Georgia	5.4	30. Ohio	67.0	29. Oklahoma	15.1
30. Wisconsin	5.2	31. Florida	66.7	30. Florida	14.9
31. New York	5.1	32. Illinois	66.5	31. Wisconsin	14.8
32. Missouri	4.7	UNITED STATES	66.5	32. North Dakota	14.8
33. North Dakota	4.4	33. North Dakota	66.4	33. Georgia	14.6
34. Louisiana	4.0	34. Indiana	66.4	34. Nevada	14.4
35. New Jersey	3.3	35. New York	66.3	35. Maine	14.4
36. Alabama	3.3	36. Oklahoma	66.0	36. Michigan	14.3
37. Maryland	3.1	37. Pennsylvania	64.7	37. South Dakota	14.0
38. Delaware	2.4	38. Missouri	63.5	38. Missouri	13.9
39. Pennsylvania	2.2	39. Texas	62.6	39. Louisiana	13.9
40. Texas	1.9	40. Virginia	62.4	40. Iowa	13.9
41. Oklahoma	1.9	41. Rhode Island	61.1	41. Ohio	13.7
42. Indiana	1.9	42. Louisiana	57.7	42. Pennsylvania	13.6
43. Massachusetts	1.6	43. Alabama	56.5	43. South Carolina	13.4
44. Nebraska	1.5	44. Georgia	56.4	44. North Carolina	13.2
45. Illinois	1.4	45. West Virginia	56.0	45. Tennessee	12.6
46. Ohio	1.2	46. Tennessee	56.0	46. Indiana	12.5
47. Kansas	1.1	47. Arkansas	55.5	47. Mississippi	12.3
48. Maine	0.8	48. North Carolina	54.8	48. Alabama	12.2
49. Rhode Island	0.7	49. Mississippi	54.8	49. Kentucky	11.1
50. Iowa	0.4	50. South Carolina	53.7	50. Arkansas	10.8
51. Connecticut	0.4	51. Kentucky	53.1	51. West Virginia	10.4

Per Capita Personal Income, 1988 (current dollars)		Rural Population, as a Percent of Total Population, 1980	
1. Connecticut	$23,059	1. Vermont	66.2%
2. New Jersey	21,994	2. West Virginia	63.8
3. District of Columbia	21,389	3. South Dakota	53.6
4. Massachusetts	20,816	4. Mississippi	52.7
5. Maryland	19,487	5. Maine	52.5
6. New Hampshire	19,434	6. North Carolina	52.0
7. New York	19,305	7. North Dakota	51.2
8. Alaska	19,079	8. Kentucky	49.1
9. California	18,753	9. Arkansas	48.4
10. Virginia	17,675	10. New Hampshire	47.8
11. Delaware	17,661	11. Montana	47.1
12. Illinois	17,575	12. Idaho	46.0
13. Nevada	17,511	13. South Carolina	45.9
14. Rhode Island	16,892	14. Iowa	41.4
15. Hawaii	16,753	15. Alabama	40.0
16. Minnesota	16,674	16. Tennessee	39.6
17. Florida	16,603	17. Georgia	37.6
18. Michigan	16,552	18. Wyoming	37.3
UNITED STATES	16,489	19. Nebraska	37.1
19. Washington	16,473	20. Indiana	35.8
20. Colorado	16,463	21. Wisconsin	35.8
21. Pennsylvania	16,233	22. Alaska	35.7
22. Kansas	15,759	23. Virginia	34.0
23. Ohio	15,536	24. Kansas	33.3
24. Wisconsin	15,524	25. Minnesota	33.1
25. Missouri	15,452	26. Oklahoma	32.7
26. Vermont	15,302	27. Oregon	32.1
27. Georgia	15,260	28. Missouri	31.9
28. Maine	15,106	29. Louisiana	31.4
29. Arizona	14,970	30. Pennsylvania	30.7
30. Indiana	14,924	31. Delaware	29.4
31. Oregon	14,885	32. Michigan	29.3
32. Nebraska	14,774	33. New Mexico	27.9
33. Iowa	14,662	34. Ohio	26.7
34. Texas	14,586	35. Washington	26.5
35. North Carolina	14,304	UNITED STATES	26.3
36. Tennessee	13,873	36. Connecticut	21.2
37. Wyoming	13,609	37. Texas	20.4
38. Oklahoma	13,323	38. Maryland	19.7
39. South Carolina	12,926	39. Colorado	19.4
40. Montana	12,866	40. Illinois	16.7
41. Alabama	12,851	41. Arizona	16.2
42. North Dakota	12,833	42. Massachusetts	16.2
43. Kentucky	12,822	43. Florida	15.7
44. South Dakota	12,755	44. Utah	15.6
45. Idaho	12,665	45. New York	15.4
46. New Mexico	12,488	46. Nevada	14.7
47. Louisiana	12,292	47. Hawaii	13.5
48. Arkansas	12,219	48. Rhode Island	13.0
49. Utah	12,193	49. New Jersey	11.0
50. West Virginia	11,735	50. California	8.7
51. Mississippi	11,116	51. District of Columbia	0

*As a percentage of all twenty-five years of age and older.

SOURCE: Edith Horner, ed., *Almanac of the Fifty States* (Palo Alto, Calif.: Information Publications, 1988 and 1991). Reprinted with permission.

288

INDEX

Boldface entries indicate pages on which key terms are defined in the text.